VOLUME 2

Exploring Inclusive & Equitable Pedagogies

Creating Space for All Learners

Melissa N. Mallon, Jane Nichols, Elizabeth Foster, Ariana Santiago, Maura Seale, and Robin Brown, editors

Association of College and Research Libraries
A division of the American Library Association
Chicago, Illinois 2023

CONTENTS

Acknowledgements

The coeditors (Ariana, Elizabeth, Jane, Maura, Melissa, and Robin) wish to thank all of our colleagues who proposed chapters for this volume. We are especially grateful for the contributing authors that spent a substantial amount of time and energy on their chapters during a time of global upheaval and anxiety. Their care and dedication to their work shines through, and we are grateful to have learned from them.

We collectively acknowledge our fellow coeditors' care and compassion as we worked on this book and appreciate the expertise shared and inspiration provided along the way. We would also like to thank Erin Nevius, content strategist at ACRL, for her wonderful editorial guidance and support over the course of this project.

Finally, we would like to thank the thousands of academic librarians out there for their commitment to creating inclusive and welcoming classroom environments that support the whole student experience.

Introduction

"We challenge you to be the instructors our students need."[1]

With this beautifully concise and prescient call to action, we join an ever-growing contingent of teaching librarians to urge our fellow instructors to explore and center equitable and inclusive pedagogies in their classrooms and libraries. To become the instructors our students need, we must adopt the mindsets and develop the underlying skills to enact inclusive and equitable teaching and learning, a theme which underpins this collection. In the contributed chapters that follow, readers will find reflections, practices, and models that deepen our collective understanding of equitable and inclusive theories and practices, presenting new grounding for both our individual teaching and our instruction programs. Adopting this framing positions library instructors to respond to Cooke and Sweeney's[2] call while opening doors for further exploration of new pedagogical ways of thinking.

Defining Inclusive and Equitable Pedagogies

Inclusive and equity-minded pedagogy is inspired by a rich array of theories including Black feminist thought, critical race theory, cultural humility, cultural competence, disabilities studies, universal design for learning, and critical information literacy, among others.[3] bell hooks and Paolo Friere's[4] anti-oppressive approaches to education are foundational to our theoretical understanding of inclusive and equitable pedagogies. Tuitt[5] integrates their theories as he outlines multiple concepts that inclusive and equitable pedagogues draw on for their daily work; concepts reflected in chapters throughout these volumes. When we base our instruction on inclusive and equitable pedagogies, we endeavor to connect authentically with students as well as to connect classroom learning to the context of their lives; we share power with students; we promote their voices, narratives, ways of learning, knowing, and being; and we strive to create a culture of care, empathy, and humility.[6] Inclusive pedagogy is further characterized by theory-based instructional design, centering students and their varied learning styles, while asking educators to be flexible and reflective.[7] As inclusive pedagogues, just as we ask students to bring their full humanity, we create space for our full humanity as well.[8] When we clearly share our objectives and expectations for a learning experience, students may better understand us and the learning context we aspire to create.[9]

In 2018 Tuitt, Haynes, and Stewart enhanced this definition based on their classroom experiences in light of ongoing shifts in higher education and society and in particular the growing Movement for Black Lives.[10] These shifts underscored their desire to "realize education as the practice of freedom"; meaning our educational practices embrace intentional praxis, voice and lived experience, interdisciplinary and diverse content, anti-racist equity mindedness, identity affirming and socially just learning environment, courageous transparency, and resilient emotional labor of love.[11]

Centering Foundational Conversations

Librarians have considered multiple aspects of equity, diversity, inclusion, and more recently, antiracism, as they relate to our profession and everyday work, to library and information science education, and to instructional activities. Several librarians have depicted the lived experiences that BIPOC library workers can face in the library and information science profession, providing much needed insight into their lived reality of systems of oppression as well as strategies for intervention (while also acknowledging that they are not representing all voices).[12] Additional efforts at changing our field and by extension, our instruction, are understanding and "problematiz(ing)" whiteness in order to develop our collective knowledge about the many manifestations of white supremacy's impact.[13] Cooke and Sweeney's *Teaching for Justice: Implementing Social Justice in the LIS Classroom*[14] centers social justice theory and pedagogy in the LIS classroom; a key location of change for the profession. Librarians have also shared new directions, or cartographies, for our work in the classroom, at the reference desk, in archives and special collections, and as a way to support librarianship in Black and Brown communities.[15] Critical librarianship, or critlib, has long been and continues to be a productive lens to interrogate librarianship as a field, including our practices, history, socioeconomics, culture, geographic locations, and our presumed neutral positionality for the purpose of becoming socially just.[16] Instruction librarians seeking to engage in equitable and inclusive practices have also applied critical theories to interrogate instructional practices while sharing the strategies and mindsets they adopted to inform their pedagogy;[17] this work has been extended to assessment practices where we are invited to consider the role of relational care when assessing our students, our instruction, and our selves.[18] Leung and López-McKnight's edited collection, *Knowledge Justice: Disrupting Library and Information Studies through Critical Race Theory*, marks a watershed of librarians applying critical race theory to librarianship and opening the possibility of our field becoming explicitly anti-racist.[19]

This collection expands on these foundational works by exploring myriad questions, such as:

- How do theories and practices related to equitable and inclusive pedagogies inspire our teaching?
- How have librarians engaged in equitable and inclusive teaching?
- How might librarians implement equitable and inclusive pedagogy in ways specific to library instruction?

Authors apply a range of theories related to equitable and inclusive pedagogies (rather than focusing on a single theory, such as social justice theory) while also featuring examples of inclusive teaching in action. This blended focus provides academic library educators with both the theoretical foundations and practical applications to adopt more inclusive teaching practices.

Book Structure

Chapters in this collection share theories and practices applicable to the range of instructional activities we undertake in our classrooms, libraries, on campus, in our communities, and especially in response to online teaching and learning. By sharing how they have re-imagined and re-interpreted their approach to these activities through the lenses of inclusive, equitable, anti-racist, anti-oppressive pedagogies, the authors in this two-volume set model inclusive and equitable ways of thinking and teaching.

We, the editors, shaped sections to expand the conversation by sharing theoretical understandings and practical applications that librarian instructors can pick up, adopt, wrangle with, and shape for their contexts. Chapters reflect the range of instructional activities in which librarians engage including special collections, information literacy, digital scholarship, and outreach and community building activities. Authors showcase the various types of academic libraries where we work: small four-year colleges, community colleges, large research universities. Some institutions have earned the minority-serving designation and others are predominately white (historically and currently). Taking an inclusive approach to content, chapters take a variety of formats such as: reflective/personal, narrative, analytical/academic, case study, autoethnography, and a zine.

Chapters are categorized into seven sections covering a variety of inclusive and equitable pedagogies: Anti-Racist Approaches; Intentional Information Literacy;

Engendering Care and Empathy; Community Building; Universal Design (including accessibility and disability studies); Instructor Identity and Positionality; and Professional Development. This organization emerged from submissions reflecting authors' current environments and is shaped by national and global concerns including the COVID-19 pandemic, systemic racism, and underfunding of social safety nets.

Sections: Volume 1

ANTI-RACIST APPROACHES

In this section, eight chapters discuss theories and practices which authors draw on to inform their journey towards becoming anti-racist teachers and community builders. Their willingness to reflect on their own positionality, privilege, and power combined with their actions contributes to dismantling whiteness in their instruction and outreach activities. Librarians may lead or participate in campus-based programs aimed at raising awareness of anti-racist pedagogies and culturally responsive practices, signaling broad based support as well as movement towards integration into individual practitioners' teaching. Individual exploration and reflection on one's theoretical approach to instruction provides rich grounding for our pedagogy. Authors share their reflections on dialogic pedagogy, epistemic justice, algorithmic literacy, and oppressive authority and how they applied these theories to a range of teaching activities.

INTENTIONAL INFORMATION LITERACY

Key to successful library educators' practice is a willingness to regularly apply, assess, and modify their pedagogy. Throughout this section, authors share how they intentionally integrate theory into their practice and reflect on outcomes for improvement. Three chapters focus on how to reframe traditional realms of library instruction in order to be more inclusive. Three chapters bring critical information literacy into conversation with other pedagogical theories and practices. Two chapters use theory to destabilize dominant understandings of academic research practices and create more inclusive classrooms and consultations.

ENGENDERING CARE AND EMPATHY

The chapters in this section emphasize empathy and care as a means of advancing equity and inclusion in the classroom. Several authors discuss how using special collections and archival materials can advance empathy by highlighting the voices and stories of those marginalized or with hidden narratives. We learn about outreach programs that similarly provide opportunities for academic communities to engage with and build empathy for their fellow humans. Finally, several authors in this section write about creating a culture of care in the classroom, particularly focusing on the student experience as researcher and contributor of new knowledge.

Sections: Volume 2

COMMUNITY BUILDING

In our daily work, we take an expansive approach to community building and the seven chapters in this section reflect that expansiveness. Chapters discuss equitable and inclusive community building in the many instructional settings familiar to library educators. The range of contexts include writing center and library instruction; individual consultations; online, hybrid, and in-person workshops; and digital scholarship projects as part of credit courses. The opportunity to create community extends to library ambassador programs where student ambassadors connect with each other and the students they present to; in particular when this model is paired with a campus student mentorship program. Course-based activities whose outcomes center trust, connection, and joy when using archival materials to produce a primary source reader are the foundations for supporting community among students and their instructors. (This chapter is delightfully presented in a zine format.) Given the centrality of our spaces, gathering student input to inform a space redesign is a natural opportunity for community building both as part of the process and the resulting effort. Developing and sustaining a practice of reflecting on one's teaching praxis as well as offering students opportunities to reflect on their research practices makes space to deepen connections among librarians and students.

UNIVERSAL DESIGN FOR LEARNING

Applying universal design for learning (UDL) principles extends equitable and inclusive instruction to address multiple learning styles as well as disabilities. Across eight chapters, library educators demonstrate how they employ UDL concepts to support student learning. Core to UDL principles is offering multiple options for learners to engage in content. Doing so, practitioners aim to reach as many students as possible and their varied learning styles and abilities. UDL has become increasingly relevant as libraries shift library instruction online, whether due to the worldwide pandemic or the rise of distance learning. Many educators adopt CAST's (formerly the Center for Applied Special Technology) helpful and practical articulation of UDL principles; a match for teaching librarians given the multidisciplinary nature of our work. Authors detail the practical implications of accessibility and UDL for library instruction and note that there is much work to do to ensure that digital learning tools and experiences are completely accessible.

INSTRUCTOR IDENTITY AND POSITIONALITY

The identity and positionality of library instructors can have a significant impact on the inclusivity of learning environments. The four chapters in this section each explore instructor identity and positionality from different perspectives, including: early-career librarians developing intentional teaching practices; reflecting on one's own social identities as an instructor, and incorporating cultural humility and funds of knowledge into praxis; the challenges unique to one-shot library instruction, with guidance on adapting inclusive teaching strategies; and as adjunct instructors in MLIS programs integrating inclusive pedagogies within the limitations of the adjunct role. It is critical to reflect on your own identities and positionality, especially terms of how they might impact students and your ability to create inclusive and equitable learning spaces.

PROFESSIONAL DEVELOPMENT

Regular professional development is crucial for librarians to continue to grow in their understanding and application of inclusive and equitable pedagogies. The four chapters in this final section share strategies and activities librarians have engaged to develop their and their colleagues' expertise. Librarians describe benefits experienced when exchanging knowledge and practices from in-house professional development activities. Key to success is creating strong relationships whether with fellow teaching librarians, library colleagues, or teaching faculty in the disciplines. Learning to effectively develop and sustain such relationships can start in the library and information science graduate school setting when working in well-crafted group projects.

Concluding Remarks

We thank all of our contributors for their willingness to engage in this project, particularly in a time period of unknown churn. We were delighted and inspired by the myriad possibilities for learning, becoming, and trying out pedagogies that support inclusivity and equity. We hope this collection inspires, educates, and stirs you to "recover, illuminate, theorize, reenvision, and enact alternative possibilities for a liberatory librarianship"[20] and praxis. Doing so will help us become the teachers our students need us to be while opening the door for their creations.

To move beyond our profession's comfort zone, we must engage in action: "Anti-racism is about action, and enacting your critical consciousness. This is the part where you engage in tangible, community-based actions."[21]

Notes

1. Cooke and Sweeney, *Teaching for Justice: Implementing Social Justice in the LIS Classroom*, 288.
2. Ibid.
3. Crenshaw, "Mapping the Margins."; Leung and López-McKnight, *Knowledge Justice*; Tervalon and Murray-Garcia, "Cultural Humility versus Cultural Competence"; Hurley, Kostelecky, and Townsend, "Cultural Humility in Libraries"; Foster, "Cultural Competence in Library Instruction"; Hodge, "Integrating Cultural Humility into Public Services Librarianship."; CAST, "Universal Design for Learning Guidelines Version 2.2."; Elmborg, "Critical Information Literacy."; Nicholson and Seale, *The Politics of Theory and the Practice of Critical Librarianship*.;.

4. Hooks, *Teaching To Transgress.*, Freire, *Pedagogy of the Oppressed.*
5. Tuitt, "Afterword."
6. Tuitt., 245-250
7. Tuitt. 251-254
8. Tuitt. 255-256
9. Tuitt. 256
10. Tuitt, Frank, Chayla Haynes, and Saran Stewart. "Transforming the Classroom at Traditionally White Institutions to Make Black Lives Matter." *To Improve the Academy* 37, no. 1 (2018). http://dx.doi.org/10.3998/tia.17063888.0037.108.
11. Ibid.
12. Chou, Pho, and Roh, *Pushing the Margins*; ; Brown, Feretti, Leung, and Méndez-Brady, "We Here: Speaking Our Truth." *Library Trends.*
13. Schlesselman-Tarango, *Topographies of Whiteness*; Brown, Feretti, Leung, and Méndez-Brady, "We Here: Speaking Our Truth." *Library Trends*
14. Cooke and Sweeney, *Teaching for Justice: Implementing Social Justice in the LIS Classroom.*
15. Schlesselman-Tarango.
16. James Elmborg, "Critical Information Literacy: Implications for Instructional Practice." *The Journal of Academic Librarianship* 32, no. 2 (2006): 192–199; Nicholson and Seale, *The Politics of Theory and the Practice of Critical Librarianship*; Drabinski, "Critical Librarianship in a Global Context";
17. Downey, A., *Critical information literacy: Foundations, inspirations, and ideas*; Pagowsky and McElroy, *Critical Library Pedagogy Handbook*; Accardi et. al., *Critical Library Instruction: Theories and Methods*; Tewell, "A decade of critical information literacy: A review of the literature."
18. Arellano Douglas, Veronica. "Moving from Critical Assessment to Assessment as Care." *Communications in Information Literacy*
19. Leung and López-McKnight, *Knowledge Justice.*
20. Honma, 2021, p. 48
21. "Reading is only a step on the path to anti-racism," PublishersWeekly.com, https://www.publishersweekly.com/pw/by-topic/industry-news/libraries/article/83626-reading-is-only-a-step-on-the-path-to-anti-racism.html

Bibliography

Accardi, Maria T., Emily Drabinski, and Alana Kumbier. Critical Library Instruction : Theories and Methods. Edited by Maria T. Accardi, Emily Drabinski, and Alana Kumbier. Duluth, Minnesota: Library Juice Press, 2010.

Arellano Douglas, Veronica. "Moving from Critical Assessment to Assessment as Care." Communications in Information Literacy 14, no. 1 (June 2020). https://doi.org/10.15760/comminfolit.2020.14.1.4.

Brown, Jennifer, Jennifer A. Ferretti, Sofia Leung, and Marisa Méndez-Brady. "We Here: Speaking Our Truth." Library Trends 67, no. 1 (2018): 163–81. https://doi.org/10.1353/lib.2018.0031.

CAST. "Universal Design for Learning Guidelines version 2.2.". Universal Design for Learning Guidelines. 2018. http://udlguidelines.cast.org.

Chou, Rose L., Annie Pho, and Charlotte Roh. Pushing the Margins: Women of Color and Intersectionality in LIS. Library Juice Press, 2018.Cooke, Nicole A. "Reading Is Only a Step on the Path to Anti-Racism." PublishersWeekly.com. Accessed January 19, 2022. https://www.publishersweekly.com/pw/by-topic/industry-news/libraries/article/83626-reading-is-only-a-step-on-the-path-to-anti-racism.html.

Cooke, Nicole A., and Miriam E. Sweeney. *Teaching for Justice: Implementing Social Justice in the LIS Classroom*. Library Juice Press, 2017.

Crenshaw, Kimberle. "Mapping the Margins: Intersectionality, Identity Politics, and Violence against Women of Color." *Stan. L. Rev.* 43 (1990): 1241.

Downey, A. (2016). *Critical information literacy: Foundations, inspirations, and ideas*. Sacramento, CA: Library Juice Press.

Elmborg, James. "Critical Information Literacy: Implications for Instructional Practice." *The Journal of Academic Librarianship* 32, no. 2 (2006): 192–99.

Foster, Elizabeth. "Cultural Competence in Library Instruction: A Reflective Practice Approach." *portal: Libraries and the Academy* 18, no. 3 (2018): 575–93.

Freire, Paulo. 1972. *Pedagogy of the Oppressed*. [New York]: Herder and Herder.

Hodge, Twanna. "Integrating Cultural Humility into Public Services Librarianship." *International Information & Library Review* 51, no. 3 (July 3, 2019): 268–74. https://doi.org/10.1080/10572317.2019.1629070.

Homna, Todd. "Introduction to Part I." In *Knowledge Justice: Disrupting Library and Information Studies through Critical Race Theory*, edited by Sofia Y. Leung and Jorge R. López-McKnight, 0. The MIT Press, 2021. https://doi.org/10.7551/mitpress/11969.003.0004.

hooks, bell. *Teaching to Transgress: Education as the Practice of Freedom*. Taylor & Francis. New York, NY: Routledge, 1994

Hurley, David A., Sarah R. Kostelecky, and Lori Townsend. "Cultural Humility in Libraries." *Reference Services Review* 47, no. 4 (November 11, 2019): 544–55. https://doi.org/10.1108/RSR-06-2019-0042.

Leung, Sofia Y., and Jorge R. López-McKnight, eds. *Knowledge Justice: Disrupting Library and Information Studies Through Critical Race Theory*. MIT Press, 2021. https://doi.org/10.7551/mitpress/11969.001.0001.

Nicholson, Karen P., and Maura Seale. *The Politics of Theory and the Practice of Critical Librarianship*. Library Juice Press, 2018.

Pagowsky, Nicole, and Kelly McElroy. *Critical Library Pedagogy Handbook*. Edited by Nicole Pagowsky and Kelly McElroy. Chicago, Illinois: Association of College and Research Libraries, a division of the American Library Association, 2016.

Schlesselman-Tarango, Gina. *Topographies of Whiteness: Mapping Whiteness in Library and Information Science*. Library Juice Press Sacramento, CA, 2017.

Tervalon, Melanie, and Jann Murray-Garcia. "Cultural Humility versus Cultural Competence: A Critical Distinction in Defining Physician Training Outcomes in Multicultural Education." *Journal of Health Care for the Poor and Underserved* 9, no. 2 (1998): 117–25.

Tewell, Eamon. "A decade of critical information literacy: A review of the literature." *Communications in information literacy* 9, no. 1 (2015): 2. https://doi.org/10.15760/comminfolit.2015.9.1.174

Tuitt, Franklin A. "Afterword: Realizing a More Inclusive Pedagogy." in A. Howell and F. A. Tuitt (Eds.), *Race and Higher Education: Rethinking Pedagogy in Diverse College Classrooms*, 243-68. Cambridge, MA: Harvard Education Publishing Group, 2003.

Tuitt, Frank, Chayla Haynes, and Saran Stewart. *Race, Equity, and the Learning Environment : The Global Relevance of Critical and Inclusive Pedagogies in Higher Education*. Vol. First edition. Sterling, Virginia: Stylus Publishing. 2016.

Tuitt, Frank, Chayla Haynes, and Saran Stewart. "Transforming the Classroom at Traditionally White Institutions to Make Black Lives Matter." *To Improve the Academy* 37, no. 1 (2018). http://dx.doi.org/10.3998/tia.17063888.0037.108.

SECTION 4
Community Building

Introduction

Jane Nichols

Core to librarian practice is being a community member and engaging in acts of building community. Many in higher education feel that their library is the heart of their community due to its physical or intellectual location. Yet we know this is not true for all in our communities. We know our spaces are not and have not been either neutral or a clearly welcoming and inclusive site for all in our communities. We know libraries have been a location of and have enacted harm. Recognizing this, across seven chapters, authors share theories and practices designed to authentically create community. We can learn from and be inspired by their experience with interventions to create spaces where education is about "community and opportunity" rather than "competition and stratification."[1]

Librarians seek innovative approaches to support online education in general and not just in response to extenuating circumstances like the COVID-19 pandemic. In chapter 23 Elliott Stevens, Madeline Mundt, and Perry Yee advocate for creating community between online and in-person graduate students, regardless of disciplinary focus, in "Bridging Physical, Online, and Community Spaces with Digital Storytelling." Building on their previous workshops, they offered an online digital storytelling workshop as a way to create community among online and in-person graduate students. This idea arose as an iteration of their existing in-person Scholar's Studio lighting talk event, which prepares campus-based graduate students to present about their research. The authors note that not being able to participate in the lightning talk activity left online graduate students feeling disconnected from the larger community of graduate students. In response, the authors designed and facilitated the fully online, free Storytelling Fellows workshop, which used a cohort model of mixed online and in-person students to develop digital storytelling skills over the course of the month.

Erin Durham, David Kelly Jr., Allison Jennings-Roche, and Elaine MacDougall explore in Chapter 24 the richness of counterstory to foster community with students in "Whose Voice Matters? Cocreating Knowledge Practices with Students in Libraries and Writing Centers." The authors discuss how they show up in their individual and group interactions with students by drawing on counterstory and embodied knowledges to resist standard language ideologies, white mainstream English in particular, and deficit pedagogies that don't value student lived experience. Each author shares vignettes about how they integrate these theories into their one-to-one and class-based instruction in writing center and library settings. Durham, Kelly, Jennings-Roche, and MacDougall argue that their positioning chips away at hierarchical relationships and dominant academic structures while creating productive space for culturally relevant epistemologies that centers their students' agency and voice.

This section continues with a focus on community building that arises when employing a student ambassador model for instruction as relayed by Gina Schlesselman-Tarango, Sara Durazo-DeMoss, and Barbara Herrera in chapter 25, "Student-Centered, Student-Delivered: Leading with Equity and Inclusion through a First-Year Library Ambassador Program at a Hispanic-Serving Institution." They discuss how they expanded their peer instructional model by partnering with the university Office of Undergraduate Studies' Student Mentoring Program (SMP). The SMP pairs upper and lower division students in a mentor-mentee relationship to demystify college life and share ways to succeed academically. In the library-SMP partnership, mentors receive training to become library ambassadors as well as mentors. Then, as Library Ambassadors, they present library services and the SMP program. A high-impact practice, the peer learning model also decreases uneven power dynamics between students and faculty (or librarians). Ambassadors visit classes in groups of two or three, which allows them to collaborate on their presentations and helps alleviate public speaking anxiety. The authors found that their program builds community and student-to-student connection while extending the reach of the Library Ambassador Program and the SMP.

In Chapter 26, presented as a zine, Kyle Denlinger, Megan Mulder, Kathy Shields, and Mir Yarfitz showcase how archives continue to be rich sites for community building in a classroom setting, even when COVID-19 necessitated moving their undergraduate history course online. The joy and community students experienced during the course and course project of designing and authoring an open-access primary source reader is keenly evident in "Making History Together: Reflections on Trust, Connection, and Finding Joy in the Archives." As the course instructors and designers, the authors framed the course to center trust, connection, and joy as course outcomes. To enact these values, they employed ungrading; they asked students to engage in self-reflection and self-assessment of their learning and of what learning looks like. These inclusive practices helped students to set their own learning goals. Several additional inclusive practices were made possible through the design of their course project. Because students were the content creators, their voices were central, necessitating authentic research, both elements of inclusive pedagogy. Sharing power among the students involved in each stage of the book's creation meant trusting students, which in turn fostered connection and joy.

Many educators appreciate course-based digital scholarship projects as a structure for students to explore openness, collaboration, collegiality and connectedness, diversity, and experimentation.[2] Librarians Rebecca Fitzsimmons and Anne Shelley outline in Chapter 27 "Inclusive Pedagogy through Digital Scholarship: A Case Study" how they forefronted these qualities in a faculty campus workshop and when facilitating a project as part of a term-long course. The authors consider recent critiques of digital scholarship where large-scale projects can be valued over smaller, student-oriented ones and where projects are private rather than open and developed with and for a local community.[3] Mindful of barriers that their K–12 school partners might face, graduate education students running the project sought out digital tools that support two-way communication and are accessible, free, and web-based. Fitzsimmons and Shelley demonstrate how librarians can extend understandings of equity and inclusivity to classroom digital scholarship projects and beyond to include community partners.

Librarians Zach Newell, Stacey Knight-Davis, and Beth Heldebrandt consider how their spaces support, or do not, their local community in Chapter 28 "Fostering Community in the Library: Diversity, Equity, and Inclusion as the Cornerstone in the Development of New Library Active Learning Spaces and Services." When faced with a redesign of their library, they recognized it as an opportunity to forefront equity, diversity, and inclusion, values that rose to the top during their strategic plan renewal. The redesigned space features mobile furniture, makerspace technology, and equipment that allows remote collaboration. The space supports student collaboration, creativity, and problem-based learning, the authors' pedagogical foundation. The authors share the importance of directly asking students about their needs in lieu of relying on assumptions. Doing so revealed a continued need for computers, digital literacy, and access to the learning center for students with mobility needs. Student input was also sought through a problem-based learning activity where they formulated proposals that solved a problem by using the learning center's resources (or resources purchased for it). Winning projects focused on providing access to statistical software as part of establishing a diplomacy lab and creating an app to address food insecurity.

Closing the section, Chapter 29 authors Zohra Saulat and Pamela Nett Kruger advocate for community building as key to first-gen students' retention and success in "Let's Take a Moment: Student Reflections and Reframing Research as a Journey." They outline the invitational education model, which states that students learn best from those who are considered trustworthy, respectful, optimistic, and intentional. By being approachable and inviting, Saulat and Nett Kruger promote an inclusive and engaging online one-shot experience and seek to allay student anxiety and nervousness as they face research assignments. Their teaching is further inspired by the slow teaching movement and their two-fold reflective practice, where they ask students to engage in self-reflective activities just as they find value in devoting time to reflecting after teaching.

As we reengage with our communities, whether online or in person, we can take inspiration from these examples to enhance, reinvigorate, or completely redesign our efforts to build community in its many manifestations. Each chapter led me to consider how I might integrate new approaches into my work, collaborations, and teaching. The range of how we practice inclusive, welcoming, and equitable community building presented here offers rich opportunity to connect with our communities to shape our libraries and services.

Note

1.   James Elmborg, foreword to *Critical Library Pedagogy Handbook*, vol. 1, ed. Nicole Pagowsky and Kelly McElroy (Chicago: Association of College and Research Libraries, 2016), viii.
2.   Lisa Spiro, "Defining Digital Social Sciences." *dh+lib*, April 9, 2014. https://acrl.ala.org/dh/2014/04/09/defining-digital-social-sciences/.
3.   Wendy F. Hsu, "Lessons on Public Humanities from the Civic Sphere." In *Debates in the Digital Humanities*, edited by Matthew K. Gold and Lauren F. Klein, 280–86. Minneapolis: University of Minnesota Press, 2016. https://doi.org/10.5749/j.ctt1cn6thb.27.

Bibliography

Elmborg, James. Foreword to *Critical Library Pedagogy Handbook*, vol. 1, edited by Nicole Pagowsky and Kelly McElroy. Chicago: Association of College and Research Libraries, 2016.

Hsu, Wendy F. "Lessons on Public Humanities from the Civic Sphere." In *Debates in the Digital Humanities*, edited by Matthew K. Gold and Lauren F. Klein, 280–86. Minneapolis: University of Minnesota Press, 2016. https://doi.org/10.5749/j.ctt1cn6thb.27.

Spiro, Lisa. "Defining Digital Social Sciences." *dh+lib*, April 9, 2014. https://acrl.ala.org/dh/2014/04/09/defining-digital-social-sciences/.

CHAPTER 23

Bridging Physical, Online, and Community Spaces with Digital Storytelling

Elliott Stevens, Madeline Mundt, and Perry Yee

In 2016, the University of Washington (UW) Libraries Research Commons and UW Libraries Instructional Design (LibID) came together to create a new, completely online digital storytelling cohort program for graduate students called Storytelling Fellows. This undertaking was a shift for our units because, at the time, the Research Commons was devoted to aiding and celebrating graduate student research through events solely in physical spaces, while LibID—a unit adept at supporting online classes—had not yet run its own freestanding cohort-based program. The result of this collaboration, Storytelling Fellows, aimed to bring the best of the Research Commons' place-based programming for on-campus graduate students to the broader audience that LibID knew so well: online and off-campus graduate students.

Many of UW's online learners are enrolled in fee-based graduate and professional programs, which receive no tuition support or subsidy from the state of Washington. As a result, these programs do not offer in-state tuition and tend to be more expensive, thereby raising concerns about equity in education. Though some students in fee-based programs are located in Seattle, they can also be spread around the United States, not to mention the globe, so they can feel disconnected from the UW's three campuses in Seattle, Bothell, and Tacoma. And because many of these programs

are completely online, separated from physical spaces and humans, they can give students a sense of disembodiment—another factor that can contribute to online students feeling that there is an unbalance regarding the equity of their education, especially when compared to that of on-campus students' experiences with the traditional contexts of higher ed.

LibID's mission is to serve online learners, and the unit has a philosophy focused on equity, learner-centered design, and respect for students as whole people. Through assessment intended to improve learning experiences for students, LibID found that online students craved opportunities to connect and share outside of their programs but were often not able to find such opportunities—or the ones that were available were solely on campus and in person. Here is one response from a survey:[*]

> [On connection outside of programs] I know everyone in my program inside and out. I don't know anyone outside of my program. I wish there were more opportunities for getting together and making friends.[1]

Though at the time LibID and the Research Commons were similar in that they both supported graduate students, they were also in great contrast because the Research Commons did so in ways that were completely on campus and in person. That is, traditional. Scholars' Studio, hosted by the Research Commons, is an example of programming tailored to graduate students that was not available to online and off-campus learners. Scholars' Studio is a successful in-person lightning-talk event that invites graduate students to give five-minute talks about their work for a general audience. This event is much more than just sharing research; Scholars' Studio makes space for students across different disciplines to tell their holistic stories with presentations on research, practice, teaching, and their intersections. For example, one graduate student in the Department of Geography presented about a walking tour he created that gives the public a window into the Queer history of a Seattle neighborhood. Another graduate student from the School of Nursing presented her proposed research in causes of children being unvaccinated and vaccine hesitancy in Seattle Public Schools. But Scholars' Studio isn't just about the big event. Before these presentations, over the course of a couple of weeks, the participants join a cohort of other graduate student researchers, and they have the chance to meet each other, make connections, practice their presentations, and get feedback about them.

Scholars' Studio had always been a successful, popular program. However—while it had always done its job of supporting graduate students in crucial ways—the more we ran it, the more we realized that it wasn't an opportunity or a resource that was open to all graduate students at the University of Washington. Because of all the

---

[*] At the UW, our institutional review board generally declines to review this kind of internal assessment done in the libraries, even when it is possible that the results will be referred to in published papers.

factors that LibID identified in its assessment, Scholars' Studio was inadvertently excluding online graduate students.

The Creation of Storytelling Fellows

Five years ago, the impetus for creating Storytelling Fellows had at least two legs: UW graduate students in fee-based programs were being underserved and not finding the communities they desired, and Scholars' Studio—a very effective program for graduate students—excluded those online students. At first, in early brainstorming sessions, we simply thought we'd make Scholars' Studio an online event via web conference. However, that was long before the COVID-19 pandemic, when Zoom accounts at the UW would become ubiquitous, so we didn't feel we had the resources—or even the models—to run such a program. (At the end of this chapter, we'll return to this idea of an online Scholars' Studio.)

Instead, we settled on a totally online, cohort-based, mostly synchronous workshop where graduate students from all disciplines, interdisciplines, campuses, and online programs would make digital stories over the course of a month with the help of a coaching team. We wanted a high-quality experience for all UW graduate students without any of the barriers presented by place-based events. We chose this design because we felt it played to the strengths of both of our units, and we selected digital storytelling because we felt it would work well in an online environment and also because we had never facilitated its creation before and wanted to try something new. Digital storytelling can be defined in many ways, so maybe it's easier to give a classic example: a short video that comprises things like digital images and video, recorded narration, sounds, music, and captioning—all of which can be found online or made with digital tools. This kind of example has been around since at least the 1990s, when Joe Lambert, founder of StoryCenter in the California Bay Area, began offering in-person workshops in digital storytelling.[2] Storytelling Fellows began with this kind of video-based digital storytelling and, through an evolution we describe at the end of this chapter, expanded to podcasting.

The rest of this chapter will describe the creation and continued evolution of Storytelling Fellows, from its inception as described above. First, we will cover the development of the program through our "Cohort as Community" approach and our choice to frame workshop leadership as coaching rather than teaching. Then we will explore the evolution of Storytelling Fellows that came about as we gave attention to inclusivity, design, and, in particular, accessibility. Finally, we will close with some reflections on the ways the Storytelling Fellows workshops have come to shape LibID and the Research Commons beyond the program itself.

An accompanying appendix at the end of this chapter will list several step-by-step instructions for starting your own Storytelling Fellows and incorporating many of the activities and events we continue to use in our workshops today.

Cohort as Community

Storytelling Fellows starts and ends with people. From participants to coaches and those who support them, the program is driven by people. People who have come to the University of Washington to learn, research, and teach; people who have stories to tell. Stories about what they learned or researched or taught, but also about their connection to learning, what drives their research, or how they aspire to influence the instructional landscape. These stories are developed, written, and told with digital tools and materials in an online space with peers and colleagues connected virtually, and in this online space, it's important to humanize the learning experience for workshop participants. They are encouraged to bring prior experiences to the workshop along with their own personal stories. We find that grounding participation in experience rather than expertise is an equitable approach to developing storytelling narratives. We adapt our workshop's structure to facilitate sharing, not telling. This facilitation encourages participants and coaches to bring their holistic selves and focus on connections. This model calls upon the works of Paulo Freire, bell hooks, and critical digital pedagogy scholars such as Sean Michael Morris and Jesse Stommel.[3]

Morris and Stommel build upon the works of Freire and hooks by interrogating instructional and educational technologies and the role these systems play in digital pedagogy.[4] Morris argues that educational technologies are often introduced for behaviorist interventions such as assessment, tracking, and grading in the learning management system. Particularly during the COVID-19 crisis, he mentions that educational technologies have moved us away from pedagogy that connects us as humans. As educators, we should strive to practice humanizing pedagogy that "protects the dignity of students and educators alike, with an aim to empower them, too."[5]

In *An Urgency of Teachers*, Morris and Stommel lay out that "building community is at the heart of the learning, whether on-ground, online, or hybrid."[6] Storytelling Fellows coaches believe in the decree that learning environments are best when open to a wide community of voices. Morris mentions the practice of critical instructional design—an "emerging attempt to get at some concrete methodologies for creating agentive spaces in online and hybrid learning environments."[7] Storytelling Fellows coaches have a similar self-perception: humans who bring experience with understanding of emotional intelligence rather than advanced technical expertise. We switched from labels of "teacher" to "coach" early in the workshop life cycle to better convey how we wish to support participants. We are here not only to teach but also to inspire, motivate, and celebrate people and their stories. We try to use "instructional design that approaches the very human task of learning, the impulse to learn, and the increasingly urgent need for learning to result in the wisdom of agency."[8]

Stories and narratives aren't prescriptive. They're personal. The job of a storytelling coach is to build a community where stories are welcome and storytellers are unafraid to speak. This is hard work, which is why co-coaching is an important part of the process. Co-coaching allows us to acknowledge our realities and share workloads in effective ways. This work also includes sharing lesson plans and teaching resources at the end of the workshop with any participant seeking to adapt the model to their classrooms. Past fellows have gone on to teach digital storytelling in geography, history, and English courses. From top to bottom, we try to build a community model through our teaching, participation, and relationships with workshop participants.

Building a Community of Storytellers

At the beginning of each workshop, participants complete an introduction activity shared with other peers in the workshop before they even meet in a synchronous setting. This serves as a personal introduction and allows participants to familiarize themselves with the workshop technology.

The kickoff session reserves thirty to sixty minutes to orient participants to the learning environment and each other. An icebreaker activity called Name Stories builds awareness of cultural contexts represented in the cohort. The activity asks participants and coaches to share the story of their name and is an opportunity to humanize participants, seek cultural humility, and encourage connection.

Community guidelines for engagement are codesigned for each cohort. These Community Agreements act as a container for synchronous sessions and are established through group decision-making. Community Agreements are a set of expectations for participants and an accountability mechanism for coaches. The structure establishes the coaches' responsibilities for ensuring agreements are upheld. Participants and coaches are encouraged to contribute to the Community Agreement at any time.

Coaches have established channels for participant support. We use Slack as a community platform, but any collaborative messaging tool works. Coaches use scheduled check-ins with participants called Nudges, based on the concept of Nudge Targeted Students in online spaces.[9] Nudges help participants develop a better defined scope of workshop output and establish a communication pipeline directly to coaches. Asynchronous time then becomes mostly reserved for peer-to-coach interactions, whereas synchronous sessions are dedicated to peer-to-peer interaction.

The draft workshop, a structured synchronous time in the latter half of the learning experience, is devoted to sharing progress and is another method of building engagement and connection. Draft workshops call on all participants and coaches to surface challenges, share pain points, and provide moments of reflection.

Supplied with feedback from other storytellers as well as coaches, participants go back to the digital edit bay in the final week of the workshop to finalize story narratives, fine-tune audio and visual edits, and put the finishing touches on their productions before attending the last community meeting: the storytelling celebration. In this session, everyone shares the final version of their stories. "Final," in this sense, does not mean perfect! Instead, we ask everyone to share the best version of their digital story so far. The community comes together to revel in the fact that they managed to create a digital story in four weeks, together, in an online-only environment. In addition to this celebration, it's also a time for us to evaluate the experience together. Coaches create a space in the session for self-reflection, hold candid conversations about the workshop experience, and provide participants an anonymous workshop evaluation form if they cannot attend or do not feel comfortable sharing with others. Coaches strongly encourage participants to continue developing their stories outside of the workshop and to reach out to the UW Libraries for any future digital storytelling needs (which they often do, particularly if they are interested in incorporating digital storytelling into their own instruction). Finally, coaches take all feedback and meet after the session to debrief and evaluate their own experience, particularly in terms of coaching, instruction, and community building. The last session is truly an opportunity to celebrate, evaluate, and iterate.

Design and Inclusivity

Storytelling Fellows begins and ends with human connections and community, but between that beginning and ending, we have to provide a learning environment and learning experience that reflect the values of the Storytelling Fellows coaching team—values like equity and inclusion—as well as meet the creativity and needs of the fellows. This program is completely digital and online, so we certainly use tools and platforms that fit those contexts, but we also strive to focus not so much on the tools themselves as on the processes in which we're using them. In our coaching team, we sometimes invoke a useful phrase we've come up with: "Process over tools."

But what does "Process over tools" even mean? Though it might sound something like the old saying "Process over product," that's not what we are talking about. "Process over product," in the context of education, seems to be about making sure that learners know that a process of research or composition or production isn't subordinate to an end result, a product. For example, if a middle-school learner were to end up with a drawing they didn't like in an art class or a failed experiment in a chemistry class, then you, as a teacher or coach, might tell them that that's not really a bad thing if the process of making the drawing or conducting the experiment was rich.

With "Process over tools," what we're trying to say is that there are processes in participating in programs like Storytelling Fellows that are crucial—processes such as communicating with one another, paying for costs, and accessing tools in the context of disability. Such processes are ones that, as designers of Storytelling Fellows, we want to identify and be aware of, and they are much more important than any particular software or tools. This is all to say that, over the years, we've realized that we'd much rather focus on the processes we think are most important and then choose tools for those processes as opposed to the other way around—clutching at particular tools first, only to come up with processes later.

Storytelling Fellows has always been totally online, and we've always wanted participants to feel they can be active and expressive within it. From the beginning, we've focused on how people can be present in the workshops, how they can communicate with the coaches and with each other—both synchronously and asynchronously—and how they can access learning materials. Ideally, there would be some kind of miraculous, magical, accessible, equitable, and inclusive single format of technology that would mesh with all those processes, but that sort of thing just doesn't exist. As a result, over the years, we've tested and experimented with many different tools.

Communication

The very first time we did a Storytelling Fellows digital storytelling workshop in early 2017, we used Adobe Connect for our web conference tool. At the time, many of the fellows were new to online, synchronous, web-based workshops, so there was some trepidation on their part about how the online learning environment would work. Unfortunately, Adobe Connect only compounded concerns about the learning environment because we'd spend the first ten minutes of every meeting troubleshooting. After that first workshop iteration, our coaching team reviewed other tools and ultimately chose to switch to Zoom. Zoom ended up presenting zero connectivity problems, so we had more time and had fewer barriers in our way as we embarked on getting to know one another, coaching one another, and making digital stories or podcasts. This is not to say that Zoom will be our forever tool for web conferencing, especially since it presents its own issues with regard to internet security and student privacy.[10]

Another example of our coaching team relying on the "Process over tools" phrase has to do with e-mail. In our first offering of Storytelling Fellows, we relied wholly on e-mail to communicate with the fellows. While this worked in some ways, e-mail also appeared to exclude fellows who tended to prefer synchronous learning. Again, after this first offering, our coaching team reviewed e-mail as a tool and ultimately found that it was not inclusive to the learning and communication preferences of fellows. At the time, Slack was still relatively new, so we chose to use that in our next program, and all the problems that we had with e-mail disappeared. In Slack, students had a far easier time contacting us individually, if they wanted to, or speaking with the rest of the group if they wanted to discuss something both asynchronously and synchronously. And, much like Zoom, though Slack does solve some of our old e-mail problems, we're not saying here that it's our forever solution for bringing about inclusive communication in Storytelling Fellows. More and more, students seem to groan at the prospect of having yet another Slack board in their collection of five or six. Further, during the pandemic, we've noticed that more and more of our graduate students are moving from Slack boards to Discord servers, so this may be an option we consider for future offerings.

Costs

In teaching media making—like making short videos or podcasts—another crucial consideration with regard to equity and inclusion has to do with monetary costs. We always knew that we didn't want participants to pay for the workshop itself, especially because other online web-based digital storytelling workshops can cost hundreds of dollars for a few days.[11] Video editors, like Adobe Premiere, iMovie, or Final Cut, can also be expensive, so we wanted to make sure, focusing on equity and inclusion as well as "Process over tools," that fellows would get a high-quality workshop and video editor for free. In order to do this, we initially used WeVideo, which is a browser-based video editor that costs the libraries only a few hundred dollars a year for fifty accounts. Sure enough, in the first iterations of Storytelling Fellows, WeVideo proved to be effective on both Macs and PCs—as well as in any browser window—but later on, we discovered its deep flaw: a lack of accessibility for people with disabilities.

Accessibility

In 2018, we worked with the University of Washington's Accessible Technologies Center and its team of accessibility testers to examine WeVideo. When UW Accessible Technologies tests something—whether that something is a website, an application, or software—it does so by scrutinizing every step in a process that someone with a disability would try to accomplish using a given program. This is the "User Journey" approach to accessibility testing,[12] and it meant that we had to demonstrate common processes that people need to carry out in WeVideo (like uploading media and then putting that media into tracks to edit). Unfortunately, UW Accessible Technologies found that the video editor had serious programmatic flaws, like inconsistent heading and landmark organization as well as pop-up toolbars navigable exclusively by a mouse. These problems meant complete design blocks for disabled people who use screen readers or who don't use a mouse. It also meant that WeVideo wasn't even up to the WCAG 2.1 A level of accessibility guidelines—let alone WCAG 2.1 AA level,* which is where we would most like to be at the University of Washington.[13] Given this information, our Storytelling Fellows coaching team had to make a decision. Do we continue to offer Storytelling Fellows digital storytelling workshops, knowing full well that one of our central tools is inaccessible? Or should we discontinue using WeVideo because it takes away from a process that we would like to be as accessible as possible?

In the end, we chose to stop offering Storytelling Fellows workshops with WeVideo and then spent some time searching for video editors that are free or low cost, functional on Macs and PCs, and accessible. We came up with nothing and continue to find nothing today. Around this time, we also started getting requests to teach podcasting workshops, and as we got deeper into testing the commonly used audio editor Audacity, we learned that it's quite accessible. Unlike WeVideo, it has detailed documentation about its accessibility, it features many standard keyboard shortcuts, and it can be navigated without a mouse.[14]

As we made accessibility for people with disabilities a bigger part of our process for selecting media-making tools in Storytelling Fellows, we also made accessibility a focus in our lesson plans for media making itself. In the first couple of iterations of the workshop, when we had taught video creation, we had never taught or emphasized captioning videos, but in later iterations we not only took fellows through the process of captioning with WeVideo and iMovie but also required it. And as we moved away from WeVideo and video creation because of our accessibility concerns, we stressed to fellows the importance of making complete transcripts for their podcasts. Often, we would frame practices like captioning and providing complete transcripts as taking part in Universal Design.[15] Our thinking was that, when media makers provide transcripts, then it's not just disabled people who benefit but, really, anyone who might benefit from the flexibility that a transcript provides. For example, being able to search a transcript via Control+F seems to be universally useful. That being said, reviewing recent scholarship like Aimi Hamraie's *Building Access* and Sasha Costanza-Chock's *Design Justice*,[16] we are coming to understand that Universal Design isn't a purely positive or benign concept but actually one that actively erases and excludes the experiences, contributions, and representation of disabled people.

---

* "WCAG" stands for "Web Content Accessibility Guidelines," and most institutions call for digital and web tools that are up to the WCAG 2.1 AA level.

Conclusion: Continuing the Story

Storytelling Fellows has taught us so much about equitable, inclusive, and accessible practice as a team and as an organization. We've learned to value flexibility and imagination, to hold ourselves to the highest standards of accessibility, to see stories as a valuable tool for equity, and to reflect critically on coaching and teaching.

Scholars' Studio was part of what brought about Storytelling Fellows, and in the end, Storytelling Fellows helped bring about a new version of Scholars' Studio. Through February 2020, we thought of Scholars' Studio as an inherently place-based event—not something that could be held online. As universities worldwide pivoted to online learning in March 2020, we suddenly had to look at our programming to see what could be shifted online and how we could do online programming inclusively, accessibly, and equitably.

Storytelling Fellows, which we had been previously seen as an online complement to our face-to-face programming, gave us a blueprint for a wide range of online events. As we planned our first virtual Scholars' Studio event, we looked to Storytelling Fellows for ways to connect with presenters and build community online. We learned that creating a new program like Storytelling Fellows wasn't useful just for what it offered students. Ultimately, it has also been crucial in expanding our understanding of what we can offer to serve all of our users in equitable community spaces.

Appendix: Starting Your Own Storytelling Fellows

1. Pick a form of media creation you'd like to offer an online workshop in. Digital storytelling? Podcasting? Digital exhibit making? Digital book making? Video game making?
2. Assemble a coaching team that can help and assist and push people in this media creation.
3. Settle on an online learning environment for synchronous meetings. Zoom? Slack? Canvas? Google Drive? Open access platforms?
4. Find a group of people who would like to participate in a one-month Storytelling Fellows workshop.

Introduction Activity

1. Come up with a media-making activity that a beginner could complete in less than an hour.
2. Make a short video that leads people through this manageable activity.
3. Share this activity with participants before the workshop starts.
4. On the first day of the workshop, look at some of these completed activities together and discuss them.
5. Check out https://libstory.github.io/assign-prework.html for an example.

Name Story

Ask participants questions like
- Who gave you your name? Why?
- What name do you prefer to be called?
- What is your relationship with your name?

Community Agreement

1. Brainstorm in a shared document about expectations you all have of the community.
2. Discuss the brainstorm and the initial preferences.
3. Put together a first draft of the Community Agreement.

4. As the workshop goes on, continue to check in about the Community Agreement. The Community Agreement is especially useful when work is shared and discussed.

Draft Workshop

1. A person shares their work. They can decide if they'd like prescriptive feedback (feedback that is more critical), descriptive feedback (feedback that's based on observations and connections), or a mix of both.
2. Using a Community Agreement as a guide, everyone in the workshop examines the work and comes up with feedback to give.
3. Everyone discusses the work, and the person sharing their work can decide how much they'd like to be part of that discussion.
4. Check in with the person who has shared their work.

Testing Tools and Websites for Accessibility

1. Search the internet to check if your tool has a Voluntary Product Accessibility Template (VPAT). No VPAT? Bad sign…
2. Search the internet to check if your tool or website has any documentation about accessibility features or if it maps to current Web Content Accessibility Guidelines (WCAG). No documentation? No mention of WCAG? Bad sign…
3. Try to navigate the tool or website without a mouse using standard keyboard commands. This is the "#NoMouse Challenge." Detailed instructions are located at https://nomouse.org.
4. Examine if the website has accessible heading structure, link text, and alt text using accessibility bookmarklets. A set of bookmarklets can be installed at https://accessibility-bookmarklets.org.

General Resources

http://tinyurl.com/uwlibstory (redirects to https://wakelet.com/wake/7vQmOhVbvpYNcWSpA-7Xs)

Notes

1. Anonymous, interview by University of Washington Libraries Instructional Design, Seattle, WA. May 11, 2016.
2. StoryCenter, "Our Story," accessed October 22, 2021, https://www.storycenter.org/history.
3. Paulo Freire, *Pedagogy of the Oppressed*, 30th anniversary ed., trans. Myra Bergman Ramos (New York: Bloomsbury Academic, 2000); bell hooks, *Teaching to Transgress* (New York: Routledge, 1994); Sean Michael Morris and Jesse Stommel, "The Discussion Forum Is Dead; Long Live the Discussion Forum," in *An Urgency of Teachers: The Work of Critical Digital Pedagogy* (Madison, WI: Hybrid Pedagogy, 2018), https://criticaldigitalpedagogy.pressbooks.com/chapter/the-discussion-forum-is-dead-long-live-the-discussion-forum/.
4. Morris and Stommel, "Discussion Forum Is Dead."
5. Sean Michael Morris, "Critical Digital Pedagogy after COVID-19," *Sean Michael Morris* (blog), December 9, 2020, https://www.seanmichaelmorris.com/critical-digital-pedagogy-after-covid-19/.
6. Morris and Stommel, "Discussion Forum Is Dead."
7. Sean Michael Morris, "Critical Instructional Design" in *An Urgency of Teachers: The Work of Critical Digital Pedagogy* Sean Michael Morris and Jesse Stommel (Madison, WI: Hybrid Pedagogy, 2018), https://criticaldigitalpedagogy.pressbooks.com/chapter/critical-pedagogy-and-learning-online/.
8. Morris, "Critical Instructional Design."
9. Flower Darby and James Lang, *Small Teaching Online* (San Francisco: Jossey-Bass, 2019), 173.
10. Jane Wakefield, "Zoom Boss Apologises for Security Issues and Promises Fixes," BBC News, April 2, 2020, https://www.bbc.com/news/technology-52133349.
11. StoryCenter, "View Workshops and Register," accessed October 22, 2021, https://www.storycenter.org/workshop.
12. Larry Lewis, "Webinar, August 19: Using Screen Readers and Testing Tools to Evaluate the Accessibility of a User Journey," TPGi, August 19, 2020, https://www.tpgi.com/webinar-august-19-using-screen-readers-and-testing-tools-to-evaluate-the-accessibility-of-a-user-journey/.
13. University of Washington, "IT Accessibility Guidelines," *Accessible Technology* (blog), accessed October 22, 2021, https://www.washington.edu/accessibility/policy-resources/guidelines/.
14. Audacity, "Accessibility," Audacity 3.2 Manual, accessed October 22, 2021, https://manual.audacityteam.org/man/accessibility.html.
15. University of Washington, "What Is Universal Design?" DO-IT: Disabilities, Opportunities, Internetworking, and Technology, accessed October 22, 2021, https://www.washington.edu/doit/what-universal-design-0.
16. Aimi Hamraie, *Building Access* (Minneapolis: University of Minnesota Press, 2017); Sasha Costanza-Chock, *Design Justice,* Information Policy Series (Cambridge, MA: MIT Press, 2020).

Bibliography

Anonymous. Interview with University of Washington Libraries Instructional Design. May 10, 2016. Seattle, WA.

Anonymous. Interview with University of Washington Libraries Instructional Design. May 11, 2016. Seattle, WA.

Audacity. "Accessibility." Audacity 3.2 Manual. Accessed October 22, 2021. https://manual.audacityteam.org/man/accessibility.html.

Costanza-Chock, Sasha. *Design Justice: Community-Led Practices to Build the Worlds We Need.* Information Policy Series. Cambridge, MA: MIT Press, 2020.

Darby, Flower, and James Lang. *Small Teaching Online: Applying Learning Science in Online Classes.* San Francisco: Jossey-Bass, 2019.

Freire, Paulo. *Pedagogy of the Oppressed*, 30th anniversary ed. Translated by Myra Bergman Ramos. New York: Bloomsbury Academic, 2000.

Hamraie, Aimi. *Building Access: Universal Design and the Politics of Disability.* Minneapolis: University of Minnesota Press, 2017.

hooks, bell. *Teaching to Transgress: Education as the Practice of Freedom.* New York: Routledge, 1994.

Lewis, Larry. "Webinar, August 19: Using Screen Readers and Testing Tools to Evaluate the Accessibility of a User Journey." TPGi, August 19, 2020. https://www.tpgi.com/webinar-august-19-using-screen-readers-and-testing-tools-to-evaluate-the-accessibility-of-a-user-journey/.

Morris, Sean Michael "Critical Digital Pedagogy after COVID-19." *Sean Michael Morris* (blog), December 9, 2020. https://www.seanmichaelmorris.com/critical-digital-pedagogy-after-covid-19/.

Morris, Sean Michael, and Jesse Stommel. *An Urgency of Teachers: The Work of Critical Digital Pedagogy.* Madison, WI: Hybrid Pedagogy, 2018. https://criticaldigitalpedagogy.pressbooks.com/.

StoryCenter. "Our Story." Accessed October 22, 2021. https://www.storycenter.org/history.

———. "View Workshops and Register." Accessed October 22, 2021. https://www.storycenter.org/workshop.

University of Washington. "IT Accessibility Guidelines." *Accessible Technology* (blog). Accessed October 22, 2021. https://www.washington.edu/accessibility/policy-resources/guidelines/.

———. "What Is Universal Design?" DO-IT: Disabilities, Opportunities, Internetworking, and Technology. Accessed October 22, 2021. https://www.washington.edu/doit/what-universal-design-0.

Wakefield, Jane. "Zoom Boss Apologises for Security Issues and Promises Fixes." BBC News, April 2, 2020. https://www.bbc.com/news/technology-52133349.

CHAPTER 24

Whose Voice Matters?

Cocreating Knowledge Practices with Students in Libraries and Writing Centers

Erin Durham, David Kelly Jr., Allison Jennings-Roche, and Elaine MacDougall

Drawing from our different positionalities as writing center directors, English department lecturers, librarians, and information literacy instructors from a minority-serving urban institution (University of Baltimore) and a midsize public research institution (University of Maryland, Baltimore County), we bring a wide range of teaching experiences and perspectives. By exploring the power of counterstory and discussing our own and others' teaching and learning experiences, we will share rhetorical moves that educators can make to interrogate and dismantle power structures that exist in college classrooms. After providing a brief overview of legacies of colonization and racism in higher education, we will each share a personal narrative of our experience working with students on the writing and research process from our different positionalities.

Social Epistemologies in Higher Education

Social epistemologies in the United States have dictated the agency and narratives of minoritized literacies as part of its colonial conquest. White Mainstream English

(WME), also known as standard English or academic English, is one of many mechanisms in the US caste system that dictate how race, class, and gender create intersectional barriers that historically erase and plunder the language cultures of minoritized peoples.[1] Academic support centers, such as writing centers and university libraries, operate under vestiges of colonial Enlightenment traditions as they are funded to "uplift" those students who are considered deficient and in need of enlightenment.[2] Similarly, vocationalism in higher education promises upward mobility, based on white mainstream normativization while undermining, in particular, minoritized learners' moral, civic, and intellectual epistems—education's purpose.[3] These origins lead to service models in libraries and writing centers that adversely affect students. As Kareem suggests, "In program-level and institutional-level writing curriculum, discursive expectations of students are centered on the properties of whiteness and Eurocentric epistemological traditions."[4] Godbee argues that "epistemic injustice—helps to explain the wrongs (micro-inequities that turn into macro injustices) that manifest when writers are stripped of their language, experience, or expertise and their attendant agency, confidence and even personhood."[5] Deficit expectations also set up troubling hierarchical barriers between students and library and writing center personnel. For example, the overwhelmingly white and female library profession is bound up with the patronizing and oppressive lady bountiful archetype and white saviorism as discussed by Schlesselman-Tarango.[6] The epistemic injustices incurred as a result of these linguistic conquests and exploitation permeate the systems and processes of writing centers, libraries, and classrooms in higher education.

Minoritized students' counter-narratives are pushed to the fringes of academia because of the exclusivity of academic English and resistance to fully embracing multicultural Englishes.[7] WME emphasizes how ways of white speaking and knowing become invisible and normative. This invisibility and normativity is made hypervisible when minoritized writers' ways of knowing evidenced in their lived experiences and writing are deemed incompatible with most universities' framing of English. Vershawn Ashanti Young tells us the pedagogy of code-switching segregates home language and school (academic) language. Code-switching suppresses minoritized writers' counter-stories and causes writers to develop "negative attitudes about themselves and their language use."[8] The asymmetrical positioning of academic English implies the political nature of English as a tool for power. Language-identity politics as a means of exercising power makes clear which English narratives are privileged in Academia and which are erased via assimilation.[9] Baker-Bell notes how "language-focused racism has been used to exclude and discriminate against linguistically and racially diverse groups." Enslaved Africans and Spanish-speaking populations were oppressed and marginalized through the institutionalization of denied literacy by law and English-only policies.[10] Baker-Bell draws upon Kynard's work and writes, "Black students learn to monitor their linguistic expression based on how they have been treated and trained to view themselves in language arts [and writing-intensive] classrooms."[11] "Eradicationist," "Respectability," and "Anti-racist Black Language" pedagogies continue to uphold white linguistic homogeneity and reinforce the oppression and minoritization of Black/POC students' linguistic expression, like the laws and policies Baker-Bell references above.[12]

The gospel of higher education needs to continually be reexamined, redefined, and committed anew to dismantling eradicationist and respectability language pedagogies that undermine minoritized writers' agency and autonomy.[13] Writing instructors, writing center directors, and librarians can choose to use their asymmetrical positions of power as deemed by the university to either serve as gatekeepers of WME or stand as accomplices who help writers push the boundaries of their disciplinary borders. Pedagogical praxes such as counterstory and respecting student epistemologies serve to resist oppression and injustice and will be explored in our narratives that follow.

The Importance of (Counter)Story in First-Year Composition: Elaine's Narrative

As a writing teacher meeting students, oftentimes, during their first semester in college, I need to be aware of how each student has experienced the identity of writer, but, more importantly, I need to recognize their wholeness as a person with unique life experiences. Similar to Jamila Kareem's reflection on her experiences with writing, I hear this familiar refrain from first-year composition (FYC) students when I ask how they feel about writing: "I hated academic writing by the time I reached the first year of my undergraduate education."[14] In an attempt to understand this fear and hatred of academic writing, I have reflected more deeply on the tenets of critical race theory, feminist theory, Black feminism, and Stephanie Cariaga's idea of "bodymindspirit as a counter-pedagogy,"[15] and how these epistemologies apply to academic writing, especially classes in the field of rhetoric and composition, "which has witnessed no sustained examination of race, racism, and the effects of both on composition instruction and effective writing program administration."[16]

Shifting to a focus on "counterstory as methodology [that] serves to expose, analyze, and challenge stock stories of racial privilege and can help to strengthen traditions of social, political, and cultural survival and resistance,"[17] I interrogate what Richard Delgado identifies as "stock stories" or "dominant narratives" that surface in my classes, both in student writing and in my instruction as a white, female, middle-aged, middle-class teacher. We start off the semester with Debra Busman's article "Silence and Stories: Honoring Voice and Agency in the College Classroom," which encourages students to "question who gets to tell the story and whose stories are not heard."[18] Many first-year students are hearing this concept for the first time, so the narrative framework of Busman's article helps them understand the importance of telling one's own story through one's lived experiences. Students seem hesitant at first to trust this process of storytelling, since many have never been encouraged to use first person in their essays. They ask, *You want to hear my voice?* I answer, *Yes, I want to hear your voice.*

Another meaningful text we discuss at the beginning of the semester is D. Watkins's book *We Speak for Ourselves: How Woke Culture Prohibits Progress.* Watkins's honest prose and storytelling "inspir[es] young people to value their stories."[19] He is also a Baltimore City native, so students at UMBC are in close proximity to the city he describes although many have not ever been there. Starting the semester with these open discussions about the power of narrative helps students begin to make meaning of their own stories.

Kareem states, "Taking a critical lens to the transitional moments from secondary to postsecondary writing experiences gives the field a critical opportunity to address deeper societal issues."[20] Through the literacy narrative assignment, as well as the follow-up reflection, I encourage first-year students to contemplate their relationship with literacy before entering college. After reading several example narratives, like the ones described above, on the themes of students' right to their own language, silenced voices, and story-telling, students are asked to share their own stories with any type of literacy. Some students choose to write about the influence of a book or teacher, while other students address discriminatory, harmful experiences they have encountered with literacy.

Although I've always valued and encouraged students' stories, reading Christina Cedillo's article "What Does It Mean to Move? Race, Disability, and Critical Embodiment Pedagogy" influenced the revisions to my literacy narrative assignment and helped me understand the "why" of literacy narratives. Cedillo states that "Literacy often refers to someone's ability to read and write, but …literacy is a complex issue that has cultural and bodily implications."[21] Her approach to the literacy narrative assignment better prepares students to fully engage with their own definitions of and experiences with literacy. Cedillo uses more invitational language to encourage students to go beyond discussing the first book they read to really discovering their relationship with literacy. Similarly, Stephanie Cariaga talks about "reconstructing the classroom" to facilitate "space for students to embrace their wholeness—including their wounds, emotions, resilience, and desires."[22]

Adopting these strategies during the literacy narrative unit allows for our class discussions and the resulting assignment to focus more genuinely on students' voices, counterstories, and lived experiences. Students are asked to give one reading presentation on a selected text, which gives them agency to discuss ideas that resonated with them and, hopefully, transfer those ideas to their own writing. One student reflection from my spring 2021 FYC course discusses how his ideas regarding writing changed as a result of this unit; while he used to dislike writing, he concluded that every person should write about their stories and appreciated the opportunity to write and reminisce about important memories. Another FYC student from summer 2021 reflected that she came to a better understanding of herself and her community through reading D. Watkins's book and writing her literacy narrative. She also realized that her words have power and can influence others.

My goal for this unit is to help students, as well as myself, "come to a deeper understanding of their place in the world, as well as their relation to others within it."[23] Although the first time I taught this unit was fully online due to the pandemic, I felt more connected to the students as a whole than I have to students in previous semesters because they revealed something authentic about themselves and practiced vulnerability through telling their stories.

Through storytelling we can arrive in the world of academia as our whole selves: body, mind, and spirit.

Valuing Personal Experience in the Research and Writing Process: Erin's Narrative

As Elaine has discussed, first-year composition (FYC) courses can provide opportunities for educators to honor student identities, agency, and counterstories. As a reference and instruction librarian and subject liaison to the English department at the University of Maryland, Baltimore County (UMBC), I support students with their research assignments in a variety of courses, including in the FYC program. This support frequently takes the form of one-shot research sessions where I serve as a guest instructor for a class session and engage students in activities to search for and discuss sources for their annotated bibliographies and final papers.

In their discussions of research instruction, library scholars and practitioners emphasize the importance of helping students draw from their own experiences as they work on research and writing assignments.[24] As Halpern and Lepore write, "By helping students to develop an authorial identity and understand how research solves problems, we hoped to …have students see themselves as agents (not visitors) to their own work."[25] Morrison emphasizes the importance for teaching librarians "to look at the diverse populations they serve, their situatedness, and make information literacy relevant."[26] She puts forth a model of "asset-based pedagogy" that honors the diverse cultural knowledges of her students.[27] This centering of student experience relates to Cedillo's work of supporting students' personal and embodied knowledges, and to Baker-Bell's critique of the harms that traditional approaches to language education have on minoritized students' sense of self and identity.[28]

While this work of engaging students with inclusive teaching practices would be best developed in a full-semester course, there are practices that can be applied in one-shot instruction or in research consultations with students. For example, Baer acknowledges the limited opportunities for librarians to get to know "students' current understandings, abilities, and interests" when teaching a one-shot session.[29] She writes that librarians can make use of "Think-Pair-Share activities" where students share their knowledge with a classmate, learn from each other, and then share out with the full class, in "a process through which individuals are exposed to a still wider range of perspectives and can further build on or challenge prior learning."[30] In research consultations, it is important to listen carefully as students discuss their research topics. In listening, we can learn about students' prior knowledge and experience with the topic, point out the value of that knowledge, and help them include their experience along with a discussion of the scholarly literature.

In helping to center student experience in research instruction and consultations, it is important to consider my own identity as a white middle-class woman and the ways my privilege and authority as a librarian might affect conversations about ways of knowing and the research process. Greater transparency and culturally relevant pedagogy are needed to dismantle barriers, build greater rapport and trust with students, and root out deficit educational models.[31] As bell hooks advocates for the liberatory power of education, she writes, "As a classroom community, our capacity to generate excitement is deeply affected by our interest in one another, in hearing one another's voices, in recognizing one another's presence."[32]

I was reminded of the importance of centering student experience during a research consultation with a FYC student in spring 2021. A few weeks after I taught a research session for an English 100 course, a student from the class reached out to me through e-mail, mentioning that he was feeling anxious about the research assignment and asking for some assistance in identifying sources for his research paper on language acquisition.

We set up a research appointment for the next day. As I logged into the Webex session the following afternoon, I met John (pseudonym), a Black student likely in his late teens or early twenties. As we started to discuss his research, I learned that John had a good deal of proficiency and experience in learning languages. He mentioned his desire to find sources that supported his experience with language immersion. As we searched for and identified relevant sources, we discussed how he could organize and present the findings from each of those sources to set up a convincing argument. Because of his success in language learning, I assumed that he would directly highlight that experience in his paper, so I asked if he was planning to discuss his language immersion experiences.

John seemed taken aback about the possibility of sharing his own experience and questioned if he was allowed to do so in a college paper. John's hesitancy speaks to failings of research and writing instruction that neglects to help students see the value of their own experiences and "authorial identity."[33] As I spoke to John, I affirmed how relevant his experience was and how it could make a compelling contribution to his paper. Our exchange impressed upon me how vital it is not to assume—but rather directly call out—the value of personal epistemologies in my teaching and reference interactions.

When calling out the value of personal experience, it is important to be aware of the harms of an education system that props up WME and research practices that ignore or dismiss student experience.[34] In practice, this may look like "nulli-fy[ing] language behaviors that do not conform to Eurocentric ways of knowing"[35] or valuing only knowledge contained in peer-reviewed articles published in prestigious research journals. In John's case, I contributed to oppressive educational norms by failing to directly discuss the value of personal experience in our English 100 research session earlier that semester. As Folk writes, "There is a rich literature that examines educational institutions and culture as sites of alienation, isolation, and marginalization for students who do not come from the culture(s) privileged in higher education."[36] To counteract these harms, librarians and writing instructors can show how scholarly literature and personal experience can be woven together to inform and advance a research argument.[37] Morrison provides a powerful example of "invit[ing] counterstorytelling" by drawing upon autoethnography and critical information literacy with students.[38] Sharing examples and pointing out the value of personal experiences can help students develop their "scholarly storytelling" abilities and unique contributions as authors.[39]

My conversation with John caused me to reflect on the balances of power in research and writing instruction, and on my own positionality as a librarian. Knowing that I was not the one who created the assignment nor would be the one grading it, I emphasized that John should check with his professor about sharing his personal experience in the research paper. My hedging clearly highlights how it can feel like a tightrope balancing act to draw upon education as a liberating force and yet also help students check the right boxes and complete the assignment according to the grading rubric in order to be "successful" college students and future job candidates.[40] My liminality as a guest instructor highlights the importance of reaching out to writing professors to advocate for the value of student voice and experience throughout the research process. Providing examples, modeling, and directly calling out the value of personal experience in the research and writing process are critical to advancing inclusive scholarship. In the future, I hope to have more nuanced conversations with writing instructors and students about the value of personal epistemologies and help students place their experiences in conversation with academic sources. Working with students to explore research topics that are personally relevant to them can shift the research process to be less about busywork and more about advancing rich and inclusive scholarly discussions.

Working in the Third Space to Foster Agency, Autonomy, and Confidence: David's Narrative

I met Rachel, a student, adult learner, and working professional, in the fall of 2019. She was referred to me by a student I taught the previous semester. Rachel had enrolled in the required writing, research, and composition course and was working toward her bachelor's degree. When I work with students, as the writing center director, my first goal is usually to identify what kind of relationship they have with writing. I learned from Rachel's recollection that she felt alienated and perhaps invisible as indicated by raceclassist disparities in her lived experience. She mentioned all that she thought she had not acquired as a youth in school; she had been out of school for over ten years. She was clearly deficiting herself, but up to that point she had passed all of her courses.

This alienation and invisibility was echoed in her minoritized status as a Black woman writer performing the discourse. Her lived experiences, entangled in racialized socioeconomic disparities, made her performance of the discourse hypervisible to the extent that she doubted her own abilities. This hypervisibility can feel like violence, plunder, erasure, or exploitation of BIPOC's bodies and language-culture identities.[41] Buchanan and Settles assert that "Differential power and marginalization are precursors for invisibility and hypervisibility given that those with status and power have the authority to render others visible, invisible, or hypervisible."[42] The stress of this hypervisibility limits the full awareness needed to compose understandings and knowledges. Godbee draws on Dowst and Berlin to propose, "When composing words, [writers] are also composing understandings and knowledges hence constructing and making sense of ideology, power, and relations"[43] The linguistic resources that Rachel relied on in other spaces were not readily valued in her academic courses because of linguistic gatekeeping that often occurs in higher education. Over the broader course of Rachel's educational experience, she, like many other minoritized students, including myself, was stripped of her "knowledge, experience, and earned expertise", as well as, her attendant agency in academic writing.[44] Minoritized writers who are disproportionately impacted by socioeconomic hardship develop their epistemological understandings in commonplaces that higher education, as a whole, is reluctant to recognize.

I am a man, a Black man, raised as an Army brat, then a civilian. My mother and father were born and raised in Baltimore City and got pregnant with me at eighteen and twenty respectively. Both of my parents come from working and middle-class backgrounds. Shortly after finding out about the pregnancy, my father enlisted in the military. I was educated on military bases or military towns from kindergarten until I graduated high school. I went to schools that afforded me the access and practice to write in White Mainstream English "good" enough for my teachers. As I think back to my own educational upbringing, I remember my teachers, many of whom were white women, noting how articulate I was; articulate in my performance of WME.

I was never singled out for writing remediation, at least not in a penalizing or deficiting way. I was able to try on the ways of knowing that Bartholomae describes in "Inventing the University."[45] Because of my relative privilege and access, I did the things Batholomae is talking about. I was given the space to try on the ways of knowing that define the discourse of the academic community;[46] granted they were from the lens of my teachers' white epistems, which reinforced my unquestioned performance of WME. So many of my experiences in school and at home were marked by how I spoke and wrote English, "proper English." I learned how to navigate using my Black Language[47] and White Mainstream English. It's literally like knowing two languages and being passive-aggressively praised only for using the one that is not entirely familiar to you, but privileged by the person(s) with authority and power; for the purpose of upholding a status quo based on arbitrary phenotypical human features—racialization. And grafted on the language bi-poles, which mirror those of the social hierarchy-caste, are implicit and explicit biases and privileges for using the preferred language in proximity to those at the top of the caste.[48] Interestingly enough, though, I was often critiqued by my friends for talking "too white," which they used to challenge the credibility of my "Blackness."

I am perhaps one of many versions of the exceptionalism and tokenism that those who subscribe to neoliberal ideologies use to validate some of the success myths about usage of WME. But what about those minoritized students who fail or struggle to mimic the grammatical and syntactic style associated with WME? And/or those who are not verbally "articulate" enough to communicate their ideas in ways that align with white mainstream epistemologies?

The thing about being a minoritized person is that both perceived deficits and strengths can be weaponized as microaggressions, making us writers who are otherwise invisible, hypervisible. The compounding effects of this injustice contradict the privilege and authority Bartholomae tells us ALL writers need.[49]

Rachel pleaded that she needed my help, asserting that she was a terrible writer, the first time we met. So many minoritized students don't get the equitable benefit to use their minoritized epistemologies to construct how they make sense of writing assignments without being remediated. This erroneous positioning is an act of violence and representative of the historical erasure, plunder, and exploitation of BIPOC's identities via their bodies and language-cultures.

Rachel's recollection of her experiences with writing throughout her life made it clear that she had been impacted by two epistemic injustices, testimonial and hermeneutical, which undermined her agency and ability to make informed rhetorical decisions in her writing. She seemed so stressed talking about the implicit aspects of her own writing process that our conversation was made explicit-hypervisible, unearthing all that she had not been given the full space to discuss before. According to Fricker, "Testimonial injustice occurs when prejudice causes a [reader] to give a deflated level of credibility to a [writer's] word."[50] Next I asked her what kind of feedback she commonly got on papers. She replied that she usually got Bs or Cs on her papers, and she most remembered commonly getting feedback about grammar. Rachel did not mention any constructive or positive feedback that she received.

The hermeneutical injustice imposed on Rachel is that of a lineage in education and other institutions where individuals in the institutions, who hold the power, enforce it though social norms aimed at maintaining the existing social order: WME.[51] Gaps in minoritized writers' collective interpretive resources—from race-class disparities, structurally put them at an unfair disadvantage, possibly because of the compounding effects of race, class, and gender, to perform their discourses compared to their counterparts who have been privileged to access and resources.[52]

Unpacking Rachel's relationship with writing made it clear that her ability and that of many other minoritized writers to invent and think through ideas is limited to their ability to communicate them in WME, which limits their articulation on paper. So what did we do during our three years working together? My focus was on her agency, autonomy, and confidence. From 2019 until the spring of 2021, when she graduated, we came together to create a space so that she could try on ways of knowing across her home language and academic performance of WME without being penalized for not mimicking standard language ideologies which reflect white linguistic and cultural norms.[53] One of the bridges that I believe is important to note is my own positionality.

I can't say for certain that I was the only Black instructor that she's ever had, but we shared similar cultural understandings-epsitems. I am expressedly interested in affirming BIPOC-minoritized epistems and prioritizing content and ideas over grammar and syntax, understanding that writing as a process that is seldom revealed to BIPOC students. Our home Englishes overlapped. We dialogued using our Black Language[54] and grafted those ideas on to writing strategies like PIE (point, information, explanation) and quote sandwiching. My task was to demystify the academic conversation being had in her assignments using writing strategies, her lived experience, and growing disciplinary knowledge.

I asked her open-ended questions that challenged her to think through her own perceived limitations, as reinforced by her experiences in the classroom. I leaned on Rachel's knowledge and expertise on the course content and her ideas as they related to the writing prompts she worked on. I affirmed and asserted her ideas, challenging her to go further with her thoughts and explanations, or provide evidence to support her explanations, or listen to her logic for organizing an assignment. Before long she was the one leading and directing our conversations, and I simply responded with questions aimed at clarifying her ideas. Her counterstory in our meetings was the mainstream narrative.

Each time we met to work on a writing assignment for her course, Rachel's confidence grew. Focusing on global-order concerns was always my priority over those at the sentence level. Any focus on the sentence level was aimed at clarifying ideas or explaining them rather than focusing on grammar and syntax itself. During our time working together I was most impressed with her growing confidence and authority to think through her ideas, rather than get hung up on grammar and syntax. Rachel scheduled a Zoom meeting with me before turning in her final undergraduate assignment. She didn't schedule the meeting to review her paper; instead, she scheduled the meeting to thank me.

I graciously accepted her appreciation and quickly expressed that the power was inside of her, and I simply helped her to make better sense of what she already knows and communicate it in the performance of her discourse through actionable writing strategies. I told her that our time and shared learning together didn't stop there for her. All of the skills, confidence, and agency that she has been honing will benefit her in her future endeavors. Her last words to me were, "I love you and if you eva have any doubts about your impact in the university, know that you impacted at least one!" We said our goodbyes, and then she was gone.

How each of us knows what we know and how we come to know it directly connects to how we articulate (verbally and written) knowledges from those epistems, in particular when resisting the white epistemic gospel of higher education. Agency, autonomy, and meaning making when incorporated through minoritized language-culture epistemologies expand discourse conventions to create new, more inclusive, and intentionally multicultural Englishes. Counterstories, code meshing, and engagement in multicultural rhetorical awareness are a few of many inclusive pedagogical practices aimed at re-imagining the student-instructor relationship in the halls of higher education.

Grappling with Vocationalism and the Education Gospel as an Embedded Librarian: Allison's Narrative

Serving as an embedded librarian in an advanced writing course is a strange role, akin to the "tightrope balancing act" that Erin mentioned above. I am neither fully an insider in the course space, nor a one-time visitor or outside consultant. When

I interact with students, though, I find I actually lean into the liminal space of my positionality as a librarian, as well as tapping into some of my own lived experiences. Individual research consultations become about so much more than locating sources. Instead, I often act as a de facto translator for students who are trapped between the twin forces of the education gospel and the vocationalism that pervades the college experience for working-class students, especially those with intersectional identities, in 2021. The outwardly contradictory but related experiences of students seeking a foot in the door and those trying to just earn the credential that will allow them to hold onto the bit of middle-class stability they already have are all a response to these larger forces of social inequality.

Working with students at an urban, minority-serving public institution lays bare the flaws inherent in this pervasive "education gospel" as described by Dr. Tressie McMillan Cottom in *Lower Ed*, every day.[55] As a society, we have upheld higher education as an unquestioned social good, often the sole road to social mobility, without considering the structures or limitations of our institutions.[56] For example, vocationalism, the push to make higher education into explicit job preparation, largely for minoritized and marginalized students, has pernicious effects for the very students this framework seeks to remediate. At its foundation, vocationalism operates from a deficit model where it seeks to assimilate students with diverse perspectives into the dominant working culture, rooted in White Mainstream English and cultural norms.[57] This deficit model is evident in the interactions I have with students ostensibly seeking research assistance, but who more often need support as they navigate opaque institutional norms and cultural expectations.

Students who are already working professionals are sometimes frustrated by what they perceive as meaningless assignments and hoops they have to jump through, and yet students with no professional background struggle to connect the career-oriented assignments to their limited life experiences. Kendra (pseudonym) was just such a student; she has many years of experience in her field of financial services. She came to me frustrated by assignments insisting she use her working experience, but the particulars of these projects did not work in her specific field; in response, she couldn't help but question her own understanding. Kendra was the expert in her own profession, and I would not presume to help in that realm; however, I was able to provide context for the course and the assignments themselves. By pulling back the covers on the academic system, I was able to help her contextualize that assignment in that broader liberal arts framework. Kendra used that information to approach research and writing with her usual professional confidence.

Derrick (pseudonym), another student, struggled to connect the career-focused assignments to a hypothetical white-collar working world that he had yet to experience firsthand. He sought out assistance from his course instructors, but likely due to intersectional external markers that to many would signal him out for exclusion and hermeneutical injustice, his very real concerns were routinely dismissed and ignored. Since we first worked together, Derrick has set research consultations with me before he submits assignments in every single one of his courses. A brilliant and hardworking scholar, he does not need my input on his content; rather, each time, he seeks affirmation that his own instincts and perspectives are valid, even in an institutional context that devalues his home cultures. The devaluation endemic in the deficit model often leads students to doubt their own instincts and to seek reassurance from others.

Because marginalized or minoritized students often cannot "immerse themselves in college life" or invent the university like their peers who come to college with more social and economic privilege, it can be harder to see the purpose of many of the demands of college life.[58] Even foundational ideas like why courses outside of a narrow career/vocational track are required for a bachelor's degree are not immediately evident to students who have been steeped in the education gospel without the explication of the foundational ideas of a liberal arts higher education in the United States.

As a former first-generation, low-income, white student (who grew up in the city our institution serves), I am one of the lucky few who has been able to transcend class barriers and achieve a level of the middle-class American dream. In so many ways my experience is not the norm; in fact "sociologists of education and widening access practitioners have persevered with the 'meritocracy' paradigm, trying to make it work for working-class students. Time and again it has been proved to work largely as a mechanism for the intergenerational reproduction of social elites."[59] In response, I strive to use my role and positionality to dismantle the hidden curriculum. Helping students decipher institutional norms, assignment instructions, and instructor feedback may not be a part of the traditional research process, but affirming student agency and autonomy is at the core of what I have come to view as my primary duty in this space. As a Gallup-Purdue poll demonstrated (affirming what many know from lived experience) that the most important thing for all students is not skill building, rigor, or specific coursework; instead, it is the relational experiences they have in college with caring faculty and staff.[60] In all of the broader discourse around dismantling inequality by providing students with the hard skills for upward mobility, aka vocationalism, both epistemic justice and our shared humanity are lost. Meritocracy may reinforce inequality, but I don't need to.

Synthesis: Why We Care

Leaning into counterstories and embodied knowledges provides a way to resist standard language ideologies and deficit pedagogies that privilege white language and culture. Daniel Solórzano and Tara Yosso argue that "although social scientists tell stories under the guise of 'objective' research, these stories actually uphold deficit, racialized notions about people of color."[61] In addition, we recognize students' adherence to the belief that only a singular, "ethical" English exists, which will not change until larger system-wide changes are implemented.[62]

Similarly, Woody points out that many students are more "interested in acquiring marketable skills than overthrowing [the] dominant discourse" of a system they are trying to enter.[63] Marketable skills equate to White Mainstream English, which equates back to a Eurocentric epistemological perspective based on white privilege.[64] Students' interest in skill building is rooted in the vocational impulses of the "education gospel," as well as each of our institutions' structural grounding in neoliberal ideology, which we collectively reject, but understand and approach with empathy in our pedagogy and interactions with students.[65]

By drawing on the work of these scholars, and through our own stories and narratives, we bring together our epistemologies centering on student voice, agency, and advocacy. Incorporating these culturally relevant pedagogical practices helps to break down academic gatekeeping and demystify the hidden academic curriculum. Students are better able to see themselves within the academy and feel that their ideas are valued, especially through their role in the cocreation of knowledge. Listening to student stories and lived experiences is our job; this is our reckoning and reflection on the power of story in both library and writing center sessions, as well as in the classroom. How we show up directly affects student experience, so we better reckon with our intentions as educators and mentors.

Notes

1. April Baker-Bell, *Linguistic Justice* (New York: Routledge, 2020).
2. Gina Schlesselman-Tarango, "The Legacy of Lady Bountiful: White Women in the Library," *Library Trends* 64, no. 4 (2016): 667–86, https://doi.org/10.1353/lib.2016.0015.
3. W. Norton Grubb and Marvin Lazerson, "Vocationalism in Higher Education: The Triumph of the Education Gospel," *Journal of Higher Education* 76, no. 1 (2005): 2.
4. Jamila Kareem, "A Critical Race Analysis of Transition-Level Writing Curriculum to Support the Racially Diverse Two-Year College," *Teaching English in the Two-Year College* 46, no. 4 (2019): 275.
5. Beth Godbee, "Writing Up: How Assertions of Epistemic Rights Counter Epistemic Justice," *College English* 79, no. 6 (2017): 595, https://core.ac.uk/download/pdf/213085398.pdf.
6. Schlesselman-Tarango, "The Legacy of Lady Bountiful."
7. Laura Greenfield, *Radical Writing Center Praxis* (Logan: Utah State University Press, 2019).
8. Erin M. Cassar, quoted in Vershawn Ashanti Young et al., *Other People's English* (New York: Teachers College Press, 2014), 3.
9. Greenfield, *Radical Writing Center Praxis*.
10. Baker-Bell, *Linguistic Justice*, 17.
11. Carmen Kynard, *Vernacular Insurrections* (Albany, NY: SUNY Press, 2013): 109, cited in Baker-Bell, *Linguistic Justice*, 128.
12. Baker-Bell, *Linguistic Justice*, 28.
13. Baker-Bell, *Linguistic Justice*.

14. Kareem, "Critical Race Analysis," 271.

15. Stephanie Cariaga, "Towards Self-Recovery: Cultivating Love with Young Women of Color through Pedagogies of Bodymindspirit," *Urban Review: Issues and Ideas in Public Education* 51, no. 1 (2019): 101–22.

16. Gary A. Olson, quoted in Aja Y. Martinez, "A Plea for Critical Race Theory Counterstory: Stock Story versus Counterstory Dialogues Concerning Alejandra's 'Fit' in the Academy," in *Performing Antiracist Pedagogy in Rhetoric, Writing, and Composition*, ed. Frankie Condon and Vershawn Ashanti Young (Fort Collins, CO: WAC Clearinghouse and Boulder: University Press of Colorado, 2016), 68.

17. Richard Delgado, quoted in Martinez, "Plea for Critical Race Theory Counterstory," 70.

18. Debra Busman, "Silences and Stories: Honoring Voice and Agency in the College Classroom," in *Ways of Being in Teaching: Conversations and Reflections*, ed. Sean Wiebe, Ellyn Lyle, Peter R. Wright, Kimberly Dark, Mitchell McLarnon, and Liz Day (Rotterdam, Netherlands: Brill, 2017), 49.

19. D. Watkins, *We Speak for Ourselves* (New York: Atria Books, 2020), 184.

20. Kareem, "Critical Race Analysis," 276.

21. Christina V. Cedillo, "What Does It Mean to Move? Race, Disability, and Critical Embodiment Pedagogy," *Composition Forum* 39 (Summer 2018), Writing Project: Literacy Narrative, https://compositionforum.com/issue/39/to-move.php.

22. Cariaga, "Towards Self-Recovery," 103.

23. Cassandra Woody, "Re-engaging Rhetorical Education through Procedural Feminism: Designing First-Year Writing Curricula That Listen," *College Composition and Communication* 71, no. 3 (2020): 484.

24. Kim L. Morrison, "Informed Asset-Based Pedagogy: Coming Correct, Counter-stories from an Information Literacy Classroom," *Library Trends* 66, no. 2 (2017): 176–218; Amanda L. Folk, "Drawing on Students' Funds of Knowledge: Using Identity and Lived Experience to Join the Conversation in Research Assignments," *Journal of Information Literacy* 12, no. 2 (December 2018): 44–59; Chelsea Heinbach et al., "Dismantling Deficit Thinking: A Strengths-Based Inquiry into the Experiences of Transfer Students in and out of Academic Libraries," *In the Library with the Lead Pipe*, February 6, 2019, http://www.inthelibrarywiththeleadpipe.org/2019/dismantling-deficit-thinking; Eamon Tewell, "The Problem with Grit: Dismantling Deficit Thinking in Library Instruction," *portal: Libraries and the Academy* 20, no. 1 (January 2020): 137–59, https://doi.org/10.1353/pla.2020.0007; Rebecca Halpern and Lisa Lepore, "Scholarly Storytelling: Using Stories as a Roadmap to Authentic and Creative Library Research," in *Not Just Where to Click: Teaching Students How to Think about Information*, ed. Troy A. Swanson and Heather Jagman (Chicago: Association of College and Research Libraries, 2015), 349–65; Andrea Baer, "Gently Stretching to Reach All Students: Inclusive Learning through Scaffolding and Flexible Pedagogy," *College and Research Libraries News* 82, no. 4 (2021): 182–85, https://crln.acrl.org/index.php/crlnews/article/view/24890/0.

25 Halpern and Lepore, "Scholarly Storytelling," 351.

26. Morrison, "Informed Asset-Based Pedagogy," 195.

27. Morrison, "Informed Asset-Based Pedagogy."

28. Cedillo, "What Does It Mean to Move?"; Baker-Bell, *Linguistic Justice*.

29. Baer, "Gently Stretching to Reach All Students," 182.

30. Baer, "Gently Stretching to Reach All Students," 182–83.

31. Tewell, "Problem with Grit"; Morrison, "Informed Asset-Based Pedagogy"; Heinbach et al., "Dismantling Deficit Thinking"; Folk, "Drawing on Students' Funds of Knowledge"; Baer, "Gently Stretching to Reach All Students."

32. bell hooks, *Teaching to Transgress* (New York: Routledge, 1994), 8.

33. Halpern and Lepore, "Scholarly Storytelling," 350.

34. Kareem, "Critical Race Analysis;" Baker-Bell, *Linguistic Justice*; Tewell, "Problem with Grit"; Morrison, "Informed Asset-Based Pedagogy;" Folk, "Drawing on Students' Funds of Knowledge."

35. Kareem, "Critical Race Analysis," 275–76.

36. Folk, "Drawing on Students' Funds of Knowledge," 46.

37. Halpern and Lepore, "Scholarly Storytelling;" Morrison, "Informed Asset-Based Pedagogy;" Folk, "Drawing on Students' Funds of Knowledge."

38. Morrison, "Informed Asset-Based Pedagogy," 192–93.

39. Halpern and Lepore, "Scholarly Storytelling," 349, see also 352–55, 361–64.

40. See for example Vikki Boliver, "Misplaced Optimism: How Higher Education Reproduces Rather Than Reduces Social Inequality," *British Journal of Sociology of Education* 38, no. 3 (2017): 423–32, https://doi.org/10.1080/01425692.2017.1281648; Grubb and Lazerson, "Vocationalism in Higher Education."

41. Baker-Bell, *Linguistic Justice*; Vershawn Ashanti Young, "Should Writers Use They Own English?" *Iowa Journal of Cultural Studies* 12, no. 1 (2010): 110–17.

42. NiCole T. Buchanan, and Isis H. Settles, "Managing (In)visibility and Hypervisibility in Workplace," *Journal of Vocational Behavior* 113 (August 2019): 2, https://doi.org/10.1016/j.jvb.2018.11.001.

43. Godbee, "Writing Up," 595, drawing on Kenneth Dowst, "The Epistemic Approach: Writing, Knowing, and Learning," in *Eight Approaches to Teaching Composition*, ed. Timothy R. Donovan and Ben W. McClelland (Urbana, IL: National Council of Teachers of English, 1980), 66, and James A. Berlin, *Rhetorics, Poetics, and Cultures* (West Lafayette, IN: Parlor, 2003), 84–87.

44. Godbee, "Writing Up," 595.

45. David Bartholomae, "Inventing the University," *Journal of Basic Writing* 5, no. 1 (1986): 4–22.

46. Bartholomae, "Inventing the University."

47. Geneva Smitherman, *Word from the Mother* (New York: Routledge, 2006), 3.

48. Baker-Bell, *Linguistic Justice*; Buchanan and Settles, "Managing (In)visibility"; Isabel Wilkerson, *Caste* (New York: Random House, 2020).

49. Bartholomae, "Inventing the University."

50. Miranda Fricker, *Epistemic Injustice* (Oxford: Oxford University Press, 2007), 598.

51. Greenfield, *Radical Writing Center Praxis*, 20.

52. Fricker, *Epistemic Injustice*.

53. Baker-Bell, *Linguistic Justice*, 5.

54. Baker-Bell, *Linguistic Justice*, 2.

55. Tressie McMillan Cottom, *Lower Ed* (New York: New Press, 2017).

56. Nicole M. Stephens et al, "Unseen Disadvantage: How American Universities' Focus on Independence Undermines the Academic Performance of First-Generation College Students," *Journal of Personality and Social Psychology* 102, no. 6 (2012): 1178–97, https://doi.org/10.1037/a0027143

57. Francesca Borgonovi and Gabriele Marconi, "Inequality in Higher Education: Why Did Expanding Access Not Reduce Skill Inequality?" *Open Education Studies* 2, no. 1 (2020): 312–43, https://doi.org/10.1515/edu-2020-0110; Baker-Bell, *Linguistic Justice*.

58. Boliver, "Misplaced Optimism"; Bartholomae, "Inventing the University."

59. Boliver, "Misplaced Optimism," 427.

60. Julie Ray and Stephanie Marken, "Life in College Matters for Life after College," Gallup, May 6, 2014, https://news.gallup.com/poll/168848/life-college-matters-life-college.aspx; John Warner, *Sustainable, Resilient, Free* (Cleveland, OH: Belt Press, 2020), 54.

61. Daniel G. Solórzano and Tara J. Yosso, "Critical Race Methodology: Counter-storytelling as an

Analytical Framework for Education Research," *Qualitative Inquiry* 8, no. 1 (February 2002): 23, https://doi.org/10.1177/107780040200800103.

62. Kynard, *Vernacular Insurrections.*
63. Woody, "Re-engaging Rhetorical Education," 483.
64. Baker-Bell, *Linguistic Justice*; Kareem, "Critical Race Analysis"; Woody, "Re-engaging Rhetorical Education."
65. Cottom, *Lower Ed.*

Bibliography

Baer, Andrea. "Gently Stretching to Reach All Students: Inclusive Learning through Scaffolding and Flexible Pedagogy." *College and Research Libraries News* 82, no. 4 (2021): 182–85. https://crln.acrl. org/index.php/crlnews/article/view/24890/0.

Baker-Bell, April. *Linguistic Justice: Black Language, Literacy, Identity and Pedagogy.* New York: Routledge, 2020.

Bartholomae, David. "Inventing the University." *Journal of Basic Writing* 5, no. 1 (1986): 4–22.

Berlin, James A. *Rhetorics, Poetics, and Cultures: Refiguring College English Studies.* West Lafayette, IN: Parlor, 2003.

Boliver, Vikki. "Misplaced Optimism: How Higher Education Reproduces Rather Than Reduces Social Inequality." *British Journal of Sociology of Education* 38, no. 3 (2017): 423–32. https://doi. org/10.1080/01425692.2017.1281648.

Borgonovi, Francesca, and Gabriele Marconi. "Inequality in Higher Education: Why Did Expanding Access Not Reduce Skill Inequality?" *Open Education Studies* 2, no. 1 (2020): 312–43. https://doi. org/10.1515/edu-2020-0110.

Buchanan, NiCole T., and Isis H. Settles. "Managing (In)visibility and Hypervisibility in the Workplace." *Journal of Vocational Behavior* 113 (August 2019): 1–5. https://doi.org/10.1016/j. jvb.2018.11.001.

Busman, Debra. "Silences and Stories: Honoring Voice and Agency in the College Classroom." In *Ways of Being in Teaching: Conversations and Reflections,* edited by Sean Wiebe, Ellyn Lyle, Peter R. Wright, Kimberly Dark, Mitchell McLarnon, and Liz Day, 47–54. Rotterdam, Netherlands: Brill, 2017.

Cariaga, Stephanie. "Towards Self-Recovery: Cultivating Love with Young Women of Color through Pedagogies of Bodymindspirit." *Urban Review: Issues and Ideas in Public Education* 51, no. 1 (2019): 101–22.

Cedillo, Christina V. "What Does It Mean to Move? Race, Disability, and Critical Embodiment Pedagogy." *Composition Forum* 39 (Summer 2018). https://compositionforum.com/issue/39/to-move. php.

Cottom, Tressie McMillan. *Lower Ed: The Troubling Rise of For-Profit Colleges in the New Economy.* New York: New Press, 2017.

Dowst, Kenneth. "The Epistemic Approach: Writing, Knowing, and Learning." *Eight Approaches to Teaching Composition,* edited by Timothy R. Donovan and Ben W. McClelland, 65–86. Urbana, IL: National Council of Teachers of English, 1980.

Folk, Amanda L. "Drawing on Students' Funds of Knowledge: Using Identity and Lived Experience to Join the Conversation in Research Assignments." *Journal of Information Literacy* 12, no. 2 (December 2018): 44–59.

Fricker, Miranda. *Epistemic Injustice: Power and the Ethics of Knowing.* Oxford: Oxford University Press, 2007.

Godbee, Beth. "Writing Up: How Assertions of Epistemic Rights Counter Epistemic Justice." *College English* 79, no. 6 (2017): 593–618. https://core.ac.uk/download/pdf/213085398.pdf.

Greenfield, Laura. *Radical Writing Center Paxis: A Paradigm for Ethical Political Engagement*. Logan: Utah State University Press, 2019.

Grubb, W. Norton, and Marvin Lazerson. "Vocationalism in Higher Education: The Triumph of the Education Gospel." *Journal of Higher Education* 76, no. 1 (2005): 1–25.

Halpern, Rebecca, and Lisa Lepore. "Scholarly Storytelling: Using Stories as a Roadmap to Authentic and Creative Library Research." In *Not Just Where to Click: Teaching Students How to Think about Information,* edited by Troy A. Swanson and Heather Jagman, 349–65. Chicago: Association of College and Research Libraries, 2015.

Heinbach, Chelsea, Brittany Paloma Fiedler, Rosan Mitola, and Emily Pattni. "Dismantling Deficit Thinking: A Strengths-Based Inquiry into the Experiences of Transfer Students in and out of Academic Libraries." *In the Library with the Lead Pipe*, February 6, 2019. http://www.inthelibrary-withtheleadpipe.org/2019/dismantling-deficit-thinking.

hooks, bell. *Teaching to Transgress: Education as the Practice of Freedom*. New York: Routledge, 1994.

Kareem, Jamila. "A Critical Race Analysis of Transition-Level Writing Curriculum to Support the Racially Diverse Two-Year College." *Teaching English in the Two-Year College* 46, no. 4 (2019): 271–96.

Kynard, Carmen. *Vernacular Insurrections: Race, Black Protest, and the New Century in Composition-Literacies Studies*. Albany, NY: SUNY Press, 2013.

Martinez, Aja Y. "A Plea for Critical Race Theory Counterstory: Stock Story versus Counterstory Dialogues Concerning Alejandra's 'Fit' in the Academy." In *Performing Antiracist Pedagogy in Rhetoric, Writing, and Composition*, edited by Frankie Condon and Vershawn Ashanti Young, 65–85. Fort Collins, CO: WAC Clearinghouse and Boulder: University Press of Colorado, 2016. https://doi.org/10.37514/ATD-B.2016.0933.2.03.

Morrison, Kim L. "Informed Asset-Based Pedagogy: Coming Correct, Counter-stories from an Information Literacy Classroom." *Library Trends* 66, no. 2 (2017): 176–218.

Ray, Julie and Stephanie Marken. "Life in College Matters for Life after College." Gallup, May 6, 2014. https://news.gallup.com/poll/168848/life-college-matters-life-college.aspx.

Schlesselman-Tarango, Gina. "The Legacy of Lady Bountiful: White Women in the Library." *Library Trends* 64, no. 4 (2016): 667–86. https://doi.org/10.1353/lib.2016.0015.

Smitherman, Geneva. *Word from the Mother: Language and African Americans*. New York: Routledge, 2006.

Solórzano, Daniel G., and Tara J. Yosso. "Critical Race Methodology: Counter-storytelling as an Analytical Framework for Education Research." *Qualitative Inquiry* 8, no. 1 (February 2002): 23–44. https://doi.org/10.1177/107780040200800103.

Stephens, Nicole M., Stephanie A. Fryberg, Hazel Rose Markus, Camille S. Johnson, and Rebecca Covarrubias. "Unseen Disadvantage: How American Universities' Focus on Independence Undermines the Academic Performance of First-Generation College Students." *Journal of Personality and Social Psychology* 102, no. 6 (2012): 1178–97. https://doi.org/10.1037/a0027143.

Tewell, Eamon. "The Problem with Grit: Dismantling Deficit Thinking in Library Instruction." *portal: Libraries and the Academy* 20, no. 1 (January 2020): 137–59. https://doi.org/10.1353/pla.2020.0007.

Warner, John. *Sustainable, Resilient, Free: The Future of Public Higher Education*. Cleveland, OH: Belt Press, 2020.

Watkins, D. *We Speak for Ourselves: How Woke Culture Prohibits Progress*. New York: Atria, 2020.

Wilkerson, Isabel. *Caste: The Origins of Our Discontents*. New York: Random House, 2020.

Woody, Cassandra. "Re-engaging Rhetorical Education through Procedural Feminism: Designing First-Year Writing Curricula That Listen." *College Composition and Communication* 71, no. 3 (2020): 481–507.

Young, Vershawn Ashanti, Rusty Barrett, Y'Shanda Young-Rivera, Kim Brian Lovejoy. *Other People's English: Code-Meshing, Code-Switching, and African American Literacy.* New York: Teachers College Press, 2014.

———."Should Writers Use They Own English? *Iowa Journal of Cultural Studies* 12, no. 1 (2010): 110–17.

CHAPTER 25

Student-Centered, Student-Delivered

Leading with Equity and Inclusion through a First-Year Library Ambassador Program at a Hispanic-Serving Institution

Gina Schlesselman-Tarango, Sara Durazo-DeMoss, and Barbara Herrera

Land Acknowledgement

We recognize that California State University, San Bernardino sits on the territory and ancestral land of the San Manuel Band of Mission Indians (Yuhaaviatam). We recognize that every member of the California State University, San Bernardino community has benefitted and continues to benefit from the use and occupation of this land since the institution's founding in 1965. Consistent with our values of community and diversity, we have a responsibility to acknowledge and make visible the university's relationship to Native peoples. By offering this Land Acknowledgement, we affirm Indigenous sovereignty and will work to hold California State University, San Bernardino more accountable to the needs of American Indian and Indigenous peoples. *-CSUSB Land Acknowledgement, CSUSB Office of Tribal Relations*

Introduction

Libraries have long used peer-to-peer models at service points (circulation and reference desks, for example), but this approach in library teaching contexts is not widely adopted.[1] Yet for those who have experimented with peer instructional models, the benefits to both those delivering and those receiving instruction are clear—peers are viewed as more approachable, serve to decrease uneven power dynamics between teacher and student, and can relate to fellow students in ways librarians or other faculty cannot.[2] As Maxson and colleagues explain,

> [peer-assisted learning] strategies center the student in the pedagogy and provide agency and empowerment through valuing students' experiences and positioning them as knowledge creators and co-creators. Seen through the lens of critical pedagogy, [peer-assisted learning] has liberatory aims in that it frees both the teacher and student from the traditional classroom… and honors students' identities and agency.[3]

Recognizing how these models are rooted in equity and inclusion, the Pfau Library instruction team decided to pilot a peer-to-peer Library Ambassador Initiative program (LAI) in 2016. This case study highlights the evolution of the Pfau Library Ambassador program from its inception to its current model. Beginning as a small initiative within the California State University, San Bernardino (CSUSB) John M. Pfau Library, the LAI program has grown into a student-centered campus partnership with the Office of Undergraduate Studies' Student Mentoring Program (SMP) and continues to reach an increasing number of first-year students.

CSUSB is a Hispanic-serving institution in Southern California and serves approximately 19,404 students, 2,286 of whom are first-year students. Sixty-six percent identify as Hispanic or Latino, and 75 percent of students are first-generation students, meaning they will be the first in their family to attain a college degree. Additionally, 51 percent of the students are Pell Grant recipients, meaning their family demonstrates financial need.[4] Of the incoming first-year students, 38 percent were identified as needing additional support in math, English, or both.

All first-year undergraduate students at CSUSB are required to take several general education courses, many of which have a critical information literacy outcome mapped onto them. In part, these courses are meant to introduce students to information literacy practices, including strategic searching for, critical selection and examination of, and ethical sharing of information.[5]

Teaching critical information literacy and developing habits and dispositions can look different in each course and even among course sections, as all faculty at CSUSB are afforded academic freedom; even in the few cases in which all sections of a course share a "signature assignment," the manner in which the content is taught and how students are prepared to complete the assignment is up to the instructor of record. However, there are key information and skills all students need to successfully engage, not only in these courses, but throughout their college careers. Due to staffing limitations, for years the CSUSB Pfau Library was unable to support first-year courses through synchronous library-led instruction and instead sought to address the lower division general education curriculum in other ways, from assisting with the facilitation of professional development for instructors[6] to the development of online tutorials tailored for beginning researchers. Despite the effectiveness of these interventions, first-year faculty still often approached the Pfau Library in search of a "face" to put to the name; in other words, they valued a personal connection to the library for their students.

Program Background and Description

Student Mentoring Program: High-Impact Practice

Kuh and the Association of American College and Universities (AAC&U) introduced high impact practices (HIPs) in education. Practices include first-year seminars, common intellectual experiences, learning communities, writing-intensive courses, collaborative assignments and projects, undergraduate research, diversity and global learning, service learning/community-based learning, internships, and capstone courses and projects. One of the key components of these nationally recognized practices includes peer-to-peer engagement in learning, and the educational benefits students gain from engaging in HIPs, specifically in terms of educational justice and closing equity gaps, are such that the AAC&U recommends incorporating them at institutions of higher education.[7]

An example of a HIP, the SMP fosters undergraduate student success by supporting academic excellence, campus connectedness and engagement, personal growth, and professional development. It began as a faculty-led initiative in 1990 and then evolved into a coordinator- and student-led program in 2013. Over time, the number of student leaders who serve as mentors increased from fifteen to forty-five, and as of fall 2021, we increased the number of student mentors to one hundred because of the positive impact peer education and student mentoring have had on reducing equity gaps in academic achievement.

First-year undergraduate students who participate in the SMP are called protégés. Student mentors attend a twelve-hour training before the academic year begins. The training consists of the following topics: time management, setting boundaries, effective communication, goal setting, campus resources, and library resources (discussed below). Typically, mentors and protégés are matched by major. Beginning every fall, student mentors conduct one-on-one meetings with protégés. During the one-on-one meetings, mentors and protégés begin to develop rapport and get to know each other. As they build on the foundation of this new relationship, mentors support the protégés through the transition from high school to university life. Student mentors guide protégés in their academic journey by creating a semester success plan, introducing campus resources, encouraging them to meet with faculty during office hours, helping them with campus engagement, and more.

Library Ambassador Initiative

In 2016, when the Library Ambassador Program was initially piloted, library staff thought it best to start small and therefore offered the service only to a first-year seminar course. Further, the team thought it logical to identify potential ambassadors from among the ranks of the many library employees. However, it quickly became apparent that only a small number of student employees were both comfortable serving as ambassadors and had work schedules that were flexible enough to allow them to participate. Because the program operates on a classroom visit model, the library found itself in the unfortunate position of having to turn down requests from faculty who taught sections in the evening, for example, because no student ambassadors were available. At other times, a librarian was able to cover for students who called in sick, but that defeated the purpose of a peer-to-peer program and was neither sustainable nor scalable.

LAI and SMP Partnership

In 2018, the Pfau Library and SMP came together to discuss the future of this program and how a partnership might prove to be mutually beneficial. Together, we decided that Library Ambassadors could be drawn from the existing pool of student mentors in the SMP. In practice, this would mean that the SMP would continue to hire and train mentors and the library would give these same students the opportunity to act as ambassadors and arrange for them to visit classes to represent the library. All student mentors, therefore, are Library Ambassadors (and vice versa). By tapping into a reserve of highly vetted upper division student mentors, most of whom, similar to the student body at CSUSB, were first-generation college students sharing similar experiences transitioning to college, the Library Ambassador program would be able to grow the initiative to serve more faculty and students. The previous pilot demonstrated that the classroom visit model allowed for curricular integration in a way that was fairly simple to manage, and the SMP was excited about how this approach might allow first-time students an additional access point to peer mentors. The SMP recognized this as an opportunity to recruit more mentees into the program resulting in increased student retention rates from first to second year for participants. In 2019, we steadily increased the number of first-year courses to which we offered Library Ambassador visits. Most recently, we offered the program to all first-year general education courses that have a critical information literacy learning outcome. Courses include Foundation Seminar (previously First-Year Seminar), Oral Communication, Written Communication, US History, and Freshman Learning Community.

As Library Ambassadors, mentors are trained in the basics of the Pfau Library, including services available to new students, how to find resources for common assignments, and how to get research help. The librarian-developed training typically includes an overview of an in-class presentation, practice addressing frequently asked questions, and discussion of presentation best practices. The trainings center and build upon student experiences with college-level research and library use, public speaking and presenting, and delivery of the Library Ambassador presentation itself. Returning mentors who have visited classrooms in past years are eager to share tips and techniques with new mentors, while all participants contribute by asking questions and sharing how they have used the library while in college.

Every semester, the coordinator of library instruction identifies instructors of targeted courses, sends them an e-mail describing the program with a link to a Library Ambassador request form, and works with the SMP to set up and confirm the forty-five-minute classroom visits. The ambassadors visit the classes in groups of two or three, which not only alleviates some public speaking anxiety but also allows the students to collaborate to deliver the presentation and answer student and faculty questions. In addition to delivering the library presentation and sharing their own journeys with research and use of the library as CSUSB students, the Library Ambassadors also distribute a brief survey at the conclusion of each visit.

The surveys provide us with information to adjust the training and initiative as necessary to ensure we are best serving students. For example, we ask students if anything about the library remains unclear, and a number have in the past indicated that they still have questions about the course reserve system. Because providing free access to required course materials is central to ensuring all students are able to fully and equitably participate in their learning—regardless of socioeconomic status—we not only follow up with students who have questions but also adjust training to ensure the ambassadors understand the system and are prepared to successfully communicate it during their classroom visits (and during one-on-one meetings with protégés if questions about textbooks arise). We also ask students what they learned and if there is anything else they wished the ambassadors had discussed.

Overall, students consistently report that as a result of the ambassador visit, they not only feel confident conducting college-level research, but also know how to get research help and support. We further use the survey data to annually advocate for program funding.

Ambassadors also share information about the SMP and how new students can build authentic peer-to-peer relationships that are instrumental in demystifying college life and academic success. Survey results show that students identify the SMP as a safe place and valuable resource to receive assistance as they learn how to navigate the university. A number of students in classes that had Library Ambassador visits later sought mentors, demonstrating that the LAI acts as a pathway into the SMP for new students.

Peer Learning, Equity, and Inclusion

The programs, LAI and SMP, are HIPs grounded in equity by connecting new students to the services and resources needed to thrive. In fact, undergraduate research is a nationally recognized HIP.[8] Taking a critical approach to both programs allows educators to engage in a transformative way of thinking where the traditional relationship between student and classroom teaching and between student and mentor shift to collaborative and empowering interactions. Centering students in teaching and learning is a core element of critical pedagogy and of mentoring that helps combat library anxiety by providing early exposure to the library while highlighting student research experiences, concerns, and needs.[9]

Both programs are intentional about creating collective, communal, and collaborative experiences that draw on the cultural and familial wealth that students possess and share.[10] During classroom visits, Library Ambassadors share their experiences as students and researchers, thereby centering the concerns and needs of students rather than what a librarian, for example, thinks students ought to know or be able to access. The students and staff involved in this program are both producers and consumers of knowledge and teaching, and by centering students and their peers, the program celebrates them as contributors to the university and ensures that staff or librarians do not inadvertently act as gatekeepers of institutional knowledge. Here, students contribute to knowledge production and defining the parameters of what information is.[11]

It is important to understand the power dynamics of the classroom and within mentoring relationships. While both can be sites of liberation and development, traditionally, they have served as mechanisms to reproduce inequity. Critical mentoring, then, is mentoring augmented by a critical consciousness, one that compels us to take collective action and to do it alongside our young people…. [it] is about helping youth to construct powerful identities and gain valuable work and school experiences that they can use in legitimate ways.[12]

Participation in the SMP and LAI, then, provides the opportunity for students to develop identities as knowledgeable leaders and acquire experience in both peer support and pedagogical exchange.

Because the LAI targets general education courses, the program alleviates some of the teaching load for the limited number of librarians at the Pfau Library who are often pulled in a variety of directions as they juggle the competing demands of promotion and tenure. Library Ambassadors are certainly not free replacement labor for librarians, however, and the program coordinators insist that participants be paid for training, preparation, and classroom visits. Paying students for their labor, paired with a focus on professional and leadership development, is an essential component ensuring the praxis is equitable and not exploitative and that students are treated as valuable employees and part of the university.

Finally, we are also beginning to consider how this program is a form of open pedagogy, or what Couros describes as "learning experiences that are open, transparent, collaborative, and social" and that "support …students in the critical consumption, production, connection, and synthesis of knowledge through the shared development of learning networks."[13] Heinbach, Rinto, and Mitola delineate core principles of open pedagogy, two of which resonate with the LAI approach: it emphasizes learner-driven curricula and educational structures and stresses community and collaboration over content.[14] When thinking about the Library Ambassador classroom visit as one potential pathway into the formation of a lasting learning network or mentor-protégé relationship, we reflect on their compelling questions:

How does this change our pedagogical practice? How might it also change how we approach our assessment, research, and student employment in libraries and higher education institutions more broadly? How might it change the way students see themselves as a part of the university?[15]

Successes, Challenges, and Lessons Learned

The COVID-19 pandemic and rapid shift to online learning in spring 2020 presented several challenges to the CSUSB community, including how the Pfau Library and

SMP would continue to partner to serve first-year students. The team ultimately decided to continue to offer the synchronous classroom-visit model and therefore shift the focus of training to how to effectively deliver information and engage students through platforms such as Zoom or Microsoft Teams. We also took this opportunity to increase student mentor involvement in the training and incorporated a student-developed and -facilitated discussion, another effort to ensure the initiative centers students' voices and experiences throughout all aspects of the program. In the future, we hope to increasingly involve mentors in the development and delivery of Library Ambassador training.

In January 2021, following midyear training, we surveyed the Library Ambassadors and confirmed that the program has had a positive impact on the mentors' familiarity with library resources, confidence conducting college-level research, knowledge of how to get research help, ability to help protégés understand and access campus resources, and leadership skills. Mentors feel more confident in their public speaking skills and are more comfortable answering questions from students—in fact, they really enjoy it when students engage in their presentations. When asked how the LAI program could be improved, mentors suggested that due to the quickly changing nature of available library services and resources as a result of the implementation and lifting of statewide stay-at-home orders, updates throughout the semester would be helpful. In spring 2021, for example, staff were ordered to stay at home for a period, and the contactless book pickup system was unavailable during this time. Once instructors began to schedule Library Ambassador visits, then, periodic Library Ambassador Refreshers were offered throughout the semester to give mentors an opportunity to ask questions, review the LAI materials, get updates, and so on in the days or weeks before they were to present.

On occasion, we have had to manage faculty expectations of the program, as mentors have reported that instructors have pressed them to cover content or skills beyond the scope of the presentation (how to cite in a particular style or locate historical newspapers, for example). Though the Library Ambassadors are trained to refer those with advanced questions to a librarian, faculty have unfortunately put the mentors on the spot or expressed disappointment with the visit. Such faculty have been identified, and we have reached out to them and reiterated the introductory nature of the presentation and underscored that Library Ambassadors are not trained to provide advanced research training or assistance. When Library Ambassador visits are confirmed with faculty, they are again reminded that the visit is meant to supplement, not replace, faculty-led critical information literacy instruction and that the goal is to center and establish connection among students, in turn decreasing library anxiety for learners new to the university.

Looking Ahead

The future of the Library Ambassador partnership is an exciting one, as moving forward we will be working with mentors and first-time students who, for the most part, have experienced online learning and all that entails, be it at CSUSB or at the high school level. Much remains to be determined, but we envision a program that is flexible and able to accommodate in-person, hybrid, and virtual classrooms. This means that for the first time, we will likely be able to make the program available to faculty, mentors, and students at CSUSB's satellite Palm Desert Campus. Situated in California's Coachella Valley, this campus serves approximately 1,600 students—93 percent of whom are undergraduates and 68 percent of whom are Hispanic or Latino[16]—and, due to its size, distance from the San Bernardino campus, and budget limitations, has often been unable to provide the same level of service to its students. Offering an online option for Palm Desert faculty and even starting up an in-person LAI using Palm Desert Campus mentors are options we are exploring in our continued commitment to access and equity for all our students.

Regardless of where students are located and learning is taking place, the LAI is an example of how libraries and their campus partners can provide programming that legitimizes students and their experiences, in turn alleviating library anxiety for those new to the university. In creating a path for students to share with their peers the ways they engage with library materials and services while developing supportive relationships, librarians and staff move from center to side stage, making space for student-to-student connections to flourish.

Notes

1. Bronwen K. Maxson et al., "The Power of Peers: Approaches from Writing and Libraries," *Reference Services Review* 47, no. 3 (2019): 314–30, https://doi.org/10.1108/RSR-03-2019-0020.
2. Brett B. Bodemer, "They CAN and they SHOULD: Undergraduates Providing Peer Reference and Instruction," *College and Research Libraries* 75, no. 2 (2014): 162–78, https://doi.org/10.5860/crl12-411; Maxson et al., "Power of Peers"; Erin Rinto, John Watts, and Rosan Mitola, eds., *Peer-Assisted Learning in Academic Libraries* (Santa Barbara, CA: Libraries Unlimited, 2017).
3. Maxson et al., "Power of Peers," 318.
4. California State University, San Bernardino, CSUSB Dashboard Landing Page, accessed June 3, 2021, https://dashboard.csusb.edu/idashboards/view?guestuser=idashguest&dashID=599&-dashId=599.
5. California State University, San Bernardino, "CIL Rubric Narrative," May 2017, John M. Pfau Library, https://www.csusb.edu/sites/default/files/upload/file/CIL-Rubric_Narrative.pdf.
6. Gina Schlesselman-Tarango, "Exploring Epistemological Lineages: Using the Gallery Walk with Students and Instructors of a First-Year Seminar Course," in *Critical Approaches to Credit-Bearing Information Literacy Courses*, ed. Angela Pashia and Jessica Critten (Chicago: Association of College and Research Libraries, 2019), 295–314.

7. Jillian Kinzie, "High-Impact Practices: Promoting Participation for All Students," *Diversity and Democracy* 15, no. 3 (2012): 13-14, https://dgmg81phhvh63.cloudfront.net/content/user-photos/Publications/Archives/Diversity-Democracy/DD_15-3_FA12.pdf; George Kuh, *High-impact Educational Practices* (Washington DC: Association of American Colleges and Universities, 2008); George Kuh and Ken O'Donnell, *Ensuring Quality and Taking High-Impact Practices to Scale* (Washington DC: Association of American Colleges and Universities, 2013).
8. Kuh, *High-Impact Educational Practices*.
9. Zoe Blecher-Cohen, "The Student Connection: Thinking Critically on Library Anxiety and Information Literacy," *Public Services Quarterly* 15, no. 4 (2019): 359–67, https://doi.org/10.1080/15228959.2019.1664361; Heather Carlile, "The Implications of Library Anxiety for Academic Reference Services: A Review of Literature," *Australian Academic and Research Libraries* 38, no. 2 (2013): 129–47, https://doi.org/10.1080/00048623.2007.10721282; Cecelia Parks, "Testing a Warmth-Based Instruction Intervention for Reducing Library Anxiety in First-Year Undergraduate Students," *Evidence Based Library and Information Practice* 14, no. 2 (2019): 70–84, https://doi.org/10.18438/eblip29548.
10. Tara J. Yosso, "Whose Culture Has Capital? A Critical Race Theory Discussion of Community Cultural Wealth," *Race Ethnicity and Education* 8, no. 1 (2005): 69–91, https://doi.org/10.1080/1361332052000341006; Sheara A. Williams and Beverly A. Dawson, "The Effects of Familial Capital on the Academic Achievement of Elementary Latino/a Students," *Families in Society* 92, no. 1 (2011): 91–98, https://doi.org/10.1606/1044-3894.4066.
11. Eamon Tewell, "A Decade of Critical Information Literacy: A Review of the Literature," *Communications in Information Literacy* 9, no. 1 (2015): 24–43, https://doi.org/10.15760/comminfolit.2015.9.1.174; Torie Weiston-Serdan, *Critical Mentoring* (Sterling, VA: Stylus, 2017).
12. Weiston-Serdan, *Critical Mentoring*, 1.
13. Alec Couros, "Developing Personal Learning Networks for Open and Social Learning," in *Emerging Technologies in Distance Education*, ed. George Veletsianos (Edmonton, AB: Athabasca University Press, 2010), 115.
14. Chelsea Heinbach, Erin Rinto, and Rosan Mitola, "Open Pedagogy: An Emerging Strategy for Challenging Deficit Thinking and Empowering Student Voices," presentation, ACRL 2021 virtual conference, March 15–18, 2021, https://drive.google.com/drive/folders/1-6ks6IpAwkZi2TP-wYTMAwPnybHpPv9bc.
15. Heinback, Rinto, and Mitola, "Open Pedagogy."
16. California State University, San Bernardino, "Palm Desert Campus Statistics," Fall 2019, https://www.csusb.edu/pdc/about-pdc/statistics (information for 2019 removed from page).

Bibliography

Blecher-Cohen, Zoe. "The Student Connection: Thinking Critically on Library Anxiety and Information Literacy." *Public Services Quarterly* 15, no. 4 (2019): 359–67. https://doi.org/10.1080/15228959.2019.1664361.

Bodemer, Brett B. "They CAN and They SHOULD: Undergraduates Providing Peer Reference and Instruction." *College and Research Libraries* 75, no. 2 (2014): 162–78. https://doi.org/10.5860/crl12-411.

California State University, San Bernardino. "CIL Rubric Narrative." May 2017. John M. Pfau Library. https://www.csusb.edu/sites/default/files/upload/file/CIL-Rubric_Narrative.pdf.

———. CSUSB Dashboard Landing Page. Accessed June 3, 2021. https://www.csusb.edu/institutional-research/dashboards.

———. "Palm Desert Campus Statistics." Fall 2019. https://www.csusb.edu/pdc/about-pdc/statistics (information for 2019 removed from page).

Carlile, Heather. "The Implications of Library Anxiety for Academic Reference Services: A Review of Literature." *Australian Academic and Research Libraries* 38, no. 2 (2013): 129–47. https://doi.org/1 0.1080/00048623.2007.10721282.

Couros, Alec. "Developing Personal Learning Networks for Open and Social Learning." In *Emerging Technologies in Distance Education,* edited by George Veletsianos, 109–128. Edmonton, AB: Athabasca University Press, 2010.

Heinbach, Chelsea, Erin Rinto, and Rosan Mitola. "Open Pedagogy: An Emerging Strategy for Challenging Deficit Thinking and Empowering Student Voices." Presentation, ACRL 2021 virtual conference, March 15–18, 2021. https://drive.google.com/drive/folders/1-6ks6IpAwkZi2TPwYTMAwPnybHpPv9bc.

Kinzie, Jillian. "High-Impact Practices: Promoting Participation for All Students." *Diversity and Democracy* 15, no. 3 (2012): 13-14. https://dgmg81phhvh63.cloudfront.net/content/user-photos/Publications/Archives/Diversity-Democracy/DD_15-3_FA12.pdf.

Kuh, George D. *High-Impact Educational Practices: What They Are, Who Has Access to Them, and Why They Matter.* Washington, DC: Association of American Colleges and Universities, 2008.

Kuh, George D., and Ken O'Donnell. *Ensuring Quality and Taking High-Impact Practices to Scale.* Washington, DC: Association of American Colleges and Universities, 2013.

Maxson, Bronwen K., Michelle E. Neely, Lindsay M. Roberts, Sean M. Stone, M. Sara Lowe, Katharine V. Macy, and Willie Miller. "The Power of Peers: Approaches from Writing and Libraries." *Reference Services Review* 47, no. 3 (2019): 314–30. https://doi.org/10.1108/RSR-03-2019-0020.

Parks, Cecelia. "Testing a Warmth-Based Instruction Intervention for Reducing Library Anxiety in First-Year Undergraduate Students." *Evidence Based Library and Information Practice* 14, no. 2 (2019): 70–84. https://doi.org/10.18438/eblip29548.

Rinto, Erin, John Watts, and Rosan Mitola, eds. *Peer-Assisted Learning in Academic Libraries.* Santa Barbara, CA: Libraries Unlimited, 2017.

Schlesselman-Tarango, Gina. "Exploring Epistemological Lineages: Using the Gallery Walk with Students and Instructors of a First-Year Seminar Course." In *Critical Approaches to Credit-Bearing Information Literacy Courses,* edited by Angela Pashia and Jessica Critten, 295–314. Chicago: Association of College and Research Libraries, 2019.

Tewell, Eamon. "A Decade of Critical Information Literacy: A Review of the Literature." *Communications in Information Literacy* 9, no. 1 (2015): 24–43. https://doi.org/10.15760/comminfolit.2015.9.1.174.

Weiston-Serdan, Torie. *Critical Mentoring: A Practical Guide.* Sterling, VA: Stylus, 2017.

Williams, Sheara A., and Beverly Araujo Dawson. "The Effects of Familial Capital on the Academic Achievement of Elementary Latino/a Students." *Families in Society* 92, no. 1 (2011): 91–98. https://doi.org/10.1606/1044-3894.4066.

Yosso, Tara. J. "Whose Culture Has Capital? A Critical Race Theory Discussion of Community Cultural Wealth." *Race Ethnicity and Education* 8, no. 1 (2005): 69–91. https://doi.org/10.1080/136 1332052000341006.

CHAPTER 26

Making History Together

Reflections on Trust, Connection, and Finding Joy in the Archives

Kyle Denlinger, Megan Mulder, Kathy Shields, and Mir Yarfitz

Introduction

In this chapter, we share our experiences designing and teaching Gender and Sexuality in World History, an undergraduate history course in which students work together to research and produce a new class volume of an open access primary source reader. In designing the course and implementing our primary strategies of ungrading and open pedagogy, we centered trust, connection, and joy as both critical structures of and desired outcomes of an equitable class community.

Accessibility note: This chapter is formatted as a zine, so it is not fully accessible to those with print disabilities in its current format. Please refer to the appendix for a text-only description and transcription of each page. A screen reader-compatible copy of the zine in Google Slides and a downloadable version of the appendix in .docx and .html formats can be found at https://doi.org/10.17605/OSF.IO/CJNBD.

MAKING HISTORY TOGETHER:
REFLECTIONS ON TRUST,
CONNECTION, & FINDING
JOY IN THE ARCHIVES

Gender and Sexuality throughout
World History: An International
Collection of 18th to 20th Century Works
Wake Forest University, HST 114/WGS 214, Fall 2020

Kyle Denlinger
Megan Mulder
Kathy Shields
Mir Yarfitz

INTRO: UNBOXING JOY

Hello, reader.

We want to share with you our experience designing and teaching "Gender and Sexuality in World History," an undergraduate history course in which students work together to research and produce a new class volume of an open access primary source reader.[1] In writing and producing a book together, students are motivated to engage in meaningful, tangible scholarship that will have an audience beyond the classroom. Recognizing the importance of each person's contributions, they trusted one another and took great pride in their work. You can read more about the course in another book.[2]

As our students opened boxes of archival documents, they often uncovered painful truths. However, the inclusive environment we created together meant that students just as often opened themselves to new ways of seeing the world and new ways of learning in community.

In designing the course, we centered **TRUST, CONNECTION,** and **JOY** as both critical structures of and desired outcomes of an equitable class community. Our primary strategies, **UNGRADING** and **OPEN PEDAGOGY,** served to challenge traditional classroom power structures that far too often lead to misplaced student motivation, antagonistic teacher-student relationships, and bias against minoritized students. As we open these boxes together, it is our hope that you might find inspiration to take risks, seek joy, and connect more deeply with students and colleagues.

With gratitude for our students,

The Authors
September 2021

oh, also: We've never produced a zine before. We knew that collaborating remotely in the middle of a global pandemic and in a genre completely new to us would be a challenge, but we were intentional in doing it this way. We feel that producing this zine has allowed us to enter into a space we asked our students to enter, to experience some small measure of generative discomfort that has ultimately produced a large measure of joy.

support for new Fall 2019 divisional HST course

BOXES

Yarfitz, Mir <yarfi   Mon, Apr 22, 2019, 2:29 PM   ☆   ↩   ⋮
o me ▾

Dear Kyle,

Hi, I am writing to request your assistance with a new course that I have been developing for the fall, in Gender and Sexuality in World History, which will hopefully repeat each semester. I've been discussing it for a while with Kathy Shields, who I believe mentioned it to you somewhat. I am hoping that you can help me design a portal page which brings together databases and other resources, and also help with the design of a collective project which will be sort of like an open source textbook. Kathy mentioned that your expertise in Hypothesis might be useful in this design, and I've also been looking at the American YAWP as a model.

Are you interested in and available to supp
semester? I wanted to give you the heads-u
if possible I'd rather wait to meet until the b

BOX 1: TRUST

Thanks very much,
Mir

BOX 2: CONNECTION

BOX 3: JOY

Premise: Design a course that:
- Shares power
- Trusts students
- Engages students in primary source research
- Involves them in the process of authentic scholarship
- Doesn't beat them down
- Embraces community
- Embodies inclusive pedagogical principles

Shifts what students think history is:
- Not just a linear timeline of prominent white people
- It's a process they're a part of and contributing to

"Overall, this was my favorite class this semester, and I felt it was also the class I was the most comfortable in, engaged the most in, and learned the most in. I felt like the work I accomplished in this class, most specifically the collaborative book project, was some of the best work I have done in college so far, and that this class made me think the most deeply about topics including gender roles, power dynamics, gender fluidity, reproductive rights, and so much more."

TRUST

Trust in our students and in each other was an essential element. Each one of us—the students, the instructor, the three librarians—played a pivotal role in the success of these books.

Students had to trust that their classmates would engage deeply as co-producers of the book. Collectively, they helped each other decide on topics and sources, copyedited their peers' drafts, organized the book into sections, and even contributed cover art. We handled much of the project management and the tech, but **the rest was up to the students**.

We entrusted the students with a great deal of power, as well. We **relinquished control** over the format and structure of the book, most of the processes by which students created their work, and the licenses under which they chose to share it. We also **relinquished power** by making the class entirely ungraded.

UNGRADING

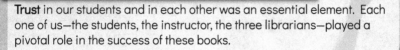

"But I really think I enjoy this class so much because I'm not afraid to fail in it."

"I rediscovered, in a way, my motivations for learning."

To make matters worse, traditional grading systems don't just affect students' perceptions of themselves; teachers, too, start to hold negative beliefs about students of color and multilingual students and their ability to succeed in school. We might say that our grading systems are fair and objective, but biases often enter our evaluation practices. For instance, a recent study conducted by David M. Quinn suggests that "racial stereotypes can influence the scores teachers assign to student work." [3]

Ungrading, and the self-reflection and self-assessment practices it encourages,[4] created space for each student to process some of their internalized beliefs about what learning is and who they are as learners. Like many students, those we work with tend to be extrinsically motivated by grades and often conflate grades with self-worth. In our class, most of these students, many of whom come from marginalized backgrounds, were for the first time **setting their own standards, pursuing their own learning goals, and taking risks they may not have otherwise taken**. Our hope was that our conversations about ungrading and the trust we demonstrated by ceding control of the grade would shift students' perceptions of themselves and the value of their work, push back against some of their internalized biases, and help mitigate any implicit biases of our own.

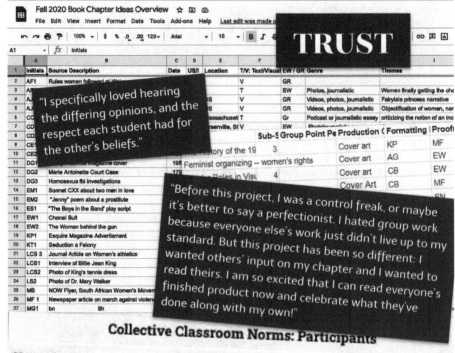

Fall 2020 Book Chapter Ideas Overview ☆ ▣ ☺
File Edit View Insert Format Data Tools Add-ons Help   Last edit was made o

↶ ↷ 🖨 🖍 | 100% ▾ | $ % .0 .00 123▾ | Arial ▾ | 10 ▾ | B I $ | **TRUST** | ∞ ▣ ⬚

A1 ▾ | fx | Initials

	Initials	Source Description	Date	US/I	Location	T/V: Text/Visual	EW / GR	Genre	Themes
2	AF1	Rules women followed at				V	GR		
3	A					T	EW	Photos, journalistic	Women finally getting the cha
4	A				s	V	GR	Videos, photos, journalistic	Fairytale princess narrative
5	A				s	V	GR	Videos, photos, journalistic	Objectification of women, nar
6	CC				assachuset	T	Gr	Podcast or journalistic essay	critizizing the notion of an inc
7	CD				reenville, St	V	EW	Photoiournalistic	
8	CD							Sub-S Group Point Pe Production (Formatting	Proofi
9	CE1						3	Cover art	KP	MF
10	CE2			tory of the 19			Cover art	AG	EW
11	DG1	roe magazine cover	195 Feminist organizing -- women's rights			Cover art	CB	EW
12	DG2	Marie Antoinette Court Case	179		Roles in Vist	4	Cover Art	CB	MF
13	DG3	Homosexua fbi investigations						SN
14	EM1	Sonnet CXX about two men in love						
15	EM2	"Jenny" poem about a prostitute						
16	ES1	"The Boys in the Band' play script						
17	EW1	Chanel Suit						
18	EW2	The Woman behind the gun						
19	KP1	Esquire Magazine Advertisment						
20	KT1	Seduction a Felony						
21	LCS 3	Journal Article on Women's athletics						
22	LCS1	Interview of Billie Jean King						
23	LCS2	Photo of King's tennis dress						
24	LS2	Photo of Dr. Mary Walker						
25	MB	NOW Flyer, South African Women's Movem						
26	MF 1	Newspaper article on march against violen						
27	MG1	bn	8h					

"I specifically loved hearing the differing opinions, and the respect each student had for the other's beliefs."

"Before this project, I was a control freak, or maybe it's better to say a perfectionist. I hated group work because everyone else's work just didn't live up to my standard. But this project has been so different: I wanted others' input on my chapter and I wanted to read theirs. I am so excited that I can read everyone's finished product now and celebrate what they've done along with my own!"

Collective Classroom Norms: Participants

Uncomfortable

Interrupting
Provocation – trolling
Personal attacks
Feeling like you can't say what
you think
Whispering, face
Assuming meani
Racially-charged
Condescension
Misgendering
Targeting people (

Optimal

Check what people meant to say
(reflect back)
One-on-one conflict / challenging
conversations

"We engaged with some heavy topics and I felt that we were able to create a safe and respectful environment in our classes. I even think we reached some of the things in the 'delightful' column because we were able to build some trust both through our discussions but also through our collaborative project."

Delightful

Trust
Knowing others as individual
Retain respect across differen
Remain aware of how much
space each of us taking up (wr
down to remember)
If someone leaves, leave them
alone unless you are friends
Open to changing minds
Talk to one another, not
facilitator
Assume others' faces,
movements, or words aren't
about you – it's about them

Repeating, getting stuck
mmediate jumping in

Sit in a circle? See t
Ask: anything else
on from topic
Ask: what are things we find
offensive in this text, that our
particular position lets us see?
Take a breather when things are
hot – ask if we want to come

In the first week of each semester, students created shared norms.

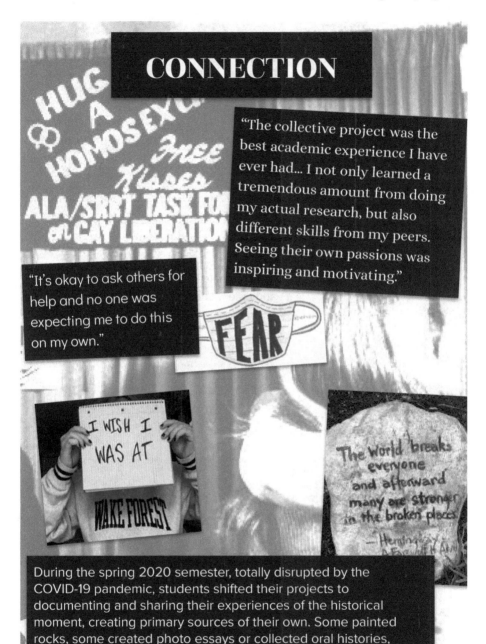

CONNECTION

"HUG A HOMOSEX... Free Kisses ALA/SRRT TASK FO... on GAY LIBERATION"

"The collective project was the best academic experience I have ever had... I not only learned a tremendous amount from doing my actual research, but also different skills from my peers. Seeing their own passions was inspiring and motivating."

"It's okay to ask others for help and no one was expecting me to do this on my own."

FEAR

I WISH I WAS AT WAKE FOREST

The World breaks everyone and afterward many are stronger in the broken places

— Hemingway, A Farewell to Arms

During the spring 2020 semester, totally disrupted by the COVID-19 pandemic, students shifted their projects to documenting and sharing their experiences of the historical moment, creating primary sources of their own. Some painted rocks, some created photo essays or collected oral histories, others made zines connecting to past crises. Slowing down to connect to their experiences and those of their classmates provided many with an emotional outlet and a source of solace.

CONNECTION & OPEN PEDAGOGY

"I believe that my classmates and I all worked very hard on our chapters to make sure they represented ourselves, as well as the class and you, well! So, although there was no pressure to 'get a good grade,' there was the pressure to make everyone proud."

"I don't know everything. I've never claimed to, but some of the best moments in this project came from someone adding on to what I had to say or offering up a suggestion."

"After completing every assignment, I try and reflect on what I have just completed and connect with within other aspects of my life, trying to apply my newfound knowledge or perspective to things like conversations, social media memes, historical stories, movies, etc."

The values of **open pedagogy**,[5] especially **access, equity, agency, connection,** and **responsibility**, are all aligned with the vision and values we had for this project. By contributing to the creation of an OER, students interrogated their own positionality, roles, and responsibilities in studying history, expanding access to marginalized stories, and writing for authentic audiences. As they positioned themselves within the legacy of knowledge production and being in conversation with future readers, students saw their work, their copyrights, and Creative Commons licenses as **relevant**.

We believe that our approach made the class more equitable, but we acknowledge that openness may be a barrier for some students.

THE POWER OF A NAME

OF A NAME

Sowebeyntta Amungo, '70'

JOY

"Visiting special collections was a joy, hands on activities make learning about history more engaging as I feel more immersed into what [I'm] reading or looking at."

Students worked with physical documents in Special Collections and Archives and with digitized documents available through the library and on the open web. An informal goal was to give students the opportunity to experience the **joy of finding connection to history** through the use of the archives.

We The BLACK WOMAN
poems by Femi Funmi Ifetayo

How do we find JOY in the archives?

2. The giving and receiving of affection is a personal thing and something which you do not to cheapen by making a spectacle of yourself. public affection is defined as any display of aff which makes those around you uncomfortab watch. Your first violation of this standard will in a verbal warning; your second, in a call-dow your third, in a campus.

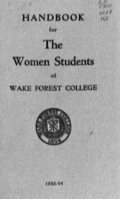

HANDBOOK
for
The
Women Students
of
WAKE FOREST COLLEGE

1953-54

JOY

"As a classroom community, our capacity to generate excitement is deeply affected by our interest in one another, in hearing one another's voices, in recognizing one another's presence.... Excitement is generated through collective effort. Seeing the classroom always as a communal place enhances the likelihood of collective effort in creating and sustaining a learning community."[6]

"[Students] want knowledge that is meaningful.... This demand on the students' part does not mean that they will always accept our guidance. This is one of the joys of education as the practice of freedom, for it allows students to assume responsibility for their choices."[7]

-bell hooks, *Teaching to Transgress*

"While I am proud of my final project, I am so much more proud of OUR final project. The fact that we wrote a 300 page textbook together entirely over Zoom and remotely is absolutely incredible. I was so giddy at our launch party to see everyone's hard work come to fruition, and I cannot wait to receive a physical copy. I literally cannot express in words how cool I think it is that we actually did it!!!"

Endnotes

1.   Wake Forest University Students. *Gender & Sexuality: A Transnational Anthology from 1690 to 1990*, 2019. https://librarypartnerspress.pressbooks.pub/gendersexuality1e/; *Crisis and History: Gender and Sexuality Reader 2.0*, 2020. https://library.biblioboard.com/viewer/59707ad7-c1e6-4be5-aa5e-79 6fa5b45ce4; *Gender and Sexuality Throughout World History*. Library Partners Press, 2020. https://librarypartnerspress.pressbooks.pub/gendersexuality3e/.

2.   Yarfitz, Mir, Kyle Denlinger, Kathy Shields, and Megan Mulder. "Developing an Open Primary Source Reader on Gender and Sexuality." In *Engaging Undergraduates in Primary Source Research*, 47–58. Lanham, Maryland: Rowman and Littlefield, 2021.

3.   Lince, Anthony. "Ungrading to Build Equity and Trust in Our Classrooms." *NCTE: National Council of Teachers of English* (blog), April 28, 2021. https://ncte.org/blog/2021/04/ungrading-build-equity-trust-classroo ms/.

4.   Stommel, Jesse. "How to Ungrade," March 11, 2018. https://www.jessestommel.com/how-to-ungrade/.

5.   Sinkinson, Caroline. "The Values of Open Pedagogy." *EDUCAUSE Review*, November 14, 2018. https://er.educause.edu/blogs/2018/11/the-values-of-open-pedagogy.

6.   hooks, bell. *Teaching to Transgress: Education as the Practice of Freedom*. New York: Routledge, 1994, p. 8.

7.   hooks, *Teaching to Transgress*, p. 19.

All images are either used with permission of the Wake Forest University Archives, excerpted from student work, or screenshots of our process documentation. Unattributed quotes are from students from classes of Fall 2019, Spring 2020, and Fall 2020.

Appendix

Making History Together: Reflections on Trust, Connection, & Finding Joy in the Archives

Kyle Denlinger, Megan Mulder, Kathy Shields, and Mir Yarfitz

Page 1: Cover

PAGE DESCRIPTION

The title of the zine appears at the top of the page, and the zine's authors are listed at the bottom of the page. The background image is a close-up of a person's hand holding a copy of a book titled Gender and Sexuality throughout World History: An International Collection of 18th to 20th Century Works. Its cover is a collage of various images, including a close-up image of a white woman's eyes, an image of Gloria Steinem in sunglasses, and an image of women of color marching in front of a "women's liberation" banner. The book is authored by students at Wake Forest University.

Page 2 - Intro: Unboxing Joy

PAGE DESCRIPTION

The top of the page is a text box with the title "Intro: Unboxing Joy." Two large blocks of text on black backgrounds are interspersed with small white boxes of text. The background is a blurred image of a propaganda poster from World War 1 depicting a woman engaged in heavy industrial work.

TEXT BOX 1, AUTHOR-SUPPLIED TEXT

Hello, reader.

We want to share with you our experience designing and teaching "Gender and Sexuality in World History," an undergraduate history course in which students work together to research and produce a new class volume of an open access primary source reader (source: Endnote 1). In writing and producing a book together, students are motivated to engage in meaningful, tangible scholarship that will have an audience beyond the classroom. Recognizing the importance of each person's contributions, they trusted one another and took great pride in their work. You can read more about the course in another book (source: Endnote 2).

As our students opened boxes of archival documents, they often uncovered painful truths. However, the inclusive environment we created together meant that students just as often opened themselves to new ways of seeing the world and new ways of learning in community.

In designing the course, we centered trust, connection, and joy as both critical structures of and desired outcomes of an equitable class community. Our primary strategies, ungrading and open pedagogy, served to challenge traditional classroom power structures that far too often lead to misplaced student motivation, antagonistic teacher-student relationships, and bias against minoritized students. As we open these boxes together, it is our hope that you might find inspiration to take risks, seek joy, and connect more deeply with students and colleagues.

With gratitude for our students,
The Authors
September 2021

TEXT BOX 2, AUTHOR-SUPPLIED TEXT

Oh, also:
We've never produced a zine before. We knew that collaborating remotely in the middle of a global pandemic and in a genre completely new to us would be a challenge, but we were intentional in doing it this way. We feel that producing this zine has allowed us to enter into a space we asked our students to enter, to experience some small measure of generative discomfort that has ultimately produced a large measure of joy.

Page 3 - Contents

PAGE DESCRIPTION

This page provides the organizing structure for the zine. At the top of the page is a text box that reads "Boxes," and three other text boxes in the middle right of the page read: "Box 1: Trust", "Box 2: Connection", "Box 3: Joy". Two other text boxes float above the background image.

The background image for the top half of the page is a screenshot of an e-mail that the professor sent to one of the librarians at the start of the project. The background image for the bottom half of the page is a box of materials from the archives.

TEXT BOX 1, A BULLETED LIST DRAWN FROM COURSE PLANNING NOTES

Design a course that:
- Shares power
- Trusts students
- Engages students in primary source research
- Involves them in the process of authentic scholarship
- Doesn't beat them down
- Embraces community
- Embodies inclusive pedagogical principles.

Shifts what students think history is:
- Not just a linear timeline of prominent white people
- It's a process they're a part of and contributing to

TEXT BOX 2, A QUOTE FROM STUDENT FEEDBACK

"Overall, this was my favorite class this semester, and I felt it was also the class I was the most comfortable in, engaged the most in, and learned the most in. I felt like the work I accomplished in this class, most specifically the collaborative book project, was some of the best work I have done in college so far, and that this class made me think the most deeply about topics including gender roles, power dynamics, gender fluidity, reproductive rights, and so much more."

Page 4 - Trust & Ungrading

PAGE DESCRIPTION

Numerous text boxes float over the background image. The background image is mostly obscured by the text, but it appears to depict a woman being thrown into the air by a group of men holding something like a trampoline. Two headings appear: the first reads "Trust," the other reads "Ungrading."

SECTION 1, "TRUST"

Text box 1, author-supplied text

Trust in our students and in each other was an essential element. Each one of us—the students, the instructor, the three librarians—played a pivotal role in the success of these books.

Students had to trust that their classmates would engage deeply as co-producers of the book. Collectively, they helped each other decide on topics and sources, copyedited their peers' drafts, organized the book into sections, and even contributed cover art. We handled much of the project management and the tech, but the rest was up to the students.

We entrusted the students with a great deal of power, as well. We relinquished control over the format and structure of the book, most of the processes by which students created their work, and the licenses under which they chose to share it. We also relinquished power by making the class entirely ungraded.

SECTION 2, "UNGRADING"

Text boxes 2 and 3, quotes from student feedback

"But I really think I enjoy this class so much because I'm not afraid to fail in it." "I rediscovered, in a way, my motivations for learning."

Text box 4, a screenshot of text

"To make matters worse, traditional grading systems don't just affect students' perceptions of themselves; teachers, too, start to hold negative beliefs about students of color and multilingual students and their ability to succeed in school. We might say that our grading systems are fair and objective, but biases often enter our evaluation practices. For instance, a recent study conducted by David M. Quinn suggests that 'racial stereotypes can influence the scores teachers assign to student work'" (source: Endnote 3)

Text box 5, author-supplied text

Ungrading, and the self-reflection and self-assessment practices it encourages (source: Endnote 4), created space for each student to process some of their internalized beliefs about what learning is and who they are as learners. Like many students, those we work with tend to be extrinsically motivated by grades and often conflate grades with self-worth. In our class, most of these students, many of whom come from marginalized backgrounds, were for the first time setting their own standards, pursuing their own learning goals, and taking risks they may not have otherwise taken. Our hope was that our conversations about ungrading and the trust we demonstrated by ceding control of the grade would shift students' perceptions of themselves and the value of their work, push back against some of their own internalized biases, and help mitigate any implicit biases of our own.

Page 5 - Trust

PAGE DESCRIPTION

At the top of the page is a text box with the title "Trust." Various text blocks float above the background. The background image is a collage of various spreadsheets used in the class for organizing the book sections. One spreadsheet depicts the student-generated "Collective Classroom Norms," which lists examples for "Uncomfortable," "Optimal," and "Delightful" classroom behaviors.

TEXT BOX 1, AUTHOR-SUPPLIED TEXT

In the first week of each semester, students created shared norms.
[Description: Nearby, in the corner of the page is a small image of the character "Norm" from the sitcom "Cheers."]

TEXT BOX 2, A QUOTE FROM STUDENT FEEDBACK

"I specifically loved hearing the differing opinions, and the respect each student had for the other's beliefs."

TEXT BOX 3, A QUOTE FROM STUDENT FEEDBACK

"Before this project, I was a control freak, or maybe it's better to say a perfectionist. I hated group work because everyone else's work just didn't live up to my standard. But this project has been so different: I wanted others' input on my chapter and I wanted to read theirs. I am so excited that I can read everyone's finished product now and celebrate what they've done along with my own!"

TEXT BOX 4, A QUOTE FROM STUDENT FEEDBACK

"We engaged with some heavy topics and I felt that we were able to create a safe and respectful environment in our classes. I even think we reached some of the things in the 'delightful' column because we were able to build some trust both through our discussions but also through our collaborative project."

Page 6 - Connection

PAGE DESCRIPTION

At the top of the page is a text box with the title "Connection." Various text boxes and images float above the background. The background image is a photograph depicting two women embracing at a booth with a sign that says "Hug a Homosexual, Free Kisses, ALA/SSRT Task Force on Gay Liberation." Three images are scattered on the page. One depicts a hand-drawn surgical mask emblazoned with the word "FEAR."

Another image is a photograph of a student holding a handwritten sign in front of their face. The sign reads "I WISH I WAS AT." The sign appears above the words "Wake Forest" on the student's sweatshirt. A final image is a photograph of a rock bearing the handwritten words, "The world breaks everyone and afterward many are stronger in the broken places—Hemingway, A Farewell to Arms."

TEXT BOX 1, AUTHOR-SUPPLIED TEXT

During the spring 2020 semester, totally disrupted by the COVID-19 pandemic, students shifted their projects to documenting and sharing their experiences of the historical moment, creating primary sources of their own. Some painted rocks, some created photo essays or collected oral histories, others made zines connecting to past crises. Slowing down to connect to their experiences and those of their classmates provided many with an emotional outlet and a source of solace.

TEXT BOX 2, A QUOTE FROM STUDENT FEEDBACK

"The collective project was the best academic experience I have ever had... I not only learned a tremendous amount from doing my actual research, but also different skills from my peers. Seeing their own passions was inspiring and motivating."

TEXT BOX 3, A QUOTE FROM STUDENT FEEDBACK

"It's okay to ask others for help and no one was expecting me to do this on my own."

Page 7 - Connection & Open Pedagogy

PAGE DESCRIPTION

At the top of the page is a text box with the title "Connection & Open Pedagogy." Numerous student quotes and other text float above the background image. The background image depicts four female-presenting students seated at a table examining primary source documents.

TEXT BOX 1, AUTHOR-SUPPLIED TEXT

The values of open pedagogy, (source: Endnote 5) especially access, equity, agency, connection, and responsibility, are all aligned with the vision and values we had for this project. By contributing to the creation of an OER, students interrogated their own positionality, roles, and responsibilities in studying history, expanding access to marginalized stories, and writing for authentic audiences. As they positioned themselves within the legacy of knowledge production and being in conversation with future readers, students saw their work, their copyrights, and Creative Commons licenses as relevant. We believe that our approach made the class more equitable, but we acknowledge that openness may be a barrier for some students.

TEXT BOX 2, A QUOTE FROM STUDENT FEEDBACK

"I believe that my classmates and I all worked very hard on our chapters to make sure they represented ourselves, as well as the class and you, well! So, although there was no pressure to 'get a good grade', there was the pressure to make everyone proud."

TEXT BOX 3, A QUOTE FROM STUDENT FEEDBACK

"I don't know everything. I've never claimed to, but some of the best moments in this project came from someone adding on to what I had to say or offering up a suggestion."

TEXT BOX 4, A QUOTE FROM STUDENT FEEDBACK

"After completing every assignment, I try and reflect on what I have just completed and connect with within other aspects of my life, trying to apply my newfound knowledge or perspective to things like conversations, social media memes, historical stories, movies, etc."

Page 8 - Joy

PAGE DESCRIPTION

At the top of the page is a text box with the title "Joy." Numerous text boxes containing student quotes and other text float above a collage of images from the students' chapters. Images include a Maoist propaganda poster depicting a smiling woman and man; a drawing of an arm with a flexed bicep inscribed with handwritten text that reads "The Power of a Name"; the cover of a poetry pamphlet called "We the Black Woman" that features three hand-drawn pictures of black women sporting afro hairstyles; the cover of the Handbook for The Women Students of Wake Forest College from 1953-1954; an excerpt from that handbook, some of which is obscured by other images, that reads: "2. The giving and receiving of affection is a personal thing and something which you do not … to cheapen by making a spectacle of yourself … public affection is defined as any display of aff … which makes those around you uncomfortab … watch. Your first violation of this standard will …in a verbal warning; your second, in a call-down … your third, in a campus."

TEXT BOX 1, A QUOTE FROM STUDENT FEEDBACK

"Visiting special collections was a joy, hands on activities make learning about history more engaging as I feel more immersed into what [I'm] reading or looking at."

TEXT BOX 2, AUTHOR-SUPPLIED TEXT

Students worked with physical documents in Special Collections and Archives and with digitized documents available through the library and on the open web. An informal goal was to give students the opportunity to experience the joy of finding connection to history through the use of the archives."

TEXT BOX 3, DECORATIVE TEXT

How do we find JOY in the archives?

Page 9 - Joy

PAGE DESCRIPTION

At the top of the page is a text box with the title "Joy." Various text boxes float above the background image. The background image for top portion of the page is an image of Black students dancing joyfully at a campus event in what appears to be the 1970s. The background image for the lower portion of the page is a screenshot of a Zoom meeting between the four chapter authors. Each author is smiling.

TEXT BOX 1, TWO QUOTES FROM BELL HOOKS

"As a classroom community, our capacity to generate excitement is deeply affected by our interest in one another, in hearing one another's voices, in recognizing one another's presence…. Excitement is generated through collective effort. Seeing the classroom always as a communal place enhances the likelihood of collective effort in creating and sustaining a learning community." (Source: endnote 6)

"[Students] want knowledge that is meaningful…. This demand on the students' part does not mean that they will always accept our guidance. This is one of the joys of education as the practice of freedom, for it allows students to assume responsibility for their choices." (Source: endnote 7) -bell hooks, *Teaching to Transgress*

TEXT BOX 3, A QUOTE FROM STUDENT FEEDBACK

"While I am proud of my final project, I am so much more proud of OUR final project. The fact that we wrote a 300 page textbook together entirely over Zoom and remotely is absolutely incredible. I was so giddy at our launch party to see everyone's hard work come to fruition, and I cannot wait to receive a physical copy. I literally cannot express in words how cool I think it is that we actually did it!!!"

Page 10 - Endnotes

PAGE DESCRIPTION

At the top of the page is a text box that reads: "Endnotes." The background image, which appears to be from the mid-20th century, shows a white, male-presenting student looking through an old card catalog.

TEXT BOX 1, ENDNOTES FOR SOURCES THAT WERE CITED IN THE CHAPTER

1. Wake Forest University Students. *Gender & Sexuality: A Transnational Anthology from 1690 to 1990*, 2019. https://librarypartnerspress.pressbooks.pub/gendersexuality1e/; *Crisis and History: Gender and Sexuality Reader 2.0*, 2020. https://library.biblioboard.com/viewer/59707ad7-c1e6-4be5-aa5e-796fa5b45ce4; *Gender and Sexuality Throughout World History*. Library Partners Press, 2020. https://librarypartnerspress.pressbooks.pub/gendersexuality3e/.

2. Yarfitz, Mir, Kyle Denlinger, Kathy Shields, and Megan Mulder. "Developing an Open Primary Source Reader on Gender and Sexuality." In *Engaging Undergraduates in Primary Source Research*, 47–58. Lanham, Maryland: Rowman and Littlefield, 2021.

3. Lince, Anthony. "Ungrading to Build Equity and Trust in Our Classrooms." *NCTE: National Council of Teachers of English* (blog), April 28, 2021. https://ncte.org/blog/2021/04/ungrading-build-equity-trust-classrooms/.

4. Stommel, Jesse. "How to Ungrade," March 11, 2018. https://www.jessestommel.com/how-to-ungrade/.

5. Sinkinson, Caroline. "The Values of Open Pedagogy." *EDUCAUSE Review*, November 14, 2018. https://er.educause.edu/blogs/2018/11/the-values-of-open-pedagogy.

6. hooks, bell. *Teaching to Transgress: Education as the Practice of Freedom.* New York: Routledge, 1994, p. 8.

7. hooks, *Teaching to Transgress, p. 19.*

TEXT BOX 2, AUTHOR-SUPPLIED TEXT

All images are either used with permission of the Wake Forest University Archives, excerpted from student work, or screenshots of our process documentation. Unattributed quotes are from students from classes of Fall 2019, Spring 2020, and Fall 2020.

CHAPTER 27

Inclusive Pedagogy through Digital Scholarship

A Case Study

Rebecca Fitzsimmons and Anne Shelley

Introduction

Cultivating a sense of community and building toward an inclusive classroom environment are central goals of teaching and learning, and ones that have been challenged in the wake of the COVID-19 pandemic. One notable and widespread response from higher education was a shift to primarily online teaching. As faculty found themselves revising how they delivered lessons and developed assignments, a shift to online classroom instruction offered opportunities to rethink what inclusive spaces and active participation looks like in a college classroom and beyond.

In her 2012 chapter "'This Is Why We Fight': Defining the Values of Digital Humanities," Lisa Spiro proposed a list of values that should be central to digital scholarship. That list included openness, collaboration, collegiality and connectedness, diversity, and experimentation.[1] These values also form the underpinnings of a complex and community-oriented classroom landscape that champions active participation and empowers students to become effective curators, communicators, and knowledge producers. In summer 2020, two librarians at Illinois State University taught a faculty development workshop on using digital scholarship tools in the classroom that encouraged faculty in a variety of disciplines to think about reshaping assignments using new methods and with Spiro's values in mind.

Following this workshop, an instructor invited the librarians to help design a group project that incorporated multimodal publishing, data visualization, and mapping methods into one of her graduate-level courses related to community building in K–12 educational institutions. The tools incorporated into the course allowed a range of collaborative possibilities between students, creating new working and communication spaces that encouraged everyone to freely share ideas and learn from each other. We challenged students to have important conversations about how they could leverage open and accessible tools as a powerful means of outreach outside the higher education classroom. The goal of these conversations was to generate ideas about how common digital scholarship tools and methods could be used to promote equity and inclusivity in communications with school partners, helping to build more participatory and engaged communities and reimagining what inclusivity and deep collaboration can accomplish in classrooms, schools, neighborhoods, and spaces beyond.

Pedagogy and Inclusivity in Digital Scholarship

The transition to online delivery of course material has led many librarians and faculty members in a wide range of disciplines to consider how they can increase a sense of engagement, equity, and inclusion in their virtual classroom spaces. Adding previously unused digital tools or revisiting the possibilities of incorporating digital scholarship methods into the classroom has proved a powerful way for many instructors to reshape interactions in changing classroom environments. Tools used in digital scholarship naturally fit into this landscape because they can support equity and inclusivity in the classroom. Many are free to use, web-based, encourage project sharing, and support collaborative group work. Furthermore, many platforms adapt easily to resource sharing and can be used to cultivate a flexible and safe space for the exploration of ideas and collective learning among peers. Discussions within the digital humanities community that have centered on the core values that drive this work are useful.[2] In the nearly ten years since Lisa Spiro proposed a list of values that should be central to digital humanities work, asserting that "instead of trying to pigeonhole digital humanities by prescribing particular methods or theoretical approaches, we can instead focus on a community that comes together around values such as openness and collaboration,"[3] much has been written about the possibilities for rethinking how digital scholarship across fields and inside classrooms can look.

First, despite the possibilities that openness and collaboration present to create less hierarchical and more flexible communities of practice, we also have to acknowledge some important critiques of the promises and limitations of digital humanities ideals. These critiques include accessibility issues, conversations around digital exceptionalism, and ethical considerations surrounding the use of student labor for DH projects.[4] Maha Bali has pointed to widespread and deeply rooted illusions of inclusivity, especially in one-size-fits-all courses, platforms, and online spaces that espouse universal values.[5] We feel that responding directly to the needs of participants and partners to tailor instruction and project goals, along with resisting the urge to encourage groups to find an immediate consensus while generating ideas, can help to offset some of these challenges to inclusion.

Suggesting there may be a waning openness to fresh perspectives and welcoming new participants to the field, Sean Michael Morris has written about academic work, conformity, and the institutionalization of digital humanities, noting, "it's also become all too discriminating about what and whom the field may include."[6] In addition, it is important to examine the resources used in creating digital projects for potential barriers to inclusivity, including the ways that some voices have been marginalized, excluded, or misrepresented in archival holdings, descriptive processes, and library catalogs. In writing about library technology, Chris Bourg has noted a need for transparency about the limitations of inclusivity and the biases embedded in technology, stating that "digital humanities frequently relies on library expertise and resources, but often in ways that are surprisingly uncritical."[7] These issues all certainly call for active and ongoing interrogation—or at least vigilance—of where the possibilities of digital scholarship, pedagogy, and community building might inadvertently eclipse inclusivity.

Another point to consider is the perceived barriers between fields of study and how breaking them down is an important step toward inclusive instruction and research possibilities. In thinking about the applications of a variety of digital tools and research methods, Lisa Spiro has drawn connections between digital humanities and digital social sciences, noting that while there are differences in approaches in the various fields of study, there is also a tremendous amount of methodological overlap, interdisciplinary work, and opportunity for scholars across disciplines to collaborate.[8] Lauren Klein and Matthew Gold, writing specifically about the expansion of digital humanities to "foreclose the question of 'who's in and who's out' by allowing the 'differently structured possibilities' of the digital humanities to emerge,"[9] have also hinted at a more universal issue in digital scholarship—namely that the same principles and methods applied in different ways throughout the various humanities fields have relevance to pedagogy in fields outside these disciplines.

These observations can easily apply to digital scholarship in closely related fields such as education (the subject of our course case study), which is often interdisciplinary, highly collaborative, and seeking to leverage digital tools. Further extending the idea of meaningful collaboration across traditional boundaries, Wendy Hsu challenges the models of one-way communication often associated with scholarship when she writes about public humanities through the lens of civic engagement, noting that, "by evoking lessons on public inclusion, community-driven inquiry, and public-benefit design, I hope that we as humanists can be inspired to contribute to the public while participating as partners with the public."[10] In particular, Hsu's assessment of how creating a "community-driven digital object" and using methods for "intervening in a civic or public process in a way that furthers a humanist agenda"[11] is extremely relevant to course work that cultivates a sense of community and produces work that can reach beyond the classroom to actively engage a broader public audience.

There are many frameworks and approaches for implementing digital scholarship activities in teaching, and much that is relevant to our course design has been written about the specific methods, information literacy skills, openness of resources, collaborative emphasis, and interactions between faculty and students in the production of digital content. Kristen Mapes builds on Lisa Spiro's earlier articulation of a set of values that should guide the digital humanities field to outline one such framework for teaching. In her presentation "Teaching Values, Not Definitions," she identifies components of digital humanities projects and syllabi, with a focus on how openness, diversity, collegiality, and collaborative project work commonly guide digital scholarship in the classroom.[12] In writing about the increasing prevalence of online materials and communications in higher education classrooms, William Thomas and Elizabeth Lorang question the oppressive focus on large-scale projects, commercial resource sets, and closed classroom communities. They note that "to a surprising degree, we have ceded control and critical perspective in response to the promised potential of volume and the large scale"[13] and that this can come at the expense of smaller, more engaging opportunities for students to create and share knowledge. In detailing the methods employed in their ongoing History Harvest project,[14] the authors share a framework for replicating this model, with the assertion that "we must insist on and enact more reciprocal, open, and community-based terms of digital engagement in higher education."[15] The K–12 community-building focus of our case study encourages this outward-looking approach that seeks to create an inclusive communication model, rather than a one-way, product-driven outcome.

Similarly focused on authentic learning experiences for students, David "Jack" Norton notes that "DH courses locate knowledge in a student-centered process" and that "they must take knowledge, interrogate it, change it, remix it, and present it."[16] This set of methods for engagement builds on ideas outlined by Thomas P. Mackey and Trudi E. Jacobson, who defined "metaliteracy" by noting that it "expands the scope of traditional information skills …to include the collaborative production and sharing of information in participatory digital environments," which "promotes empowerment through the collaborative production and sharing of information."[17] When truly supported, information sharing among peers increases equity because it draws on the strengths of multiple contributors and encourages different perspectives to be included in discussions and project deliverables. This practice is built into the school-community focus of our project, with the intention that this practice will extend to ongoing projects that students implement in their own school environments. Common to all the methods covered in this section is a focus on making digital scholarship in the classroom flexible, collaborative, and inclusive, which is the most significant element of our case study that will be explored in detail.

Digital Scholarship Background at Illinois State University

In March 2019, the library convened a Digital Humanities Task Force to investigate the campus's current activities and interest in digital scholarship to determine the types and levels of library support needed. The task force used internal and external environmental scans, a faculty survey, and a focus group to produce a white paper describing findings from its investigations and recommendations for better supporting digital scholarship at Illinois State University.

We learned that faculty are teaching using a variety of digital methods, including but not limited to data visualization, mapping, and virtual reality. In addition to identifying existing campus resources to support digital scholarship work, the task force identified needs, such as the ability to collaborate across disciplines, find project partners, or procure a specific type of support or expertise. They do not feel there is currently a place or mechanism on campus for them to do so.

Milner Library has been able to address some of these needs by offering new digital-scholarship-related programming and professional development opportunities. One example is enhancing the library's partnership with our campus's Center for Teaching, Learning, and Technology (CTLT) to offer faculty workshops that focus on using digital scholarship tools, methods, and values in teaching.

COVID/Shift to Online Teaching

In mid-March 2020, ISU abruptly shifted all classes from in-person to virtual, and CTLT rapidly expanded support for instructors' transition to online teaching. We saw an opportunity to offer faculty more information about digital scholarship tools and methods that might fit well with online learning and support group projects in a virtual environment. Further, because all students in the class have a chance to be creators and contribute intellectually toward a shared project—rather than the bulk of the knowledge being imparted by the instructor—digital scholarship projects naturally allow for an inclusive and equitable environment of sharing expertise. We offered a workshop on using digital scholarship tools and methods in the classroom as part of CTLT's 2020 Summer Institute. A workshop participant then asked us to collaborate on a project to incorporate mapping, multimodal publishing, and data visualization methods into her fall 2020 course.

Working with Educational Administration and Foundations 587—Community Relations Seminar

Instructor Goals

Educational Administration and Foundations 587—Community Relations Seminar is part of a Carnegie Project on the Education Doctorate (CPED) program that "is framed around questions of equity, ethics, and social justice to bring about solutions to complex problems of practice."[18] Most students enrolled in the course were current educational administrators. Both sections were taught online, with students in one section local to Bloomington–Normal and students in the other section from the Chicago area. The instructor wanted students to create an online group project related to school-community engagement that included a community engagement audit, plan for long-term increases in community partnership, and an interactive community asset map.

Librarian Roles

The collaboration on the course began with a basic workshop on using digital scholarship tools in the classroom to promote exploration, creative research directions, and collaboration. The course instructor reached out to inquire if we thought Scalar—a multimedia digital authoring tool—could work for a major project that would include two sections of the seminar and nine groups who needed to share information in highly collaborative ways. After some discussion of the goals and expected outcomes, we agreed to co-teach two sessions per section, covering uses of Scalar and Tableau Public. As the sessions took shape, we adjusted the contents to meet the needs of students, including working on creating and embedding Google maps, using Canva to create multimedia graphics, and using Datawrapper as an easier alternative to Tableau.

We taught initial two-hour sessions on using Scalar and Tableau early in the semester, followed near the end of the semester by another two-hour workshop on creating and embedding a multilayered Google map. Throughout the semester we provided support to students that included individual and group meetings. These sessions ranged in length depending on specific student needs and included troubleshooting technical issues in real time, conversations about how to enhance the communication of ideas, and discussion about uses of Scalar as a community-building tool outside the classroom.

Instruction Methods

We offered a diverse array of instructional strategies to support students in the teaching style that would best meet their needs, including direct demonstration, written directions, video tutorials, and in-person working sessions with individuals and groups. Through these instructional strategies, all of the students enrolled in the course were able to successfully work in groups using Scalar to complete a finished chapter section of a class book that included all the required elements of a community assessment and action plan.

The learning outcomes of the sessions were tied to several sections of the Association of College and Research Libraries (ACRL) *Framework for Information Literacy for Higher Education*, which reinforced valuable skills related to digital scholarship. The learning objectives for the project extended beyond acquiring technological skills and included work that particularly reinforced the frames "Information Has Value" and "Scholarship as Conversation."[19] Students not only located data and information about the schools and surrounding communities that formed the basis for their projects, but also considered ways that they could use a range of digital tools to communicate that information. Since the focus of the class (and the Scalar project) was on developing ways to enhance educational initiatives by creating a sense of true community engagement and involvement in local schools, the students considered ways to leverage digital tools to increase active participation. The students are current K–12 teachers and administrators, so the potential for these digital methods to enhance equity and inclusivity in the classroom extends beyond the course. The interactive aspects and two-way communication features embedded in their digital projects can be a first step in using these tools to begin building and nurturing local communities to support educational practices. This goal of partnering with the public around digital objects such as asset maps and other information objects, while offering ways to actively solicit input and engage in creating civic dialogues and defining creative interactions within the local school community, embodies Wendy Hsu's ideals of "community-driven inquiry and public-benefit."[20]

Implications for Equity and Inclusion

It was important to us to recommend options to the students that are free and web-based rather than costly proprietary software. While there are potential access issues related to free, web-based platforms for some users, they are still more equitable choices for most people. We wanted anyone with an internet connection to have equal access to the platforms and the same opportunities to fully engage with the resources. This strategy has potential to benefit users beyond the classroom. As administrators and educators themselves, the students we worked with can also recommend these tools to teachers in their schools to use with their students.

After ensuring that students had equal access to the online platforms they would use for this assignment, our next priority was addressing the spectrum of student confidence in using the tools. Students across both sections had different comfort levels and prior experience with web-based publishing, and we sought to even out these circumstances by making ourselves freely available to help students feel as comfortable as possible using the tools.

Digital scholarship projects are inherently collaborative, and we brought this focus to our instructional approach. Often each person in a project group has a unique role or specialized knowledge they bring to the project. This arrangement promotes inclusivity as everyone's efforts are necessary to the project's success. We encouraged students to freely share knowledge and ideas within their groups, but also to look at the contributions other groups were making to a shared Scalar resource. The ability to look at the work of classmates, examining different ideas and ways of communicating information, is a benefit when trying to support a robust learning community. The ability to examine the technical aspects of other students' work is also invaluable. While our focus is not always tied to a specific platform, the use of Scalar for this group was strategic because it can support inclusive practices beyond the people enrolled in or teaching a particular class; for example, the social annotation tool hypothes.is can be enabled, allowing members of the public to engage with Scalar sites by commenting on or questioning what they read there. The shared space allows equitable collaboration within, but also across group projects and creates opportunities to share knowledge and skills both synchronously and asynchronously, actively and indirectly. Our work with this class succeeded in incorporating all of Spiro's defined values while effectively supporting a model of community engagement that should extend beyond the classroom. We will continue to be mindful of building on such important guiding principles in our teaching and future project collaborations with faculty and students.

Conclusion

COVID-19 has presented and will continue to present numerous and varied challenges to higher education. Many institutions' responses to the virus revealed or magnified inequities among students, faculty, and staff, including but not limited to lack of technology needed for online learning, access to spaces conducive to study, differences in job requirements and ability to work remotely, and availability of library resources. Depending on one's circumstances, however, reactions to COVID have also offered opportunities for experimentation and growth. In this case study we have described how we librarians, the course instructor, and the students experimented with new tools and methods that supported inclusive online group work. We see the potential going forward to have important conversations about how we can continue to help expand equity and inclusion across campus through supporting digital scholarship in and out of the classroom. From our perspective we were pedagogically and technologically stretched—but largely not strained. More importantly, this valuable experience continues to inform how we speak with faculty and students about teaching, learning, and community building around digital scholarship.

Notes

1. Lisa Spiro, "'This Is Why We Fight:' Defining the Values of Digital Humanities," in *Debates in the Digital Humanities*, ed. Matthew K, Gold (Minneapolis: University of Minnesota Press, 2012), 16–35, https://dhdebates.gc.cuny.edu/read/untitled-88c11800-9446-469b-a3be-3fdb36bfbd1e/section/9e014167-c688-43ab-8b12-0f6746095335#ch03.
2. This chapter references digital humanities as well as digital scholarship. While definitions for both terms vary, *digital scholarship* is—at the time of this writing—generally recognized as an umbrella term that includes digital humanities. In particular, the literature review includes a number of references to digital humanities, as groundbreaking projects that used digital methods were largely driven by humanities researchers, and seminal analyses of these projects and their goals and ideals maintained a similar disciplinary focus.
3. Spiro, "This Is Why We Fight," 16.
4. On accessibility issues, see George H. Williams, "Disability, Universal Design, and the Digital Humanities," in *Debates in the Digital Humanities*, ed. Matthew K. Gold (Minneapolis: University of Minnesota Press, 2012), 202–12, http://www.jstor.org/stable/10.5749/j.ctttv8hq.15. On digital exceptionalism, see Michelle Moravec, "Exceptionalism in Digital Humanities: Community, Collaboration, and Consensus," in *Disrupting the Digital Humanities*, ed. Dorothy Kim and Jesse Stommel (Santa Barbara, CA: Punctum Books, 2018), 169, https://doi.org/10.2307/j.ctv19cwdqv.15, for a discussion of how "digital exceptionalism is suffused with techno-optimism around what the digital can do and with the belief that the digital represents a marked, and presumably better, break with all that came before," including a discussion of ways that conversations in digital humanities communities may actually eclipse inclusion through an overly optimistic framing of the collaborative potential of the field. Also see Diane Jakacki, "Is There Such a Thing as Digital Exceptionalism …?" *Diane K. Jakacki—"Tam Arte Quam Marte"* (blog), October 6, 2013, http://dianejakacki.net/is-there-such-a-thing-as-digital-exceptionalism/ (site

discontinued) for an early discussion raising the question of what digital exceptionalism might mean, the pitfalls of the term *exceptionalism*, and the potential of embracing digital scholarship methods while treading carefully with the notion that they are better simply because they are digital. On student labor, see Spencer D. C. Keralis, "Disrupting Labor in Digital Humanities; or, The Classroom Is Not Your Crowd," in *Disrupting the Digital Humanities*, ed. Dorothy Kim and Jesse Stommel (Santa Barbara, CA: Punctum Books, 2018), 273–94, https://doi.org/10.2307/j. ctv19cwdqv.20.

5. Maha Bali, "The 'Unbearable' Exclusion of the Digital," in *Disrupting the Digital Humanities*, ed. Dorothy Kim and Jesse Stommel (Santa Barbara, CA: Punctum Books, 2018), 295–320, https:// doi.org/10.2307/j.ctv19cwdqv.21.

6. Sean Michael Morris, "Digital Humanities and the Erosion of Inquiry," in *Disrupting the Digital Humanities*, ed. Dorothy Kim and Jesse Stommel (Santa Barbara, CA: Punctum Books, 2018), 221, https://doi.org/10.2307/j.ctv19cwdqv.16.

7. Chris Bourg, "The Library Is Never Neutral," in *Disrupting the Digital Humanities*, ed. Dorothy Kim and Jesse Stommel (Santa Barbara, CA: Punctum Books, 2018), 468, https://doi. org/10.2307/j.ctv19cwdqv.29.

8. Lisa Spiro, "Defining Digital Social Sciences," dh+lib, April 9, 2014, https://acrl.ala.org/ dh/2014/04/09/defining-digital-social-sciences/.

9. Lauren F. Klein and Matthew K. Gold, "Digital Humanities: The Expanded Field," in *Debates in the Digital Humanities*, ed. Matthew K. Gold and Lauren F. Klein (Minneapolis: University of Minnesota Press, 2016), x, https://doi.org/10.5749/j.ctt1cn6thb.3.

10. Wendy F. Hsu, "Lessons on Public Humanities from the Civic Sphere," in *Debates in the Digital Humanities*, ed. Matthew K. Gold and Lauren F. Klein (Minneapolis: University of Minnesota Press, 2016), 280, https://doi.org/10.5749/j.ctt1cn6thb.27.

11. Hsu, "Lessons on Public Humanities," 284.

12. Kristen Mapes, "Teaching Values, Not Definitions: Experiences and Research in the Introductory Digital Humanities Course" (presentation, Digital Humanities and the Undergraduate Experience Conference, Edwardsville, IL, April 26, 2019), http://www.kristenmapes.com/siue2019/.

13. William Thomas and Elizabeth Lorang, "The Other End of the Scale: Rethinking the Digital Experience in Higher Education," *EDUCAUSE Review* 49, no. 5 (2014): 44, https://er.educause. edu/-/media/files/article-downloads/erm1452.pdf.

14. William G. Thomas, Patrick D. Jones, and Andrew Witmer, "History Harvests: What Happens When Students Collect and Digitize the People's History?" *Perspectives on History*, January 1, 2013, https://www.historians.org/publications-and-directories/perspectives-on-history/ january-2013/history-harvests offers a good overview of History Harvests and the methods for developing one.

15. Thomas and Lorang, "Other End of the Scale," 44.

16. David "Jack" Norton, "Making Time: Workflow and Learning Outcomes in DH Assignments," in *Debates in the Digital Humanities*, ed. Matthew K. Gold and Lauren F. Klein (Minneapolis: University of Minnesota Press, 2019), https://dhdebates.gc.cuny.edu/read/untitled-f2acf72c-a469-49d8-be35-67f9ac1e3a60/section/f1b1d9a6-974b-46c4-afde-7606bf238fc3#ch25.

17. Thomas P. Mackey and Trudi E. Jacobson, *Metaliteracy* (Chicago: ALA Neal-Schuman, 2014); see also Thomas P. Mackey and Trudi E. Jacobson, "Reframing Information Literacy as a Metaliteracy," *College and Research Libraries* 72, no. 1 (2011): 64.

18. Illinois State University, "Doctoral Degree in Education Administration and Foundations: P–12 Administration," accessed June 4, 2021, https://education.illinoisstate.edu/edd_p12/.

19. Association of College and Research Libraries, *Framework for Information Literacy for Higher Education* (Chicago: Association of College and Research Libraries, 2016), https://www.ala.org/ acrl/standards/ilframework. The frame Information Has Value is described in this way: "Infor-

mation possesses several dimensions of value, including as a commodity, as a means of education, as a means to influence, and as a means of negotiating and understanding the world. Legal and socioeconomic interests influence information production and dissemination." The frame Scholarship as Conversation is described in this way: "Communities of scholars, researchers, or professionals engage in sustained discourse with new insights and discoveries occurring over time as a result of varied perspectives and interpretations."

20.   Hsu, "Lessons on Public Humanities," 284.

Bibliography

Association of College and Research Libraries. *Framework for Information Literacy for Higher Education*. Chicago: Association of College and Research Libraries, 2016. https://www.ala.org/acrl/standards/ilframework.

Bali, Maha. "The 'Unbearable' Exclusion of the Digital." In *Disrupting the Digital Humanities*, edited by Dorothy Kim and Jesse Stommel, 295–320. Santa Barbara, CA: Punctum Books, 2018. https://doi.org/10.2307/j.ctv19cwdqv.21.

Bourg, Chris. "The Library Is Never Neutral." In *Disrupting the Digital Humanities*, edited by Dorothy Kim and Jesse Stommel, 455–472. Santa Barbara, CA: Punctum Books, 2018. https://doi.org/10.2307/j.ctv19cwdqv.29.

Hsu, Wendy F. "Lessons on Public Humanities from the Civic Sphere." In *Debates in the Digital Humanities*, edited by Matthew K. Gold and Lauren F. Klein, 280–86. Minneapolis: University of Minnesota Press, 2016. https://doi.org/10.5749/j.ctt1cn6thb.27.

Illinois State University. "Doctoral Degree in Education Administration and Foundations: P–12 Administration." Accessed June 4, 2021. https://education.illinoisstate.edu/edd_p12/.

Jakacki, Diane. "Is There Such a Thing as Digital Exceptionalism …?" *Diane K. Jakacki—"Tam Arte Quam Marte"* (blog), October 6, 2013. http://dianejakacki.net/is-there-such-a-thing-as-digital-exceptionalism/ (site discontinued).

Keralis, Spencer D. C. "Disrupting Labor in Digital Humanities; or, The Classroom Is Not Your Crowd." In *Disrupting the Digital Humanities*, edited by Dorothy Kim and Jesse Stommel, 273–94. Santa Barbara, CA: Punctum Books, 2018. https://doi.org/10.2307/j.ctv19cwdqv.20.

Klein, Lauren F., and Matthew K. Gold. "Digital Humanities: The Expanded Field." In *Debates in the Digital Humanities*, edited by Matthew K. Gold and Lauren F. Klein. Minneapolis: University of Minnesota Press, 2016. https://doi.org/10.5749/j.ctt1cn6thb.3.

Mackey, Thomas P., and Trudi E. Jacobson. *Metaliteracy: Reinventing Information Literacy to Empower Learners*. Chicago: ALA Neal-Schuman, 2014.

———. "Reframing Information Literacy as a Metaliteracy." *College and Research Libraries* 72, no. 1 (2011): 62–78.

Mapes, Kristen. "Teaching Values, Not Definitions: Experiences and Research in the Introductory Digital Humanities Course." Presentation, *Digital Humanities and the Undergraduate Experience Conference*, Edwardsville, IL, April 26, 2019. http://www.kristenmapes.com/siue2019/.

Moravec, Michelle. "Exceptionalism in Digital Humanities: Community, Collaboration, and Consensus." In *Disrupting the Digital Humanities*, edited by Dorothy Kim and Jesse Stommel, 169–96. Santa Barbara, CA: Punctum Books, 2018. https://www.jstor.org/stable/10.5749/j.ctttv8hq.15.

Morris, Sean Michael. "Digital Humanities and the Erosion of Inquiry." In *Disrupting the Digital Humanities*, edited by Dorothy Kim and Jesse Stommel, 217–26. Santa Barbara, CA: Punctum Books, 2018. https://doi.org/10.2307/j.ctv19cwdqv.16.

Norton, David "Jack." "Making Time: Workflow and Learning Outcomes in DH Assignments." In *Debates in the Digital Humanities*, edited by Matthew K. Gold and

Lauren F. Klein. Minneapolis: University of Minnesota Press, 2019. https://dhdebates.gc.cuny.edu/read/untitled-f2acf72c-a469-49d8-be35-67f9ac1e3a60/section/f1b1d9a6-974b-46c4-afde-7606bf238fc3#ch25.

Spiro, Lisa. "Defining Digital Social Sciences." dh+lib, April 9, 2014. https://acrl.ala.org/dh/2014/04/09/defining-digital-social-sciences/.

———. "'This Is Why We Fight:' Defining the Values of Digital Humanities." In *Debates in the Digital Humanities*, edited by Matthew K. Gold. Minneapolis: University of Minnesota Press, 2012. https://dhdebates.gc.cuny.edu/read/untitled-88c11800-9446-469b-a3be-3fdb36bfbd1e/section/9e014167-c688-43ab-8b12-0f6746095335#ch03.

Thomas, William G., Patrick D. Jones, and Andrew Witmer. "History Harvests: What Happens When Students Collect and Digitize the People's History?" *Perspectives on History*, January 1, 2013. https://www.historians.org/publications-and-directories/perspectives-on-history/january-2013/history-harvests.

Thomas, William, and Elizabeth Lorang. "The Other End of the Scale: Rethinking the Digital Experience in Higher Education." *EDUCAUSE Review* 49, no. 5 (2014): 34–48. https://er.educause.edu/-/media/files/article-downloads/erm1452.pdf.

Williams, George H. "Disability, Universal Design, and the Digital Humanities." In *Debates in the Digital Humanities*, edited by Matthew K. Gold. Minneapolis: University of Minnesota Press, 2012. https://www.jstor.org/stable/10.5749/j.ctttv8hq.15.

CHAPTER 28

Fostering Community in the Library

Diversity, Equity, and Inclusion as the Cornerstone in the Development of New Library Active Learning Spaces and Services

Zach Newell, Stacey Knight-Davis, and Beth Heldebrandt

The creation of a new space is an exciting and challenging time. There are many decisions to be made that will shape the physical environment and choices that will strongly influence who uses the space and how. At Booth Library, when renovating library spaces, our goal is to create spaces that center diversity, equity, and inclusion (DEI). We also strive to create programs and services within the space that encourage participation from a diverse group of students, offer equitable access to resources, and are as inclusive as possible.

Booth Library is located on the campus of Eastern Illinois University in Coles County, Illinois, a rural area three hours south of Chicago. The residents of Coles County are more than 90 percent white, and the individual poverty rate exceeds 20 percent.[1] The EIU campus, however, has a much more diverse population and more students who fall into the category of low income. In fall 2019, 43 percent of students

enrolled at EIU were minority students and more than half —51 percent—were low income, evidenced by their eligibility for Pell Grants. It is important to meet the needs of these students and make them feel welcome here in Charleston, Illinois, and at EIU. With that in mind, DEI considerations drove decisions on pedagogy, technology, and services within the library's new Center for Student Innovation (CSI).

It is important to note that the planning stages for the Center for Student Innovation happened alongside the development of a new library mission statement, vision statement, and five-year strategic plan.[2] The strategic planning process primed us to think of our core values and how we wanted to see the library develop. This introspective and future-focused mindset allowed and encouraged the ideas and conversations that formed the concept of the CSI. Once we centered DEI in our organizational goals, it naturally followed that DEI was also centered in the creation of a new learning space.

When approached with the opportunity to design our library's Center for Student Innovation, centering DEI drove our decisions on pedagogy, technology, and services. The library building was redesigned in the late 1990s and reopened in 2002. At that time, print periodicals were an essential part of library services. Over time, the space needed for housing, displaying, and processing new print periodicals shrank dramatically. Staffing lines for periodicals processing had already been restructured to create and support an institutional repository, but prime floor space sat occupied by low-use bound periodicals and VHS tapes. Clearly there was a use for the space that would encourage learning rather than storing media that was older than the majority of students. Structuring the purpose and audience for the space sprang from intentional pedagogical choices: collaboration, creativity, and problem-based learning.

Review of the Literature

There is a convergence of ideas that come into play when implementing a center for student innovation. The authors acknowledge the need to establish more flexible space; look toward the future and what that means for transformations in teaching, learning, and scholarship; and consider ways to more fully engage our robust, diverse student population in these changes. Davies and colleagues explain that there is reasonable evidence across a number of studies that the space within a classroom or workshop should be capable of being used flexibly to promote students' creativity.[3] In the article "Leading Creative Practice Pedagogy Futures," the studio (a place for art and design) is discussed as a space where learning emerges through action.[4] The action-oriented space is described as facilitating an investigative and creative process that also fosters exploration and experimentation, critique and reflection.[5] As an active learning classroom with a technology hub, the CSI promotes an investigative and reflective process. The integrative process of the space—encouraging movement among students, interaction, collaboration, and problem-based learning—facilitates extended interaction. In discussing the studio (space and tools), the positive studio community culture highlights student engagement and commitment, with a high level of interaction and effective collaboration among students. High-quality projects reflect a variety of real-world studio outcomes and involve academic and student connections with the industry or profession. Space shapes the way we learn and the way we interact.

It is widely accepted that collaborative and blended learning environments emphasizing peer learning and the co-construction of knowledge can be effective motivators for learners.[6] The studio in multiple forms can enact this for students: "Competitive pressure from globalized access to education, the ubiquity of content and content providers, and the focus on different sorts of outputs from higher education are all driving change and innovation."[7] James and Brookfield, in their book *Engaging Imagination,* discuss the effect of spaces on the way we learn—that learning spaces can make us more aware of how we think about experience.[8] This, in turn, can lead to a "transformational overhaul" of personal beliefs.[9] The learning space itself becomes a mechanism for enhancing creativity in teaching and learning, and both a physical and theoretical platform to enable transformation. The space itself also forces us, through varied pedagogical practices, to confront our peers in engaging and flexible ways. The library is confronted by the changing needs of students in the way they collaborate and learn.

Miller, in an article on the future of teaching and learning in an academic research library, discusses student needs for a wide range of technologies and a variety of spaces to work with.[10] This comes as a repositioning of students at the center of our work in libraries.[11] Digital technologies, the internet, and mobile devices are enabling students to learn, connect, and collaborate with one another and the world outside in a way that was impossible for previous generations.[12] Students are diverse in background and experience, career goals, interests, and passions. The library acts as a nexus for preparing a diverse student body for what comes next—harnessing a great deal of energy and diversity.

These creative and inclusive aspects of collaboration are further enhanced and realized by the development of the physical space. Elmborg presents the idea of Third Space as both a teaching and learning concept.[13] The idea of the Third Space reinvents the library from the premise that libraries and librarians can develop ways of working with diverse populations in increasingly dynamic contexts. The learning space itself becomes a mechanism for enhancing inclusionary aspects of teaching and learning, and both a physical and theoretical platform to enable transformation.

Third Space is described as the "borderland between Representations of Space (spaces dominated by structures and concepts) and Representational Space (the symbolic and personal)."[14] Elmborg explains that represented space is "rigid, controlled, policed, and defined"[15] and that Third Space can be viewed as an area of "cultural, social, and epistemological change in which the competing knowledges and discourse of different spaces is brought into conversation to challenge and reshape identities."[16] It is the physical space that brings the theoretical in enhancing the learning environment. More specifically, Third Space can be conceived as a space where the librarian might function as a companion or guide for giving direction to the "displaced."[17] Elmborg contends that librarians who practice in this way might strive to see the library from the view of the "cultural other."[18]

Elmborg relates Third Space to the teaching of information literacy, which involves "understanding who people are, what they care about, and how to engage them to find personal meaning in information."[19] One way of thinking about Elmborg's approach is for the library and the librarian to operate from the perspective of a growth mindset in an active learning environment. Third Space becomes a new democratic space where librarians and students work together to create real and meaningful conversations about information and how we use it to "make our points and live our lives."[20]

This allows us to teach and learn in a collaborative space that is critically inclusionary in bringing a variety of students, their voices and their needs, into a participatory realm. To further underscore the importance of learning in a dynamic context, active learning employs group work that develops students' problem-solving skills. Active learning is grounded in constructivist theory, which maintains that people learn by actively using new information and experiences to modify their existing models of how the world works. The positive impact of active learning on our underrepresented student population is evidenced in a detailed study that explores how active learning narrows the achievement gap.

Theobald and colleagues analyzed 9,238 student examinations from fifteen studies across the country and data on student failure rates from twenty-six studies covering 44,606 total students.[21] They concluded that active learning accounted for a 33 percent reduction in achievement gaps on examinations in the STEM disciplines. For both examination scores and passing rates, the amount of active learning that students do is positively correlated with narrower achievement gaps. The research found that, on average, active learning narrowed gaps in pass rates by 45 percent for low-income and racially underrepresented groups, including students who are Black, Indigenous, or People of Color (BIPOC).[22] More intensive classes in which students spend two-thirds of their course time in active learning narrow the gap in test scores and pass rates even further. High-intensity active learning is correlated to a 42 percent reduction in the achievement gap relative to traditional lecturing and a 76 percent reduction in the achievement gap relative to passive learning.[23]

In an article summarizing the data from Theobald and colleagues, Witcher discusses the advantages of active learning in positioning students as participants in their own knowledge growth.[24] Witcher refers to this as having a growth mindset.

The view is that active learning is more inclusion-oriented. The inclusionary aspect of active learning fosters a growth mindset, one that embraces a desire to learn and embrace challenges. According to Theobald and colleagues,

> Small gaps are associated with faculty who have a growth or challenge mindset, which emphasizes the expandability of intelligence and is inclusion-oriented, while larger gaps are correlated with faculty who have a fixed mindset, which interprets intelligence as innate and immutable and is therefore exclusion- or selection-oriented.[25]

The strong evidence favors active learning as a model for inclusionary learning. Witcher refers to this as a "heads-and-hearts" strategy.[26] The hearts aspect makes underrepresented students feel welcome. The goal is to get students and instructors in a space working together, not around each other. This is the inclusionary aspect of active learning—finding lessons and inspiration in the success of others in an environment where students can persist, learn, and develop.

Active Learning in the CSI

Our foundational concepts of problem-based learning, creativity, and collaboration drove decisions on the layout of the Center for Student Innovation and the type of technology included. The space has no fixed layout. All furnishings are easily movable and can be repositioned quickly. The space can move from an in-the-round demonstration to small breakout groups in a matter of minutes. Large flat-panel monitors were chosen instead of a projection system, so the screens can move as needed. The monitors can sync together to offer the same content to different parts of the room or be used individually by smaller groups. This flexibility allows the instructor to demonstrate a new concept to the full class and then have smaller groups explore that concept and report back using the same screens. Robust wireless network access is available in the space, allowing students to have several connected devices.

Creativity is enabled with the availability of 3D scanning and printing equipment, 360-degree cameras, virtual reality viewing equipment, and digital design software. Faculty have already taken advantage of printing options to make anatomical models for teaching. Independent study students have discussed digitally modeling historical housing to better understand how spaces functioned. The 360-degree cameras were used by psychology students to produce videos used in treating clients with anxiety. These creative, hands-on projects allow for deeper engagement with concepts. The technology is a support to new approaches. Students and faculty come to the center with ideas, and we discuss how we can all work together to develop those ideas.

New technology is added as needed to support student projects. We take care in selecting equipment that offers access to technology in a manner that is approachable and less intimidating. For example, we recognize there is a steep learning curve to computer-assisted design and that even the name of the technology can put up a barrier for some students. To provide a more welcoming and accessible entry point to the technology, we will be adding a cutting machine that can be used to make fabric transfers and decals. The machine is a CAD machine, but it is packaged as a crafting tool rather than a manufacturing machine. Decorating a T-shirt with a computer-cut design still involves many of the same computer numerical control concepts as 3D printing, but the entry-level knowledge required is much lower for a machine with a friendly graphical interface. Motivation is greater and apprehension is lower for a project like cutting a decal, encouraging more students to become creators.

Including voices from outside the space is encouraged as part of the library's strategic goal to "emphasize communication and collaborative partnerships" both on and off campus.[27] With this in mind, the team selected teleconferencing equipment that can bring in students or guest speakers. The CSI offers a Google Jamboard, a self-contained whiteboard device that runs the Google Jamboard platform. This equipment encourages collaboration around the board, allows for recording sessions, and helps learners to connect remotely. The technology is familiar to students who came from high schools using Google systems. Using the free Jamboard app or any web browser, participants can share information with the Jamboard. Another collaboration tool is a 360-degree autofocusing camera and microphone system. The unit allows a large group to easily interact with a remote participant. The system has already been used for several guest lectures, and it is planned to be used for collaboration between student research teams and the US Department of State (more on this below).

While the center was created with remote collaboration in mind, the closure of physical classrooms in March 2020 to prevent the spread of COVID-19 quickly made it obvious that our students were not equally prepared to meet the challenges of remote learning. Students sought laptops, webcams, microphones, and internet access. Although some students had personal equipment available to use, a significant number were excluded from learning by lack of equipment or network access. Sometimes the lack of equipment or network access was an economic issue; low-income students had used public computing areas that became inaccessible when computer labs closed. In some cases, lack of network access was a geographic issue. Our university serves students who live in rural areas without broadband support. With no existing programs on campus to meet these needs, students came to the library looking for help.

With funds provided by the state of Illinois Governor's Education Emergency Relief (GEER) Fund, the library was able to provide the needed computing equipment.[28]* As described in Illinois Board of Higher Education documentation, about 6 percent of the education relief funds were reserved for "targeted initiatives to enroll and retain underrepresented, first-generation, and high-need students." A circulating equipment service was established in the CSI, allowing any EIU student to check out a laptop, microphone, or camera. Those without network access could borrow a 4G cellular hotspot with unlimited data. This technology allowed students to participate in remote learning while classrooms were closed. When limited in-person instruction resumed, several students used the circulating equipment while confined to their rooms after suspected COVID exposure.

Although the library is in the center of campus, the distance from the library to student housing can be a barrier, especially in the winter and for students with mobility disabilities. A satellite location for the CSI was opened in a residence hall to lower this barrier. Thomas Hall, the hall chosen to host the satellite CSI, is in the housing complex where students in the Freshman Connection program reside. The Freshman Connection provides mentoring and academic support for students who are first-generation, rural, Pell-eligible, or BIPOC. We know from speaking with students that many of them find the size of the library intimidating. The goal for the satellite CSI is to offer an environment that supports hands-on learning and creativity within a residential space where students are comfortable. The space is staffed by a diverse group of graduate and undergraduate student workers representing domestic and international students from a range of backgrounds. It was our intention that the space be staffed by the peers of the students using the space. The Thomas Hall CSI exists to lower barriers to technology and library services, providing more equitable access.

How to Know What Students Need? Just Ask Them!

In addition to the previously described GEER-funded technology checkout, the library also was awarded GEER funding for a problem-based learning initiative for BIPOC, first-generation, and Pell-eligible students. Students competed for scholarship funds by submitting a proposal describing how they would solve a problem using resources in the CSI or with resources the CSI could obtain to support their project. Collaboration and problem-based learning were the key pedagogical strategies used to construct this pitch competition.

---

* Equipment in Booth Library's Center for Student Innovation was purchased with funds from the Illinois State Library, Governor's Emergency Education Relief Fund (GEER), and Eastern Illinois University. Physical renovations were funded by the Charleston Area Charitable Foundation.

Winning students were awarded an academic scholarship, improving retention by lowering economic barriers. In addition, technology and materials will be purchased to support their winning proposals.

Improving Student Engagement

The first-place winners will develop services and equipment offerings in the CSI as a way to increase creativity and student engagement. The student competitors said they felt that lack of engagement was a key risk factor for students leaving the university. Suggestions included purchasing technology and equipment to encourage collaboration, as well as creating increased publicity for the CSI to raise its visibility.

Diplomacy Lab

The second-place team will establish a Diplomacy Lab as a part of a US State Department program. The library will provide the required statistical software to participate in the program and the required teleconferencing equipment. This project enables many more problem-based projects to occur and allows students to collaborate with the State Department to solve real-world problems.

App Development

Food insecurity is a major issue for many students, and the third-place winner is working to establish an app to complement the new on-campus food pantry. The goal is to develop an application for students to use to request food. The final winner is also developing an application to encourage community building and connection. She noted the lack of closeness during the pandemic and hoped to create an app that will help people play together while physically distanced.

Our competition winners were already well acquainted with basic technologies and were ready to explore app development, digital design, video production, and other advanced digital techniques. But some students and potential students lack basic skills like using e-mail or recognizing bias in online media. This lack of digital literacy deepens the digital divide. To address this issue, Booth Library applied for and received funding from the Illinois Department of Commerce and Economic Opportunity's Broadband READY program[29] to create a digital literacy program for the Southeast Central area of Illinois.* Through the grant, a digital literacy coordinator was hired to develop a series of digital citizenship, digital literacy, and information literacy workshops. The pedagogical foundation for the citizenship workshops balances a rights-and-responsibilities approach with concepts of digital advocacy. Digital literacy sessions are driven by inquiry and collaboration. Training sessions for this program were held in the CSI, utilizing the space as a hub to include the larger community beyond the university. While making the CSI technology available is important to our mission, it is also vital that we provide training to help patrons who may be new to the technology and online platforms. These patrons are eager to embrace the new technology, but it's important that they also learn the skills needed to use these resources safely and critically. As an equity issue, not all students had exposure to explicit digital literacy education in high school. Some are lacking in basic computer literacy. It is important to acknowledge and address these differences in preparation, many of which are tied to socioeconomic factors. Through digital literacy outreach, the CSI becomes a more inclusive space.

Conclusion

All of these programs and initiatives support the library's strategic goal to build a culture that supports diversity and inclusion. This goal states

> Our institution and our library embrace the strength of our diverse student and scholar population in an environment that fosters inclusivity, equity, and respect. Accordingly, we will be intentional in support of diversity and inclusion.[30]

Being inclusive means not making assumptions. We had assumed most students had access to a computer. We were wrong, and that assumption excluded students. With our development of inclusive learning spaces and focus on digital literacy education, we are committed to ensuring students have access to the tools and skills they need to be successful in college. Thinking of the larger environment, thinking systemically, and doing it intentionally is our strategy to build a culture that supports diversity and inclusion.

We have created the CSI as a space that supports active learning, a pedagogy that can narrow achievement gaps for underrepresented students. We provide space, equipment, expertise, and financial resources to support problem-based learning. We intentionally listen to our students and create new programs to meet their needs.

---

* Booth Library is a member of the Illinois Broadband READY Southeast Region, under the Broadband Regional Engagement for Adoption and Digital Equity Community Technology Center Grant Program, grant number 21-034001.

As we further develop the space and programs, we will be mindful of physical accessibility, representation in staff and publicity materials, and barriers to using the services. We hope to lower barriers to technology use and collaboration for our students and lower barriers to problem-based and active learning pedagogies for instructors.

Acknowledgements

The authors recognize Nate Carlson, digital literacy coordinator, Illinois Broadband READY Southeast Region, for his research and development of the digital literacy and digital citizenship workshops described in this chapter.

Notes

1. US Census Bureau, "Quick Facts, Coles County, Illinois," 2020, https://www.census.gov/quickfacts/colescountyillinois.
2. Booth Library Strategic Planning Committee, "2020–2025 Strategic Plan," Eastern Illinois University, Spring 2020, https://thekeep.eiu.edu/lib_strategic_plan/1/.
3. Dan Davies et al., "Creative Learning Environments in Education—A Systematic Literature Review," *Thinking Skills and Creativity* 8 (April 2013): 84, https://doi.org/10.1016/j.tsc.2012.07.004.
4. J. Fiona Peterson et al., "Leading Creative Practice Pedagogy Futures," *Art, Design and Communication in Higher Education* 14, no. 1 (2015): 72, https://doi.org/10.1386/adch.14.1.71_1.
5. Peterson et al., "Leading Creative Practice," 72.
6. Peterson et al., "Leading Creative Practice," 73.
7. Peterson et al., "Leading Creative Practice," 73.
8. Alison James and Stephen Brookfield, *Engaging Imagination* (Hoboken, NJ: Jossey-Bass, 2014).
9. James and Brookfield, *Engaging Imagination*, 139.
10. Kelly Miller, "Imagine! On the Future of Teaching and Learning and the Academic Research Library," *portal: Libraries and the Academy* 14, no. 3 (July 2014): 331, https://doi.org/10.1353/pla.2014.0018.
11. Miller, "Imagine!" 332.
12. Miller, "Imagine!"
13. James K. Elmborg, "Libraries as the Spaces between Us: Recognizing and Valuing the Third Space," *Reference and User Services Quarterly* 50, no. 4 (2011): 338–50, https://doi.org/10.5860/rusq.50n4.338.
14. Elmborg, "Libraries as the Spaces between Us," 344.
15. Elmborg, "Libraries as the Spaces between Us," 344.
16. Elmborg, "Libraries as the Spaces between Us," 347.
17. Elmborg, "Libraries as the Spaces between Us," 346.
18. Elmborg, "Libraries as the Spaces between Us," 346.
19. Elmborg, "Libraries as the Spaces between Us," 348.
20. Elmborg, "Libraries as the Spaces between Us," 348.
21. Eli J. Theobald et al., "Active Learning Narrows Achievement Gaps for Underrepresented Students in Undergraduate Science, Technology, Engineering, and Math," *Proceedings of the National Academy of Sciences of the United States of America* 117, no. 12 (2020): 6476.

22.   Theobald et al., "Active Learning," 6476, 6478.
23.   Theobald et al., "Active Learning," 6478.
24.   T. R. Witcher, "Active Learning Helps Diverse Groups with STEM Subjects," *Source: Civil Engineering Magazine*, November 10, 2020, https://source.asce.org/active-learning-helps-diverse-groups-with-stem-subjects/.
25.   Theobald et al., "Active Learning," 6480.
26.   Witcher, "Active Learning."
27.   Booth Library Strategic Planning Committee, "2020–2025 Strategic Plan."
28.   Illinois Board of Higher Education. "Governor's Emergency Education Relief Fund." https://www.ibhe.org/Geer-Grant-RFP.html.
29.   Illinois Department of Commerce and Economic Opportunity. "Connect Illinois." https://www2.illinois.gov/dceo/ConnectIllinois/Pages/default.aspx.
30.   Booth Library Strategic Planning Committee, "2020–2025 Strategic Plan."

Bibliography

Booth Library Strategic Planning Committee. "2020–2025 Strategic Plan." Eastern Illinois University, Spring 2020. https://thekeep.eiu.edu/lib_strategic_plan/1/.

Davies, Dan, Divyal Jindal-Snape, Chris Collier, Rebecca Digby, Penny Hay, and Alan Howe. "Creative Learning Environments in Education—A Systematic Literature Review." *Thinking Skills and Creativity* 8 (April 2013): 80–91. https://doi.org/10.1016/j.tsc.2012.07.004.

Elmborg, James K. "Libraries as the Spaces between Us: Recognizing and Valuing the Third Space." *Reference and User Services Quarterly* 50, no. 4 (2011): 338–50. https://doi.org/10.5860/rusq.50n4.338.

Illinois Board of Higher Education. "Governor's Emergency Education Relief Fund." https://www.ibhe.org/Geer-Grant-RFP.html.

Illinois Department of Commerce and Economic Opportunity. "Connect Illinois." https://www2.illinois.gov/dceo/ConnectIllinois/Pages/default.aspx.

James, Alison, and Stephen D. Brookfield. *Engaging Imagination: Helping Students Become Creative and Reflective Thinkers*. Hoboken, NJ: Jossey-Bass, 2014.

Miller, Kelly E. "Imagine! On the Future of Teaching and Learning and the Academic Research Library." *portal: Libraries and the Academy* 14, no. 3 (July 2014): 329–51. https://doi.org/10.1353/pla.2014.0018.

Peterson, J. Fiona, Noel Frankham, Louise McWhinnie, and Graham Forsyth. "Leading Creative Practice Pedagogy Futures." *Art, Design and Communication in Higher Education* 14, no. 1 (2015): 71–86. https://doi.org/10.1386/adch.14.1.71_1.

Theobald, Eli J., Mariah J. Hill, Elisa Tran, and Scott Freeman. "Active Learning Narrows Achievement Gaps for Underrepresented Students in Undergraduate Science, Technology, Engineering, and Math." *Proceedings of the National Academy of Sciences of the United States of America* 117, no. 12 (2020): 6476–83. https://doi.org/10.1073/pnas.1916903117.

US Census Bureau. "Quick Facts, Coles County, Illinois." 2020. https://www.census.gov/quickfacts/colescountyillinois.

Witcher, T. R. "Active Learning Helps Diverse Groups with STEM Subjects." *Source: Civil Engineering Magazine*, November 10, 2020. https://source.asce.org/active-learning-helps-diverse-groups-with-stem-subjects/.

CHAPTER 29

Let's Take a Moment

Student Reflections and Reframing Research as a Journey

*Zohra Saulat and Pamela Nett Kruger**

Introduction

Nervous. Anxious. Stressed. Uncertain. These are consistently the most common responses from students when asked how they feel about their upcoming research assignment at the start of our information literacy one-shot sessions. As instruction librarians, we (the authors) seek to eliminate library anxiety and build research confidence in our students. Reframing research as a journey and tackling its uncertainty, as well as making space for reflection, in the one-shot can encourage students to engage more meaningfully with their research and with the library. For many universities, the university library is considered the academic heart of the campus. This positions the university library to contribute to the success of its students. In order to ensure student success, understanding the various life experiences of students on a campus is crucial. California State University, Chico (Chico State), resides in rural northeastern

---

* Zohra Saulat (she/her/hers) is a first-generation South Asian (Pakistani descent), Midwest US–born, straight, cis, able-bodied woman. At the time of writing, Zohra is an early career academic librarian in a non-tenure-track faculty position at Lake Forest College. Pamela Nett Kruger (she/her/hers) is California US–born, white, straight, cis, with invisible disabilities. She was a first-generation college student, and currently a mid-career librarian in a tenure-track faculty position at California State University, Chico.

California on ancestral Mechoopda land. Most of our student population comes from the larger metropolitan areas of Los Angeles and the San Francisco Bay area.[1] Unlike most of the other campuses in the California State University system, the Chico State campus is a residential university, offering a new experience to the majority of our student population, who are not from the surrounding rural communities that make up the designated university service area.[2] Additionally, 52 percent of the student population identifies as first-generation (FG) college students,[3] 36 percent identify as Latine, and 77 percent receive financial aid.[4] Cognizant of all these factors, we aim to create a welcoming and inclusive one-shot environment for all of our students. This case study will discuss our inclusive instructional design process and our experience with implementing reflections for student researchers and instructional librarians. Our hope is that readers can take away this two-part reflective approach to better support students as well as themselves in the one-shot library classroom.

Background

We both identify as first-generation college students and a first-generation immigrant and we continually explore new ways to develop our teaching practice in order to improve the college experience of FG students at Chico State. There have been various criteria for what constitutes FG student status, but generally FG students are students whose parents have either minimal or no college experience and have not completed their bachelor's degree. According to the Center for First-Generation Student Success, "The term 'first-generation' implies the possibility that a student may lack the critical cultural capital necessary for college success because their parents did not attend college."[5] FG students face unique challenges compared to their non-FG peers while navigating the university system.[6] Additionally, FG students tend to be people of color, female, and from lower socioeconomic status, as noted by Nguyen and Nguyen.[7] An FG student may juggle additional responsibilities such as working many hours to support themselves or their families while trying to figure out the university system.[8] FG students at Chico State have shared with one of the authors that they also experience microaggressions or isolation. However, because of these same challenges, FG students often demonstrate remarkable dedication, persistence, and resilience. Though FG students may not have cultural capital,[9] they do have other strengths, which include familial and aspirational capital,[10] that can be leveraged by universities to support FG student success. It is important to approach FG student success from a strengths-based and intersectional approach. Using these approaches to support the diverse experiences of FG students is inherently inclusive in benefiting all students.[11]

Cultivating a sense of belonging is critical in supporting the retention and success of FG students. Arch and Gilman suggest approaching library services from a "student ready" focus rather than assuming students—FG or other students—are "college ready" in order to improve library experiences. They note that an important step in overcoming the hesitancy to seek help is to make a connection with students and to normalize asking for research assistance.[12] Students, especially FG students, are more likely to approach their peers for assistance due to fear of being perceived as inferior or inadequate by authority figures, such as a librarian.[13] These are all attributes of library anxiety.[14] To mitigate these challenges and minimize library anxiety, Graf also suggests normalizing asking for help and redefining the role of authority. Graf writes,

> Librarians seeking to support FG students should actively pursue and earn their trust; leading with expertise does not necessarily create relationships. Caring about students and giving them reasons to connect can be more valuable, even if building these relationships may seem outside of traditional librarian duties.[15]

Libraries can support a sense of belonging for FG students in a variety of different ways. Librarians can build student research confidence by validating student experiences and feelings. These include affirming the struggles and challenges that often come with library research, allowing for the librarian to build trust with the students. The one-shot, in particular, is the prime opportunity for the librarian to engage with the strengths of FG students and foster a sense of belonging. Given that students can be hesitant to approach the reference desk or make appointments for research consultations on their own, the one-shot is a good first point of contact because students are guided to library resources by their course instructor in the comfort of a group setting. To encourage students to ask for help beyond the one-shot, we began to emphasize connection and contemplation through research reflections.

We first implemented research reflection prompts in a joint, in-person information literacy session in the fall of 2019. For this paper-based activity, we would periodically pause after explaining a concept to allow students to write down their thoughts in response to the reflection prompts. These guided prompts gave students time to process the new information and use writing to assimilate their learning. From this experience, we saw the value of research reflections as a teaching tool and sought to enhance our reflection prompts with the needs and strengths of FG students in mind. We designed our new student research reflections prompts based on Kuhlthau's Information Search Process (ISP) model (see figure 29.1). The ISP model charts the *thoughts, feelings,* and *actions* of the researcher during the search process and demonstrates the iterative and complex nature of the research journey from beginning to end.[16] Consequently, through each reflection prompt, students are tasked to examine their own thoughts, feelings, and actions regarding their learning of the research process. By utilizing the ISP model, we aim to demystify the process and allay any potential research anxiety by normalizing the variety of feelings and struggles that occur during the research journey. With the transition to all online learning at our campus in the spring of 2020 and the 2020–21 academic year, we found that dedicating time to reflection for our students and ourselves enhanced our virtual classroom experience. Research reflections allowed us to connect with our students and build community online in a new and more supportive way.

Model of the Information Search Process							
	Initiation	Selection	Exploration	Formulation	Collection	Presentation	Assessment
Feelings (Affective)	Uncertainty	Optimism	Confusion Frustration Doubt	Clarity	Sense of direction/ Confidence	Satisfaction or Disappointment	Sense of accomplishment
Thoughts (Cognitive)	vague		⟶	focused	increased	interest	Increased self-awareness
Actions (Physical)	seeking	relevant Exploring	information	seeking	pertinent Documenting	information	

Figure 29.1

Kuhlthau's Information Search Process model.
(Source: Carol C. Kuhlthau, "Information Search Process," Rutgers School of Information and Communication, accessed June 7, 2021, http://wp.comminfo.rutgers.edu/ckuhlthau/information-search-process/.)

Lesson Plan: Research Reflections in the One-Shot

Our transferrable one-shot lesson plan (see appendix) is designed to reframe research as a journey building student research confidence and can be used across multiple disciplines. Whether in person or online, it is important to begin the session in a personable tone. We often devote seven minutes of a fifty-minute session to the introduction. We introduce ourselves with a fun fact and emphasize that we enjoy working with and supporting students. We take a moment to ask students if they know exactly what a librarian does so they understand our role in supporting their research. Based on our experience, this discussion generates student interest in the session and serves as a nice transition to the agenda. The agenda is based on the student learning outcomes determined by the course instructor and the librarian in collaboration. Using terms and phrases such as "goals" and "you will be able to …," we purposefully worded the student learning outcomes from a positive student perspective to help build student confidence. Additionally, as part of our accessible and transparent instructional practice, we avoid education or library jargon. By spending a significant amount of time making connections at the beginning, and throughout the one-shot, we hope that students will feel more comfortable using library resources.

With the switch to virtual learning in the spring of 2020, we began presenting the research reflections prompts on Poll Everywhere, a live audience response tool. Poll Everywhere offers open-ended responses, word clouds, and ranked polls. Students are prompted to enter their response on a web browser or via text message, and they can watch as their peers anonymously contribute. The librarian can expect to take a minute or two to assist participants in using the tool. Whether in person or online, Poll Everywhere creates a great opportunity for student engagement. Poll Everywhere can be embedded into Google Slides, allowing for a seamless presentation for the facilitator. Though the original intention of research reflections was to encourage students to take a moment to individually process their learning without having to share their answers, we found that using Poll Everywhere for research reflections can build a better sense of community by allowing students to see how their classmates are responding. This further helps students see that they are not alone in their reactions to the research process. As the results display, the librarian can facilitate a discussion, speaking to student belonging and research confidence.

Our initial two research reflections prime the students to consider the ISP model (see figures 29.2 and 29.3). The first research reflection asks students to define research. By asking students to share their definitions of research, the librarian invites student authority. Doing so can potentially lead students to be more invested in the lesson. This is also a good point to check student understanding of the research assignment. Our second research reflection immediately follows the first one. We ask students how they are currently feeling about their research assignment. As stated in the introduction, throughout all of our one-shots, the most common answers are "nervous," "anxious," or "unsure" (see figure 29.3). Making space for students to be vulnerable anonymously can help to build a sense of community by showing they are not alone in their struggles with academic stress and uncertainty. Students are able to see that their peers may be feeling the same and thus may not feel as isolated. We use this opportunity to be vulnerable with our students by sharing our own struggles with research. We do this to humanize our authority and build trust in order to make us more approachable to students.

" gathering/reading/analyzing information "

" To study and analyze the world around us "

" Testing hypotheses through experiments and studies and seeing if your results support or do not support your hypotheses "

" Finding answers or results to question you and others have "

" study of materials and sources in order to establish facts "

" Trying to figure out what is unknown in the world "

Figure 29.2
Sample reflection responses to "What is research?"

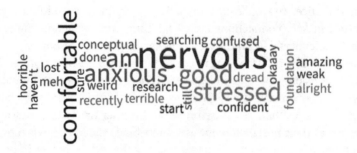

Figure 29.3
Sample reflection responses to "In one word, how do you feel about your research right now?"

After the discussion of the second research reflection prompt, we present and explain the ISP model (step 5b of the lesson plan, see appendix). The ISP model serves as an excellent teaching tool as it breaks down a research journey by providing the steps of conducting research. The model also acknowledges potential feelings and thoughts—either positive or negative—that a student might experience while they navigate the process. The ISP model also visually provides students with a sense of direction, encouraging research persistence. At this point in the discussion, we reframe research as a self-discovery journey. We encourage students to pick a topic that is related to their identity or personal experiences. As instructors, we emphasize that we all bring our own unique perspectives and experiences and that research is an opportunity to build on that knowledge. We point out that the research journey can be frustrating, but research can be more rewarding and less frustrating if students pick topics of genuine interest. Additionally, we mention that research is a collaborative endeavor and does not occur in isolation. Even as students work individually on assignments, we tell students to seek out additional services on campus, such as the writing center, to support their research journey. Communicating to students that they are part of the scholarly conversation is also important in making students feel included and confident at the university.

After going over library content as well as research resources and strategies—such as mind mapping or source evaluation—(steps 6–8 of the lesson plan, see appendix), we return to our final research reflections to close the session. In the third and fourth research reflections, we ask students to consider the tools and strategies they learned and what their plan of action is (see figures 29.4 and 29.5). The final research reflection is a summative evaluation that revisits the student learning outcomes presented at the beginning of the session. It is our hope that research reflections provide students a break from passively receiving lesson content and instead invite them to connect with the research process more deeply and with more confidence.

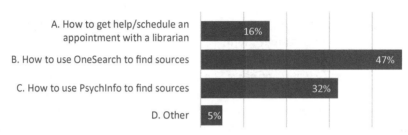

Figure 29.4
Sample reflection responses to "What was the most useful research skill or tool that you learned today?"

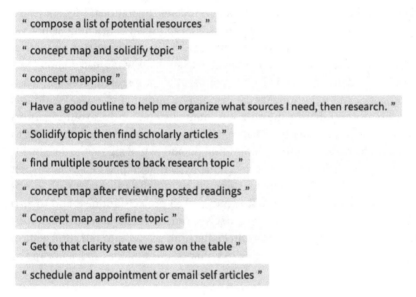

Figure 29.5
Sample reflection responses to "What is your plan of action for this research assignment?"

Inclusive Instructional Design

Instructional design is a process, and as we implemented research reflections in our one-shots, we continued to look for additional ways to create a more inclusive and engaging online one-shot experience. The instruction librarian is responsible for setting and maintaining the classroom energy. Librarians can take this opportunity to intentionally create a welcoming environment to cultivate a sense of community and increase feelings of student belonging, even in the one-shot. We found that incorporating elements of invitational education and slow teaching complemented our goals with the research reflections.

We were inspired by the holistic approach to FG students by Ward, Siegel, and Davenport in *First-Generation College Students,* particularly their application of the invitational education model. They emphasize the value of college students and their advanced educational capabilities and state that students learn best from people who exhibit approachable and inviting qualities.[17] The model was developed from the concept that schools can play a positive role in ensuring that students, and people in general, matter and in encouraging students to embrace the many opportunities the educational setting has to offer.[18] The four basic assumptions of invitational education are *trust, respect, optimism,* and *intentionality.* These assumptions respond especially well to the needs *and* strengths of FG students. Invitational education also encourages a balance of a personal and professional approach to teaching, which we found helpful as we wanted to show more authenticity in our professional practice. We want to be both approachable and accessible to students while also demonstrating that we have extensive knowledge to support student research. Building trust, respect, optimism, and intentionality can happen in a number of ways. We do this first in the classroom by sharing information about ourselves and also our eagerness to meet with students. We mention that we all bring our own unique knowledge to any research project and recommend building on and exploring that prior knowledge. As instruction librarians, we project a happy and often playful attitude when conducting our sessions. We enjoy working with students and make sure to not only mention that, but also show it. It is our goal to project kindness and to also show our vulnerability and humanize ourselves during this brief encounter with students. By incorporating the invitational education model into our information literacy one-shot sessions, we were able to enhance the student experience in the virtual library classroom.

With the shift to virtual instruction and pandemic life, we found the thoughtful and reflective nature of the slow teaching approach particularly helpful. Even prior to the COVID-19 pandemic, as instruction librarians we felt at times overwhelmed in our roles. This was exacerbated during the pandemic, which brought uncertainty and changes. Wanting to make personal connections with our students online allowed an opportunity to revisit and improve our instruction skills. In *Slow Teaching: On Finding Calm, Clarity and Impact in the Classroom,* Thom encourages being a mindful and reflective educator in order to foster classrooms where everyone is presently engaged through listening, focus, and reflecting on their learning.[19] While written to support a semester- or year-long instruction, *Slow Teaching* can also be applied in the one-shot session. Despite the temptation to jam-pack a one-shot session with as many student learning outcomes as possible, slow teaching has empowered us to simplify our one-shot instruction and reinforced prioritizing reflection in the classroom. Slow teaching and invitational education have allowed us to create a more inclusive one-shot experience and connect more authentically with our students.

On Reflection

The value of reflective pedagogy and the impact of reflection on student learning have been explored in various disciplines, and thus reflection has been defined in various ways.[20] Exploring reflection primarily in the context of rhetoric and compo-sition education, Kathleen Blake Yancey considers reflection as "identifying what we know and …understanding how we come to know."[21] Yancey relates reflection to goal setting and self-assessment as learning occurs.[22] It is through reflection that students can cultivate their agency.[23] Helping students recognize that they are agents of their own learning is key to student success. Yancey writes: "Reflection makes possible a new kind of teaching. The portraits of learning that emerge here point to a new kind of classroom: one that is coherently theorized, interactive, oriented to agency."[24] This new form of teaching and new form of classroom are envisaged further by Whitver and Riesen in the context of information literacy instruction:

> Librarians have a history of innovating teaching practices to meet the chal-lenges and limitations of the library instruction classroom to engage students in deep learning. Applying reflection as a structured learning construct within library instruction classrooms (course-embedded single session and short multi-session series) may offer librarians a methodology for accom-plishing the kinds of learning that transcend the present, providing students with a passport to future research contexts.[25]

Surveying library literature, Whitver and Riesen have found that, although reflec-tion has been explored by librarians, reflection in one-shots has been primarily used as an assessment tool, after student learning has taken place instead of as it takes place.[26] While semester-long information literacy courses have allowed librar-ians to incorporate reflection, this does not address the challenge of incorporating student-centered reflection opportunities in the one-shot.[27] To that end, Whitver and Riesen apply the work of Yancey and others to offer instruction librarians various reflection opportunities and tips for one-shot engagement. These include scaffolding reflection throughout the library instruction, introduction of key terms, readings in reflection, structured reflection through activities, freewriting, mind mapping, strategizing, and end-of-class reflection.[28] Our research reflection lesson plan incor-porates many of these suggestions, and most importantly allows students multiple reflection opportunities throughout the one-shot.

Reflection is also essential for us as instructors, not just for our students. After each of our information literacy sessions, we take time for self-reflection to assess our teaching. Recognizing that we are constantly evolving as instructors, we take about five to fifteen minutes on our own to reflect on the library instruction session. After the one-shot, we compare our delivery with our original intention for the session. We assess what worked well and what did not work. We also note the classroom dynamics, such as participation and engagement, as well as any other thoughts that come to mind. As Brookfield states, "Critical reflection is, quite simply, the sustained and intentional process of identifying and checking the accuracy and validity of our teaching assumptions."[29] Librarian self-reflection as a critical process has been explored by others.[30] As instructors, we come into the one-shot with assumptions about engagement, connection, and delivery of material. Each class brings its own unique characteristics and dynamics to the planned library lesson. To ground us in our practice, we use the ISP model to note our *thoughts, feelings,* and *actions.* We seek feedback regarding the course instructor's objectives for the class assignment. As we implemented research reflections, we regularly discuss classroom experiences with our fellow librarians . We identify instructional needs, share our observations, and explore pedagogy together. This layered and continuous collaborative approach of reflection has been effective in refining our instructional practice and increasing our confidence as instructors. By reflecting on our teaching, we aim to create an inclusive experience in our one-shots. Building off the work of Brookfield,[31] Graf states: "Teachers who desire just and loving classrooms must engage in critical reflection in order to recognize their own role in these dynamics, especially if they hope to challenge or change existing inequalities."[32]

Conclusion

The ACRL *Framework for Information Literacy for Higher Education* emphasizes critical thinking and self-reflection.[33] Our critical approach includes asking students to reflect on the research experience itself. At the beginning of our session, students approach their research assignment with uncertainty or anxiousness. At the end of our session, students are able to identify clear action plans and recall various support resources available to them, relaying a sense of direction and confidence. Making space for sharing vulnerabilities by way of research reflections in the one-shot has led to a noticeable shift in our connections with our students. We have found that acknowledging struggles and identifying feelings can create agency and build confidence, especially for FG students. Prioritizing time to self-reflect after each one-shot session, we have been able to continually improve our own instruction practice and sustain confidence as instructors as we endeavor to build the confidence of our students. As we strive for more inclusive classrooms for FG and all students, we invite instructional librarians to reframe research as a journey and create space for reflection.

Appendix

Sample Research Reflection Lesson Plan

1. **Welcome**
   a. Librarian Introduction
      i. Personable Fun Fact
      ii. Engagement Opportunity: Ask *"What does a librarian do?"*
         1. Emphasize supporting students and research help
   b. Agenda: Ask *"What are we going to do today?"*
      i. Research Process—ISP model
      ii. Discussion/Activity for Student Learning Outcome #1
      iii. Discussion/Activity for Student Learning Outcome #2
      iv. Demonstration of Relevant Library Resources
2. **Research Reflection Poll #1: What is research?**
   a. Ask: "Can someone tell me the research assignment for this class?"
3. **Research Reflection Poll #2 : In ONE word, how are you feeling about your research right now?**
   a. Engagement Opportunity: Acknowledge and assure
4. **Our Goals (SLOs)**
   a. You will be able to _____ in order to _____(Student Learning Outcome #1)
   b. You will be able to _____ in order to _____(Student Learning Outcome #2)
   c. You will be able to confidently navigate library catalog in order to find sources
   d. You will be able to schedule an appointment with a librarian in order to get help
5. **Research Process**
   a. Research is iterative
      i. Frustrating: this is normal
      ii. Rewarding: pick a topic that will sustain your interest
      iii. Collaborative: utilize campus resources
   b. Kuhlthau's Information Search Process model
      i. Engagement Opportunity: Ask *"What point in the research process are you at?"*
6. **Discussion/Activity for Student Learning Outcome #1**
7. **Discussion/Activity for Student Learning Outcome #2**

8. **Demonstration of Relevant Library Resources**
9. **Research Reflection Poll #3: Next Steps: What is your plan of action for this research assignment?**
10. **Research Reflection Poll #4: What was the most useful skill or resource you learned today?**
    a. How to _____ (Student Learning Outcome #1)
    b. How to _____ (Student Learning Outcome #2)
    c. How to use the library catalog to find sources
    d. How to get help/how to schedule an appointment with a librarian
    e. Other
11. **Questions? Ask a Librarian**
    a. Restate helping students
    b. Contact information (provide different methods)
    c. Office/Student research assistance hours (emphasize flexibility)

Research Reflection Polls highlighted

Notes

1. California State University, Chico, "Chico Facts," last modified Fall 2020, https://www.csuchico.edu/about/chico-facts.shtml.
2. California State University, Chico, "Chico Facts." Chico State's service area includes the following California counties: Butte, Colusa, Glenn, Lassen, Modoc, Plumas, Shasta, Siskiyou, Sutter, Tehama, Trinity, and Yuba.
3. Chico State defines first-generation college students as "First-generation university students are those students whose parent(s) have not attained a college degree. These students, who have little or no family collegiate history, may enter a college or university with limited knowledge about the jargon, traditions, and patterns of expected behavior. These factors may prevent first-generation students from fully engaging in a university setting and may contribute to early departure from the university before the completion of a degree. No matter how intelligent and capable, first-generation students may benefit from additional support as they adjust to a new environment." California State University, Chico, "Resources," Equity, Diversity, and Inclusion, accessed September 9, 2021, https://www.csuchico.edu/diversity/associations/first-gen/resources.shtml.
4. California State University, Chico, "Data and Demographics," last modified Fall 2020, https://www.csuchico.edu/diversity/demographics.shtml.
5. Center for First-Generation Student Success, "Defining First-Generation," *Center for First-Generation Student Success* (blog), November 20, 2017, https://firstgen.naspa.org/blog/defining-first-generation
6. Lee Ward, Michael J. Siegel, and Zebulun Davenport, *First-Generation College Students* (San Francisco: Jossey-Bass, 2012), 106.
7. Thai-Huy Nguyen and Bach Mai Dolly Nguyen, "Is the 'First-Generation Student' Term Useful for Understanding Inequality? The Role of Intersectionality in Illuminating the Implications of an Accepted—Yet Unchallenged—Term," *Review of Research in Education* 42, no. 1 (March 2018): 148, https://doi.org/10.3102/0091732X18759280.

8. Anne Jumonville Graf, "First-Generation Students and Libraries: Beyond the Deficit Narrative," in *Supporting Today's Students in the Library: Strategies for Retaining and Graduating International, Transfer, First-Generation, and Re-entry Students*, ed. Ngoc-Yen Tran and Silke Higgins (Chicago: Association of College and Research Libraries, 2019), 3–21, https://digitalcommons. trinity.edu/cgi/viewcontent.cgi?article=1108&context=lib_faculty

9. According to the *Oxford Dictionary of Sociology*, cultural capital is "A term introduced by Pierre Bourdieu to refer to the symbols, ideas, tastes, and preferences that can be strategically used as resources in social action. By analogy with economic capital, such resources can be invested and accumulated and can be converted into other forms. Bourdieu sees this cultural capital as formed into a 'habitus', an embodied socialized tendency or disposition to act, think, or feel in a particular way. Thus, middle-class parents are able to endow their children with the linguistic and cultural competences that will give them a greater likelihood of success at school and at university. Working-class children, without access to such cultural resources, are less likely to be successful in the educational system." John Scott, *Oxford Dictionary of Sociology*, 4th ed. (Oxford: Oxford University Press, 2014), Oxford Reference, https://doi.org/10.1093/ acref/9780199683581.001.0001.

10. Tara J. Yosso, "Whose Culture Has Capital? A Critical Race Theory Discussion of Community Cultural Wealth," *Race Ethnicity and Education* 8, no. 1 (2005), 78. https://doi.org/10.1080/1361 332052000341006.

11. Xan Arch and Isaac Gilman, "First Principles: Designing Services for First-Generation Students," *College and Research Libraries* 80, no. 7 (2019): 997, https://crl.acrl.org/index.php/crl/article/ view/23615/30927.

12. Arch and Gilman, "First Principles," 1003.

13. Graf, "First-Generation Students and Libraries," 14.

14. According to Heather Carlile, the definition of library anxiety is "the negative and uncomfortable feelings experienced by many university students when using, or contemplating using, the academic library." Heather Carlile, "The Implications of Library Anxiety for Academic Reference Services: A Review of Literature," *Australian Academic and Research Libraries* 38, no. 2 (2007), 129, https://doi.org/10.1080/00048623.2007.10721282.

15. Graf, "First-Generation Students and Libraries," 9.

16. Carol C. Kuhlthau, "Information Search Process," Rutgers School of Information and Communication, accessed June 7, 2021, http://wp.comminfo.rutgers.edu/ckuhlthau/information-search-process/.

17. Ward, Siegel, and Davenport, *First-Generation College Students*, 113.

18. William Watson Purkey, "What Is Invitational Education and How Does It Work?" (presentation, Annual California State Conference on Self-Esteem, Santa Clara, CA, February 22–24, 1991), 3, https://eric.ed.gov/?id=ED334488.

19. Jamie Thom, Slow Teaching (Woodbridge, UK: John Catt Educational, 2018), 12.

20. Luigina Mortari, "Reflectivity in Research Practice," *International Journal of Qualitative Methods* 14, no. 5 (August 2015): 1–4, https://doi.org/10.1177/1609406915618045.

21. Kathleen Blake Yancey, *Reflection in the Writing Classroom* (Logan: Utah State University Press, 1998), 6.

22. Yancey, *Reflection in the Writing Classroom*, 5.

23. Yancey, *Reflection in the Writing Classroom*, 5.

24. Yancey, *Reflection in the Writing Classroom*, 8.

25. Sara Maurice Whitver and Karleigh Knorr Riesen, "Reiterative Reflection in the Library Instruction Classroom," *Reference Services Review* 47, no. 3 (January 2019): 278, https://doi. org/10.1108/rsr-04-2019-0023

26. Whitver and Riesen, "Reiterative Reflection," 270.

27. Whitver and Riesen, "Reiterative Reflection," 271.
28. Whitver and Riesen, "Reiterative Reflection," 274–77.
29. Stephen Brookfield, *Becoming a Critically Reflective Teacher* (San Francisco: Jossey-Bass, 2017), 3.
30. Graf, "First-Generation Students and Libraries," 3–21.
31. Brookfield, Becoming a Critically Reflective Teacher, 19.
32. Graf, "First-Generation Students and Libraries," 10.
33. Association of College and Research Libraries, *Framework for Information Literacy for Higher Education* (Chicago: Association of College and Research Libraries, 2016), https://www.ala.org/acrl/standards/ilframework.

Bibliography

Arch, Xan, and Isaac Gilman, "First Principles: Designing Services for First-Generation Students." *College and Research Libraries* 80, no. 7 (2019): 996–1012. https://crl.acrl.org/index.php/crl/article/view/23615/30927.

Association of College and Research Libraries. *Framework for Information Literacy for Higher Education*. Chicago: Association of College and Research Libraries, 2016. https://www.ala.org/acrl/standards/ilframework.

Brookfield, Stephen. *Becoming a Critically Reflective Teacher*. San Francisco: Jossey-Bass, 2017.

California State University, Chico. "Chico Facts." Last modified Fall 2020. https://www.csuchico.edu/about/chico-facts.shtml.

———. "Data and Demographics." Equity, Diversity, and Inclusion. Last modified Fall 2020. https://www.csuchico.edu/diversity/demographics.shtml.

———. "Resources." Equity, Diversity, and Inclusion. Accessed September 9, 2021. https://www.csuchico.edu/diversity/associations/first-gen/resources.shtml.

Carlile, Heather. "The Implications of Library Anxiety for Academic Reference Services: A Review of Literature." *Australian Academic and Research Libraries* 38, no. 2 (2007), 129–47. https://doi.org/10.1080/00048623.2007.10721282.

Center for First-Generation Student Success. "Defining First-Generation." *Center for First-Generation Student Success* (blog), November 20, 2017. https://firstgen.naspa.org/blog/defining-first-generation.

Graf, Anne Jumonville. "First-Generation Students and Libraries: Beyond the Deficit Narrative." In *Supporting Today's Students in the Library: Strategies for Retaining and Graduating International, Transfer, First-Generation, and Re-entry Students*, edited by Ngoc-Yen Tran and Silke Higgins, 3–21. Chicago: Association of College and Research Libraries, 2019. https://digitalcommons.trinity.edu/cgi/viewcontent.cgi?article=1108&context=lib_faculty.

Kuhlthau, Carol C. "Information Search Process." Rutgers School of Information and Communication. Accessed June 7, 2021. http://wp.comminfo.rutgers.edu/ckuhlthau/information-search-process/.

Mortari, Luigina. "Reflectivity in Research Practice." *International Journal of Qualitative Methods* 14, no. 5 (August 2015). https://doi.org/10.1177/1609406915618045.

Nguyen, Thai-Huy, and Bach Mai Dolly Nguyen. "Is the 'First-Generation Student' Term Useful for Understanding Inequality? The Role of Intersectionality in Illuminating the Implications of an Accepted—Yet Unchallenged—Term." *Review of Research in Education* 42, no. 1 (March 2018): 146–76. https://doi.org/10.3102/0091732X18759280.

Purkey, William Watson. "What Is Invitational Education and How Does It Work?" Presentation, Annual California State Conference on Self-Esteem, Santa Clara, CA, February 22–24, 1991. https://eric.ed.gov/?id=ED334488.

Scott, John. *Oxford Dictionary of Sociology*, 4th ed. Oxford: Oxford University Press, 2014. Oxford Reference. https://doi.org/10.1093/acref/9780199683581.001.0001.

Thom, Jamie. *Slow Teaching: On Finding Calm, Clarity and Impact in the Classroom*. Woodbridge, UK: John Catt Educational, 2018.

Ward, Lee, Michael J. Siegel, and Zebulun Davenport. *First-Generation College Students: Understanding and Improving the Experience from Recruitment to Commencement*. San Francisco: Jossey-Bass, 2012.

Whitver, Sara Maurice, and Karleigh Knorr Riesen. "Reiterative Reflection in the Library Instruction Classroom." *Reference Services Review* 47, no. 3 (January 2019): 268–79. https://doi.org/10.1108/rsr-04-2019-0023.

Yancey, Kathleen Blake. *Reflection in the Writing Classroom*. Logan: Utah State University Press, 1998.

Yosso, Tara J. "Whose Culture Has Capital? A Critical Race Theory Discussion of Community Cultural Wealth." *Race Ethnicity and Education* 8, no. 1 (2005): 69–91. https://doi.org/10.1080/1361332052000341006.

SECTION 5

Universal Design for Learning

An Important Benchmark

Robin Brown

One of the most important benchmarks in the pursuit of equitable and inclusive instruction is the universal design for learning movement (UDL). Instructors who practice UDL stress multiple means of offering learning content and multiple options for engagement. The idea is to reach as many students as possible, addressing different learning styles, as well as disabilities. This has become increasingly relevant as libraries are dealing with shifting library instruction online due to the worldwide pandemic. There is a lot of work to be done to ensure that digital learning tools developed by libraries are completely accessible. CAST summarizes the basic principles of UDL.[1] A "Keeping up with" post from ACRL gives a good overview of UDL and libraries.[2] Among the many sources it recommends, TEAL (Teaching Excellence in Adult Literacy) stand out.[3] The papers in this chapter each go into detail about the practical implications of accessibility and UDL for library instruction.

Kern and Elliott ("Developing Lasting Inclusive and Equitable Teaching Practices: A Tasting Menu (Ch30)) acknowledge the impact of the pandemic on the instructional program of their library. They offer a menu of activities, all demonstrating the principles of UDL, suggesting that librarian instructors can pick, depending on what is most appropriate. They begin with an acknowledgement of the challenges of college instruction with some classrooms being a mix of remote and in-person students. The librarians developed lesson plans and worked to help classroom instructors understand how collaborative activities influenced by UDL can support mixed classrooms. They also promoted the value of open educational resources (OERs) when the library was closed. They provide a portfolio of activities that can be adapted.

Wittek and Fager ("Prioritizing Accessibility in Synchronous and Asynchronous Learning Environments (Ch 31)) make the very good point that accessibility is often reactive, keyed to a student coming forward with a specific request. UDL practitioners advocate making accessibility part of the initial design of materials. It is a proactive way to meet the needs of many different types of students. Wittek and Fager do a nice job of summarizing the fact that UDL benefits many more students than just the ones who are disabled. The authors want accessibility to become a habit. They provide a significant amount of practical guidance for the librarian who wants to produce accessible instruction.

Ruggiero ("Using an Interactive Tutorial to Achieve Inclusivity in a Flipped Literacy Class (Ch 32)) describes the process of designing a tutorial using LibWizard (Springshare) while applying UDL principles. Tutorials are particularly valuable for asynchronous instruction during the pandemic. The author describes the tutorial design process, working with a specific class. She began with a survey to discover the students' learning styles. This was notable because it allowed the design of the tutorial to meet specific needs. The format of the tutorial is described, along with ensuring that it is accessible. The author also gives an overview of micro learning, the idea of offering information in small chunks. The tutorial was used to flip the classroom.

Wilson ("Choose Your Own Adventure: The Use of Flexible Online Asynchronous Instruction for Information Literacy" Ch 33) describes the redesign of a credit bearing information literacy course, applying universal design for learning. Wilson begins by reviewing the legislation that governs accessibility when using technology for education. Universal design for learning is described as being useful for everybody. Wilson describes the different steps that she took to make the course more accessible. Through dividing the lesson into shorter segments, and exploring different ways to present topics, students have choices. The best way to describe this type of teaching is flexibility. Wilson also considers technology equity issues.

Brunk ("Lived and Learned Experience with Accessible and Inclusive Pedagogy" (Ch 34)) offers a reflective essay, discussing accessibility as a person with low vision. The author stresses that making library instruction accessible is not always perfect. She reviews the social model of disability and stresses the importance of how instructors treat disabled students. She speaks frankly about the challenges of library instruction, including acknowledging its purposes. She describes communicating with a class beforehand, describing what is going to happen. Students are invited to get in touch if they have questions. Brunk's suggestions are very thought provoking

Kingsbury ("Bodies Matter: What Disability and Watching People Learn to Sing Taught Me about Teaching Information Literacy" (Ch35)) uses the experience of observing singing lessons as a frame for insights on how instruction librarians interact with students. She begins by describing how her own experiences led her to discover disabilities studies as a field. Research for her doctoral dissertation led to observing singing lessons. She identified insights into inclusion and library instruction. It is important not to make assumptions about whether or not somebody can do something. Success is about collaboration. Do we acknowledge the emotional states of our students?

Notes

1. CAST, "The UDL Guidelines," https://udlguidelines.cast.org/.
2. Robin Brown, Zach Welhouse, and Amy Wolfe. "Keeping up with… Universal Design for Learning," 2020, Association of College and Research Libraries. https://www.ala.org/acrl/publications/keeping_up_with/udl
3. Teaching Excellence in Adult Literacy, "TEAL Center Fact Sheet No. 2: Universal Design for Learning," 2010, https://lincs.ed.gov/sites/default/files/2_TEAL_UDL.pdf.

Bibliography

Brown, Robin, Zach Welhouse, and Amy Wolfe. "Keeping Up with… Universal Design for Learning." 2020. Association of College and Research Libraries. https://www.ala.org/acrl/publications/keeping_up_with/udl.

CAST. "The UDL Guidelines." https://udlguidelines.cast.org/.

Teaching Excellence in Adult Literacy. "TEAL Center Fact Sheet No. 2: Universal Design for Learning." 2010. https://lincs.ed.gov/sites/default/files/2_TEAL_UDL.pdf.

CHAPTER 30

Developing Lasting Inclusive and Equitable Teaching Practices

A Tasting Menu

Sara C. Kern and Christine R. Elliott

Introduction

When inclusive teaching practices are done well, they can appear to be a well-thought-out, multicourse meal. In reality, the preparations and practices are often similar to a takeout menu: disparate ideas coming together to achieve a common goal. Pre-pandemic, the menu offered by the Juniata College library covered a wide range of activities, presenting instructors and students with straightforward ways to engage with research in the in-person classroom. With a sudden shift to online instruction, our librarians prioritized ensuring our highly engaging in-class activities would translate into an equitable learning experience where some students were online and remote while others were in person. Many students and instructors desired a meaningful sense of community while we learned together from myriad online locations. How could librarians aid the college in building and growing a sustainable online academic community that equaled in-class experiences?

This chapter presents an updated menu—an offering of newly interpreted activities and program ideas grounded in universal design for learning to aid other academic librarians as they transition to supporting remote learners in their shift

back to normalcy. This customizable format allows educators to sample and select the methods best suited to their context. Aside from an explanation of the theoretical framework that informed our collection of activities, readers can dive into the following sections: instructional methods and departmental outreach.

Instructional methods include detailed examples for designing library instruction activities based in universal design for learning concepts and ways to advocate for faculty to adopt those practices. These lesson plans highlight effective ways to use tutorials, collaborative documents, and other engagement tools to connect students and instructors in their information-seeking goals in a remote, in-person, or hybrid setting.

Departmental support spans liaison and outreach activities. This section explains how we supplemented our instruction efforts with a liaison program and used those connections to champion open educational resources to support a culture of accessibility on campus.

Any combination of these shared ideas provides an accessible start to integrating inclusive and equitable teaching practices in library instruction and outreach efforts.

Theoretical Frameworks

During the onset and duration of COVID-19's effects on college classes, students at our college were provided with flexible options for attendance, either in person or online, which gave students the ability to decide how they wanted to comfortably interact with their courses on a session-by-session basis. While more convenient for students, these opportunities created unique obstacles for instructors in building student connections within the classroom. Many instructors struggled to develop activities that engaged remote and in-person attendees equally while establishing clear channels for peer-to-peer interactions. In some situations, remote students had a hard time hearing their peers speak in class, while those in class had trouble interacting with remote students in small-group activities. Remote students who accessed all of their courses online dealt with expectations of consistent class participation in an unfamiliar format with web cameras. Extended screen time also resulted in an onslaught of "Zoom fatigue" for both students and instructors.[1] Zoom fatigue stemmed from a sudden increase in screen time, combined with the worries of continuing their education during a pandemic and dealing with the far-reaching effects of COVID on their health, social, professional, and personal lives.

At Juniata College, the librarians decided that an effective method of addressing this type of technology fatigue is to utilize familiar applications that require minimal instruction. Companies like Google and Microsoft have created collaborative suites that enable individuals to work in a shared medium. These applications can be shared as openly or restrictively as the instructor desires, allowing a class to engage in collaborative note-taking or submitting responses to in-class prompts and activities in real time. Using software that students are already familiar with enables students and faculty to interact with each other through a medium with a lower threshold of access and usability.

Librarians at our institution increasingly saw a need to develop accessible and collaborative lesson plans. We used universal design for learning (UDL) principles as the foundation for newly developed activities and lesson plans. UDL emphasizes incorporating multiple means of engagement, representation, and expression in instruction. Lessons rooted in UDL principles focus more on students reaching a learning objective and less on how they reach it. For example, learners can present information verbally and visually, or students may have the option of completing a final paper or creating a video that demonstrates the same knowledge or skills. These multiple options support all learners and provide flexibility in hybrid educational environments.[2] Being provided with additional options for engagement, students could maintain meaningful class participation through a lower-stakes format with the freedom to use their cameras as desired. Students were dealing with uncertainty and learning to navigate online learning; UDL's focus on the learning objective, rather than the process of getting there, reduces barriers to that learning goal. Using UDL principles as a foundation, librarians and instructors can address possible concerns about peer-to-peer engagement in hybrid courses by resetting how students connect with each other and with course content.

As our librarians developed and updated lesson plans to incorporate UDL principles, they simultaneously promoted open educational resources (OERs) as another way of fostering accessibility. OERs complement our use of UDL principles because they are freely available on the internet for any individual to download and access without the additional strains of financial, legal, or technical barriers.[3] This open access model is a contrast to the requirements for students to purchase access to their digital or physical course materials. Restricted access to campus prompted a handful of instructors at Juniata College to consider using OERs to meet the unique needs of students who were unable to access physical course materials when college buildings were temporarily closed due to the pandemic. While the library had existing OERs and Creative Commons LibGuides about the evaluation and use of open and shared academic resources, OERs became part of the course development workflow when instructors contacted librarians for assistance.[4]

Instructional Methods

The activities provided below were developed to allow students to test their understanding of key information literacy concepts and practice their digital literacy skills. With a foundation in accessibility and equity, many of these library instruction sessions can be effectively designed to utilize a flipped-classroom approach to dedicate class time toward meaningful interactions between content and students. These lessons require internet access, but can be delivered remotely, in a hybrid model, or in person, which allows them to continue to be used in post-pandemic instruction.

We provide these lessons as a menu in this chapter; an instructor can select several activities and piece them together to develop a full class session. Our librarians offered the same for our instructors: we collected expanded versions of the lesson plans below as a digital Information Literacy Toolbox, organized by class level and applicable frames from the ACRL *Framework for Information Literacy for Higher Education.*[5] Like those below, each activity included a summary, learning objectives, pre-assignment tasks, activity instructions, post-assignment engagement prompts, and assessment guidelines. We offered flexible delivery options to tie into the library's continued efforts to build inclusive teaching practices into shared learning objects. Offering information literacy lesson plan options allowed us to better collaborate with faculty and provide more targeted information literacy sessions for students.

Pre-class Asynchronous Tutorials[6]

- Learning Objective: Students will be able to identify types of and search for resources using the library website.
- Assignment: Prior to the start of class, students are assigned an online form or worksheet with a series of questions tied to video tutorials. Each student independently watches these videos, each of which focuses on one particular concept, such as searching for e-books or using limiters. Afterward, the student answers a guided question that asks them to practice skills from the video by finding a source related to their topic. At the end of the worksheet, they are asked to reflect on this experience. Different questions and tutorials can be used to accommodate different level classes.
- Rationale: Tutorial worksheets allow you to incorporate a flipped classroom approach and assign a worksheet to students to introduce them to library research. Students are introduced to skills at their own pace and discover sources that are directly tied to their research. By collaborating with the instructor, the librarian has access to the completed worksheets prior to class and can use class time to reinforce topics where students struggled. This approach also ensures that students with poor or limited internet access can work at their own pace, when or where they have the best internet access. While they may not be able to participate as actively in the classroom, they still have the opportunity to gain research skills.
- Format: Google or Microsoft Forms or text document; YouTube tutorials
- Level: First-year to graduate level

- UDL Tie-In: Students are able to engage with captioned videos and work at their own pace to begin their research. For students with limited internet access, asynchronous tutorials provide them with flexibility while ensuring they have access to core concepts. They are also able to submit questions or request additional help directly through the form. They may also return to the tutorials to reinforce particular skills. The librarian is able to revisit concepts and answer questions during the synchronous class session.

Icebreaker[7]

- Learning Objective: Students will be able to use a collaborative document.
- Assignment: Include one or two questions in the collaborative document at the beginning of your presentation. One might relate directly to the class, like "What do you think makes a source credible?" while the other might be more fun, like "What is your favorite study snack?" One librarian was able to use the debate over toaster pastry flavors as an example throughout an entire class (e.g., "You want to make sure you have credible sources if you want to prove strawberry is superior!"), which kept the students laughing and interested during the lesson.
- Rationale: This activity introduces students to using collaborative documents by asking them to answer a low-stakes question. In addition to building that skill, this activity allows the instructor to establish a connection with them and gauge some of their knowledge on the subject of your lesson.
- Format: Google Doc or Slide or Microsoft online document with full editing permissions
- Level: First-year to graduate level
- UDL Tie-In: Students are introduced to the multiple response options, which would be used for the remainder of the class. This activity provides a check to ensure students can find at least one way to communicate, be it through speaking, typing in the collaborative document, or chat features.

Collaborative Note-Taking[8]

- Learning Objective: Students will be able to assess what information should be included in notes and practice working as a team to record information from the lesson.
- Assignment: Share an editable document with the students with lesson prompts and questions for students to contribute to for the duration of the class.

- Rationale: Throughout a session, students can use a single document to contribute notes, submit questions about content, and take part in peer-to-peer intercommunication through a collaborative note-taking object. This activity increases student interactivity with the content, allowing them to comfortably utilize the learning method that works best for them without adding additional pressures on the instructor. These documents can be used to assess in-class participation and identify where students were able to challenge themselves in the research and evaluation process.
- Format: Google Doc or Slide or Microsoft online document with full editing permissions
- Level: First-year to graduate level
- UDL Tie-In: Creating, sharing, and archiving collaborative note-taking objects for students and instructors to reference through the span of a course serves as a key example of equitable teaching practices. Collaborative notes can be used and referenced by various types of learners, and democratizes their access to course content, in-class discussion, and resources found and evaluated during class time: all without the need to request for additional accommodations.

Source Evaluation Activity[9]

- Learning Objective: Students will be able to identify, compare, and assess various sources.
- Assignment: Individually or in groups, students compare and contrast two different sources that are linked in a shared document. This activity can be scaled to different levels—it could be as simple as students identifying the similarities and differences between popular and scholarly periodicals, or more complex, where students assess how the same information or event is presented in different ways to support different conclusions.
- Rationale: Collectively, students are able to enter their observations or comments on the document, which enables them to immediately identify similarities and contrasts in their contributions. These documents can be used to assess in-class participation, identify where students were able to challenge themselves in the evaluation process, and highlight concepts that need to be revisited in follow-up instruction.
- Format: Google Form or Slide or Microsoft online document with full editing permissions
- Level: First-year introductory activity; warm-up activity for upper-level students

- UDL Tie-In: Students work together to learn about types of sources. While the material is primarily presented visually, students can respond verbally, through the collaborative document, or through a chat feature.

Trivia[10]

- Learning Objective: Students will demonstrate their existing knowledge on a given subject.
- Assignment: Individually or in groups, students can play an introductory game. The game can be embedded into the main lesson platform (slides, LMS module, worksheet, etc.) so that students can collectively play a basic trivia game, reviewing content or introducing new concepts prior to the lesson.
- Rationale: This activity is an icebreaker that can be used by the instructor to observe baseline comprehension students have of class content and allows students to share and learn basic library services and trivia. The use of an online instructional game provides them a real-time, in-the-moment competitive experience as they challenge each other to answer the most questions quickly and correctly.
- Format: Slido or Kahoot! account and learning object embedded in lesson
- Level: First-year to senior-level
- UDL Tie-In: This activity allows for multiple modes of assessment early in a session. Students answer questions throughout the game, but also talk about their answers. It also helps to bring all of the students to the same level of base knowledge prior to the start of the session as they learn from their peers any answers they may not have already known.

Departmental Outreach

Inclusive instructional practices can be applied to institutional communication efforts. Building and utilizing new hybrid lessons opens new opportunities for instructors to view librarians as teaching partners: working together to identify accessible course materials and to inspire instructors to step away from lecture-based formats. For libraries already utilizing a liaison model for working with specific departments, these connections offer valuable opportunities for using existing trust and partnerships to promote accessible tools and methods. The authors recognize that not all libraries have a liaison program, but many librarians still have relationships with faculty.

One of the strongest partnerships at our library has been with First Year Experience courses—a series that includes Foundations, an introduction to college life; Composition, an introduction to college writing; and Seminar, an introduction to critical thought and discussion. Our college had recently adopted a new curriculum, and librarians were invited to participate in several committees to develop that curriculum. We used this opportunity to successfully advocate for two required library sessions for First Year Composition classes. These required sessions have provided opportunities for librarians to test out accessible teaching methods and receive feedback from both instructors and students.

While much liaison work has focused on recommending instruction sessions, librarians have also used these relationships to champion accessible resources and promote other ways to reduce barriers to student learning.

Advocating for Open Educational Resources

OERs lower barriers for students in several ways: they remove financial barriers, can be customized to fit a class, and are often already compatible with accessible technologies. To normalize conversations around OERs, it is important to plan within your existing menu of instruction activities, especially around scholarly communication and resource evaluation. Routinely including an exercise around OER publications and how one goes about contributing to open scholarship encourages students and faculty to think beyond the bias of considering free resources online to be nonacademic or not always peer-reviewed.[11] These conversations can naturally open up opportunities for librarians and instructors to discuss access to course materials and how OER textbooks and courseware can be found, evaluated, and incorporated in a class.

At Juniata College, the learning services and assessment librarian completed a survey to determine student perceptions on the cost and accessibility of textbooks. The librarian shared the results of this study with faculty to highlight that certain subject areas (i.e., sciences, business, art) habitually assigned expensive textbooks that a majority of registered students either shared with each other or did not buy. To have Juniata College students openly share their struggles with high textbook costs inspired some faculty to invite librarians to assist them in finding open materials. Having a librarian execute the initial OER search and resource gathering lowered the perceived challenges faculty had regarding how to start finding OERs related to their subject areas. The following "lesson" can be used to guide librarians in their efforts to broach this conversation with faculty and students. Explore the prompts below:

- Engaging Instructors: Faculty may be unaware of the costs or challenges that students may have in acquiring certain titles or editions of textbooks.

Either in person or virtually, when a faculty member inquires about the availability of course materials in the library collection, we recommend that you consider the following steps:

○ Ask for the titles of previous assigned materials.
○ Search for titles, book chapters, or articles in the library catalog that cover similar material.
○ Search for two to three OERs that cover similar content.

Provide links and descriptions in a summative e-mail or document that you share with your instructor. This allows them to conveniently explore easily accessible materials without feeling overwhelmed. The Juniata College's "Open Educational Resources Guide" contains a curated selection of search aids for anyone to explore OERs for any subject type.[12]

• Engaging Students: An OER search activity can be formatted just like any other source evaluation activity, best tied to an existing course assignment or on a student's field of interest. Prompt students to use the Mason OER Metafinder or another OER search service on Juniata College's "Affordable Learning Resources Guide."[13] This can lead to further conversations about why open publishing is essential to conversations around scholarly communications. This ties well to equity, diversity, and inclusion efforts that address access to information as a privilege. Openly published information and academic sources are more broadly available to individuals who may or may not have access to expensive databases.

Conclusions

The 2020–21 academic year challenged educators to rethink their teaching strategies. To meet the remote needs of both students and instructors, it was important to integrate inclusive teaching practices. These practices had the additional benefit of addressing unique learning styles and providing new active learning opportunities. As learning institutions transition to fully in-person instruction, it is important to reflect on engagement methods that can be sustained when all students are in the classroom. Many remote objects can be just as effective to bring a new layer of engagement to class instruction, such as collaborative notetaking. The activities in this chapter, once created for a specific class or need, are easy to maintain and share, allowing instructors and librarians to maintain successful practices beyond the effects of COVID-19 in higher education.

Notes

1. Brenda K. Wiederhold, "Connecting through Technology during the Coronavirus Disease 2019 Pandemic: Avoiding 'Zoom Fatigue,'" editorial, *Cyberpsychology, Behavior, and Social Networking* 23, no. 7 (2020): 437–38, https://doi.org/10.1089/cyber.2020.29188.bkw.
2. CAST, "Universal Design for Learning Guidelines," ver. 2.2, The UDL Guidelines, 2018, http://udlguidelines.cast.org. We chose to use CAST for our citation, rather than another of the many sources about UDL because our campus Accessibility Office uses CAST when introducing faculty to UDL. In a desire to be supportive of their efforts and to remain consistent across our campus, we present CAST here as well. But we encourage you to check out many of the other resources available.
3. BOAI, Budapest Open Access Initiative, 2017, https://www.budapestopenaccessinitiative.org/boai15/.
4. Christine Elliott, "Juniata's Affordable Learning Resource Guide," Juniata College Library, November 12, 2020, https://libguides.juniata.edu/oer (page content changed).
5. Association of College and Research Libraries, *Framework for Information Literacy for Higher Education* (Chicago: American Library Association, 2016).
6. Deb Roney and Sara Kern, "Library Research Worksheet," Google Drive, June 4, 2021, https://drive.google.com/file/d/1CrrbShgHzMRA7tzHUcgUXqhR-d3nRiwE/view.
7. Juniata College Library, "First Year Seminar Google Docs Example," Google Drive, January 15, 2021, https://docs.google.com/document/d/1INRU0HmrkDq6KbIzfCY6ANM1TQntGpg1N-0TaTICj-c4/edit. The icebreaker activity is included near the beginning of the document.
8. The following two examples show different ways of presenting similar lessons using Google Docs and Google Slides. Juniata College Library, "First Year Seminar Google Slides Example," Google Drive, June 4, 2021, https://docs.google.com/presentation/d/1yb7WUOFWqoVXU34Y-WHGtUK56nMFE5LOOoNJL9hGk4SE/edit#slide=id.p; Juniata College Library, "First Year Seminar Google Docs Example."
9. Juniata College Library. "ITP Chapter Evaluation Activity", Google Drive, June 3, 2021, https://drive.google.com/file/d/1OCVTD-KwBQP_bDPlGVed55R_Ob1J9lPF/view.
10. Juniata College Library, "ITP Chapter Trivia Gamification," Google Drive, June 3, 2021, https://drive.google.com/file/d/1CLxdL6VUNgSORDOQyEbn6PTl1o1gM1ha/view.
11. Annie Gaines, "From Concerned to Cautiously Optimistic: Assessing Faculty Perceptions and Knowledge of Open Access in a Campus-wide Study." Journal of Librarianship and Scholarly Communication 3, no. 1 (2015): eP1212, https://doi.org/10.7710/2162-3309.1212; John Hilton III, "Open Educational Resources and College Textbook Choices: A Review of Research on Efficacy and Perceptions," *Educational Technology Research and Development* 64 (2016): 573–90, https://doi.org/10.1007/s11423-016-9434-9.
12. Elliott, "Juniata's Affordable Learning Resource Guide."
13. Juniata College Library. "Evaluating OER Sources Worksheet," Google Drive, August 17, 2021, https://docs.google.com/document/d/1bzN98MPPzEhyNgA7s03oZo3xUlXzabY_/edit.

Bibliography

Association of College and Research Libraries. *Framework for Information Literacy for Higher Education*. Chicago: Association of College and Research Libraries, 2016.

BOAI. Budapest Open Access Initiative, 2017. https://www.budapestopenaccessinitiative.org/boai15/.

CAST. "Universal Design for Learning Guidelines," ver. 2.2. The UDL Guidelines. 2018. http://udlguidelines.cast.org.

Elliott, Christine. "Open Educational Resource Guide." Juniata College Library, November 12, 2020. https://libguides.juniata.edu/oer (page content changed).

Gaines, Annie. "From Concerned to Cautiously Optimistic: Assessing Faculty Perceptions and Knowledge of Open Access in a Campus-wide Study." *Journal of Librarianship and Scholarly Communication* 3, no. 1 (2015): eP1212. https://doi.org/10.7710/2162-3309.1212.

Hilton, John, III. "Open Educational Resources and College Textbook Choices: A Review of Research on Efficacy and Perceptions." *Educational Technology Research and Development* 64 (2016): 573–90. https://doi.org/10.1007/s11423-016-9434-9.

Juniata College Library. "Evaluating OER Sources Worksheet." Google Drive, August 17, 2021. https://docs.google.com/document/d/1bzN98MPPzEhyNgA7s03oZo3xUlXzabY_/edit.

———. "First Year Seminar Google Docs Example." Google Drive, January 15, 2021. https://docs.google.com/document/d/1INRU0HmrkDq6KbIzfCY6ANM1TQntGpg1N0TaTICj-c4/edit.

———. "First Year Seminar Google Slides Example." Google Drive, June 4, 2021. https://docs.google.com/presentation/d/1yb7WUOFWqoVXU34YWHGtUK56nMFE5LOOoNJL9hGk4SE/edit#slide=id.p.

———. "ITP Chapter Evaluation Activity." Google Drive, June 3, 2021. https://drive.google.com/file/d/10CVTD-KwBQP_bDPlGVed55R_Ob1J9lPF/view.

———. "ITP Chapter Trivia Gamification." Google Drive, June 3, 2021. https://drive.google.com/file/d/1CLxdL6VUNgSORDOQyEbn6PTl1o1gM1ha/view.

Roney, Deb, and Sara Kern. "Library Research Worksheet." Google Drive. June 4, 2021. https://drive.google.com/file/d/1CrrbShgHzMRA7tzHUcgUXqhR-d3nRiwE/view.

Wiederhold, Brenda K. "Connecting through Technology during the Coronavirus Disease 2019 Pandemic: Avoiding 'Zoom Fatigue.'" Editorial. *Cyberpsychology, Behavior, and Social Networking* 23, no. 7 (2020): 437–38. https://doi.org/10.1089/cyber.2020.29188.bkw.

CHAPTER 31

Prioritizing Accessibility in Synchronous and Asynchronous Learning Environments

Lauren Wittek and Rachel Fager

Introduction

Traditional education design tends to be a one-size-fits-all approach: functionality for the majority of users is the goal and accommodations for "nontraditional" users are developed reactively as new demands make themselves known. The burden is on the student to disclose their needs and request accommodations. Universal design for learning (UDL), in contrast, seeks to meet the needs of as many students as possible from the beginning. By providing students with multiple means of engagement and representation, as well as action and expression, UDL reduces barriers to learning, not only for those with disabilities, but also non-native English speakers, those with limited access to technology, and students with various learning styles and preferences.[1] The flexibility built into UDL actively supports a more diverse student population.

Libraries must meet the legal and ethical standards set forth by state and federal laws, including the Americans with Disabilities Act of 1990 and Section 504 of the Rehabilitation Act of 1973, to create an inclusive learning environment for all students of all abilities. Beyond meeting standards, consider accessibility as a habit—it is not special or by request only. Accessibility is part of one's routine, what is by default, and something that can be reinforced and built upon just by doing it. Using accessibility practices effectively complements UDL by removing barriers to content for all users, not just individuals who require an accommodation.

Approaching accessibility as a holistic design endeavor can quickly feel overwhelming while thinking about how much work and preparation is involved in creating and retrofitting course or lesson content. This chapter discusses the foundations of UDL and how it has been applied to the authors' library instruction; details common obstacles experienced by students living with disabilities; provides ideas, resources, and tools for overcoming these barriers for synchronous and asynchronous sessions; and suggests ways to continue to expand upon one's knowledge, skills, and community of practice.

Disabilities in the United States

According to the Centers for Disease Control and Prevention, one in four American adults live with a disability—this translates to 61 million people.[2] In this instance, the term *disability* is not limited to issues with mobility, cognition, and vision. It can also include challenges with self-sufficiency and the ability to live independently. Within these five dimensions of disability, there is a wide variety of conditions (e.g., autism, blindness, rheumatoid arthritis, bipolar disorder), and individuals may identify as having more than one disability. Some disabilities are permanent (e.g., loss of a limb), some are situational (e.g., weather dependent), and some are temporary (e.g., recovering from surgery). However, to be protected under the Americans with Disabilities Act (ADA), disability is defined as "a physical or mental impairment that substantially limits one or more major life activities, a person who has a history or record of such an impairment, or a person who is perceived by others as having such an impairment."[3] In 2008, the definition of "major life activities" was expanded to include major body functions, such as digestion, circulation, and respiratory functions. While the term *disability* is used to describe a subset of the population, it fails to fully capture the wide variety of symptoms, treatments, and needs across this population. Different disabilities carry with them discreet challenges, and no single accommodation can satisfy the needs of all disabled individuals.

According to the American College Health Association's National College Health Assessment, the top five reported disabilities among college students are attention deficit and hyperactivity disorder (12.1%), a learning disability (3.6%), blind/low vision (3.4%), deafness/hearing loss (2.1%), and autism spectrum disorder (2%).[4] About 19 percent of undergraduate students report having a disability.[5] In actuality, this percentage may be higher because not every student needs or wants to report their disability to receive an accommodation through their institution's disability support office.[6] However, the composition of the disability community will vary greatly from institution to institution and even year to year as the student population changes.

Universal Design for Learning (UDL)

Traditionally, products and spaces have been designed for the average user—any modifications needed for those with disabilities are often an afterthought. Universal design (UD), however, is creating environments to be usable by as many people as possible without the need for modifications. The concept of UD was developed in the late 1990s by a group of engineers, architects, and researchers at North Carolina State University's Center for Universal Design and contains seven core principles: equitable use, flexibility in use, simple and intuitive use, perceptible information, tolerance for error, low physical effort, and size and space for approach and use.[7] This group recognized the importance of baking accessibility into the design stage rather than retrofitting it to a finished environment or product once an issue or complaint has emerged. Some common applications of UD include adjustable desks, high-contrast signage with easy-to-read fonts, multisensory alarms, and automatic doorways.

So, how can librarians address accessibility issues in the library? The concept of universal design for learning (UDL) builds on the idea of UD by addressing educational barriers for all students, not just those living with a disability. UDL can be broken down into three areas:[8]

- *Representation:* Present information in multiple ways, such as providing a video lecture with closed captioning and a text-based transcript of that lecture. This provides students with a variety of means by which to access the information.
- *Action and Expression:* Students are given multiple opportunities to demonstrate what they have learned—meaning instructors may give students assignment options and they pick one that speaks to their interests and skills. For instance, librarians teaching for-credit courses could assign students a paper or allow them to create a podcast episode demonstrating the course or assignment objectives. For librarians teaching one-shot

sessions, consider allowing students to share what they have learned verbally and in writing, which could include responding to an interactive poll, sharing their experiences with the class, drawing a diagram, and more.

- *Engagement:* It is important to find multiple ways for students to engage with the content, their fellow students, and the instructor in order to make the material more meaningful. Some examples of this could be creating pair and group activities, dividing overarching course or session goals into smaller short-term objectives, or asking students to reflect on how the course or session connects to their personal learning goals.

UDL can also help institutions meet federal and state legal mandates. These laws help ensure students have equal access to learning materials and seek to eliminate discrimination based on disability.

Implementing UDL may benefit students without disabilities. Utilizing this approach can help English language learners, those with different learning styles, or those who have trouble concentrating and need multiple methods of absorbing course content, to name just a few. This helps to promote a more inclusive learning environment by offering various ways to access and engage with the material. UDL helps to reduce stigma by preemptively providing options without forcing students to make a request for alternative content formats.

Accessibility

Accessibility is about removing barriers for students; it's not about checking a box. When creating instructional content, consider how the students will perceive and engage with the learning object and the class as a whole. A beginning step to this work is to evaluate where your accessibility practices are today: What methods are being employed that make your content accessible? What other, different methods can be employed? To assist with that self-reflection and to help move forward in building accessibility habits, a guide has been included (see appendix B, "Guide of Accessibility Habits")—it is not all-inclusive; rather, it should be used as a starting point to understand where you are currently. This guide presents many of the basic tasks for different content and formats.

As you dive into these practices, you will be able to find a multitude of resources—accessibility guides, videos, and checklists—to expand your skills.[9] Your institution may already have a checklist or guide, and online resources abound, including The A11y Project's checklist, WebAIM's WCAG 2 checklist, and the University of Washington's IT accessibility checklist.[10] There are tools, technology, and resources to improve or evaluate accessibility (see appendix A, "Resources"). Please take these strategies and resources as a starting point; companies are working to make their products more accessible, and technology and the law are always evolving.[11]

Asynchronous Learning

Think about how documents, handouts, presentations, or any other learning object will be shared with students as you create them. Is the document going to be shared in a digital format, a printout, or both? There are basic accessibility practices that should be followed with all documentation, but some are vital for a digital format.

DOCUMENTS

The discussion in this section (see table 31.1) is focused on good accessibility practices for documents, but many of these also apply to materials such as flyers, forms, and social media posts.

Table 31.1

Accessibility practices for documents. Many of the resources mentioned are listed in appendix A.

Accessibility Habit	Notes
Use appropriate font size.	At least 12-point font for documents and 18-point font for slides.
Use appropriate font.	Simple fonts, e.g., Verdana or Arial for online reading and Times New Roman or Georgia for print.*
Use sufficient white space.	Line spacing of 1.2 or more; white space is as important as the font for ease of reading.
Use high color contrast.	Choose a color that has high contrast with the background. Black text on a white background is always a good choice. There are color contrast checkers online to help evaluate color combinations, including from WebAIM and Ally.
Use more than color to convey meaning.	Use color to reinforce (but not to create) meaning. That visual cue will not be helpful for those who cannot see, those with color-blindness, or those who print the document in black and white. There are technologies to re-create what an image looks like to those with different types of color-blindness. For example, Coblis demonstrates this using a sample or an uploaded image.

* Nafiseh Hojjati and Balakrishnan Muniandy, "The Effects of Font Type and Spacing of Text for Online Readability and Performance," *Contemporary Educational Technology* 5, no. 2 (April 2014), https://doi.org/10.30935/cedtech/6122.

Table 31.1

Accessibility practices for documents. Many of the resources mentioned are listed in appendix A.

Accessibility Habit	Notes
Use headings.	For those using a screen reader, the headings are navigational beacons that can be used to get an outline of the document and provide shortcuts to desired sections. This creates a consistent and expected structure, so the document can be easily scanned by all students. It also enables the easy creation and updating of a table of contents by inserting the table of contents from the toolbar or menu.
Adjust format of headings.	The font, size, and spacing of the headings can be changed within the document or can be altered to a preferred default.
Use the built-in bulleted or numbered list feature.	Use the system's bulleted or numbered list option to create an underlying structure that can be interpreted by screen readers. A list using tabs or numbers does not create that structure, and someone with a screen reader might not know when the list starts or ends.
Add alternative text (alt text) to images.	Use alt text to describe images, charts, diagrams, and other visual information. Alt text should be concise but give the user all the information needed to understand the content of the image. Alt text is read by the screen reader so that the user is aware of the content without needing to view the image. Alt text will appear if an image does not load, for example, due to a poor internet connection.
Use descriptive links.	A descriptive link is a description of what the user will link to as the hyperlink rather than the URL text. In a digital format, the descriptive link is preferred because the screen reader will identify the text as a link and read the descriptive name rather than the string of letters and characters that make up the URL. Linking text that says "click here" is not descriptive, especially if there are several links that all say "click here" as the text. If providing a printout, type out the URL but still provide the name of the website.

Table 31.1

Accessibility practices for documents. Many of the resources mentioned are listed in appendix A.

Accessibility Habit	Notes
Use descriptive file names.	Use descriptive names for files so a student knows what to expect when opening or downloading a document. This also makes finding the file easier later.
Use a descriptive name for each sheet in a workbook.	If a workbook has more than one sheet, rename the sheets to describe the information they contain.
Make accessible tables	Avoid merged and split cells. Add a header row to all tables.
Set the reading order of slide contents.	Best done as the last step before sharing slides. Check the order of the boxes to ensure the reading order for the computer is correct.
Use slide numbers and unique titles.	Number the slides. The computer can do this automatically. Every slide has a unique title to differentiate it.
Use Save As or Export to a PDF file.	Microsoft Office, Adobe InDesign, LibreOffice, and OpenOffice keep structures that support accessibility when a file is saved as or exported to a PDF file. The Print to PDF option will lose the heading structure, alternative text, and any other tag structure. A screen reader user may still be able to access the text of a PDF created in this way, but it is not as accessible.
Scan readable documents with high color contrast.	Ensure the entire page is included in the scan and legible. Scan in black/white or 24-bit color and maintain a high color contrast. Scan one print page as one electronic page.
Scan with appropriate DPI for text and images.	Text-based documents scan at 300–400 dots per inch (DPI). 600 DPI may be required for content that is image-heavy. These DPI settings make the scan easier for people to view and improve the ability of conversion software to identify characters.

Table 31.1

Accessibility practices for documents. Many of the resources mentioned are listed in appendix A.

Accessibility Habit	Notes
Apply optical character recognition (OCR) to scans.	Use a scanner or a system that has optical character recognition (OCR). Often, this option is identified as saving a document as a searchable PDF.
	OCR turns pictures of text into computer-readable text, allowing users to highlight and copy text and use Ctrl+F to search for text.
	If the scanner does not have OCR, software such as Adobe Acrobat Pro can recognize text and save that information to the file. Any images in the PDF should be tagged with alt text to make the PDF more accessible.
Use accessibility checkers for documents, slides, etc.	Use the Check Accessibility feature within Microsoft Office. This will scan the document for errors, explain why these errors should be remedied, and list the steps to fix them.
	Google does not currently have a native accessibility check feature. One potential work-around is to download the Google document as an equivalent Microsoft file (e.g., downloading Google Docs as Microsoft Word files) and use the Microsoft accessibility checker. Revise any errors or warnings and upload the file back to Google Drive.
Use accessibility checker for LibGuides and websites.	Use tools to check the accessibility of websites. The World Wide Web Consortium (W3C) keeps a list of web accessibility evaluation tools. WAVE from WebAIM is one free example that offers several options.

VIDEOS/PRESENTATIONS

This section discusses accessibility practices for videos and presentations (table 31.2). Note that the terms *subtitles* and *captions* are often used interchangeably, but there are distinct differences. Subtitles are the dialogue or translation of the dialogue in text format. Captions are the text of dialogue and sounds (e.g., music, sound effects, and off-screen noises) that accompany a video. The term *caption* is sometimes used for what is better described as a subtitle. Closed captions can be displayed or hidden; open captions are embedded in a video file and are always displayed on screen.

Table 31.2

Accessibility practices for videos and presentations. See appendix A for a listing of the resources mentioned.

Accessibility Habit	Notes
Describe visual elements aloud.	Describe any images, charts, or visual elements. Decorative images do not need to be described, but any visual that is informative or specifically referenced should be succinctly described aloud for those who cannot see the visual content.
Subtitle or caption videos.	Add subtitles or captions to videos. There are tools that will automatically add subtitles. These computer-generated subtitles are helpful but should be reviewed and edited for accuracy. Amara allows users to create or improve upon a video's captions or subtitles. Amara is free to users but offers the option to pay for captioning or translation services.
Edit computer-generated subtitles or captions.	Edit for accuracy, and pay particular attention to acronyms, homonyms, names, and punctuation.
Create a transcript for video.	A transcript is different from video captions or subtitles because it is independent of the video or audio. A transcript can be read and searched because it is a text document. The free web app oTranscribe lets users upload an audio or video file or enter a link to a YouTube video for manual transcription within the same page.

Synchronous Learning

If you teach a semester-long class, students or your institution's disability support office may notify you regarding what accommodations are needed. If you are teaching a one-shot class, ask the professor if there are accommodations you should plan to include for that session. Not every accommodation needs to be shared with you; however, if a student has an interpreter, records every class, or uses a particular software to interface with the computer, it can be helpful to know ahead of time. The habits and resources discussed here (table 31.3) are a good baseline, but be responsive to a student's request as they know what works best for them.

Table 31.3

Accessibility practices for synchronous learning

Accessibility Habit	Notes
Use live-captioning software.	The best option is Communication Access Realtime Translation (CART), where a professional provides captioning for the class or event. This is not free, but a 98 percent total accuracy rate is considered entry-level quality for a CART captioner.*
	Machine-generated captions are not as accurate but are often free and easily applied. Your institution may already pay for a service that provides live captioning. Google Slides and Zoom offer free live captioning when presenting.
Consider options for student engagement.	It is important to provide options, let students know what their options are, and work out any kinks as early as possible. Will students be allowed or encouraged to unmute and speak? Will they use chat? Will you use a polling feature? Will you use another platform like a shared document, Padlet, or other technology?
	It is best practice to repeat participant questions and comments that come from the chat before responding so everyone knows what question you are responding to, both live and in the recording.
	Consider sharing materials and slides in advance so that students can review them ahead of time and be more engaged during the session. Let students know if you are recording and whether the recording will be provided after the session. Send a recap that includes a summary of topics discussed and links to relevant websites, online resources, and other materials mentioned. These practices can ease the cognitive load and make it easier for students to fully engage for the duration of the session.
Familiarize yourself with accessibility software in your library.	Learn what accessibility software is available in the library's classrooms and on which machines. For example, ZoomText, which enlarges and enhances text for low-vision users, may be installed only on certain terminals. If that is the case, make sure that a student who needs that software is seated at that computer. It might not be on any of the classroom computers but on a laptop the student can borrow. Your library's or institution's IT department may need to install the program on one of the computers before a session with that student.

*NCRA Broadcast and CART Captioning Committee, *Guidelines for CART Captioners (Communication Access Realtime Translation Captioners*, revised October 2016, https://www.ncra.org/docs/default-source/uploadedfiles/governmentrelations/guidelines-for-cart-captioners.pdf.

Getting Involved at Your Campus

Internal Library Work

You can bring a lens of accessibility to your work and any committee on which you sit. Make accessibility a regular part of conversations with committee colleagues. On a user experience committee, consider the accessibility of your website, LibGuides, and physical spaces. On a collection development committee, consider the usability of the vendor's platform before purchasing or during renewal. The University of Washington has gone through all 500+ of its database subscriptions and evaluated each for basic keyboard navigation. [12] This information can be used when negotiating with vendors because they often have an incomplete picture as to how accessible their products are.

A simple way to convey a welcoming environment and the importance of accessibility to library users is to compile information into an accessibility page on the library's website.[13] Creating a central place for all this information to live helps save users from having to search the entire website in order to determine what services and features are available at the library. Consider providing the following details:

- Facilities: Nearest parking with designated disabled parking spots; elevator access; restrooms; and sensory information (lighting, sound levels, private/quiet rooms, and study areas).
- Services and equipment: Stacks retrieval help; proxy borrower policy; relevant equipment available for checkout (e.g., headphones, laptops, voice recorders, etc.).
- Database assistance: Brief description of accessibility and/or help sections within databases and relevant library contact information if navigation assistance is needed.

This page could be added by a small team that updates the website or as part of a larger website redesign project.

Campus Partnerships and Committees

Another way to be formally involved on campus is to join your campus's accessibility or disability support committee. These committees are typically made up of a cross-section of faculty and staff from various departments around campus, such as human resources, IT, disability support, and facilities. These committees seek to address accessibility issues and make recommendations while raising awareness about disability issues. If your campus does not have such a committee, consider creating one.

Conclusion

Librarians have the opportunity and responsibility to create an inclusive and equitable learning environment for all students. Whereas a library's online presence and virtual offerings were once just a part of the library's overall services and spaces, they are now a primary means of serving and demonstrating value to our institutions. As we all continue adjusting to an uncertain future, providing and improving instruction to students virtually via synchronous and asynchronous modalities takes on an increased significance. This chapter may be a starting point if you are new to UDL and accessibility or give you some new insights if you are already familiar with them. Librarians should utilize UDL guidelines as a framework to build learning opportunities for students and continue to make accessibility practices a habit. No matter what your current level of familiarity or funding, there is so much beneficial information and training out there for you to learn and grow to better serve your students.

Appendix A: Resources

Accessibility Certification

International Association of Accessibility Professionals (IAAP) certification—
https://www.accessibilityassociation.org/s/certification
> A not-for-profit organization focused on building individual and organizational accessibility skills and integrating accessibility into services and products. IAAP offers five different certification options, including core competencies and web accessibility, which are valid for three years.

Project ENABLE—https://projectenable.syr.edu/
> Offers free, asynchronous module-based training for librarians and library staff interested in developing foundational knowledge focused on disability awareness and creating more inclusive library spaces.

Universal Design for Learning

CAST—https://www.cast.org/
> A nonprofit education research and development organization that is credited with creating the universal design for learning framework. The site offers learning resources, online tools, UDL-focused projects, and events.

Accessibility Training/Information

Accessibility: Designing and Teaching Courses for All Learners (from SUNY)—
https://www.canvas.net/browse/empirestate/empirestate-buffalostate/courses/
accessibility-designing-teaching
> Self-paced online accessibility course created by faculty and staff at SUNY Empire State College and SUNY Buffalo State College focused on reducing barriers for students by using UDL and accessibility practices.

Accessibility Self-Paced Training (from the University of Washington)—https://
canvas.uw.edu/courses/1351896
> This self-paced online accessibility course from the University of Washington includes modules on the basics of accessibility, creating accessible materials, and advocacy.

Digital Library Federation Digital Accessibility Working Group (DAWG)—
https://wiki.diglib.org/Digital_Accessibility_Group
> The Digital Accessibility Working Group promotes accessibility through its work of reviewing digital accessibility of galleries, libraries, archives, and museums; creating and collecting accessibility best practices; and promoting information sharing.

DO-IT (Disabilities, Opportunities, Internetworking, and Technology) Center—https://www.washington.edu/doit/

Resources and news for educators and students, including a knowledge base with over 800 case studies, Q&As, and more.

Northwest Higher Education Accessibility Technology (NWHeat) Group—https://nwheat.org/

NWHeat is a joint project between the Orbis Cascade Alliance and the Northwest Academic Computing Consortium. Noninstitutional members can view archived webinar recordings and download any related presentation materials and transcripts.

RespectAbility: Fighting Stigmas. Advancing Opportunities—https://www.respectability.org/

A disability-led nonprofit dedicated to fighting stigmas and advancing awareness about the importance of accessibility. Offers dozens of free on-demand webinars and compiles current events and news.

Section508.gov—https://www.section508.gov/

The US General Services Administration is responsible for supporting government agencies with compliance with Section 508 of the Rehabilitation Act.

Web Accessibility Initiative—https://www.w3.org/WAI/

The World Wide Web Consortium's (W3C) Web Accessibility Initiative creates technical standards and related training for making the web accessible to those with disabilities.

WebAIM—https://webaim.org/

A nonprofit organization focused on web accessibility through trainings, resources, certification, and consulting. The site provides many resources, including a color contrast checker.

Accessibility Tools

W3C Web Accessibility Evaluation Tools List—https://www.w3.org/WAI/ER/tools/

A compilation of web accessibility tools compiled by the World Wide Web Consortium (W3C).

WAVE Web Accessibility Evaluation Tool—https://wave.webaim.org/

WebAIM's WAVE is a free online tool that provides feedback on a page's accessibility. Users can also download the WAVE Toolbar, which is an extension for Firefox, Chrome, and Edge browsers.

A11y Color Contrast Accessibility Validator—https://color.a11y.com/

Users may enter two hexadecimal (hex) color codes to ensure color contrast is appropriate per WCAG 2.1. Users may also test a specific web page for contrast issues.

Coblis—Color Blindness Simulator—https://www.color-blindness.com/
coblis-color-blindness-simulator/

> A website that demonstrates the effects of the different types of color-blindness
> using a sample image or user-uploaded image.

oTranscribe—https://otranscribe.com/

> A web app that lets users upload an audio or video file or enter a link to
> a YouTube video for transcription within the same page. Users can pause,
> rewind, and fast-forward without taking their hands off the keyboard. Users
> can export the transcript to Markdown, plain text, and Google Docs.

Amara—https://amara.org/en/

> A free web app that allows users to create or improve upon a video's captions
> or subtitles. After users have created the captions for a video, they can export
> them as a text file.

YouDescribe—https://youdescribe.org/

> A free web-based platform that allows users to add audio descriptions of the
> actions taking place within YouTube videos. Users can search and browse for
> previously completed videos or create a wishlist, and the site offers step-by-
> step instructions for adding one's own audio descriptions.

Web Captioner—https://webcaptioner.com/

> A free real-time automated captioning service that requires only a browser and
> a microphone. Web Captioner recognizes over forty languages and dialects
> and allows users to edit the transcript and censor words or make substitutions
> as needed.

Appendix B: Guide to Accessibility Habits

Use this checklist as a reflective training document to assess where you are now and how you can move forward. Mark in the appropriate column which accessibility habits you need to learn more about, which you currently do, and which you do so well and consistently you could teach someone else. A notes column has been included to jot down any additional thoughts.

Learn	Do	Teach	Accessibility Habit	Notes
			Use appropriate font size and sufficient white space.	
			Use high color contrast.	
			Use more than color to convey meaning.	
			Use headings.	
			Adjust format of headings.	
			Use the built-in bulleted or numbered list feature.	
			Add alt text to images.	
			Use descriptive links.	
			Use descriptive file names.	
			Use a descriptive name for each sheet in a workbook.	
			Make accessible tables.	
			Set the reading order of slide contents.	
			Use unique slide titles.	
			Use Save As or Export to a PDF file.	
			Scan readable documents with high color contrast.	

Learn	Do	Teach	Accessibility Habit	Notes
			Scan with appropriate DPI for text and images.	
			Apply OCR to scans.	
			Use accessibility checkers for documents, slides, etc.	
			Use accessibility checkers for LibGuides and websites.	
			Describe visual elements aloud.	
			Subtitle or caption videos.	
			Edit computer-generated subtitles or captions.	
			Create a transcript for video.	
			Use live captioning software.	
			Consider options for student engagement.	
			Familiarize yourself with accessibility software in your library.	

Notes

1. Eva Chen, "The Importance of Universal Design for Learning," Usable Knowledge, Harvard Graduate School of Education, December 20, 2008, https://www.gse.harvard.edu/news/uk/08/12/importance-universal-design-learning.
2. Centers for Disease Control and Prevention, "Disability Impacts All of Us," infographic, September 16, 2020, https://www.cdc.gov/ncbddd/disabilityandhealth/infographic-disability-impacts-all.html.
3. US Department of Justice, Civil Rights Division, "Introduction to the ADA," accessed June 6, 2021, https://www.ada.gov/ada_intro.htm.
4. National College Health Assessment, "Percentage of U.S. College Students That Reported Select Disabilities or Health Conditions as of Fall 2021," chart, September 5, 2022, Statista. https://www.statista.com/statistics/827023/disabilities-among-us-college-students/
5. National Center for Education Statistics, "Students with Disabilities," accessed June 17, 2021, https://nces.ed.gov/fastfacts/display.asp?id=60.

6. Allie Grasgreen, "Dropping the Ball on Disabilities," Inside Higher Ed, April 2, 2014, https://www.insidehighered.com/news/2014/04/02/students-disabilities-frustrated-ignorance-and-lack-services; David Leake, "Problematic Data on How Many Students in Postsecondary Education Have a Disability," *Journal of Postsecondary Education and Disability* 28, no. 1 (2015): 73–87, https://files.eric.ed.gov/fulltext/EJ1066327.pdf.

7. Bettye Rose Connell et al., "The Principle of Universal Design," ver. 2.0, Center for Universal Design, North Carolina State University, April 1, 1997, https://web.stanford.edu/class/engr110/2007/PUD.pdf.

8. CAST, "Universal Design for Learning Guidelines," ver. 2.2, 2018, http://udlguidelines.cast.org.

9. For a video, see Rachel Fager and Lauren Wittek, "Quickly Implementing Accessibility Tools" (presentation, ACRL Presents Webcasts, April 3, 2020), YouTube video, 52:34, https://www.youtube.com/watch?v=EAqH6T2wHoY.

10. A11Y Project, "Checklist," accessed October 19, 2021, https://www.a11yproject.com/checklist; WebAIM, "WebAIM's WCAG 2 Checklist," last modified February 26, 2021, https://webaim.org/standards/wcag/checklist; University of Washington, "IT Accessibility Checklist," accessed October 19, 2021, https://www.washington.edu/accessibility/checklist/

11. C. Low, "Accessibility in Tech Improved in 2020, but More Must Be Done." Engadget, December 23, 2020, https://www.engadget.com/accessibility-in-tech-2020-150002855.html.

12. University of Washington Libraries, "Library E-Resource Accessibility Testing," last modified July 9, 2021, https://www.lib.washington.edu/services/accessibility/e-resource-testing.

13. Amelia Brunskill, "'Without That Detail, I'm Not Coming': The Perspectives of Students with Disabilities on Accessibility Information Provided on Academic Library Websites," *College and Research Libraries* 81, no. 5 (2020): 768–88, https://doi.org/10.5860/crl.81.5.768.

Bibliography

A11Y Project. "Checklist." Accessed October 19, 2021. https://www.a11yproject.com/checklist.

Brunskill, Amelia. "'Without That Detail, I'm Not Coming': The Perspectives of Students with Disabilities on Accessibility Information Provided on Academic Library Websites." *College and Research Libraries* 81, no. 5 (2020): 768–88. https://doi.org/10.5860/crl.81.5.768.

CAST. "Universal Design for Learning Guidelines," ver. 2.2. 2018. http://udlguidelines.cast.org.

Centers for Disease Control and Prevention. "Disability Impacts All of Us." Infographic. September 16, 2020. https://www.cdc.gov/ncbddd/disabilityandhealth/infographic-disability-impacts-all.html.

Chen, Eva. "The Importance of Universal Design for Learning." Usable Knowledge. Harvard Graduate School of Education. December 20, 2008. https://www.gse.harvard.edu/news/uk/08/12/importance-universal-design-learning.

Connell, Bettye Rose, Mike Jones, Ron Mace, Jim Mueller, Abir Mullick, Elaine Ostroff, Jon Sanford, et al. "The Principles of Universal Design," ver. 2.0. Center for Universal Design, North Carolina State University. April 1, 1997. https://web.stanford.edu/class/engr110/2007/PUD.pdf.

Fager, Rachel, and Lauren Wittek. "ACRL Presents: Quickly Implementing Accessibility Tools." Presentation, ACRL Presents Webcasts, April 3, 2020. YouTube video, 52:34. https://www.youtube.com/watch?v=EAqH6T2wHoY.

Grasgreen, Allie. "Dropping the Ball on Disabilities." Inside Higher Ed, April 2, 2014. https://www.insidehighered.com/news/2014/04/02/students-disabilities-frustrated-ignorance-and-lack-services.

Hojjati, Nafiseh, and Balakrishnan Muniandy. "The Effects of Font Type and Spacing of Text for Online Readability and Performance." *Contemporary Educational Technology* 5, no. 2 (April 2014): 161–74. https://doi.org/10.30935/cedtech/6122.

Leake, David. "Problematic Data on How Many Students in Postsecondary Education Have a Disability." *Journal of Postsecondary Education and Disability* 28, no. 1 (2015): 73–87. https://files.eric.ed.gov/fulltext/EJ1066327.pdf.

Low, C. "Accessibility in Tech Improved in 2020, but More Must Be Done." Engadget, December 23, 2020, https://www.engadget.com/accessibility-in-tech-2020-150002855.html.

National Center for Education Statistics. "Students with Disabilities." Accessed June 17, 2021. https://nces.ed.gov/fastfacts/display.asp?id=60.

National College Health Assessment. "Percentage of U.S. College Students That Reported Select Disabilities or Health Conditions as of Fall 2021." Chart. September 5, 2022. Statista. https://www.statista.com/statistics/827023/disabilities-among-us-college-students/.

NCRA Broadcast and CART Captioning Committee. *Guidelines for CART Captioners (Communication Access Realtime Translation Captioners)*. Revised October 2016, https://www.ncra.org/docs/default-source/uploadedfiles/governmentrelations/guidelines-for-cart-captioners.pdf.

University of Washington. "IT Accessibility Checklist." Accessed October 19, 2021. https://www.washington.edu/accessibility/checklist/.

University of Washington Libraries. "Library E-Resource Accessibility Testing." Last modified July 9, 2021. https://www.lib.washington.edu/services/accessibility/e-resource-testing.

US Department of Justice, Civil Rights Division. "Introduction to the ADA." Accessed June 6, 2021. https://www.ada.gov/ada_intro.htm.

WebAIM. "WebAIM's WCAG 2 Checklist." Last modified February 26, 2021. https://webaim.org/standards/wcag/checklist.

CHAPTER 32

Using an Interactive Tutorial to Achieve Inclusivity in a Flipped Information Literacy Class

Madeline Ruggiero

The pandemic brought opportunities for librarians who teach information literacy to reflect on how students learn online as the hegemony of the printed text was disrupted. During the sudden shift to online learning in March 2020, tutorials became exponentially more popular for information literacy instruction. Learning with asynchronous online tutorials allows for more students to be reached anywhere and anytime.[1] Research studies provide evidence that online library tutorials can be as effective as in-person library instruction.[2] As more colleges are enrolling a greater number of students from various linguistic backgrounds and with various learning abilities, an inclusive educational environment becomes crucial to providing effective teaching. Advances in neurosciences tell us that we all learn differently and learners are diverse: "Brain-imaging technologies have helped to demonstrate that learning styles and needs can be as unique as fingerprints or DNA."[3] Presenting content to students in the digital environment allows for flexibility in teaching to meet the needs of most learners where students are "actively mastering skills and strategies and not merely consuming information."[4] This chapter will discuss the tutorial design I created using Springshare's LibWizard, a subscription-based interactive tutorial software program, as a learning tool to flip, or invert, a community college information literacy class in psychology for online or in-person instruction.

The software capabilities of LibWizard offer inherent flexibility to design content with clear goals that use a variety of media and materials and that adopt effective teaching methods such as ongoing feedback through formative assessment. Research shows that utilizing technology to invert instruction so that direct instruction occurs outside the classroom improves instruction inside the classroom and can be beneficial to learners in inclusive settings.[5]

LibWizard's capabilities for designing tutorials align with the three core principles of universal design for learning (UDL), an inclusive pedagogical framework developed by the Center for Applied Special Technologies (CAST). "UDL turns the knowledge that has been gained from brain research into a guide for differentiating instruction to accommodate many different modes of learning."[6] UDL principles include (1) multiple means of engagement, offering options to motivate learners; (2) multiple means of representation, presenting content in different ways; and (3) multiple means of action and expression, allowing options in how learners demonstrate what they know.[7]

After clarifying learning outcomes and segmenting, or breaking, course content into subtopics, UDL strategies are applied to goals, materials, methods, and assessments.[8] Evmenova states

> This iterative process allows educators to explore ways to support the diversity of 'students with atypical backgrounds in the dominant language, cognitive strategies, culture, or history of the average classroom, who … face barriers in accessing information when presented in a manner that assumes a common background among all students.'"[9]

Review of the Literature

Although lesson plan design for distance e-learning is underrepresented in the literature, research does point to UDL principles used to deliver information literacy instruction. Research reveals inclusivity as an outcome of implementing UDL's three core principles to develop information literacy instruction.[10] Peter and Clement recount a study conducted to teach Boolean logic to students in an information literacy class in 2012, with an activity that is given in multiple accessible formats, such as using a PowerPoint presentation, providing handouts, and articulating information.[11] Hoover and colleagues participated in a project to provide inclusive library instruction, primarily to students with learning disabilities, using UDL principles. Peter and Clement state that as a result of the Hoover study, "with the implementation of UDL, librarians noticed increased confidence in information literacy skills for all students."[12] In 2009, librarians in Vermont who were focused on learning disabilities developed a concept they called Universal Design for Instruction and Learning and stated "an instructional climate has instruction …designed to be welcoming and inclusive …[with]… high expectations for …all students."[13] The Association of College and Research Libraries (ACRL) *Guidelines for Instruction Programs in Academic Libraries* align with UDL principles by recognizing "the diverse nature of the learning community, including the varieties of learning styles" and that "Learning styles should be considered and multiple modes should be incorporated whenever possible"[14]

UDL and CAST

UDL began in 1984 with the incorporation of CAST.[15] In the early 1990s CAST developed UDL as a framework to instill flexibility for the design of educational content that allows for more effective support for all learners.[16] UDL as a concept was influenced by the universal design (UD) movement in architecture, where the needs of individuals who require assistance are taken into account at the outset when implementing a design.[17] UDL is a process that supports the creation of content whose clear goals, materials, methods, and assessment serve widely diverse learners. According to CAST, "learners differ markedly in the ways in which they can be engaged or motivated to learn."[18] Providing a variety of modalities to teach content for a diverse population of students allows for options and choices that suit many learning styles.[19] When UDL principles are implemented in instructional design, by providing clear goals for engagement, offering alternative ways to represent content, using multiple media for communication, and allowing for assessment and feedback, equity and accessibility to mainstream education are a tacit outcome.[20] The three primary principles of UDL are rooted in cognitive psychology, and CAST has set up three sets of broad teaching methods that support each of them.[21] The student profile of the class is taken into account when designing a UDL-based lesson plan. The content is grounded in clear learning goals, allowing students to engage with explicit expectations.[22] Content is presented in multiple ways to achieve these learning objectives. Students are then provided with feedback and multiple options for showing their knowledge and monitoring their progress. Burgstahler states, in an article written for the Disabilities, Opportunities, Internetworking, and Technology Center, that the UDL framework considers the needs of students with known and unknown disabilities, those with a variety of learning preferences and technical expertise, English language learners, older adults, and members of specific racial and ethnic groups.[23] She goes on to affirm, "Embracing UDL reduces systemic barriers and exclusionary practices in order to create more inclusive spaces, technology, instruction, and services."[24] The goal of UDL is to support and improve instruction for all learners, and although UDL is not solely a technology-based approach, digital materials can be critical to its implementation due to the malleability of technology.[25] Equity, or providing all students with what they need to be successful, is essential today since colleges are enrolling more students with a wide variety of disabilities.[26] Digital material enables content to be represented and customized in a variety of formats such as digital text, images, sound, or video, which meets the needs of most students.

Applying UDL and CAST: LibWizard Tutorial and Learning Needs Survey

I applied UDL and CAST principles to design and teach a flipped psychology information literacy class featuring an interactive tutorial using LibWizard and designed with student input. The objective of the tutorial is to teach students how to read and find a scientific article. The tutorial, distributed in advance of the library session, introduces foundational concepts and actively engages students in learning how to find and read a scientific article. Self-paced interactive tutorials are defined as the "ability of a student to do tasks, answer questions, or receive feedback during the course of a tutorial" as opposed to video tutorials or screencasts, which do not include interactive elements.[27] By completing the tutorial before coming to class, students establish baseline knowledge of the content that they apply during the IL session.

The tutorial begins with asking about their learning needs through a survey. Using surveys to include student voices to help with the design is an inclusive approach to designing lessons. By following the UDL guidelines and placing students' needs at the center of the design, I require the psychology instructor to administer survey questions that I develop to learn how students want to engage with the tutorial's content to maximize their learning styles. Survey sample:

> We'd like to know more about you as a learner. For the following statements please indicate to what extent the statement describes you. If you do not have an opinion, please indicate 'neutral'.
>
> (Agree, Disagree, Neutral).
>
> - I prefer to get my information by watching a video.
> - I have a better understanding of material if it is spoken rather than written.

- It is easy for me to understand information by reading.
- I can mentally juggle lots of information and many ideas at the same time.
- I require breaks to process information I just learned.
- I prefer multiple choice questions rather than fill in the blank questions in a quiz.

To be an instructor who supports learning, it is essential to determine the format, such as text or video, students prefer to interact with to learn content. Gauging whether students prefer content delivered in text format or through videos enables me to accommodate how they process information. Knowing that students may require breaks or need more time to complete a task or reflect on what they have learned informed the decision to include a reflection prompt. Students are given feedback on their knowledge through multiple-choice quizzes since the surveys revealed this to be the preferred assessment format.

LibWizard and Aligning to UDL

Beyond issues of skill and access, motivational issues can inhibit engagement and progress. Therefore, clear goals and objectives of what the students are expected to learn are communicated in a video at the beginning of the tutorial where I introduce myself, welcome the students, and explain the tutorial's layout. The introductory video sets a positive tone for what to expect in the contents of the tutorial, explains why the tutorial is important, and informs students of ways to e-mail me with challenges or questions. To motivate students to engage and take on this challenging work, I tell them they will be learning strategies on how to find, read, and comprehend a scientific article. Students are assured that they all have the ability to learn the material if they pay attention to the strategies and skills I teach in the tutorial. The class is told that these skills will be valuable for research in other subjects, such as biology, chemistry, and the social sciences, and that they will learn critical thinking skills, which can be useful for securing jobs and promotions when securing jobs and promotions. Students are informed that by practicing these strategies, they will be able to find and k now the order in which to read a scientific article so it makes sense. The introduction video enables students to learn what is expected of them, including the relevancy and value of the information and the easy navigation of the tutorial.

The format of the tutorial is a split screen, with the left frame giving directions for tasks to complete and quiz questions to answer. The right frame allows the learner to engage autonomously with materials presented in video format, images, or text. The tutorial consists of six modules, each lasting about three to five minutes; students can plan to spend about twenty-five to thirty minutes completing the tutorial. For example, I relay that they will be given step-by-step guidance on how to find a peer-reviewed article in a psychology database and will be able to interact with the library database as they learn how to limit the search to a scientific article. Next, they learn the five components of a scientific article and key features of each. Then they learn the order in which to read a scientific article for maximum comprehension. I further explain that they will be given quizzes after each module or section, which they can take as many times as needed. This lucid and specific explanation of what to expect moving forward should put the students at ease and provide a supportive introduction to the tutorial. It corresponds to the engagement portion of the UDL framework, which recommends "recruiting interest through purpose …and promoting expectations and beliefs that optimize motivation."[28]

Using a UDL-based online tutorial to impart knowledge relies on microlearning, where instructors offer bite-sized learning units containing just enough information to help learners achieve a specific goal. This gives students the option of either approaching the tutorial one section at a time or jumping between sections. Modules provide information in small blocks, breaking up details into parts while providing step-by-step acquisition of skills so students are not overwhelmed by information. Research by Harding and Shepard on the life cycle of a library tutorial found that tutorials based on UDL principles of bite-sized modules, interactivity, and use of multimedia are effective teaching strategies.[29] Delivering information in small segments is affirmed by CAST researchers in their seminal book *The Universally Designed Classroom*: "for students with learning challenges …material can be marked and chunked to support improved comprehension."[30] Optimal learning takes place when there is "less information to process at any given time."[31] By splitting information into short chunks, my tutorial allows the brain to retain information more easily, facilitates learning, and minimizes cognitive load.

The first module of the seven sections of the tutorial shows students strategies and skills for database searching in PsycInfo to retrieve a scientific article. The six remaining modules highlight distinguishing features of the five sections of an article—the abstract, introduction, methods, results, and conclusion—and the order in which to read a scientific article. Each module is followed by a quiz at the end.

While text-based materials and presenting content in a single format dominates the classroom, LibWizard offers media and materials that bypass the fixed nature of texts and allows content to be presented in a variety of formats to meet the learning needs of most students. Students are given options to view an embedded YouTube video with American Sign Language (ASL) captioning or closed captions that demonstrates the format of a scientific article by highlighting its five sections. These options increase access and learning opportunities, as some students can be considered print-disabled due to visual impairments or sensory or motor challenges. English language learners can also benefit from videos and images if they lack the vocabulary needed to read print text. A link to a text version is embedded in the tutorial, so students who prefer to read text have that option. Images are used to highlight some definitions, such as the meaning of the word *abstract*. An image of a painting and a summary to differentiate the concept is embedded into the tutorial. Using imagery benefits visual learners.

LibWizard allows learners to interact with real-time web content. Each side of the split screen can display a web page, an embedded video, an image file, a PDF, or a composed text block. The learner engages with the actual real-time, fully featured web, making it a richer, more dynamic experience than captured content like screencasts, slides, or storyboards.[32] For example, the student is given step-by-step instruction on the left side of the screen on how to format a search in a psychology database to retrieve scientific articles. On the right side of the screen, they are prompted to navigate to the library databases with a direct link to the library home page, where they can follow the instructions on the left while performing a database search. This self-directed learning environment is intuitive and user-friendly. Students will not experience ambiguity or a complex user interface and can focus on developing their knowledge.

Expanding access to tutorials, LibWizard contains many accessibility features and supports interaction with content using a variety of devices. It is compatible with smartphones: the small phone screen will change the display so the content on the right will display underneath the text and questions on the left, rather than side-by-side, making it user-friendly. Creators can preview the tutorial in desktop, tablet, and mobile view to gain a sense of how students using various devices will view the information. The learner interface is Section 508–compliant, including compatibility with screen-reading software and screen readers. In addition, content can be enhanced or modified to support a wide range of ways students interact with web-based learning. For example, creators can customize color contrast and enter text into fields for defining link titles. The learner can navigate with a keyboard, mouse, or other assistive hardware.

Formative assessment is provided at the end of each module in a quiz format. The learning experience is made effective through the learner's self-guided discovery that brings each student to the same point of knowledge and understanding by offering nongraded quizzes. Each module is followed by quizzes, which are designed for formative learning and assessment to ascertain the student's ability to achieve the learning outcomes. Since the student survey reveals that most students in this class prefer multiple-choice questions, the five quizzes are set up as multiple-choice questions at the end of each module. Students must answer all four questions correctly before they can move on to the next section; they have an unlimited number of attempts to answer correctly. Students receive feedback for both correct and incorrect answers. The designer can access the students' tutorial data, including the quiz results.

Flipped Classroom

After students engage with the twenty-to-twenty-five-minute tutorial, they compose a list of questions that are e-mailed to me by the psychology instructor. Fielding questions about information learned before class allows me to intentionally plan a class specific to students' needs. The students set the pace for individualized instruction. The quality of a student's questions suggests their engagement and use of critical thinking skills, for example:

- Does the box labeled methodology contain all the studies that the database holds or are there more in other sections?
- When looking for a research study, do we always have to press the category "methodology"?

This demonstrates that the student can understand the use of limiters when searching a database as per the instructions in the tutorial. The student is also thinking beyond the information provided in the tutorial.

Receiving student questions before the IL class session helps me to design a lesson that focuses on students' challenges with the information. Most of the class focuses on applying the knowledge they learned while interacting with the tutorial. Facilitating a flipped class allows me to differentiate instruction according to individual student needs to clarify misunderstandings, rather than showing the same basic skill to all students. This creates space for those who struggle to get the most help. Students collaborate on issues or challenges since each student has interacted with the same material before class. This creates active participation. They are helping each other learn rather than relying on the instructor. They discuss with peers a database search query and help each other with questions. My role in a flipped class is to guide students as a facilitator when they have questions. Although no formal evaluation of the students' reaction to the flipped class format has been carried out, anecdotal evidence from the students and psychology instructor is positive. Students report liking the tutorial and appreciating the one-on-one interaction rather than watching an in-class demonstration.

Conclusion

Using an online tutorial to flip an information literacy class provides an opportunity to teach research strategies without presenting information in a lecture format where students remain passive and unengaged. Inclusivity is not achieved when learners are not actively participating or are unable to follow the instruction in a traditional lecture or demonstration class. Active learning is shown to meet the needs of a larger range of learners.[33] Using an interactive tutorial allows students to learn information at their own pace, which supports a wide range of learners.

Notes

1. Katherine Stiwinter, "Using an Interactive Online Tutorial to Expand Library Instruction," *Internet References Services Quarterly* 18, no. 1 (2013): 16, https://doi.org/10.1080/10875301.2013.777 010.
2. Stiwinter, "Using an Interactive Online Tutorial," 16.
3. David H. Rose, Anne Meyer, and Chuck Hitchcock, "Introduction," in *The Universally Designed Classroom: Accessible Curriculum and Digital Technologies*, ed. David H. Rose, Anne Meyer, and Chuck Hitchcock (Cambridge, MA: Harvard Education Press, 2005), 9.
4. Anne Meyer and David H. Rose, "The Future Is in the Margins: The Role of Technology and Disability in Educational Reform," in *The Universally Designed Classroom: Accessible Curriculum and Digital Technologies*, ed. David H. Rose, Anne Meyer, and Chuck Hitchcock (Cambridge, MA: Harvard Education Press, 2005), 26.
5. Sara Arnold-Garza, "The Flipped Classroom Teaching Model and Its Use for Information Literacy Instruction," *Communications in Information Literacy* 8, no. 1 (2014): 11–12, https://files. eric.ed.gov/fulltext/EJ1089137.pdf.
6. Meyer and Rose, "Future Is in the Margins," 24.
7. Tracy Hall, Anne Meyer, and Nicole Strangman, "UDL Implementation: Examples Using Best Practices and Curriculum Enhancements," in *The Universally Designed Classroom: Accessible Curriculum and Digital Technologies*, ed. David H. Rose, Anne Meyer, and Chuck Hitchcock (Cambridge, MA: Harvard Education Press, 2005), 151.
8. Anya S. Evmenova, "Walking the Walk: Designing an Online Course about UDL," *Journal of Applied Instructional Design*, 10, no. 1 (2021): 2.
9. Evmenova, "Walking the Walk," 2.
10. Samantha H. Peter and Kristina A. Clement, "One Step at a Time: A Case Study of Incorporating Universal Design for Learning in Library Instruction," *Scholarship of Teaching and Learning Innovative Pedagogy* 2 (Fall 2020): article 3, p. 30.
11. Peter and Clement, "One Step at a Time," 31.
12. Peter and Clement, "One Step at a Time," 32.
13. Peter and Clement, "One Step at a Time," 32.
14. Association of College and Research Libraries, *Guidelines for Instruction Programs in Academic Libraries* (Chicago: Association of College and Research Libraries, 2003, rev. 2011), https://www. ala.org/acrl/standards/guidelinesinstruction.
15. Terese C. Jimenez, Victoria L. Graf, and Ernest Rose, "Gaining Access to General Education: The Promise of Universal Design for Learning," *Issues in Teacher Education* 16, no. 2 (Fall 2007): 45.
16. CAST, "Provide Multiple Means of Engagement," Universal Design for Learning Guidelines, ver. 2.2, 2018, https://udlguidelines.cast.org/engagement.
17. Chuck Hitchcock, Anne Meyer, David H. Rose, and Richard Jackson, "Equal Access, Participation, and Progress in the General Education Curriculum," in *The Universally Designed Classroom: Accessible Curriculum and Digital Technologies*, ed. David H. Rose, Anne Meyer, and Chuck Hitchcock (Cambridge, MA: Harvard Education Press, 2005), 55.
18. Hall, Meyer, and Strangman, "UDL Implementation," 150.
19. CAST, "Multiple Means of Engagement."
20. Hall, Meyer, and Strangman, "UDL Implementation," 150.
21. Peter and Clement, "One Step at a Time," 30.
22. Peter and Clement, "One Step at a Time," 30.
23. Sheryl Burgstahler. "A Framework for Inclusive Practices in Higher Education: Applying Uni-

versal Design Principles to All Campus Offerings." Disabilities, Opportunities, Internetworking, and Technology (DO-IT), University of Washington, 2021, 1, https://www.washington.edu/doit/framework-inclusive-practices-higher-education.

24. Burgstahler. "Framework for Inclusive Practices," 1.

25. Rose, Meyer, and Hitchcock, "Introduction," 3; Meyer and Rose, "Future Is in the Margins," 19

26. Hall, Meyer, and Strangman, "UDL Implementation," 152.

27. Peter and Clement, "One Step at a Time," 28.

28. Kathy A. Watts, "Tools and Principles for Effective Online Library Instruction: Andragogy and Undergraduates," *Journal of Library and Information Services in Distance Learning* 12, no. 1–2 (2018), 50, https://doi.org/10.1080/1533290X.2018.1428712.

29. Julie Harding and Ryan Shepherd, "The Lifecycle of a Research Tutorial: From Concept to Implementation and Beyond," *Journal of Electronic Resources Librarianship* 32 no. 1 (2020), 30, https://doi.org/10.1080/1941126X.2019.1709734.

30. Rose, Meyer, and Hitchcock, "Introduction," 8.

31. Claire McGuiness and Crystal Fulton, "Digital Literacy in Higher Education: A Case Study of Student Engagement with E-tutorials Using Blended Learning," *Journal of Information Technology Education: Innovations in Practice* 18 (2019), 7, https://doi.org/10.28945/4190.

32. Graham Sherriff. "Interactive Tutorials—The Platform Matters: Learning from a Comparative Evaluation of Tutorial Platforms," *College and Research Libraries News* 78, no. 4 (April 2017): 213.

33. Clark Nall, "Academic Libraries and the Principles of Universal Design for Learning: Representation beyond Courses," *College and Research Libraries News* 76, no. 7 (2015): 374–75, https://doi.org/10.5860/crln.76.7.9345.

Bibliography

Arnold-Garza, Sara. "The Flipped Classroom Teaching Model and Its Use for Information Literacy Instruction." *Communications in Information Literacy* 8, no. 1 (2014): 7–22. https://files.eric.ed.gov/fulltext/EJ1089137.pdf.

Association of College and Research Libraries. *Guidelines for Instruction Programs in Academic Libraries*. Chicago: Association of College and Research Libraries, 2003, rev. 2011. https://www.ala.org/acrl/standards/guidelinesinstruction.

Burgstahler, Sheryl. "A Framework for Inclusive Practices in Higher Education: Applying Universal Design Principles to All Campus Offerings." Disabilities, Opportunities, Internetworking, and Technology (DO-IT), University of Washington, 2021. https://www.washington.edu/doit/framework-inclusive-practices-higher-education.

CAST. "Provide Multiple Means of Engagement." Universal Design for Learning Guidelines, ver. 2.2. 2018. https://udlguidelines.cast.org/engagement.

Evmenova, Anya S. "Walking the Walk: Designing an Online Course about UDL." *Journal of Applied Instructional Design* 10, no. 1 (2021). https://doi.org/10.51869/101/ae.

Harding, Julie, and Ryan Shepherd. "The Lifecycle of a Research Tutorial: From Concept to Implementation and Beyond." *Journal of Electronic Resources Librarianship* 32, no. 1 (2020): 29–35. https://doi.org/10.1080/1941126X.2019.1709734.

Jimenez, Terese C., Victoria L. Graf, and Ernest Rose. "Gaining Access to General Education: The Promise of Universal Design for Learning." *Issues in Teacher Education* 16, no. 2 (Fall 2007): 41–54.

McGuiness, Claire, and Crystal Fulton. "Digital Literacy in Higher Education: A Case Study of Student Engagement with E-tutorials Using Blended Learning." *Journal of Information Technology Education: Innovations in Practice* 18 (2019): 1–28. https://doi.org/10.28945/4190.

Nall, Clark. "Academic Libraries and the Principles of Universal Design for Learning: Representation beyond Courses." *College and Research Libraries News* 76, no. 7 (2015): 374–75. https://doi.org/10.5860/crln.76.7.9345.

Peter, Samantha H., and Kristina A. Clement. "One Step at a Time: A Case Study of Incorporating Universal Design for Learning in Library Instruction." *Scholarship of Teaching and Learning, Innovative Pedagogy* 2 (Fall 2020): article 3. https://digitalcommons.humboldt.edu/sotl_ip.

Rose, David H., Anne Meyer, and Chuck Hitchcock, eds. *The Universally Designed Classroom: Accessible Curriculum and Digital Technologies*. Cambridge, MA: Harvard Education Press, 2005.

Sherriff, Graham. "Interactive Tutorials—The Platform Matters: Learning from a Comparative Evaluation of Tutorial Platforms." *College and Research Libraries News* 78, no. 4 (April 2017): 212–16.

Stiwinter, Katherine. "Using an Interactive Online Tutorial to Expand Library Instruction." *Internet References Services Quarterly* 18, no. 1 (2013): 15–41. https://doi.org/10.1080/10875301.2013.777010.

Watts, Kathy A. "Tools and Principles for Effective Online Library Instruction: Andragogy and Undergraduates." *Journal of Library and Information Services in Distance Learning* 12, no. 1–2 (2018): 49–55. https://doi.org/10.1080/1533290X.2018.1428712.

CHAPTER 33

Choose Your Own Adventure

The Use of Flexible Online Asynchronous Instruction for Information Literacy

Megan Wilson

Over the last few decades online learning has emerged as a popular alternative to traditional in-person instruction, particularly in higher education. Online courses and programs often attract a wide variety of students, including those from low socioeconomic backgrounds, those with disabilities, adult students returning to finish a degree, and international and military students, as well as first-generation students.[1] Asynchronous online offerings can provide more flexible instructional delivery alternatives to individuals working with geographical, scheduling, or learning difficulties. Asynchronous online learning can also provide an attractive alternative for students who suffer from social anxiety and prefer to avoid a traditional classroom setting and those who have scheduling conflicts due to work, family, or other obligations.

The needs of each of these diverse groups vary and the students thrive best under different teaching strategies. This includes a need to balance active engagement with the instructor and classmates with the flexibility for students to work within their own limitations and needs. This chapter demonstrates how a credit-bearing information literacy course was redesigned using universal design for learning principles to allow students in disparate situations, with unique constraints, and with varying levels of technological experience and knowledge to have multiple options for meaningful engagement with the content as well as the instructor. By using flexible and creative instructional strategies, course designers can foster equitable and inclusive

learning and respond to student learning needs in a way that improves student retention and engagement.

Accessibility Considerations

Accessibility considerations are a major component of designing any online materials. Federal legislation such as Section 508 of the Rehabilitation Act of 1973 and the Individuals with Disabilities Education Act (IDEA) mandate that federal agencies provide electronic and information technology in a format accessible to users with disabilities.[2] Over time these requirements have been used to develop web accessibility criteria such as the "Web Content Accessibility Guidelines" (WCAG) that are used by web designers to lower barriers to users with disabilities, particularly those with auditory or visual concerns.[3] Common accommodations for disabilities in online course design include providing captioning or transcripts for videos, avoiding the use of color and text enhancement, and streamlining content to be accessible to individuals using assistive technology.[4]

General accommodations for disabilities can also be leveraged to provide options for students who do not require or request accommodations. For example, a transcript of a recorded lecture can be helpful not only to students with hearing difficulties but also to students who struggle with note-taking skills or prefer to receive content in a written format. Preemptively providing such content for all students may remove barriers for individuals who have undiagnosed concerns, are concerned about stigma, or have difficulty requesting assistance from student disability services.[5]

Universal Design for Learning

In contrast to designing for accessibility, which is typically a reactive process wherein a student requests a set of prescribed accommodations to address specific concerns, the principle of universal design takes the idea of optimizing access to content and resources and encourages designers to become proactive in accommodating a user's needs. The term *universal design* describes the general concept of developing products that are usable by everyone to the greatest extent possible. Though this concept began as an approach to architecture, the principle has grown to include all types of development, including instructional design.

Universal design for learning (UDL) takes the basic principle of universal design and applies it to instructional design. Designing curriculum with the UDL principles in mind allows a course to be more accessible and engaging for all types of students regardless of individual limitations, whether those limitations fall under the jurisdiction of student disability services or are caused by a situational need.[6] Using the UDL principles complements traditional accessibility needs by focusing on decreasing or eliminating barriers to learning in the online classroom.

CAST, previously known as the Center for Applied Special Technology, outlines three core principles of universal design for learning: to provide (1) multiple means of engagement, (2) multiple means of representation and (3) multiple means of expression for students.[7] This guidance is designed to offer students choices with the overarching goals of increasing access to all individuals. It is important to remember that this approach is intended to provide a more inclusive and equitable experience for all students rather than developing narrow accommodations for individual student needs or tailoring instruction to particular learning styles.

Background

INF 101: Research in the Information Age is a three-credit-hour course on information literacy that is offered as a University Studies elective, as well as being a foundation course for the Information Studies minor offered at Murray State University. The class is popular among student athletes as well as adult students returning to school to complete their degree. Due to the focus on research, students who are required to complete an undergraduate thesis find it particularly helpful.

I have previously taught this class in person as a night course, which focused on a flipped classroom model, with students asked to complete selected readings, attend a weekly lecture, then participate in class discussions and activities. When the course initially moved online I used a similar model, replacing the in-person lecture with a recorded one and having assignments and discussion forums completed asynchronously.

Multiple Means of Representation

When I first began teaching online, it was easy to fall into the basic idea of providing a recorded lecture, adding in a discussion board and a weekly assignment, and calling it a day. Though this method of online instruction can work, it is also limiting in how engaged students can be with the material. Students generally are not enthused to watch an hour-long video each week in the best of circumstances.[8] It has long been recognized that breaking up material into smaller segments that can be consumed at the student's pace can improve student outcomes.[9]

A common instruction strategy known as the segmenting principle operates under the idea that segmenting or chunking material, particularly audiovisual materials, into smaller, bite-sized lessons can avoid overwhelming students and potentially improve information retention.[10] The primary design in my credit-bearing course follows the chunking method, breaking up the traditional hour-long lecture into several smaller lessons using a multimedia format. In my course this means that each week's module is broken up into multiple lessons, typically three per week, that contain a mixture of text, images, and short videos. Videos and images are used primarily to supplement the text rather than replace text content. This allows the content to be accessible to all students while also providing students with more than one medium with which to process the lesson, a practice that studies show can improve the retention of information.[11] Though the chunking method is more typically applied to text-based multimedia formats, the principle can also be applied to the virtual lecture format. Design considerations such as splitting the material into multiple videos or using time markers will allow students easier navigation to relevant sections. Sharing the original slides with notes or providing a full transcript of the lecture can also help to provide choices to students in this scenario.

When allowing students to choose their own adventure through the material, the primary concern is to provide multiple opportunities and modalities to access the information being taught. This principle should take into account students' varying attention spans and time constraints, seeking to provide the same information in multiple formats. This allows each student to determine the most appropriate format for themselves and to manage their time more effectively.

Although multimedia formats are an excellent way to illustrate the material, I have found that some students still prefer a more traditional learning experience with regularly scheduled lectures. In order to facilitate this preference, the course is set up to provide both synchronous and asynchronous lectures about course content alongside the more text-based lessons. The use of multiple modalities gives students options for how to engage with the information and to review content in a new way. Studies suggest that seeing the same content in different formats may improve the students' engagement with the material.[12] Providing the lesson using a synchronous option as well, in this case through weekly live lectures, gives students the opportunity to see the content in different modalities. Live lecture sessions are provided via web conferencing at preset times, enabling students to ask questions in real time if they choose to do so. These lectures are also recorded and made available for all students the following day. This provides the option for students who were unable to attend or wish to review the material to do so at their own convenience. This option is also paired with a requirement for students to periodically check in with the instructor so that students can count attendance at a live lecture session as one of their required interactions.

Multiple Means of Engagement

Providing adequate engagement between students and the instructor can be tricky in an online asynchronous course. To adjust for this, and to provide a greater sense of community with the course, I have implemented a system of check-ins. Students in the course are required to check in periodically with the instructor—the overarching goal being to mitigate student anxiety about asking for help as well as making the instructor more approachable to all students.

To offset the scheduling concerns and to be sensitive to students who may have social anxiety, each student is given multiple options for completing the requirement as long as the interaction occurs in real time. Students are provided with the option of attending any of the weekly live lectures, which is generally a group setting, joining open online office hours, or setting up individual appointments with the instructor. Special considerations may need to be made for students in other time zones, including any military personnel overseas or international students.

Multiple Means of Action and Expression

To meet the final principle of UDL, the course provides multiple means of expression by allowing students options on how to demonstrate their learning where it is possible to do so. This can be particularly important for students who struggle with language fluency or with test-taking skills. There are several approaches that I have used here, in combination. The first is to provide assignments that use a variety of approaches. For example, over the course of a semester students may be asked to complete different types of assignments that might include discussion posts, worksheets, gaming activities, recorded presentations, and so on. To adjust for individuals who may struggle in a particular area, the lowest grade is dropped and students are provided an opportunity to make up for a single failed assignment by redoing it.

A second opportunity to provide multiple means of expression is in providing options within a given assignment, where possible. Being able to leverage the flexibility of technology means that students can be creative in how they approach assignments such as presentations. Students can choose the type of presentation that they wish to create or to write a paper instead. While this does include additional prep work, such as developing multiple rubrics, the option allows students to choose the method they feel matches them and their capabilities best while also providing options for students who may have difficulty with the technology required.

For any given assignment I ask myself two questions: (1) What concerns might the student have about the assignment? (2) What substitutions or variations will reach the same objective? Take, for example, a traditional library scavenger hunt assignment. In an in-person environment students may be asked to go find items or locations in the library and then asked to take selfies of themselves near certain locations or answer questions related to particular services. In pre-pandemic times, students in an online section might be asked to visit a local library or, if a library is not available, to complete an alternative that uses the library website. As the assignment is intended to familiarize the student with library services, both approaches are still effective.

These questions can also extend to other types of assessment, including quizzes. In my online course students are allowed to take weekly quizzes, known as comprehension checks, up to three times. This decision was made after I determined that it is more important that the students be able to learn the material than be able to quickly memorize and then forget it. If students are given the option to retake the quiz, they are more likely to revisit material that they missed or did not understand on the first pass.

Equity and Technological Considerations

Another major concern for making online courses inclusive is equity in technology use. Though online tools can greatly benefit access, improve student satisfaction, and increase accessibility for some students, it also increases the risk of technical problems and can create equity issues if students have limited access to hardware or the internet. These issues can be mitigated through careful design considerations.

For example, students may have limited access to web cameras or primarily use devices such as netbooks or phones that do not support or do not adequately support programs that may be required by the course. A common concern for our students in 2020 was that Chromebooks did not support the use of virtual proctoring software such as LockDown Browser from Respondus. On-campus students had the option of using a library desktop or laptop, but off-campus students who owned Chromebooks were often frustrated by a lack of options. Additional concerns have arisen with students who primarily rely on mobile apps, which may have less functionality than their desktop or web counterparts, if a mobile version exists at all. Mitigation efforts should include alternatives within a given assignment wherever technological concerns exist. A 2021 distance education report showed that nearly 40 percent of all online students used a mobile device such as a tablet or smartphone to access coursework.[13] This statistic highlights the need to design materials that can be viewed on mobile devices as well as providing advance notice if an assignment might require the use of a PC or other technology so alternative arrangements can be made if needed.

It is important to identify problem points ahead of time and be aware of any technology issues that may arise if students procrastinate. Where consistent issues with links or assignments crop up, providing troubleshooting tips in the instructions or providing a simpler alternative can prevent a deluge of e-mails from students trying to complete an assignment at the last minute.

Another design consideration is that students in an online course may have vastly different levels of knowledge and experience with using technology, and even so-called digital natives may have limited exposure to vocabulary and technologies such as e-mail, online document managers, research databases, and learning management systems (LMSs).[14] In order to address these technological concerns, several strategies can be used—in particular providing incentives for students to familiarize themselves with the technologies needed to complete an assignment well before an assignment is due and including pages or sections with frequently asked questions and links to helpful resources and tutorials.[15]

For example, my course requires students to take a number of screenshots for assignments. In order to help students familiarize themselves with this process, the first assignment students complete requires them to download Microsoft Word from the university's website, create a header, take and embed a screenshot, turn the document into a PDF, and then submit the PDF to Canvas. In order to help students with this task, I provide links to tutorials and an FAQ page that they can reference. Likewise, if an assignment requires the use of programs outside of the LMS, I provide additional instruction and tutorials on how to access and use the system required.

Conclusion and Recommendations

In this chapter we have looked at how one course was designed with UDL principles in mind, highlighting practical ways that instructors can anticipate student concerns and needs to provide a more inclusive learning experience. One of the biggest challenges in designing a course using universal design principles is to not forget the needs of the instructor. Many of the considerations reviewed in this chapter can be demanding on the instructor, particularly the requirement for the check-in. As an instructor I tend to be overly generous with my time, but I have found that students will work around your schedule if you set expectations early.

Though this chapter focuses on the experience of designing a credit-bearing course, similar methods can and have been used for one-shot instruction or tutorial design. Although one-shot instruction design is generally guided by the course instructors, library instructors can provide multiple modalities through the use of online instructional materials such as research guides, video tutorials, and modules. These methods can be used in combination with each other for online and hybrid classes or can be used to supplement traditional face-to-face instruction.

As you develop your own classes, remember that every course is different and to keep in mind the needs of the students that the course is being designed for. Consider how many students might be in your course, how many of those are off campus, and if there are special considerations you need to accommodate, such as a student who is deployed overseas. Much of my design work has been based on observations and feedback from students in my courses. Every year I make adjustments to my course design as I learn more about pedagogical strategies and as both student preferences and technological capabilities change.

Notes

1. Statista, "Target Populations of Online Education Programs U.S. 2019," accessed June 7, 2021, https://www.statista.com/statistics/731146/percentage-online-programs-that-were-de-signed-with-special-student-characteristics-in-mind-by-target-population-us/.
2. Section508.gov, "IT Accessibility Laws and Policies," accessed June 4, 2021, https://www.section508.gov/manage/laws-and-policies.
3. W3C Web Accessibility Initiative (WAI), "Web Content Accessibility Guidelines (WCAG) Overview," accessed June 2, 2021, https://www.w3.org/WAI/standards-guidelines/wcag/.
4. Lauren Cifuentes et al., "A Working Model for Complying with Accessibility Guidelines for Online Learning," *TechTrends* 60, no. 6 (2016): 557–64, https://doi.org/10.1007/s11528-016-0086-8.
5. Robert A. Stodden et al., "Postsecondary Education across the USA: Experiences of Adults with Disabilities," *Journal of Vocational Rehabilitation* 22, no. 1 (2005): 41–47.
6. Catherine Shea Sanger, "Inclusive Pedagogy and Universal Design Approaches for Diverse Learning Environments," in *Diversity and Inclusion in Global Higher Education: Lessons from Across Asia*, ed. Catherine Shea Sanger and Nancy W. Gleason (Singapore: Springer, 2020), 31–71, https://doi.org/10.1007/978-981-15-1628-3_2.
7. CAST, "The UDL Guidelines," accessed June 1, 2021, https://udlguidelines.cast.org/?utm_source=castsite&lutm_medium=web&utm_campaign=none&utm_content=aboutudl.
8. Diego Méndez-Carbajo and Scott A. Wolla, "Segmenting Educational Content: Long-Form vs. Short-Form Online Learning Modules," *American Journal of Distance Education* 33, no. 2 (2019): 108–19, https://doi.org/10.1080/08923647.2019.1583514.
9. Richard E. Mayer and Celeste Pilegard, "Principles for Managing Essential Processing in Multimedia Learning: Segmenting, Pre-training, and Modality Principles," in *The Cambridge Handbook of Multimedia Learning*, 2nd ed., Cambridge Handbooks in Psychology (New York: Cambridge University Press, 2014), 316–44, https://doi.org/10.1017/CBO9781139547369.016.
10. Ruth Colvin Clark and Richard E. Mayer, *E-Learning and the Science of Instruction*, 3rd ed. (San Francisco: Wiley, 2016).
11. Russell N. Carney and Joel R. Levin, "Pictorial Illustrations Still Improve Students' Learning from Text," *Educational Psychology Review* 14, no. 1 (2002): 5–26, https://doi.org/10.1023/A:1013176309260.

12. Dung C. Bui and Mark A. McDaniel, "Enhancing Learning during Lecture Note-Taking Using Outlines and Illustrative Diagrams," *Journal of Applied Research in Memory and Cognition* 4, no. 2 (2015): 129–35, https://doi.org/10.1016/j.jarmac.2015.03.002.

13. EducationData, "Distance Learning Statistics 2021: Online Education Trends," accessed June 7, 2021, https://educationdata.org/online-education-statistics.

14. Wan Ng, "Can We Teach Digital Natives Digital Literacy?," *Computers and Education* 59, no. 3 (November 2012): 1065–78, https://doi.org/10.1016/j.compedu.2012.04.016.

15. Mohamed Eltahir Osman, "Students' Reaction to WebCT: Implications for Designing On-Line Learning Environments," *International Journal of Instructional Media* 32, no. 4 (Fall 2005): 353.

Bibliography

Bui, Dung C., and Mark A. McDaniel. "Enhancing Learning during Lecture Note-Taking Using Outlines and Illustrative Diagrams." *Journal of Applied Research in Memory and Cognition* 4, no. 2 (2015): 129–35. https://doi.org/10.1016/j.jarmac.2015.03.002.

Carney, Russell N., and Joel R. Levin. "Pictorial Illustrations Still Improve Students' Learning from Text." *Educational Psychology Review* 14, no. 1 (2002): 5–26. https://doi.org/10.1023/A:1013176309260.

CAST. "The UDL Guidelines." Accessed June 1, 2021. https://udlguidelines.cast.org/?utm_source=castsite&lutm_medium=web&utm_campaign=none&utm_content=aboutudl.

Cifuentes, Lauren, Alexandra Janney, Lauran Guerra, and Jennifer Weir. "A Working Model for Complying with Accessibility Guidelines for Online Learning." *TechTrends* 60, no. 6 (2016): 557–64. https://doi.org/10.1007/s11528-016-0086-8.

Clark, Ruth Colvin, and Richard E. Mayer. *E-Learning and the Science of Instruction: Proven Guidelines for Consumers and Designers of Multimedia Learning*, 3rd ed. San Francisco: Wiley, 2016.

EducationData. "Distance Learning Statistics: Online Education Trends." Accessed June 7, 2021. https://educationdata.org/online-education-statistics.

Mayer, Richard E., and Celeste Pilegard. "Principles for Managing Essential Processing in Multimedia Learning: Segmenting, Pre-training, and Modality Principles." In *The Cambridge Handbook of Multimedia Learning*, 2nd ed., 316–44. Cambridge Handbooks in Psychology. New York: Cambridge University Press, 2014. https://doi.org/10.1017/CBO9781139547369.016.

Méndez-Carbajo, Diego, and Scott A. Wolla. "Segmenting Educational Content: Long-Form vs. Short-Form Online Learning Modules." *American Journal of Distance Education* 33, no. 2 (2019): 108–19. https://doi.org/10.1080/08923647.2019.1583514.

Ng, Wan. "Can We Teach Digital Natives Digital Literacy?" *Computers and Education* 59, no. 3 (November 2012): 1065–78. https://doi.org/10.1016/j.compedu.2012.04.016.

Osman, Mohamed Eltahir. "Students' Reaction to WebCT: Implications for Designing On-Line Learning Environments." *International Journal of Instructional Media* 32, no. 4 (Fall 2005): 353–62.

Sanger, Catherine Shea. "Inclusive Pedagogy and Universal Design Approaches for Diverse Learning Environments." In *Diversity and Inclusion in Global Higher Education: Lessons from across Asia*, edited by Catherine Shea Sanger and Nancy W. Gleason, 31–71. Singapore: Springer, 2020. https://doi.org/10.1007/978-981-15-1628-3_2.

Section508.gov. "IT Accessibility Laws and Policies." Accessed June 4, 2021. https://www.section508.gov/manage/laws-and-policies.

Statista. "Target Populations of Online Education Programs U.S. 2019." Accessed June 7, 2021, https://www.statista.com/statistics/731146/percentage-online-programs-that-were-designed-with-special-student-characteristics-in-mind-by-target-population-us/.

Stodden, Robert A., Peter W. Dowrick, John Anderson, Katharina Heyer, and Joie Acosta. "Postsecondary Education across the USA: Experiences of Adults with Disabilities." *Journal of Vocational Rehabilitation* 22, no. 1 (2005): 41–47.

W3C Web Accessibility Initiative (WAI). "Web Content Accessibility Guidelines (WCAG) Overview." Accessed June 2, 2021. https://www.w3.org/WAI/standards-guidelines/wcag/.

CHAPTER 34

Lived and Learned Experience with Accessible and Inclusive Pedagogy

Angie Brunk

I have always walked in two different worlds. Because I am low vision, not blind, I know the joy of seeing and capturing the perfect image in my digital camera's viewfinder. I know the joy of teaching a dance class. I know what it's like to be perceived as abled. Because I am low vision, not "normal," I know the frustration and sometimes humiliation of a teacher caring more about their seating plans or their favorite activity than my ability to participate fully in class. I know the frustration of missing parts of presentations because the presenter did not explain visual content on a slide. I know what it feels like to have an instructor ignore accessibility needs that you have clearly articulated. I know the humiliation of people commenting on the appearance of my eyes. I know what it is to be underestimated or not taken seriously because of preconceived notions about my capabilities.[1]

In the course of my professional life, I have been involved in library instruction, taught journalism classes, and even taught a recreational dance class. I have served on ADA committees at three different universities. I have learned a great deal from all of this. I have made mistakes along the way. I have not always lived up to my ideal of making accessibility my first priority. I do not have all the answers and will not use this chapter to tell you what to do.

I will offer you a different perspective on creating accessible instruction. I will introduce you to the unique challenges of library instruction as it relates to accessibility. I will walk through all the gray areas and possible solutions. Each institution and librarian is unique. It is not possible to offer the ultimate solution to accessible

library instruction. Instead, I will offer my experience and my perspective to help my fellow librarians develop their own professional philosophy on accessibility.

Let's get a little more specific about my biases to start. I am a strong proponent of the social or social justice model of disability. I believe this model best fits the values of most libraries as well. In a nutshell, the social justice model strives to make the experience for disabled people as similar to the experience of temporarily able-bodied people as possible. I say temporarily able-bodied because most of us will experience disability due to injury, illness, or aging. When defining solutions to problems, the dignity and autonomy of the individual is as important as function! That means students, with appropriate support, should be expected to meet the same academic standards as their nondisabled peers. Yes, this does mean that if a little tough love might be appropriate for a nondisabled student, it would be appropriate for a disabled student. In other words, the fact that Sally uses a wheelchair does not change the fact that beginning your search for materials twelve hours before your paper is due is really not a good idea. It does not change the fact that many students, including many of us reading this chapter, had to learn this lesson the hard way.

Perhaps a slight detour to unpack language is in order here. You might have noticed that I use identity-first language. That is to say, I use phrases like "disabled student." You might have been told that person-first language, such as "student with a disability," is preferred. Outside of North America, use of person-first language is rare. Within North America, it is a controversial topic, and a Google search would yield many varying opinions. I prefer identity-first language and will use it in most cases. When I am the one speaking, I hope my humanity does not need to be explicitly stated. However, when speaking with the institutional voice, person-first language may still be appropriate. This is one of those cases where you need to know your community.

The last of my biases that are relevant here is that I believe library instruction is primarily library marketing. While many of us have grand visions of being integrated into the curriculum and scaffolding our instruction, let's not lose sight of reality. Some of us do get to teach for-credit information literacy classes. I have found the experience very rewarding when I have had that opportunity. However, just as many of us know we need to be prepared to deliver our dog-and-pony show with short notice. (I think one hour notice has been my shortest so far, but I'm only midway through my career; I'm sure there will something even tighter.) We are banging our heads against a wall to get the professor who assigns a research paper to give us just one class session to talk to their students about library resources. Sometimes that professor gives us only fifteen minutes. We cannot get all of our content to stick in that time. The most important thing we can do with that time is make students more comfortable with the library and more likely to use reference help.

Whether we are willing to admit it or not, I think most of us know that instruction is really marketing. We try everything we can think of to make it fun and exciting.

We even try to make it a game. Unfortunately, making it fun can make it inaccessible or highlight a student's disability in a way they are uncomfortable with. This is not good marketing.

Let's fly up to the 30,000-foot level to look at instruction strategy. (My apologies to anyone afraid of heights.) For most of us, classroom instruction is only a small part of our instruction strategy. We're embedded in online classes. We produce LibGuides and tutorials. We've probably even done a few YouTube videos. Many of us have created a LibGuide for every single instruction session or class, even though much of the information is a duplication of the departmental guide. But is that really the best use of our time? Let me be clear, creating accessible content from the design process forward is much less time-consuming than fixing content that is not accessible. However, creating accessible content does require more time and effort than just creating content. If accessibility is to be a priority for your library, the focus needs to be on creating accessible content. In short, you need to give up on a librarian's penchant for reinventing the wheel! If you are a department head or otherwise "in charge" of instruction, examine your policies and expectations. Is there really a reason to have Your University branded tutorial on Academic Search Complete, or would an accessible tutorial made by another university or even the vendor serve your purpose just as well?

Now, let's drop to 10,000 feet and talk about content strategy. Think like a marketer here. You wouldn't expect your students to know about a library event if your only marketing strategy was to stick some posters up on the bulletin board in the union. Creating accessible content is no different. Adaptive strategies used by disabled people are complex and unique to the individual. Sometimes, they can be contradictory. A blind or visually impaired student may not be able to get key concepts from a video. For that student, a screen reader or magnification-friendly text-heavy document may be the preferred format. Don't get me wrong, I love playing with new technology as much as anybody, but sometimes the simple Luddite format is the most accessible format.

Let's drop down further and hover just above the classroom, both in meatspace and in cyberspace. Let's start with what happens when a student needs a reasonable accommodation to complete academic work. I cannot tell you exactly how the process functions at your institution, but I can summarize my experience as both a student needing accommodation and a faculty member deeply involved in accessibility at several institutions. The student will meet with the university official or department responsible for student accommodations and present the required documentation to substantiate their diagnosis and need for accommodations. The student's accommodation will be documented and communicated to all faculty members teaching that particular student each semester. The faculty member will not be informed of the student's specific diagnosis or disability. The instructor is not to offer additional accommodations to the student. I would add, though, that nothing is preventing the instructor from realizing something that might benefit the student and offer the same opportunity to the entire class. I hope you can begin to see some of the challenges unique to libraries and the gray areas I have been alluding to. We will discuss them in greater detail in a bit.

Let us now plant our feet on terra firma in the classroom. One of the unique challenges of library instruction, and one of the greatest for creating an accessible classroom, is, chances are, you will not know if you have a disabled student in class. Even if you ask, the instructor may not be able to provide useful information about student needs. That does not, however, mean there is nothing you can do. Assuming you have ample notice of an instruction session, you can ask the professor to forward an e-mail to the class. Introduce yourself and explain the purpose of the class and any activities you have planned. If there are any areas of your library that are not easily accessible, your e-mail should include that information as well as how disabled students could still access these services. This might also be a good time to remind students that library records and conversations with librarians are protected by state and local laws. Ask students to contact you if they have questions or concerns about any activities you have planned or questions about the library in general. While directly asking any students that come forward about their disability is probably not advisable, you can let the student know that you are a safe person and eager to hear any information they wish to share that would help you provide a more supportive environment.

Meanwhile back in reality where you have not had the luxury of reaching out to the class for one of many, many reasons, you can still have a positive classroom experience even if you notice there is a student who uses a wheelchair and your plans called for students to go to that one area of your library that isn't really wheelchair accessible. Perhaps it might be best to skip that area this time. The most important thing is to be flexible and be sensitive. When you walk into the classroom, have a plan for modifying any activities for various disabilities. It can be very tempting to use a new cool app you've heard about for instruction. Let's assume you've overcome the technical and digital divide issues by putting the app on library-supplied devices for each team or student. Is that app accessible? Do you know how to activate any accessibility features or make it play nicely with the built-in accessibility features on the device? Could you quickly and discreetly help a disabled student use the accessibility features? Until you can answer "Yes!" to all of those questions, it might be best to find another tool that meets your needs. When you are planning activities, use task analysis to determine the physical and cognitive demands of an activity, and plan modifications to meet various needs. Dale Monobe and I have explored modification of active learning exercises in depth in two papers. "Don't Make the Kid Who Is Blind Play Dodge Ball" is available as an open-source document, and "Level Up! Making Games Accessible" is available in another ACRL anthology.[2]

Whether you are familiar with the concept or not, you've probably been using task analysis on at least an informal basis in your professional life. Task analysis is breaking a task into all of its many steps. Think about all the physical and cognitive demands next time you play your favorite card game. Can you shuffle by hand? Can you comfortably hold a fanned-out hand of cards? (There are devices available to assist, suggesting this is common problem.) Can you remember all the rules and keep a strategy straight in your head? How difficult was it for you to learn those rules and strategies? Now, think about a time when you were sick or injured. How much more difficult did each of these activities become? A very good and straightforward guide to task analysis is available at usability.gov.[3]

Now back to those gray areas I've been hinting at. What if a student is uncomfortable with your planned walking tour or scavenger hunt? Is your priority making the student comfortable or making sure they meet the same standards as other students? While there may be a time where standards matter, I would argue that in most cases, the student's comfort, dignity, and autonomy are more important. Questions of standards versus dignity always bring me back to my high school marching band days. I'm glad I was a high school student in the early 90s. Like band nerds in many small towns in the US, being a part of band meant participating in marching band, whether I wanted to or not. As I'm sure you can imagine, trying to hold a tight formation while playing trombone is challenging if you have neither depth perception nor peripheral vision. Today, the "solution" is to have the visually impaired musician literally led around the field by a sighted student. I found the exercise humiliating the one time I tried it and might have given up on music had I been forced to continue. It is fortunate my band teacher and I were able to decide that field marching really wasn't for me. I was still able to participate fully in music and maintain my dignity. If the disability rights movement has a prime directive, it is "Nothing about us without us." Disabled people should always be consulted about accommodations. Sometimes not participating in a particular activity is the right accommodation for that person.

Let's drill down to a more practical example. You have scheduled an instruction session for a first-year experience (FYE) class. The planned activities for this class session are a brief walking tour of the library and a scavenger hunt in small teams. All students will complete a worksheet for the class. You are approached by a student who is uncomfortable with the activity because navigating a new space is made more difficult by their disability. (There are several disabilities that could apply.) The student could have several concerns. If this is a team event, they may be concerned about whether or not they are able to do their "fair share" of the work for the team. They may not be "out" about their disability and do not want their classmates to learn about it in this way. I've certainly felt both of these things at various points. There are several ways to make the student feel more comfortable. Perhaps this student could fully participate in the class exercise if they are given a slower paced private tour before the class meeting. This private tour might even help the student feel more confident and like they are an asset to the team rather than a liability. Another solution might be for the student to do the scavenger hunt worksheet at their own pace outside of class. The student refusing to do the worksheet is a whole other matter and should be treated like any student refusing to do the worksheet. The aim of this exercise is really to get the student more comfortable with the library. Rigid requirements for how the student obtains the information to fill out the worksheet will not accomplish that goal. Demonstrating that librarians are flexible and willing to meet students where they are at will accomplish that goal.

Instruction planning is about priorities. If accessibility is a priority, then other priorities need to shift. While one librarian can make a difference by promoting accessibility in their practice, creating an accessible experience for all students requires the cooperation of the entire instruction program, including any departments heads or others setting goals and priorities for library instruction. Creating quality, accessible content takes time. It may mean there is less time to produce more content. However, prioritizing accessibility often creates a better experience for all. If you have a smart phone, you are already using a technology originally designed for disabled people. As much as we may curse predictive text, many of us still rely on it when composing text messages. If you use curb cuts, ramps, or elevators, you are using assistive and adaptive technology. Yes, accessible design does take more time, but it is good design and thoughtful design that we all use. Prioritizing accessibility can help you meet several goals shared by many libraries. Accessible design prioritizes human needs, which helps us meet student needs and increase library use. As much as I do believe sharing my perspective is important, hearing one disabled person's experience is not enough. I've included a few of my favorite writers and blogs to get you started.[4] Now, settle down by the fire and get cozy with some gray areas!

Notes

1. Paul K. Longmore, "Why I Burned My Book," in *Why I Burned My Book and Other Essays on Disability* (Philadelphia: Temple University Press, 2003), 231–60.
2. Angie Brunk and Dale Monobe, "Don't Make the Kid Who Is Blind Play Dodge Ball: Making Interactive Library Instruction Accessible to Students with Disabilities" (presentation, Brick and Click Libraries: An Academic Library Symposium, Northwest Missouri State University, Maryville, MO, November 1, 2013), https://files.eric.ed.gov/fulltext/ED545375.pdf; Angie Brunk and Dale Monobe, "Level Up! Making Games Accessible," in *Games and Gamification in Academic Libraries*, ed. Stephanie Crowe and Eva Sclippa (Chicago: Association of College and Research Libraries, 2020), 49–61.
3. US General Services Administration, "Task Analysis," How To and Tools: Methods, User Research Methods, accessed December 8, 2021, https://www.usability.gov/how-to-and-tools/methods/task-analysis.html.
4. Mike Ervin, "Blogger: User Profile: Smart Ass Cripple," *Smart Ass Cripple* (blog), accessed December 8, 2021, https://www.blogger.com/profile/13017074589165581514; Kim Sauder, "About—crippledscholar," *crippledscholar* (blog), accessed December 8, 2021, https://crippledscholar.com/about/; Elin Williams, "About—My Blurred World," *My Blurred World* (blog), accessed December 8, 2021, https://myblurredworld.com/about-2/.

Bibliography

Brunk, Angie, and Dale Monobe. "Don't Make the Kid Who Is Blind Play Dodge Ball: Making Interactive Library Instruction Accessible to Students with Disabilities." Presentation, Brick and Click Libraries: An Academic Library Symposium, Northwest Missouri State University, Maryville, MO, November 1, 2013. https://files.eric.ed.gov/fulltext/ED545375.pdf

———, "Level Up! Making Games Accessible." In *Games and Gamification in Academic Libraries*, edited by Stephanie Crowe and Eva Sclippa, 49–61. Chicago: Association of College and Research Libraries, 2020.

Ervin, Mike. "Blogger: User Profile: Smart Ass Cripple." *Smart Ass Cripple* (blog). Accessed December 8, 2021. https://www.blogger.com/profile/13017074589165581514.

Longmore, Paul K. "Why I Burned My Book." In *Why I Burned My Book and Other Essays on Disability*, 231–60. Philadelphia: Temple University Press, 2003.

Sauder, Kim. "About—crippledscholar." *crippledscholar* (blog). Accessed December 8, 2021. https://crippledscholar.com/about/.

US General Services Administration. "Task Analysis." How To and Tools: Methods; User Research Methods. Accessed December 8, 2021. https://www.usability.gov/how-to-and-tools/methods/task-analysis.html.

Williams, Elin. "About—My Blurred World." *My Blurred World* (blog). Accessed December 8, 2021. https://myblurredworld.com/about-2/.

CHAPTER 35

Bodies Matter

What Disability and Watching People Learn to Sing Taught Me about Teaching Information Literacy

Maria Kingsbury

This chapter emerges from discomfort, moments without focus. I tried pressing them into a smooth chronology that suggested that I had, or have, a sense of how those encounters come together to make clear meaning. I found, though, that so doing rubs away their distinction and texture, the ways that those moments persist as distinctive kernels, refusing to resolve themselves into a larger whole. I've constructed this chapter to try to mirror how I've experienced these ideas, like an unfinished, slowly assembled bricolage, a collection of found objects placed next to one another. As in bricolage, it is my hope that meaning gradually emerges from this assemblage of ideas and moments.

The things I'm placing next to one another—disability studies, singing lessons, and library instruction—are unlikely companions. Years into my job as an academic librarian, I was surprised, too, to find myself in a tiny cinderblock office with two other people and a grand piano, watching for hours while one of those people learned to sing. As my thighs burned, keeping the wobbly, sixty-year-old, bright orange molded plastic chair I sat on from squeaking, I definitely didn't anticipate the connections I'd see to my experience as a person with disabilities. Neither did I anticipate both of those things—disability and voice lessons—prompting me to rethink how I did library instruction.

I sit uncomfortably with the insights I offer. I'm not sure that my interventions are properly matched to the scale of the issues I see. The things I suggest reject many of

the assumptions I absorbed over time about what library instruction is and how it should work, which seems to be in the absence of messy physical bodies. In this chapter, through and with the uneasiness, I'll describe my changing relationship to the implicit assumptions I communicate to students about their ability to perform "good" research. I'll argue that even as our purpose in library instruction is encouraging students' individual critical thinking, we should muddy the waters by emphasizing how information consumption and production are dependent as well as independent activities. Finally, I'll say that I think that librarians should become more adept with dealing with emotions and affect in research, even though feelings are hard to discuss. But I'm not sure that any of this is enough to create a meaningful illustration of the potential changes that centering embodied experience in library instruction could make.

While I cannot offer any sweeping conclusions, I hope you will see the inclusive potential that emerges between these seemingly unlike things and in these uncomfortable spaces. The main thing I noticed, and that I will try to communicate, is how disability studies and singing lessons bring the experience of the human body to the center of their practices. Together, those approaches offer me, as a teaching librarian, openings for exploring how I can make my classroom and practice inclusive for students of all bodies and abilities.

(Not) Defining Disability

The word *disability* evades easy definition. Its meaning, which scholars contest, changes context to context, person to person. I find useful for this chapter Rosemarie Garland-Thomson's explanation of disability as constituting four interrelated aspects:

> First, it is a system for interpreting and disciplining bodily variations; second, it is a relationship between bodies and their environments; third, it is a set of practices that produce both the able-bodied and the disabled; fourth, it is a way of describing the inherent instability of the embodied self.... Disability is an identity category that anyone can enter at any time, and we will all join it if we live long enough.[1]

Disability, then, is not as simple as a dry medical diagnosis or legal definition. It is a series of systems and relationships that are active in our real world and individual experiences. Disability shows up in the vague and abstract processes that go into a society's defining "normal" bodies and behaviors, in the practical decisions around how sidewalks on a city street should look, and in the deeply intimate anxieties each individual has around their own physical bodies and sensations. All of us, Garland-Thomson reminds us, have and will occupy disability; we are all, whether we acknowledge disability or not, moving in and out of that category.

I came to disability studies through experience of disability. "Disability demands a story," said Michael Bérubé,[2] but mine isn't overly dramatic. I have a small spectrum of mental illnesses, complex post-traumatic stress disorder, and in my early twenties had an accident that left one of my arms without sensation or strength from my shoulder to my fingertips. Now, in my late thirties, much of the strength has returned, but I still experience limited sensation.

These experiences led me to scholars and activists writing and speaking about disability, and I found (and find) in them an ethos of pragmatism, dedication, and compassion that I also find in my librarian colleagues. The compelling and enriching combination of librarianship and disability studies can be found in the work of scholars like JJ Pionke, Robin Brown and Scott Sheildlower, Jessica Schomberg and Wendy Highby, and Christine Moeller, among others[3]—and I think the opportunity for further study is vast.

Doing disability studies is hard because of, among other things, the galaxy of definitions, the stigma disability carries, and the discomfort that comes from trying to move what is on the margins to the center of the conversation. And yet, as a centerpiece of my imaginary bricolage, I call upon Rosemarie Garland-Thomson again: "Understanding how disability operates as an identity category and a cultural concept will enhance how we understand what it is to be human, our relationships with one another, and the experience of embodiment."[4] I can't put down this idea that disability might serve as the connective tissue that links existential notions of humanity, social and interpersonal relations, and our own silent experiences of our own bodies. It makes a kind of stunningly obvious sense: all humans have bodies, and all of those bodies variously break or are always already subject to breaking. It's as close to a truly universal human experience as I can think of. And even so, I couldn't figure out how to pull these profound ideas into my information literacy instruction.

A Voice Studio

I'd been carrying around pieces taken from disability scholars like Garland-Thomson when I found myself in another uncomfortable place: an undergraduate voice studio. This particular studio focused on teaching undergraduates singing in the Western classical tradition (think Schubert and Mozart), and I was there because I needed a project for my doctoral dissertation in technical communication and rhetoric. Musical instruction is rich, as it happens, in interesting forms of technical communication, and I have a personal interest in music, although I'm not a musician myself.

I'll call the voice instructor who generously allowed me into her space to watch her teach Ariadne, but that name, as well as those of the student singers I'll mention, are pseudonyms. When I observed her, Ariadne was an experienced voice teacher with a doctorate in music performance and a lively career outside the studio singing art songs and the blues.

Those five months in the voice studio were outside my wheelhouse: I am not a trained musician, but, more importantly, I also discovered I had invited myself into a deeply vulnerable space. In that singing studio, students talked about what their bodies felt like when they sang, their romantic lives, their fears, their parents, their homework woes. They demonstrated imperfection, made strange sounds, and allowed their bodies to be reshaped by thinking about raw eggs in the backs of their throats or their breath support as a paddling duck.

As I saw students' bodies and the experience of the body move to the center of the instructional setting, I began to discern and draw faint lines of connection between what happened there and my experiences in disability studies and library instruction. This voice studio was inclusive in ways that my library instruction classrooms were not. By drawing on the frailties and affordances of embodied experience, Ariadne connected her students to otherwise hopelessly abstract concepts and helped their bodies perform mysterious and complex internal movements to change the qualities of their voices.

What follows are a few of those things I've placed next to one another and am trying to connect.

Ability Is a Construction

In my first interview with her, Ariadne told me without hubris or guile, "As long as they're willing to work, I can teach anyone to sing." Her words startled me at the time, probably because I, like many of the rest of us, have gone through my life assuming that the most important quality a singer needed to have was an elusive thing called "talent." That was the key ingredient in being "able" to sing. Or so I thought.

Fifteen to twenty percent of the general population self-identify as tone-deaf—even though the vast majority of those same people don't have any physical or cognitive impairments that inhibit their ability to produce music.[5] Under 5 percent of the population actually exhibits "tone-deafness,"[6] and yet multiple studies indicate that most people regularly underestimate their own capacities for musical production.[7] Arguably, then, many more of us could derive enjoyment and community from singing, but we don't try because we think our bodies are incapable.

This misperception also works the other way. "A lot of people," Ariadne said of a few of the talented students she'd taught, "don't want to admit music isn't for them or that music is a lot of work, because [doing] that challenges this idea they have in their head about what music is and who does it." Instead, Ariadne said, she'd rather have a student who didn't self-identify as a "good" singer but is willing to keep at the work that made them a better singer, the kind of work that on its face might not seem to have much to do with performance, such as practicing thoughtfully and often and responding to critique.

And then there were things about singing ability that went beyond individual students. Ariadne said of Wendell, a student who initially didn't identify as a singer at all,

> Wendell has become one of my very favorite students and one of my greatest success stories because he works so hard.... His intonation has improved a ton. His ability to count has improved a ton. When he came here, he couldn't even read music. Because we don't have an audition [to get access to voice lessons] he has been allowed to grow and develop.

Rather than suggest that Wendell alone ought to be credited for his growth as a singer, Ariadne included the undergraduate music program's lack of an audition system; audition systems vet incoming students on the basis of their demonstrated ability in order to permit them varying access to educational and performance experiences. In other words, it was an accessible structure that, when combined with a good teacher and a willing student, facilitated Wendell's abilities. Had the program possessed an audition system, Wendell would never have had access to the resources he needed to develop his voice.

I recognize that I, as an academic librarian, am part of just such a disabling structure. In *Academic Ableism: Disability and Higher Education*, Jay Dolmage argues, "Academia powerfully mandates able-bodiedness and able-mindedness, as well as other forms of social and communicative hyperability, and this demand can best be defined as ableism. In fact, few cultural institutions do a better or more comprehensive job of promoting ableism."[8] The way Ariadne thought about Wendell's growth sitting next to Dolmage's words prompts me to wonder about how I construct my students' ability to perform research. We have habits of mind and research behaviors encoded in standards like the Association of College and Research Libraries' *Framework for Information Literacy*—but what tacit assumptions do students carry with them about being able to research, as they might about their ability to sing?

As a way of beginning to explore and respond to that discomfort these moments inspire, I've begun spending time during library instruction sessions asking students what makes them "able" to do research. This allows me both to learn what my students' assumptions are about their abilities and to respond to misconceptions I might be inadvertently reinforcing. For instance, students assume I want them to do their research in the library building. I will counter by asking how many times they've had good ideas or remembered something while in the shower. Doing research, in other words, isn't all about the ability to sit still and concentrate.

We Can't Judge Our Own Sound

Nearing the end of my time in Ariadne's voice studio, I asked her about the most important thing she wanted her students to learn. She told me:

> I think the least successful but most important one are the same thing: trying to put into words what something felt like. Because we can't judge our sound. We are so terrible at judging our sound. I mean, you've experienced it: you hear your voice on somebody's voicemail and you're like, *That's what my voice sounds like?!*

> We have a very different auditory experience of ourselves, so you can't really trust what you're hearing. You really have to trust other people.

A singer can only trust the *feeling* of producing their voice, then, not the sound of it. They have to rely on others to tell them how they sound as they feel those different sensations. Their voices develop and improve, in other words, only through a trusting relationship with other people. A singer simply cannot get better alone. Becoming a singer is to acknowledge dependence.

This still strikes me, as a product of American culture and a Western education, as a radical notion. Disability scholar Lennard Davis speaks directly to such discomfort as he says, "Impairment is the rule, and normalcy is the fantasy. Dependence is the reality, and independence grandiose thinking."[9] This dismissal of "normal" and "independence" as pillars of a desirable life still makes me anxious in its kicking over of central guideposts of "progress"; those ideas are central not only to the myths of the United States, but also to tenets we verbalize and also tacitly reward in higher education. And yet, if that isn't exactly the ethos Ariadne was describing and the activity I saw in her voice studio, it was close.

Librarians learn early in their training about the vast webs of people and systems and technologies that go into producing, distributing, and consuming information in general and how those things impact libraries in particular. But I, for one, in trying desperately to help students to internalize sound approaches to telling reliable information from its opposite, often push away the complications and murkiness that dependence introduces. Dependence is difficult to explain because it is often invisible, and it is a story that I don't have easy analogues and language to draw upon to tell.

From an architectural standpoint, academic libraries are embracing collaborative learning spaces that facilitate interdependent learning,[10] but I am struggling to figure out how to take this ethos beyond the built environment, to suggest that even when we appear to be doing solitary research and speaking in our "own" voices, we are influenced by and responding to the voices of others.

For now, I ask students to volunteer to read aloud brief, preselected passages from different sources, each expressing a unique point of view. We then spend time talking about why a student might have picked a particular passage, why they responded to it as they did, and what it felt like in their bodies to read that passage. We then speculate what it might feel like to read a passage that didn't resonate, or, perhaps, clashed with their beliefs, aloud. We then try to explore the origins of those beliefs and ideas about the world. I intend these simple exercises to introduce how our own voices are shaped without exception by the voices of others.

Emotions Are Embodied

Even if I didn't know Matthew well, it would have been clear when he came for his voice lesson one October day that he was not happy. I did what many introverts and descendants of Norwegian immigrants are apt to when I saw his slumped shoulders and face obscured by his hoodie: nothing.

Ariadne, on the other hand, addressed it directly. When Matthew responded to her greeting of "How's it going?" with a headshake, she said, "Let's use this time to find a sense of what to do when your voice is really tired, and when you're a little overwhelmed with other things." She first quizzed him on how many hours of sleep he should get, how much water he should drink (I learned singers need a little more than sixty-four ounces daily to keep their vocal folds moisturized), how much he should exercise, and how much time he should relax a day. I thought it would end there. But she went on, "There are some things we can do vocally to keep using our voice but being as gentle with it as possible." She then demonstrated, and had Matthew practice, vocal exercises worked with his mood and still worked techniques he was developing.

Many disability scholars, in contrast to the cultural reflex of repression or medicalization, recognize the complex, embodied, psychosocial, and powerful potential of emotional experience. In fact, the experience of emotion can never definitively be attributed to a single bodily condition or perceptual experience or external factor—it's all of them at once.[11] To deny emotion, then, is to deny the body. Because the human voice is probably one of the most vivid and intimate expressions both of a body and of an affective state,[12] in vocal instruction, a teacher can't simply ignore either. I see another line here between voice instruction and library instruction.

Our students' bodies and their attendant emotional states are always already present when they research as well. Miriam Matteson pragmatically points out, "Librarians should enrich their IL instruction with techniques and strategies that consider the whole student—paying attention to their emotional and cognitive development—if they are to increase the teaching and learning of IL skills."[13] But library school didn't do much to help me learn to address emotions, mine or anyone else's, and while that's not an excuse, I find myself wanting language and strategies and scripts to help navigate these conversations about the role of emotion in students' research experiences.

In that spirit, I now spend at least five minutes in each of my instruction sessions talking about the emotions students are likely to experience in performing research. Verbally naming these emotions can take away their mystique and sting, I hope, and deny them mastery over students' behavior when they emerge. Taking a cue from Ariadne, I also make suggestions about what students can do when those emotions are present so they don't get too sidelined. This is a small step, but just as singers must eventually learn to name what it is they're feeling in order to control it, student researchers might as well.

Last Notes

As I finish this chapter, I am acutely aware of how inconclusive my conclusions are. Putting it simply, I think we as library instructors, as we intentionally go about trying to make our instructional spaces and approaches more inclusive, can learn from practices and theories that center the human body, in its instabilities and idiosyncrasies, at the core of student experiences. This isn't to suggest that we abandon the important intellectual and critical work that we're asking of students—particularly at this moment in history, those habits of mind are crucial. But I think there's space and opportunity to explore disability and embodiment as approaches that complement the skills and concepts that we (or at least I) are struggling to convey.

What I've tried to illustrate in this chapter are how I'm seeing connections between seemingly unlike things, and how those things, juxtaposed to one another, changed not only my thoughts around, but my approach to library instruction. I'm admittedly still uneasy about even sharing these approaches and thoughts, because they seem very particular to me. That said, I hope that you at least found a small piece of this chapter interesting and that you can carry that piece where your library instruction journey next takes you.

Notes

1. Rosemarie Garland-Thomson, "Integrating Disability, Transforming Feminist Theory," in *The Disability Studies Reader*, ed. Lennard Davis (New York: Routledge, 2013), 336, 346.
2. Michael Bérubé, "Disability and Narrative," *PMLA* 120, no. 2 (2005): 570.
3. J. J. Pionke, "Library Employee Views of Disability and Accessibility," *Journal of Library Administration* 60, no. 2 (2020): 120–45; Robin Brown and Scott Sheidlower, "Claiming Our Space: A

Quantitative and Qualitative Picture of Disabled Librarians," *Library Trends* 67, no. 3 (2019): 471–86; Jessica Schomberg and Wendy Highby, *Beyond Accommodation* (Sacramento, CA: Litwin Books, 2020); Christine Moeller, "Disability, Identity, and Professionalism: Precarity in Librarianship," *Library Trends* 67, no. 3 (2019): 455–70.

4. Garland-Thomson, "Integrating Disability," 336.
5. John A. Sloboda, Karen J. Wise, and Isabelle Peretz, "Quantifying Tone Deafness in the General Population," *Annals of the New York Academy of Sciences* 1060, no. 1 (2005): 256.
6. Isabelle Peretz, Anne Sophie Champod, and Krista Hyde, "Varieties of Musical Disorders: The Montreal Battery of Evaluation of Amusia," *Annals of the New York Academy of Sciences* 999, no. 1 (2003): 59.
7. Lola L. Cuddy et al., "Musical Difficulties Are Rare: A Study of 'Tone Deafness' among University Students," *Annals of the New York Academy of Sciences* 1060, no. 1 (2005): 311–24.
8. Jay Dolmage, *Academic Ableism* (Ann Arbor: University of Michigan Press, 2017), 7.
9. Lennard Davis, "The End of Identity Politics and the Beginning of Dismodernism," in *The Disability Studies Reader*, ed. Lennard Davis (New York: Routledge, 2013), 276.
10. Fatt Cheong Choy and Su Nee Goh, "A Framework for Planning Academic Library Spaces," *Library Management* 37, no. 1/2 (2016): 13–28.
11. Tom Shakespeare, "The Social Model of Disability," in *The Disability Studies Reader*, ed. Lennard Davis (New York: Routledge, 2013), 218.
12. James Stark, *Bel Canto* (Toronto: University of Toronto Press, 1999), 182.
13. Miriam L. Matteson, "The Whole Student: Cognition, Emotion, and Information Literacy," *College and Research Libraries* 75, no. 6 (2014): 874.

Bibliography

Bérubé, Michael. "Disability and Narrative." *PMLA* 120, no. 2 (2005): 568–76.

Brown, Robin, and Scott Sheidlower. "Claiming Our Space: A Quantitative and Qualitative Picture of Disabled Librarians." *Library Trends* 67 no. 3 (2019): 471–86.

Choy, Fatt Cheong, and Su Nee Goh. "A Framework for Planning Academic Library Spaces." *Library Management* 37, no. 1/2, (2016): 13–28.

Cuddy, Lola L., Laura-Lee Balkwill, Isabelle Peretz, and Ronald R. Holden. "Musical Difficulties Are Rare: A Study of 'Tone Deafness' among University Students. *Annals of the New York Academy of Sciences* 1060, no. 1 (2005): 311–24.

Davis, Lennard. "The End of Identity Politics and the Beginning of Dismodernism." In *The Disability Studies Reader,* edited by Lennard Davis, 263–77. New York: Routledge, 2013.

Dolmage, Jay. *Academic Ableism: Disability and Higher Education.* Ann Arbor: University of Michigan Press, 2017.

Garland-Thomson, Rosemarie. "Integrating Disability, Transforming Feminist Theory." In *The Disability Studies Reader,* edited by Lennard Davis, 333–53. New York: Routledge, 2013.

Matteson, Miriam L. "The Whole Student: Cognition, Emotion, and Information Literacy," *College and Research Libraries* 75, no. 6 (2014): 862–77.

Moeller, Christine. "Disability, Identity, and Professionalism: Precarity in Librarianship." *Library Trends* 67, no. 3 (2019): 455–70.

Peretz, Isabelle, Anne Sophie Champod, and Krista Hyde. "Varieties of Musical Disorders: The Montreal Battery of Evaluation of Amusia." *Annals of the New York Academy of Sciences* 999, no. 1 (2003): 58–75.

Pionke, J. J. "Library Employee Views of Disability and Accessibility." *Journal of Library Administration* 60, no. 2 (2020): 120–45.

Schomberg, Jessica, and Wendy Highby. *Beyond Accommodation: Creating an Inclusive Workplace for Disabled Library Workers.* Sacramento, CA: Litwin Books, 2020.

Shakespeare, Tom. "The Social Model of Disability." In *The Disability Studies Reader,* edited by Lennard Davis, 214–21. New York: Routledge, 2013.

Sloboda, John A., Karen J. Wise, and Isabelle Peretz. "Quantifying Tone Deafness in the General Population." *Annals of the New York Academy of Sciences* 1060, no. 1 (2005): 255–61.

Stark, James. *Bel Canto: A History of Vocal Pedagogy.* Toronto: University of Toronto Press, 1999.

Instructor Identity and Positionality

Introduction

Ariana Santiago

In this section, each chapter discusses the impact of instructor identity or positionality on inclusive library instruction, with explorations relating to career stage, social identities, and agency in the classroom. The authors' reflections illustrate how instructor identity and positionality can affect students and the care that should be taken to ensure inclusivity. A common thread in this section is the importance of acknowledging students' personal identities and how your identities as an instructor relate to those of students. I found each chapter to be thought-provoking, and collectively these insights speak to the challenges and possibilities inherent in intentional acknowledgement of identity and positionality in teaching and learning.

In Chapter 36, "Embracing the Early Career: Reflections on Creating Space as Teachers and Learners in Library Instruction," Carol Fisher and Sam Buechler offer the perspective of early-career academic library instructors. They examine intuitive practices to transform them into intentional practices that create a more inclusive classroom environment, particularly by supporting mutual learning between instructor and students, minimizing classroom hierarchy, and directly acknowledging library and information anxieties and personal identities in the classroom. Fisher and Buechler's early-career reflections will be relatable to many, and their insights on inclusive teaching approaches are applicable across career stages.

In Chapter 37, "Learning to Put People First: Cultural Humility, Funds of Knowledge, and Information Literacy Instruction with First-Generation Students," Darren Ilett shares key learning moments from his teaching experience that shifted his perspective toward cultural humility and funds of knowledge, as well as resulting changes to his professional praxis. In the key learning moments, Ilett highlights the importance of considering how your identities relate to and impact your students' identities and the unintentional harm instructors can inflict on students due to unconscious biases. Ilett's honest reflection and self-assessment is a reminder to constantly examine our own biases and practice cultural humility.

Breanne Crumpton and Michelle K. Mitchell focus on adapting inclusive teaching practices to the one-shot format in Chapter 38, "Applying Columbia University's

Guide for Inclusive Teaching to the One-Shot: A Reflective Essay." Using Columbia University's *Guide for Inclusive Teaching at Columbia* as a starting point, the authors summarize the guide's principles, offer practical guidelines for adapting these inclusive teaching strategies in the context of one-shot library instruction, and reflect on the challenges of implementing inclusive teaching strategies that are typically geared toward faculty who teach credit-bearing courses. The authors' practical guidance on incorporating inclusive teaching strategies will be useful for the many academic librarians who know firsthand the unique and often challenging positionality of teaching one-shot sessions.

Nicole Pagowsky, Shanti Freundlich, Rachel Gammons, and Emily Drabinski explore inclusive pedagogies through the lens of their own experiences as adjunct instructors in MLIS programs in Chapter 39, "Teaching from the Outside: Inclusive Pedagogy and the Adjunct Instructor." The authors highlight the challenging positionality of adjunct instructors and share teaching practices that balance the limitations of this positionality with the need to integrate inclusive pedagogies. Pagowsky, Freundlich, Gammons, and Drabinski each reflect on an aspect of adjuncting: teaching philosophies as a grounding practice for both instructors and students; designing authentic and meaningful assignments; the restrictions of standardized expectations; and the importance of bringing transparency to course policies. This chapter brings a breadth of perspectives and practical applications that can benefit many in the LIS field, not limited to adjunct instructors.

CHAPTER 36

Embracing the Early Career

Reflections on Creating Space as Teachers and Learners in Library Instruction

Carol Fisher and Sam Buechler

Prior to graduate school, *pedagogy* was a peculiar, exclusive and intimidating word used by academics entrenched in an ivory tower and completely divorced from our (the authors') experiences within the classroom as students and learners. Our move from graduate school to early-career library instructors has allowed us space to understand pedagogy as a result of our own teaching practices. In our experience, pedagogy as a concept has not stopped being elusive and elitist, but it has provided us context outside of our practices to help us grow as teachers and learners to create equitable and inclusive instruction spaces. Throughout this chapter, we will use reflection to explore the ways that being early-career academic library instructors has affected how we intuitively approach teaching. Specifically, we will define how our intuitive practices foster a foundation to break down the hierarchical instructor-student relationship and the ways that identity and discussions of library and information anxiety contribute to the instruction we participate in. We will also explore ways to turn intuitive practices into intentional ones by tying our personal experiences to Paulo Freire's concept of "banking education"[1] and Dr. Alison Cook-Sather's research on students as partners in learning and teaching, as well as additional library-specific scholarship. As we transition from early career to mid-career and beyond, it's essential that the pedagogies we use and employ now are met with this level of reflection and intentionality in order to build lasting equitable and inclusive practices.

On Being Early-Career

Despite having experience teaching in a variety of contexts prior to graduate school, entering the library profession was the first time we encountered formal training and expectations surrounding instruction. The transition from student to teacher was swift, and there was limited time to cultivate an understanding of who we were in the classroom and how we wanted to present ourselves in this new role. What we found natural in this transition was to rely on our experiences as students within a classroom to inform our instruction—we knew what we found beneficial or not in our own class experiences and could see the ways to incorporate that into our own teaching. Through the practice of seeing teaching as an extension of learning in this way, we've been able to understand our roles in the classroom more intuitively. Assuming a new professional identity is difficult, even more so when considering how that identity will be reflected in a classroom full of students. For us, the practice of accepting and acknowledging our "newness" in teaching has become vital to surviving it.

When we enter instructional environments, we take a moment to inform students of who we are within our institution—this includes disclosing how long we've been in the profession and that we are still learning. In the beginning of our teaching careers, this framing had little to do with pedagogy and more to do with self-preservation. It was mostly an attempt at cushioning any failure in our roles and detracting from the idea that we should be seen as the holder of knowledge during instruction or in the classroom. As we critically examined this intuitive practice, both through reflection and research, we were able to discover that this practice could become more than survival and can actually evolve into more equitable and inclusive library instruction.

By explicitly positioning ourselves as learners through our professional identities, we are able to minimize the inherent hierarchy within the classroom—a concept that is supported in a variety of seminal and emerging critical pedagogies. In the second chapter of *Pedagogy of the Oppressed*, Paulo Freire brings forth concepts and experiences that feel intrinsically linked to how we have approached instruction within our early career.[2] We find this connection specifically in Freire's description of the "'banking' concept of education" and his methods for dismantling it. Freire describes banking education as "an act of depositing, in which the students are the depositories, and the teacher is the depositor. Instead of communicating, the teacher issues communiqués and makes deposits which the students patiently receive, memorize, and repeat."[3] In order to dismantle oppressive banking education models, Freire assigns instructors the responsibility of addressing the fallacy that they are all-knowing, as well as the inverse that students come to their class as wholly ignorant; in doing so space is created where "both [parties] are simultaneously teachers *and* students."[4] In this regard, Freire has described a positioning similar to what we have intuitively employed as early career professionals—we dismantled the teacher as depositor by informing our students that we are new and we are still learning. Given our position as early-career professionals, as well as our nearness to our own experiences as students, we are able to adapt our classroom to what we are referring to as a model of "mutual learning." By sharing learning responsibilities, we are also providing space for students to participate, through their own experiences and perspectives, in teaching.

The action of shifting classroom structure and dynamics to one of a partnership is beneficial in several ways; the pressure to perform as "all-knowing" instructors is reduced, and hopefully, students can feel more empowered and gain a sense of ownership over their own learning and subsequent teaching. This is not new, and the idea of students as partners in learning and teaching has been heavily scaffolded upon within publications over the last fifty-plus years.[5] Cook-Sather has written extensively on centering student voices in the classroom and on how to transition to a classroom where students are partners in teaching and learning.[6] While Cook-Sather is not speaking directly to library-instruction context, we find that the content of her work establishes a necessary expansion to library-based scholarship and is still applicable to our desire to create equitable and inclusive library instruction experiences.

Understanding the roots and pedagogy of mutual learning while we are in our early career allows us the space to feel more secure in our status as "teacher *and* student" during our instruction sessions.[7] While the connections between this stage of our careers and mutual learning are easily traced, mutual learning can become a lasting practice only once it is leveraged with intentionality. Without continued reflection, recommitment to intentionality, and a deeper understanding of student needs and experiences, our approach to instruction can hastily devolve into something that's formulaic and jaded. As we travel further away from being early-career, it's essential that we continue to embody the aspects of being new beyond our expiration as early-career library instructors.

Library and Information Anxiety

The related phenomenon of library anxiety and information anxiety has been well-documented and extensively researched.[8] In this section, we'll be exploring these anxieties and their related experiences from two distinct perspectives—the first perspective being the phenomenon of anxiety that students experience, and the second, the personal anxiety that we, as early-career instructors, experience. Our reflection is an attempt at leveraging our personal anxiety about teaching to encourage authenticity and work toward demystifying what constitutes both a library instructor and academic research as a whole.

Eklof describes the difference between library anxiety and information anxiety as "closely related concepts, but [they] have important distinctions: where library anxiety refers to the nervousness surrounding the use of the physical library space and collections, information anxiety refers to the nervousness surrounding the use of, and access to, information sources."[9] Eklof, Jiao, and Onwuegbuzie also describe information anxiety as "the result of many different factors: technological barriers, information overload, unfamiliarity with library databases, and, as is the case for many adult students, the expectation to find just the right piece of information on the first attempt."[10]

While research holds that library instruction in itself can lower library anxiety, we recognize that there is importance in directly naming, explaining, and legitimizing the very real experiences of library and information anxiety to students.[11] If our pedagogy merely holds library anxiety and information anxiety behind a curtain of tools and interventions, we are acting in antithesis to a mutual learning environment. Alternatively, when we name and describe anxieties associated with libraries and information seeking during our instruction, we are providing a moment for both students and ourselves to consider how we interact and exist within institutions and how they interact with us. We are taking steps to move away from a model of deposit learning—where students are only informed on how to use the library and what it offers—and instead allowing space for conversation and inquiry on libraries as places of power with long histories of gatekeeping.[12] Through being explicit in describing a common experience, and expressing that it is not a deficiency on the part of students, but of the institution, we can bring a modicum of transformation to library instruction.

It's become evident that disclosure of our own classroom anxiety is vital to opening dialogue about what it means to exist in academia. If we disclose to our students that we too feel anxious walking into a classroom to teach, then perhaps one of the many barriers that exist in academia will erode just a bit more. This act of acknowledgement and legitimization serves to challenge the existing narrative that instructors are unfazed by their inherent classroom power. If we can shift the narrative into one that supports the notion that the classroom should be equal on all fronts, then we are beginning to work toward an inclusive and equitable classroom experience for both students and instructors. However, it is understood that the act of disclosure can be uncomfortable and difficult, especially when speaking on our own fears. Reframing our own anxieties by positing ourselves not as experts, but as learners, is one way of approaching the experience without explicitly stating, "I'm anxious to be here," in front of a class.

Identities in the Classroom

Approaching personal identity in the classroom as an inclusive pedagogical tool has helped alleviate some of the anxieties we face as instructors as well as helping deconstruct the hierarchical instructor-student relationship. This is in alignment with the idea of both instructors and students acting as teachers and learners. However, identity in the classroom extends far beyond just acknowledging honest feelings in the moment. Bringing identity into the classroom as an intentional act requires self-identification—both due to the nature of invisible identities and as a recognition of power that is held by the individual. Depending on one's own identity, this in itself can be a radical, albeit sometimes dangerous, act but one that can reflect positively on our teaching.

We are more than early-career library instructors, and our existence outside of teaching and library work can hold value inside the classroom. The intersections of our professional identity includes being LGBTQ+, having invisible disabilities, having a protected veteran status, and possessing the innate privilege of being white.[13] These intersections shape how we both operate in the world, and how we see library work, and library instruction more specifically. They mold our interactions with students and help illuminate opportunities to enact positive change in the classroom. Our experiences in both teaching and learning are not wholly divorced from the experiences of the students that we teach, and the shared aspects of existing as a teacher and learner can be used to create an equitable and inclusive instruction experience.

Instructor identities can be disclosed in several different ways; however, this disclosure must also recognize systemic power and privilege. For us, our whiteness is our most prominent identity. If we were to address our intersections without acknowledging how this identity has contributed to a long history of oppressive and violent narrative of neutrality within libraries, then we would effectively be empowering the white supremacist structure already in place.[14] No amount of intersection can negate our whiteness and its implications. Our awareness of all our identities in an instructional setting becomes a priority in our pedagogy for this reason.

Disclosing components of our identity as instructors is an act that extends far beyond ourselves and is also a direct attempt at making room for students in the classroom. By working toward eroding some staunch and clinical boundaries between teacher and student, we are hoping to make space for the experiences that influence the way both instructors and students approach their academic work. Acknowledgement of the pure existence of these identities (and associated privileges) is a start, but is not the end of the work. Referring back to chapter two of *Pedagogy of the Oppressed*, the goal of creating a mutual learning environment is, "not to 'integrate' [the oppressed] into the structure of oppression, but to transform that structure so that they can become 'beings for themselves.'"[15]

Open self-identification of your expectations and who you are as a person helps to orient toward this solution by giving students space to be with the class holistically versus in the class simply as students. By sharing our personal backgrounds and identities, we are attempting to level the playing field to acknowledge our shared and differing experiences, hopefully working toward reframing the power dynamic away from us (the teacher) versus them (the students). An equitable partnership between instructors and students is one that includes respect for each other and our respective identities and histories.

Conclusion

Freire describes a version of oppressive education through a lens of reality: "The teacher talks about reality as if it were motionless, static, compartmentalized, and predictable. Or else he expands on a topic completely alien to the existential experience of his students."[16] Our newness as formal instructors, and as degree-holding library workers, has created the space for raw curiosity. In order to understand our environment and positionality as teachers (and library faculty), we've had to question everything around us, which in turn has provided us with the opportunity to build the reflective tools and attitudes we now hold. We are able to reflect on our practices solely because we questioned our environment, institutional expectations, and ourselves. By engaging our classroom in a mutual learning model—in tandem with our early-career pedagogical reflections, implementation of library and information anxiety discussions, and the prevalence of identity-based experiences—we are able to create a reality that is transformative; evolving and molding itself to fit the needs of students. How can we expect our students to be open, curious, flexible learners if we ourselves do not model that behavior? If a student walks out of our classroom knowing nothing more about us than the fact that we are a library worker who teaches, have we really done a good job at communicating our role to them? Further, if they do walk out of our classroom understanding little about us and our role in the institution, have we truly done a good job at highlighting all the different ways people can participate in higher education?

Part of inclusive and equitable pedagogy means actively and directly challenging the structures that exist in the first place. If we are to challenge structures, we need to recognize the experiences of our students in a way that allows instruction to move beyond integration and into transformation. The idea that instructors are sole sources of what is "right" and "knowledgeable" is not only hard to live up to but can also be dangerous. If we do not actively discourage the power dynamics at play, then we are inherently aligning with them. As early-career instructors we can leverage our inexperience and continued learning to build lasting philosophies and practices. We can begin, and build upon, a constant and rigorous reframing of the classroom from an authority-based perspective to one that situates the early-career library instructor as both a student and a learner, alongside students who are also functioning as both students and learners.

Notes

1. Paulo Freire, *Pedagogy of the Oppressed*, 50th anniversary ed., trans. Myra Bergman Ramos (New York: Bloomsbury Academic, 2018), 71–86.
2. Freire, *Pedagogy of the Oppressed*, 71–86.
3. Freire, *Pedagogy of the Oppressed*, 72.
4. Freire, *Pedagogy of the Oppressed*, 72.
5. Maria T. Accardi, *Feminist Pedagogy for Library Instruction* (Sacramento, CA: Library Juice Press, 2013); Maria T. Accardi, "Teaching against the Grain: Critical Assessment in the Library Classroom," in *Critical Library Instruction: Theories and Methods*, ed. Maria T. Accardi, Emily Drabinski, and Alana Kumbier (Duluth, MN: Library Juice Press, 2010), 251–64; Joshua F. Beatty, "Reading Freire for First World Librarians" (presentation, Canadian Association of Professional Academic Librarians conference, Ottawa, Ontario, Canada, June 2, 2015); bell hooks, *Teaching to Transgress* (New York: Routledge, 1994); Gretchen Keer, "Critical Pedagogy and Information Literacy in Community Colleges," in *Critical Library Instruction: Theories and Methods*, ed. Maria T. Accardi, Emily Drabinski, and Alana Kumbier (Duluth, MN: Library Juice Press, 2010), 149–59; Bryan M. Kopp and Kim Olson-Kopp, "Depositories of Knowledge: Library Instruction and the Development of Critical Consciousness," in *Critical Library Instruction: Theories and Methods*, ed. Maria T. Accardi, Emily Drabinski, and Alana Kumbier (Duluth, MN: Library Juice Press, 2010), 55–67; Sharon Ladenson, "Paradigm Shift: Utilizing Critical Feminist Pedagogy in Library Instruction," in *Critical Library Instruction: Theories and Methods*, ed. Maria T. Accardi, Emily Drabinski, and Alana Kumbier (Duluth, MN: Library Juice Press, 2010), 105–12; Lucy Mercer-Mapstone and Sophia Abbot, eds., *The Power of Partnership* (Elon, NC: Elon University Center for Engaged Learning, 2020); Caroline Sinkinson and Mary Caton Lingold, "Re-visioning the Library Seminar through a Lens of Critical Pedagogy," in *Critical Library Instruction: Theories and Methods*, ed. Maria T. Accardi, Emily Drabinski, and Alana Kumbier (Duluth, MN: Library Juice Press, 2010), 81–88; Carmen Werder and Megan M. Otis, eds., *Engaging Student Voices in the Study of Teaching and Learning* (Sterling, VA: Stylus, 2010).
6. Alison Cook-Sather, "Unrolling Roles in Techno-pedagogy: Toward Collaboration in Traditional College Settings," *Innovative Higher Education* 26, no. 2 (2001): 121–39; Alison Cook-Sather, "Authorizing Student's Perspectives: Toward Trust, Dialogue, and Change in Education," *Educational Researcher* 31, no 4 (2002), 3–14; Alison Cook-Sather, "Re(in)forming the Conversations: Student Position, Power, and Voice in Teacher Education," *Radical Teacher* 64 (2002): 21–28; Alison Cook-Sather, "Movements of Mind: The Matrix, Metaphors, and Re-imagining Education," *Teachers College Record* 105, no. 6 (2006): 946–77; Alison Cook-Sather, *Education Is Translation* (Philadelphia: University of Pennsylvania Press, 2006); Alison Cook-Sather, "The 'Constant Changing of Myself': Revising Roles in Undergraduate Teacher Preparation," *Teacher Education* 41, no. 3 (2006): 187–206; Alison Cook-Sather, "Sound, Presence, and Power: Exploring 'Student Voice' in Educational Research and Reform," *Curriculum Inquiry* 36, no. 4 (2006): 359–403; Alison Cook-Sather, "Resisting the Impositional Potential of Student Voice Work: Lessons for Liberatory Educational Research from Poststructuralist Feminist Critiques of Critical Pedagogy," *Discourse* 28, no. 3 (2007): 389–403; Alison Cook-Sather, "What Would Happen if We Treated Students as Those with Opinions That Matter? The Benefits to Principals and Teachers of Supporting Youth Engagement in School," *NASSP Bulletin* 91, no. 4 (2007): 343–62; Alison Cook-Sather, "'What You Get Is Looking in the Mirror, Only Better': Inviting Students to Reflect (on) College Teaching," *Reflective Practice* 9, no. 4 (2008): 473–83; Alison Cook-Sather, "From Traditional Accountability to Shared Responsibility: The Benefits and Challenges of Student Consultants Gathering Midcourse Feedback in College Classrooms," *Assessment and Evaluation*

in Higher Education 34, no. 2 (2009): 231–41; Alison Cook-Sather, "Translation: An Alternative Framework for Conceptualizing and Supporting School Reform Efforts," *Educational Theory* 59, no. 2 (2009): 217–31; Alison Cook-Sather, *Learning from the Student's Perspective* (Boulder, CO: Paradigm, 2009); Alison Cook-Sather, Catherine Bovill, and Peter Felten, *Engaging Students as Partners in Learning and Teaching* (San Francisco: Jossey-Bass, 2014).

7. Freire, *Pedagogy of the Oppressed*, 71–86.

8. Mary Jane Swope and Jeffrey Katzer, "Why Don't They Ask Questions?" *Reference Quarterly* 12, no. 2 (1972): 161–66; Desmond B. Hatchard and Phyllis Toy, "The Psychological Barriers between Library Users and Library Staff: An Exploratory Investigation," *Australian Academic and Research Libraries* 17, no 2 (1986), 63–69; Sharon Lee Bostick, "The Development and Validation of the Library Anxiety Scale" (PhD diss., Wayne State University, 1992); Qun G. Jiao and Anthony J. Onwuegbuzie, "Antecedents of Library Anxiety," *Library Quarterly* 67, no. 4 (1997): 372–89; Qun G. Jiao and Anthony J. Onwuegbuzie, "Perfectionism and Library Anxiety among Graduate Students," *Journal of Academic Librarianship* 24, no. 5 (1998): 365–72; Qun G. Jiao and Anthony J. Onwuegbuzie, "Self-Perception and Library Anxiety: An Empirical Study," *Library Review* 48, no. 3 (1999): 140–47; Qun G. Jiao and Anthony J. Onwuegbuzie, "Sources of Library Anxiety among International Students: Study of Undergraduates at an Urban University in the Northeast," *Urban Library Journal* 11, no. 1 (2001): 16–26; Qun C. Jiao, Anthony J. Onwuegbuzie, and Art A. Lichtenstein, "Library Anxiety: Characteristics of 'At-Risk' Students," *Library and Information Science Research* 18, no. 2 (1996): 151–63; Anthony J. Onwuegbuzie, "Writing a Research Proposal: The Role of Library Anxiety, Statistics Anxiety, and Composition Anxiety," *Library and Information Science Research* 19, no. 1 (1997): 5–33; Anthony J. Onwuegbuzie and Qun G. Jiao, "Academic Library Usage: A Comparison of Native and Non-native English Speaking Students," *Australian Library Journal* 46, no. 3 (1997): 258–69; Anthony J. Onwuegbuzie and Qun G. Jiao, "I'll Go to the Library Later: The Relationship between Academic Procrastination and Library Anxiety," *College and Research Libraries* 61, no. 1 (2000): 45–54.

9. Ashley Eklof, "Understanding Information Anxiety and How Academic Librarians Can Minimize Its Effects," *Public Services Quarterly* 9, no. 3 (2013): 246–58, quoted in Rebecca Halpern, "Active Learning Works! Until It Doesn't: Measuring the Effectiveness of Activity-Based Learning Exercises on Information Anxiety," *Journal of Library and Information Services in Distance Learning* 10, no. 3-4 (2016): 244.

10. Jiao and Onwuegbuzie, "Perfectionism and Library Anxiety," quoted in Halpern, "Active Learning Works!" 244.

11. Brian Detlor et al., "Student Perceptions of Information Literacy Instruction: The Importance of Active Learning," *Education for Information* 29, no. 2 (2012): 147–61, quoted in Halpern, "Active Learning Works!" 243; Alanna Ross and Christine Furno, "Active Learning in the Library Instruction Environment: An Exploratory Study," *portal: Libraries and the Academy* 11, no. 4 (2011): 953–70, quoted in Halpern, "Active Learning Works!" 243; Shannon R. Simpson, "Google Spreadsheets and Real-Time Assessment: Instant Feedback for Library Instruction," *College and Research Libraries News* 73, no. 9 (2012): 528–49, quoted in Halpern, "Active Learning Works!" 243.

12. Todd Homna, "Introduction to Part I," in *Knowledge Justice: Disrupting Library and Information Studies through Critical Race Theory*, ed. Sofia Y. Leung and Jorge R. López-McKnight (Cambridge, MA: MIT Press, 2021), 45–48; Anastasia Chiu, Fobazi M. Ettarh, and Jennifer A. Ferretti, "Not the Shark but the Water: How Neutrality and Vocational Awe Intertwine to Uphold White Supremacy," in *Knowledge Justice: Disrupting Library and Information Studies through Critical Race Theory*, ed. Sofia Y. Leung and Jorge R. López-McKnight (Cambridge, MA: MIT Press, 2021), 49–71.

13. Fiona Blackburn, "The Intersection between Cultural Competence and Whiteness in Libraries,"

In the Library with the Lead Pipe, December 1, 2015, http://www.inthelibrarywiththeleadpipe. org/2015/culturalcompetence/; Kawanna Bright, "A Woman of Color's Work Is Never Done: Intersectionality, Emotional, and Invisible Labor in Reference and Information Work," in *Knowledge Justice: Disrupting Library and Information Studies through Critical Race Theory*, ed. Sofia Y. Leung and Jorge R. López-McKnight (Cambridge, MA: MIT Press, 2021), 163–95; Jennifer Brown and Sofia Leung, "Authenticity vs. Professionalism: Being True to Ourselves at Work," in *Knowledge Justice: Disrupting Library and Information Studies through Critical Race Theory*, ed. Sofia Y. Leung and Jorge R. López-McKnight (Cambridge, MA: MIT Press, 2021), 329–47; Chiu, Ettarh, and Ferretti, "Not the Shark"; Veronica Arellano Douglas and Joanna Gadsby, eds., *Deconstructing Service in Libraries* (Sacramento, CA: Litwin Books, 2020); April Hathcock, "White Librarianship in Blackface: Diversity Initiatives in LIS," *In the Library with the Lead Pipe*, October 7, 2015, https://www.inthelibrarywiththeleadpipe.org/2015/lis-diversity/; April M. Hathcock and Stephanie Sendaula, "Mapping Whiteness at the Reference Desk," in *Topographies of Whiteness: Mapping Whiteness in Library and Information Science*, ed. Gina Schlesselman-Tarango (Sacramento, CA: Library Juice Press, 2017), 227–56; Homna, "Introduction to Part I"; Melissa Kalpin Prescott, Kristyn Caragher, and Katie Dover-Taylor, "Disrupting Whiteness: Three Perspectives on White Anti-racist Librarianship," in *Topographies of Whiteness: Mapping Whiteness in Library and Information Science*, ed. Gina Schlesselman-Tarango (Sacramento, CA: Library Juice Press, 2017); Megan Watson, "White Feminism and Distributions of Power in Academic Libraries," in *Topographies of Whiteness: Mapping Whiteness in Library and Information Science*, ed. Gina Schlesselman-Tarango (Sacramento, CA: Library Juice Press, 2017), 143–74.

14. Blackburn, "Intersection between Cultural Competence"; Bright, "Woman of Color's Work"; Chiu, Ettarh, and Ferretti, "Not the Shark"; Hathcock, "White Librarianship in Blackface"; Hathcock and Sendaula, "Mapping Whiteness"; Homna, "Introduction to Part I"; Prescott, Caragher, and Dover-Taylor, "Disrupting Whiteness"; Watson, "White Feminism and Distributions of Power."
15. Freire, *Pedagogy of the Oppressed*, 74.
16. Freire, *Pedagogy of the Oppressed*, 71.

Bibliography

Accardi, Maria T. *Feminist Pedagogy for Library Instruction*. Sacramento, CA: Library Juice Press, 2013.

———. "Teaching against the Grain: Critical Assessment in the Library Classroom." In *Critical Library Instruction: Theories and Methods*, edited by Maria T. Accardi, Emily Drabinski, and Alana Kumbier, 251–64. Duluth, MN: Library Juice Press, 2010.

Beatty, Joshua F. "Reading Freire for First World Librarians." Presentation, Canadian Association of Professional Academic Librarians conference, Ottawa, Ontario, Canada, June 2, 2015.

Blackburn, Fiona. "The Intersection between Cultural Competence and Whiteness in Libraries." *In the Library with the Lead Pipe*, December 1, 2015. http://www.inthelibrarywiththeleadpipe.org/2015/culturalcompetence/.

Bostick, Sharon Lee. "The Development and Validation of the Library Anxiety Scale." PhD diss., Wayne State University, 1992.

Bright, Kawanna. "A Woman of Color's Work Is Never Done: Intersectionality, Emotional, and Invisible Labor in Reference and Information Work." In *Knowledge Justice: Disrupting Library and Information Studies through Critical Race Theory*, edited by Sofia Y. Leung and Jorge R. López-McKnight, 163–95. Cambridge, MA: MIT Press, 2021.

Brown, Jennifer, and Sofia Leung. "Authenticity vs. Professionalism: Being True to Ourselves at Work." In *Knowledge Justice: Disrupting Library and Information Studies through Critical Race Theory*, edited by Sofia Y. Leung and Jorge R. López-McKnight, 329–47. Cambridge, MA: MIT Press, 2021.

Chiu, Anastasia, Fobazi M. Ettarh, and Jennifer A. Ferretti. "Not the Shark but the Water: How Neutrality and Vocational Awe Intertwine to Uphold White Supremacy." In *Knowledge Justice: Disrupting Library and Information Studies through Critical Race Theory*, edited by Sofia Y. Leung and Jorge R. López-McKnight, 49–71. Cambridge, MA: MIT Press, 2021.

Cook-Sather, Alison. "Authorizing Student's Perspectives: Toward Trust, Dialogue, and Change in Education." *Educational Researcher* 31, no 4 (2002): 3–14.

———. "The 'Constant Changing of Myself': Revising Roles in Undergraduate Teacher Preparation." *Teacher Education* 41, no. 3 (2006): 187–206.

———. *Education Is Translation: A Metaphor for Change in Learning and Teaching*. Philadelphia: University of Pennsylvania Press, 2006.

———. "From Traditional Accountability to Shared Responsibility: The Benefits and Challenges of Student Consultants Gathering Midcourse Feedback in College Classrooms." *Assessment and Evaluation in Higher Education* 34, no. 2 (2009): 231–41.

———. *Learning from the Student's Perspective: A Sourcebook for Effective Teaching*. Boulder, CO: Paradigm, 2009.

———. "Movements of Mind: The Matrix, Metaphors, and Re-imagining Education." *Teachers College Record* 105, no. 6 (2006): 946–77.

———. "Re(in)forming the Conversations: Student Position, Power, and Voice in Teacher Education." *Radical Teacher* 64 (2002): 21–28.

———. "Resisting the Impositional Potential of Student Voice Work: Lessons for Liberatory Educational Research from Poststructuralist Feminist Critiques of Critical Pedagogy." *Discourse* 28, no. 3 (2007): 389–403.

———. "Sound, Presence, and Power: Exploring 'Student Voice' in Educational Research and Reform." *Curriculum Inquiry* 36, no. 4 (2006): 359–403.

———. "Translation: An Alternative Framework for Conceptualizing and Supporting School Reform Efforts." *Educational Theory* 59, no. 2 (2009): 217–31.

———. "Unrolling Roles in Techno-pedagogy: Toward Collaboration in Traditional College Settings." *Innovative Higher Education* 26, no. 2 (2001): 121–39.

———. "What Would Happen if We Treated Students as Those with Opinions That Matter? The Benefits to Principals and Teachers of Supporting Youth Engagement in School." *NASSP Bulletin* 91, no. 4 (2007): 343–62.

———. "'What You Get Is Looking in the Mirror, Only Better': Inviting Students to Reflect (on) College Teaching." *Reflective Practice* 9, no. 4 (2008): 473–83.

Cook-Sather, Alison, Catherine Bovill, and Peter Felten. *Engaging Students as Partners in Learning and Teaching: A Guide for Faculty*. San Francisco: Jossey-Bass, 2014.

Detlor, Brian, Lorne Booker, Alexander Serenko, and Julien Heidi. "Student Perceptions of Information Literacy Instruction: The Importance of Active Learning." *Education for Information* 29, no. 2 (2012): 147–61.

Douglas, Veronica Arellano, and Joanna Gadsby, eds. *Deconstructing Service in Libraries: Intersections of Identities and Expectations*. Sacramento, CA: Litwin Books, 2020.

Eklof, Ashley. "Understanding Information Anxiety and How Academic Librarians Can Minimize Its Effects." *Public Services Quarterly* 9, no. 3 (2013): 246–58.

Freire, Paulo. *Pedagogy of the Oppressed*, 50th anniversary ed. Translated by Myra Bergman Ramos. New York: Bloomsbury Academic, 2018.

Halpern, Rebecca. "Active Learning Works! Until It Doesn't: Measuring the Effectiveness of Activi-ty-Based Learning Exercises on Information Anxiety." *Journal of Library and Information Services in Distance Learning* 10, no. 3–4 (2016): 242–53.

Hatchard, Desmond B., and Phyllis Toy. "The Psychological Barriers between Library Users and Library Staff: An Exploratory Investigation." *Australian Academic and Research Libraries* 17, no 2. (1986): 63–69.

Hathcock, April. "White Librarianship in Blackface: Diversity Initiatives in LIS." *In the Library with the Lead Pipe*, October 7, 2015. https://www.inthelibrarywiththeleadpipe.org/2015/lis-diversity/.

Hathcock, April M., and Stephanie Sendaula. "Mapping Whiteness at the Reference Desk." In *Topographies of Whiteness: Mapping Whiteness in Library and Information Science*, edited by Gina Schlesselman-Tarango, 227–56. Sacramento, CA: Library Juice Press, 2017.

Homna, Todd. "Introduction to Part I." In *Knowledge Justice: Disrupting Library and Information Studies through Critical Race Theory*, edited by Sofia Y. Leung and Jorge R. López-McKnight, 45–48. Cambridge, MA: MIT Press, 2021.

hooks, bell. *Teaching to Transgress: Education as the Practice of Freedom.* New York: Routledge, 1994.

Jiao, Qun G. and Anthony J. Onwuegbuzie. "Antecedents of Library Anxiety." *Library Quarterly* 67, no. 4 (1997): 372–89.

———. "Perfectionism and Library Anxiety among Graduate Students." *Journal of Academic Librari-anship* 24, no. 5 (1998): 365–72.

———. "Self-Perception and Library Anxiety: An Empirical Study." *Library Review* 48, no. 3 (1999): 140–47.

———. "Sources of Library Anxiety among International Students: Study of Undergraduates at an Urban University in the Northeast." *Urban Library Journal* 11, no. 1 (2001): 16–26.

Jiao, Qun G., Anthony J. Onwuegbuzie, and Art A. Lichtenstein, "Library Anxiety: Characteristics of 'At-Risk' Students." *Library and Information Science Research* 18, no. 2 (1996): 151–63.

Keer, Gretchen. "Critical Pedagogy and Information Literacy in Community Colleges." In *Critical Library Instruction: Theories and Methods*, edited by Maria T. Accardi, Emily Drabinski, and Alana Kumbier, 149–59. Duluth, MN: Library Juice Press, 2010.

Kopp, Bryan M., and Kim Olson-Kopp. "Depositories of Knowledge: Library Instruction and the Development of Critical Consciousness." In *Critical Library Instruction: Theories and Methods*, edited by Maria T. Accardi, Emily Drabinski, and Alana Kumbier, 55–67. Duluth, MN: Library Juice Press, 2010.

Ladenson, Sharon. "Paradigm Shift: Utilizing Critical Feminist Pedagogy in Library Instruction." In *Critical Library Instruction: Theories and Methods*, edited by Maria T. Accardi, Emily Drabinski, and Alana Kumbier, 105–12. Duluth, MN: Library Juice Press, 2010.

Mercer-Mapstone, Lucy, and Sophia Abbott, eds. *The Power of Partnership: Students, Staff, and Faculty Revolutionizing Higher Education.* Elon, NC: Elon University Center for Engaged Learn-ing, 2020.

Onwuegbuzie, Anthony J. "Writing a Research Proposal: The Role of Library Anxiety, Statistics Anxi-ety, and Composition Anxiety." *Library and Information Science Research* 19, no. 1 (1997): 5–33.

Onwuegbuzie, Anthony J., and Qun G. Jiao. "Academic Library Usage: A Comparison of Native and Non-native English Speaking Students." *Australian Library Journal* 46, no. 3 (1997): 258–69.

———. "I'll Go to the Library Later: The Relationship between Academic Procrastination and Library Anxiety." *College and Research Libraries* 61, no. 1 (2000): 45–54.

Prescott, Melissa Kalpin, Kristyn Caragher, and Katie Dover-Taylor. "Disrupting Whiteness: Three Perspectives on White Anti-racist Librarianship." In *Topographies of Whiteness: Mapping White-ness in Library and Information Science*, edited by Gina Schlesselman-Tarango. Sacramento, CA: Library Juice Press, 2017.

Ross, Alanna, and Christine Furno. "Active Learning in the Library Instruction Environment: An Exploratory Study." *portal: Libraries and the Academy* 11, no. 4 (2011): 953–70.

Simpson, Shannon R. "Google Spreadsheets and Real-Time Assessment: Instant Feedback for Library Instruction." *College and Research Libraries News* 73, no. 9 (2012): 528–49.

Sinkinson, Caroline, and Mary Caton Lingold. "Re-visioning the Library Seminar through a Lens of Critical Pedagogy." In *Critical Library Instruction: Theories and Methods*, edited by Maria T. Accardi, Emily Drabinski, and Alana Kumbier, 81–88. Duluth, MN: Library Juice Press, 2010.

Swope, Mary Jane, and Jeffrey Katzer. "Why Don't They Ask Questions?" *Reference Quarterly* 12, no. 2 (1972): 161–66.

Watson, Megan. "White Feminism and Distributions of Power in Academic Libraries." In *Topographies of Whiteness: Mapping Whiteness in Library and Information Science*, edited by Gina Schlesselman-Tarango, 227–56. Sacramento, CA: Library Juice Press, 2017.

Werder, Carmen, and Megan M. Otis, eds. *Engaging Student Voices in the Study of Teaching and Learning*. Sterling, VA: Stylus, 2010.

CHAPTER 37

Learning to Put People First

Cultural Humility, Funds of Knowledge, and Information Literacy Instruction with First-Generation Students

Darren Ilett

Introduction

When I accepted an information literacy (IL) librarian position at a midsize public university four years ago, I was excited to start my new career. I would teach IL courses and one-shot sessions and serve as the liaison for two federally funded TRIO programs that foster the academic success of "low-income individuals, first-generation college students, and individuals with disabilities."[1] Yet I also felt I had much to prove—to students, colleagues, administrators, and myself. After having failed midpoint tenure review in another field and subsequently weathering six years of under- and unemployment, I viewed this new job as my last chance for success in academia.

Fortunately, I have learned much from TRIO students and from colleagues dedicated to student success. They have helped me move from a self-conscious focus on my own performance to an emphasis instead on cultural humility, learning about students' lived experiences as assets, and fostering their success. I have begun to recognize some of the harm I have caused as an instructor with mostly privileged

social identities, including white, middle-class, cisgender, and male, who works with students who have mostly minoritized identities, such as first-generation, low-income, and Black, Indigenous, and People of Color (BIPOC). In this essay, I share key learning moments in my development as an educator, use the lenses of cultural humility and funds of knowledge to reflect critically on those moments, and share ways I have changed my professional praxis as a consequence.

Key Learning Moments

Two early experiences in my current position challenged my approach to teaching. Part of my approach was to "catch" students in "bad" behavior. I worried that common student behaviors—looking at cell phones, working on assignments from other classes, missing class, and so on—were a referendum on my teaching. To me, they were signs that I was not engaging enough and that students were not taking the material seriously. I feared that students would "get away with" not preparing for class or learning course content. This approach demanded constant vigilance. It was exhausting for me and hurtful to students.

The first key learning moment unsettled this perspective. I was moving about the classroom, checking on students during a group activity. I stopped at Miguel's (a pseudonym) group and said, "Oh, *now* you're watching the video! That was homework." My intention was to manage time and improve future behavior by signaling that I noticed the group's lack of preparation. As I turned away, Miguel muttered, "*baboso!*" (idiot, creep). I turned back around, laughed, and asked incredulously what he had said. Fortunately, Miguel was willing to share why he was angry. I had insulted his group by assuming they were unprepared. Not only was I mistaken, my comment also echoed a history of racist and classist abuse. "Everyone always thinks we're bad students," he told me. This comment stuck with me. I had been thinking only of my own perspective and had not considered my impact on students. I was not thinking consciously about my own social identities as a white, cisgender, male professor or their identities as low-income, first-generation, BIPOC students when I made the comment, but both played a central role in the students' experience of the incident. My tendency toward control and not letting any "misbehavior" go unremarked alienated students, reinforced stereotypes about BIPOC students, and sent the message that they did not belong in college, whether or not they did their work. I was harming the very people I had been hired to support. Miguel's willingness to share his perspective was an invaluable gift that made me aware of some of the impact I had on students.

A second learning moment came a year later when Jennifer (a pseudonym) missed several class sessions and deadlines. She also appeared withdrawn from classmates. I knew she had recently joined the TRIO program, while the others had bonded the previous semester. Several times I asked how she was doing, offered help, and encouraged her to attend TRIO events. She dismissed my concerns, insisting everything was all right. Eventually, I discovered an obstacle in our communication: me. I did not understand her research interest, namely the role of internalized misogyny in women's perpetuation of sexism. I arrogantly assumed and therefore perceived only ignorance and confusion because Jennifer's description of her project was not packaged in academic language. My default lens was deficit thinking,[2] and it caused me to overlook Jennifer's complex and important research topic and the intellectual contribution she could make based on lived experience. My dismissiveness and frustration were steeped in the sexism, racism, and classism typical of academia. Once I finally understood and expressed my enthusiasm for her project, Jennifer was also more excited and sought out my help. She also shared some struggles outside of college, including family issues. As with Miguel, Jennifer's continuing willingness to engage with me despite my hurtful behavior was a gift. This incident made me wonder how often I had allowed the elitist, gatekeeping language and conventions of the academy to hinder my understanding of students and consequently limit their ability to pursue their research interests, succeed in my classes, and attain a sense of belonging in college. Jennifer and I developed a level of trust only because she did not give up on me.

As a result of such incidents, I now understand that student behavior usually has little or nothing to do with my performance as a teacher. Instead, it hints at the pressures in their lives: working several jobs, caring for family, and dealing with food and housing insecurity, among many others. Their lives are full and complex; they are much more than students in my class. I now approach students with an eagerness to learn from them in recognition of the fact that I do not know what stressors they are facing, what their cultures are and what role those cultures play in their college experiences, what they have already accomplished, and what they are capable of. When issues arise, my goal is to provide care and support rather than admonishment. I have also switched from deficit thinking to asset-based approaches and assume that students are competent learners, creative thinkers, and effective problem solvers and that they bring to the IL classroom knowledge and skills from their lives outside formal education. This change in perspective often contributes to an improved classroom atmosphere and increased student motivation to learn IL content, as other LIS researchers have also found.[3] Ironically, though I thought I was emphasizing content in the past, my policing of behavior often ignored the students in the room as full human beings, thereby impeding their development of deeper connections with the IL content I cared so much about. My priorities were backward. People have to come first.

Theory

What I have learned from Miguel, Jennifer, and others aligns with cultural humility. Melanie Tervalon and Jann Murray-García introduced the term in the context of physician training as a corrective to cultural competence understood narrowly as "an easily demonstrable mastery of a finite body of knowledge."[4] Instead, cultural humility emphasizes a lifelong process of self-evaluation, addressing power imbalances, and cultivating "mutually beneficial and non-paternalistic partnerships."[5] Since its emergence over two decades ago, cultural humility has found resonance in such fields as social work and education. Recent explorations of cultural humility in librarianship have deepened my understanding of the concept in my own praxis as an IL librarian.

First, cultural humility has several affective features. David A. Hurley, Sarah R. Kostelecky, and Lori Townsend argue that cultural humility does not consist of self-deprecation—as *humility* might imply—but rather a willingness to engage in accurate self-assessment along with an orientation outward toward other people.[6] It requires a realization that "*my norms aren't the only norms, and unfamiliar norms aren't necessarily wrong*."[7] In addition, cultural humility calls for openness to the importance of culture in an interaction "without anticipating what exactly it will be."[8] We must accept that we cannot fully know what someone brings to an interaction because each person experiences their culture in unique ways, including the intersection of multiple social identities.[9] Yet not all aspects of one's identity or culture play equal roles in an interaction, and instead may vary by context.[10] Further, Twanna Hodge argues that we should not reduce people to "their visible group affiliation," for there may be others of equal or greater significance to them.[11] Cultural humility involves remaining open-minded, avoiding a sense of superiority, acknowledging gaps in one's knowledge, and seeking to learn rather than instruct.[12]

This can prove challenging for instructors who feel the need to project control. Yet a second aspect of cultural humility is the imperative to identify and redress power imbalances inherent in such controlling approaches. Several LIS authors call for learning about one's own cultures and biases, as well as the (unconscious) social scripts one follows in interactions.[13] One of my scripts is the need to appear knowledgeable about course content and competent in classroom management. This relates to my insecurities as a new librarian and as a first-generation student myself. However, adherence to this script only compounds my authoritative role in the classroom and places students in a relatively powerless position. When I called out Miguel's group for apparently not being prepared, I did not consider my own privileged identities and relatively powerful position as their instructor and representative of the library and university.[14]

Third, practicing cultural humility requires that I examine the (unconscious) biases I bring to the classroom. With Miguel's group, I was focused on time management. However, my implicit bias that BIPOC students, low-income students, and first-generation students are unprepared was at play, even if unconsciously. In addition, we should consider not only our own biases, but also how others see us.[15] As Miguel shared with me, my actions were part of a history of abuse he experienced with teachers. My role as instructor and my privileged social identities exacerbated the imbalance of power and added to his history of abuse. Hodge calls on us to be "aware that communities suffer from historical trauma."[16] I had the privilege of ignoring the power imbalance and remaining unaware of his history of trauma, but Miguel did not. Yet cultural humility calls on us to pay attention and learn, even and especially when it proves difficult. It involves identifying our own biases and scripts, considering how others may see us, avoiding stereotyping, and not reducing people to their visible social identities.[17]

A fourth aspect of cultural humility is relationship building.[18] The affective features, consideration of power dynamics, and self-evaluation described above help create the foundation for mutually beneficial relationships. However, Hodge also urges us to honor what people bring to an interaction and to meet people where they are rather than where we expect them to be.[19] These aspects of cultural humility resonate with another pedagogical approach, namely funds of knowledge. Norma González, Luis C. Moll, and Cathy Amanti write that the term "is based on a simple premise: People are competent, they have knowledge, and their life experiences have given them that knowledge."[20] Though originally practiced in elementary education, funds of knowledge can also serve as a strong foundation for further learning in college.[21] For example, if I had encouraged Jennifer to share and explore the funds of knowledge she developed outside of college, I could have better understood her proposed research topic relating to her lived experience. Discussing and building on students' funds of knowledge demonstrates that who they are and what they know matters in college-level learning. Furthermore, valuing students' funds of knowledge can help redress power imbalances by including their input when selecting course content. Learning from students and sharing our own funds of knowledge can help foster more reciprocal and mutually beneficial relationships in the classroom and therefore aligns with cultural humility.

Praxis

My interactions with students, critical reflection, and engagement with research have informed several changes in how I show up in the classroom and how I structure IL instruction. First, I work to redress power imbalances in the classroom by including students in decisions about what and how we learn together. Using an online discussion board, students in my credit courses provide anonymous input about course policies regarding attendance, class participation, and late work. I make this first step anonymous to encourage them to share openly. Then we decide on the policies together, giving them ownership over course policies.

In credit courses, students also nominate topics and vote on them in a March-Madness-style bracket.[22] The winning topic becomes the example throughout the course. Students serve as research consultants to develop a research question, search for sources, identify themes in the literature, and so on. We find solutions to challenges together. Recently, students chose vaccines as the topic, and we narrowed it to the medical field's historical and continuing abuse and neglect of Black communities and the consequent impact on COVID-19 vaccination rates. Students display enthusiasm when they are actively involved in decisions affecting their learning and can choose topics relating to their lived experiences.[23] Activities like this position students as experts and capable members of the college community, just as they are outside school.

A second aspect of cultural humility, building relationships, is equally important. At the beginning of credit courses students complete a confidential online survey about their research experience, interests, and responsibilities outside of college. They can also tell me their name (if different from the one in the roster), their pronouns, and anything else they would like to share. In one-shot instruction sessions, I employ a similar activity using online discussion boards with fewer questions. The information allows me to gauge students' research experience, assist them in developing research topics, and understand their stressors outside of college. It also shows that I care about them as people. Since relationships are reciprocal, I share similar information about myself to serve as a model and build trust.

Additionally, in credit classes students check in with each other about how they are dealing with stress, keeping in touch with family, and doing in their lives generally. At these times, I also share my own challenges. We brainstorm strategies for time management, self-care, and other life areas. Such activities build community and normalize both struggling and help-seeking.

Another strategy for building community in both credit classes and one-shot sessions is to dedicate class sessions to family members, friends, coaches, or teachers. Students share how someone supported them or helped them get to college. This honors their social networks, which is particularly important for first-generation students who often experience tension between college and home.[24] I also share about my own experiences as a first-generation student and dedicate class sessions to my sister who inspired and supported me to go to college.

A third aspect of cultural humility and also funds of knowledge is to build on what students bring to college. In credit courses and one-shot sessions, students brainstorm issues relating to their lives at the level of family, community, the US, and the world. I share examples from my own life, including being bullied for being gay in a conservative town in Oregon, working in my father's carpentry shop as a child, and being a first-generation student. Sharing how my identities inform my current research demonstrates that lived experiences and identities are valid foundations for research. Recently, students pursued projects related to their identities and future careers: a business major conducted a project on Latina entrepreneurs, and an education major researched first-generation students and barriers to higher education.

Another strategy in credit courses and one-shot sessions is to encourage students to use information sources they are already aware of. Students frequently interview friends, family, or community members. One student found YouTube interviews with Deaf students about their school experiences because published research excluded their perspectives. If students are encouraged to build on their funds of knowledge, including sources of information outside typical IL curricula, they often choose to do so, are more motivated to complete research projects, and experience more meaningful learning.[25]

Making inclusion and equity a central part of my own and my library's professional praxis requires ongoing commitment. Several practices help hold me accountable, another important feature of cultural humility.[26] I regularly journal after teaching, particularly regarding inclusion and equity issues. An area of improvement for me would be to include questions about equity and inclusion when I ask students for feedback on IL instruction. Colleagues and I observe each other's sessions and give feedback on whatever aspect the respective instructor has chosen to focus on, such as encouraging discussion among students or incorporating diverse topics and information sources. With the aim of encouraging candid dialogue, participation is voluntary and not tied to performance reviews. On an institutional level, my department holds regular meetings where we take turns choosing readings and leading discussions on inclusion and equity topics. These are held off campus and not related to performance reviews to foster a brave space to challenge each other and be honest in self-evaluation. My library also holds professional development sessions on inclusion and equity issues. I led a session on funds of knowledge, and colleagues and I are discussing a future session on cultural humility. In these ways, we make working toward inclusion and equity an integral and ongoing part of our individual and collective professional praxis.

Conclusion

A combination of key learning moments with students, self-reflection, and exploring inclusive and equitable theories has helped me begin putting people first instead of concerns about course content and behavior. I encourage IL librarians to remain open to learning from the difficult, messy moments when we inadvertently cause students harm. Rather than castigating ourselves, we can use those moments to learn how to work with students more equitably by honoring who they are and what they contribute to our shared learning. Inclusive and equitable approaches such as cultural humility and funds of knowledge provide IL librarians practices we can engage in to work toward those goals.

Notes

1.   US Department of Education, Federal TRIO Programs home page, last modified July 23, 2021, https://www2.ed.gov/about/offices/list/ope/trio/index.html.

2.   Richard R. Valencia, *Dismantling Contemporary Deficit Thinking* (New York: Routledge, 2010), chap. 1, https://doi.org/10.4324/9780203853214.

3.   Amanda L. Folk, "Drawing on Students' Funds of Knowledge: Using Identity and Lived Experience to Join the Conversation in Research Assignments," *Journal of Information Literacy* 12, no. 2 (December 2018): 44–59, https://doi.org/10.11645/12.2.2468; Kim L. Morrison, "Informed Asset-Based Pedagogy: Coming Correct, Counter-stories from an Information Literacy Classroom," *Library Trends* 66, no. 2 (Fall 2017): 176–218, https://doi.org/10.1353/lib.2017.0034.

4.   Melanie Tervalon and Jann Murray-García, "Cultural Humility versus Cultural Competence: A Critical Distinction in Defining Physician Training Outcomes in Multicultural Education," *Journal of Health Care for the Poor and Underserved* 9, no. 2 (1998): 118, https://doi.org/10.1353/hpu.2010.0233.

5.   Tervalon and Murray-Garcia, "Cultural Humility," 123.

6.   David A. Hurley, Sarah R. Kostelecky, and Lori Townsend, "Cultural Humility in Libraries," *Reference Services Review* 47, no. 4 (2019): 548, https://doi.org/10.1108/RSR-06-2019-0042.

7.   Hurley, Kostelecky, and Townsend, "Cultural Humility in Libraries," 549.

8.   Hurley, Kostelecky, and Townsend, "Cultural Humility in Libraries," 550.

9.   Elizabeth Foster, "Cultural Competence in Library Instruction: A Reflective Practice Approach," *portal: Libraries and the Academy* 18, no. 3 (2018): 579, https://doi.org/10.1353/pla.2018.0034.

10. Hurley, Kostelecky, and Townsend, "Cultural Humility in Libraries," 551.

11. Twanna Hodge, "Integrating Cultural Humility into Public Services Librarianship," *International Information and Library Review* 51, no. 3 (2019): 271, https://doi.org/10.1080/10572317.2019.1629070.

12. Hodge, "Integrating Cultural Humility," 271; Hurley, Kostelecky, and Townsend, "Cultural Humility in Libraries," 549; Foster, "Cultural Competence in Library Instruction," 580.

13. Xan Y. Goodman and Ruby L. Nugent, "Teaching Cultural Competence and Cultural Humility in Dental Medicine," *Medical Reference Services Quarterly* 39, no. 4 (2020): 318, https://doi.org/10.1080/02763869.2020.1826183; Hodge, "Integrating Cultural Humility," 269; Hurley, Kostelecky, and Townsend, "Cultural Humility in Libraries," 553; Rajesh Singh, "Promoting Civic Engagement through Cultivating Culturally Competent Self-Reflexive Information Professionals," *Journal of the Australian Library and Information Association* 69, no. 3 (2020): 313, https://doi.org/10.1080/24750158.2020.1777635; Julie Winkelstein, "Social Justice in Action: Cultural Humility, Scripts, and the LIS Classroom," in *Teaching for Justice: Implementing Social Justice in the LIS Classroom*, ed. Nicole A. Cooke and Miriam E. Sweeney (Sacramento, CA: Library Juice Press, 2017), 153.

14. Winkelstein, "Social Justice in Action," 155.

15. Hodge, "Integrating Cultural Humility," 269.

16. Hodge, "Integrating Cultural Humility," 271.

17. Hurley, Kostelecky, and Townsend, "Cultural Humility in Libraries," 550; Hodge, "Integrating Cultural Humility," 271.

18. Foster, "Cultural Competence in Library Instruction," 580; Goodman and Nugent, "Teaching Cultural Competence," 319; Tervalon and Murray-García, "Cultural Humility versus Cultural Competence," 123.

19. Hodge, "Integrating Cultural Humility," 271, 273.

20. Norma González, Luis C. Moll, and Cathy Amanti, preface in *Funds of Knowledge*, ed. Norma

González, Luis C. Moll, and Cathy Amanti (New York: Routledge, 2005), ix–x.
21. Cecilia Rios-Aguilar and Judy Marquez Kiyama, "Introduction: The Need for a Funds of Knowledge Approach in Higher Education Contexts," in *Funds of Knowledge in Higher Education: Honoring Students' Cultural Experiences and Resources as Strengths*, ed. Judy Marquez Kiyama and Cecilia Rios-Aguilar (New York: Routledge, 2018), 5.
22. Darren Ilett, "Course Topic Bracket Lesson Plan," Open Educational Resources, Information Literacy, no. 25, University of Northern Colorado, June 2021, https://digscholarship.unco.edu/infolit/25/.
23. Folk, "Drawing on Students' Funds of Knowledge," 54–56.
24. Rashné Rustom Jehangir, *Higher Education and First-Generation Students* (New York: Palgrave Macmillan, 2010), 21–24; Lee Ward, Michael J. Siegel, and Zebulun Davenport, *First-Generation College Students* (San Francisco: Jossey-Bass, 2012), 73–74.
25. Folk, "Drawing on Students' Funds of Knowledge," 54–56
26. Goodman and Nugent, "Teaching Cultural Competence," 318; Winkelstein, "Social Justice in Action," 151.

Bibliography

Folk, Amanda L. "Drawing on Students' Funds of Knowledge: Using Identity and Lived Experience to Join the Conversation in Research Assignments." *Journal of Information Literacy* 12, no. 2 (December 2018): 44–59. https://doi.org/10.11645/12.2.2468.

Foster, Elizabeth. "Cultural Competence in Library Instruction: A Reflective Practice Approach." *portal: Libraries and the Academy* 18, no. 3 (2018): 575–93. https://doi.org/10.1353/pla.2018.0034.

González, Norma, Luis C. Moll, and Cathy Amanti, eds. *Funds of Knowledge: Theorizing Practices in Households, Communities, and Classrooms.* New York: Routledge, 2005.

Goodman, Xan Y., and Ruby L. Nugent. "Teaching Cultural Competence and Cultural Humility in Dental Medicine." *Medical Reference Services Quarterly* 39, no. 4 (2020): 309–22. https://doi.org/10.1080/02763869.2020.1826183.

Hodge, Twanna. "Integrating Cultural Humility into Public Services Librarianship." *International Information and Library Review* 51, no. 3 (2019): 268–74. https://doi.org/10.1080/10572317.2019.1629070.

Hurley, David A., Sarah R. Kostelecky, and Lori Townsend. "Cultural Humility in Libraries." *Reference Services Review* 47, no. 4 (2019): 544–55. https://doi.org/10.1108/RSR-06-2019-0042.

Ilett, Darren. "Course Topic Bracket Lesson Plan." Open Educational Resources, Information Literacy, no. 25. University of Northern Colorado, June 2021. https://digscholarship.unco.edu/infolit/25/.

Jehangir, Rashné Rustom. *Higher Education and First-Generation Students: Cultivating Community, Voice, and Place for the New Majority.* New York: Palgrave Macmillan, 2010.

Morrison, Kim L. "Informed Asset-Based Pedagogy: Coming Correct, Counter-stories from an Information Literacy Classroom." *Library Trends* 66, no. 2 (Fall 2017): 176–218. https://doi.org/10.1353/lib.2017.0034.

Rios-Aguilar, Cecilia, and Judy Marquez Kiyama. "Introduction: The Need for a Funds of Knowledge Approach in Higher Education Contexts." In *Funds of Knowledge in Higher Education: Honoring Students' Cultural Experiences and Resources as Strengths*, edited by Judy Marquez Kiyama and Cecilia Rios-Aguilar, 3–6. New York: Routledge, 2018.

Singh, Rajesh. "Promoting Civic Engagement through Cultivating Culturally Competent Self-Reflex-ive Information Professionals." *Journal of the Australian Library and Information Association* 69, no. 3 (2020): 303–16. https://doi.org/10.1080/24750158.2020.1777635.

Tervalon, Melanie, and Jann Murray-García. "Cultural Humility versus Cultural Competence: A Critical Distinction in Defining Physician Training Outcomes in Multicultural Education." *Journal of Health Care for the Poor and Underserved* 9, no. 2 (1998): 117–25. https://doi.org/10.1353/hpu.2010.0233.

US Department of Education. Federal TRIO Programs home page. Last modified July 23, 2021. https://www2.ed.gov/about/offices/list/ope/trio/index.html.

Valencia, Richard R. *Dismantling Contemporary Deficit Thinking: Educational Thought and Practice.* New York: Routledge, 2010. https://doi.org/10.4324/9780203853214.

Ward, Lee, Michael J. Siegel, and Zebulun Davenport. *First-Generation College Students: Understanding and Improving the Experience from Recruitment to Commencement.* San Francisco: Jossey-Bass, 2012.

Winkelstein, Julie. "Social Justice in Action: Cultural Humility, Scripts, and the LIS Classroom." In *Teaching for Justice: Implementing Social Justice in the LIS Classroom*, edited by Nicole A. Cooke and Miriam E. Sweeney, 139–68. Sacramento, CA: Library Juice Press, 2017.

CHAPTER 38

Applying Columbia University's *Guide for Inclusive Teaching* to the One-Shot

A Reflective Essay

Breanne Crumpton and Michelle K. Mitchell

Land Acknowledgement

We would like to acknowledge the stolen lands our institutions currently stand on. Appalachian State University is on the lands of the Cherokee and the Catawba native peoples. Syracuse University is on the lands of the Onondaga and the Haudenos-aunee native peoples. We recognize and acknowledge their displacement, dispossession, and continuing presence.

Introduction

Around the country, colleges and universities are increasingly recognizing the power and benefits of inclusive teaching and learning.[1] Inclusive teaching includes goals such as creating an inclusive course climate, getting to know students as individuals, ensuring diverse content, and creating space for productive discussions and cultural learning.[2] Many campuses offer centers for teaching and learning or workshops and programs related to inclusive teaching for faculty members' development.[3] However, these are often directed only at teaching faculty with credit-bearing courses and not customized to the type of teaching done by librarians. Some programs include adjunct faculty, or refer to participants as instructors, but do not actively recognize or include librarians in the narrative.[4] There is a gap in the literature surrounding teaching practices in higher education about including librarians within the centers for teaching and learning.* Academic instruction librarians have a responsibility to students to incorporate inclusive teaching practices into library instruction sessions. In this reflective essay, the authors consider how inclusive teaching training for faculty can be applied to the teaching done by librarians, particularly in relation to the one-shot format.

Critical reflection is an important part of inclusive teaching. To be inclusive teachers, we need to understand what kind of teacher we are, how our identities and beliefs impact the decisions we make in lesson planning, and how our positionality affects classroom dynamics. The authors acknowledge their own positionality as both cis, white women, and early-career librarians who are at the beginning of their inclusive pedagogical journey. As librarians, we need to consistently reflect and evaluate what assumptions we are making about students, how they learn, and what they need to know to succeed. As you read through our reflective essay, we also ask you to reflect on who you are, how you carry your identity, and how the biases and assumptions you have can hinder you from creating an inclusive lesson plan.

In 2016, Columbia University created an Inclusive Teaching Working Group on the back of a successful Inclusive Teaching Forum.[5] This working group, co-chaired by Dr. Christine Simonian Bean and Dr. Amanda M. Jungels, decided an inclusive teaching guide would be the best way to continue the work. The authors of this reflective essay expand upon the working group's efforts through examining how the inclusive teaching guide can be extended to library instruction. Therefore, the authors will focus on the *Guide for Inclusive Teaching at Columbia* released in fall 2017 by the Inclusive Teaching Working Group and its five principles outlined around inclusive teaching (Guide, 6-7).[6] Librarians looking to change their teaching strategies can benefit from inclusive teaching practices. The authors will give a brief overview of each principle, identify relevant teaching strategies, and discuss

---

* The authors acknowledge there is an abundance of literature exploring critical librarianship practices, which encompasses inclusive teaching. For deeper understanding of what we are referring to, please check out the following: Andrea Wright et al., "Inclusive Pedagogy for Library Instruction: Complete Annotated Bibliography," Inclusive Pedagogy for Library Instruction, last modified June 5, 2020, https://library.sewanee.edu/ip4li/annotated_bib; Emily Drabinski, "What Is Critical about Critical Librarianship?" *Art Libraries Journal* 44, special issue no. 2 (2019): 51, https://doi.org/10.1017/alj.2019.3.

considerations when adapting the principles for library instruction. We acknowledge that incorporating these practices takes time and these ideas for incorporating inclusive teaching practices into your instruction can happen slowly and not all at once.

Principle 1: Establish and Support a Class Climate That Fosters Belonging for All Students

One of the most pervasive aspects through the Columbia guide is creating a class climate that is inclusive and addresses the learning needs of all students (Guide, 8). We see the importance of class climate throughout the five principles, along with having a robust understanding of students' identities and experiences they bring with them into the classroom (Guide, 8). Instructors often default to teaching based on their own "beliefs and assumptions about what students do and should know and what they can do and should be able to do" if they do not take the time to learn about their students (Guide, 8). Appert and colleagues explain that the course climate manifests itself in the "design and delivery of [the] course," a commitment to help students achieve "high standards," and seeking opportunities for "shared meaning" between students and the instructor (Guide, 8, 10, 8). The rapport between instructors and students, and also between students themselves, can contribute to an inclusive course climate. Instructors need to be aware of microaggressions to avoid using them and to know how to address them as they arise in the classroom.

Adapting Relevant Teaching Strategies from the Guide

- "Build instructor-student rapport," (Guide, 9).
  - o "Reduce anonymity" through learning students' names (Guide, 10). In an online environment, it is easy to learn students' names as they are often built into the virtual classroom. This can be mimicked in a physical classroom through allowing students to create placards where they can display their preferred names and pronouns. Be sure to model this yourself either through a name tag or through prominently displaying your name and pronouns somewhere in the classroom space.

○ Use a pre-class survey to help you learn more about the students' prior knowledge and experiences they are bringing to your classroom.

○ Share information about yourself, including how you choose to approach research.

○ Be up-front about any struggles you have with research and in navigating databases and other concepts. Oftentimes because we are limited to the one-shot, we have practiced examples that can make research seem easier than it is. Soliciting search suggestions from students and allowing yourself to become flustered or not conduct a "perfect" search can help break down barriers for the students and how they view their own ability to research.

○ Solicit topics from students to show an interest in their ideas. When a student volunteers an answer, consider repeating their answer back to them to validate their words. This will reinforce the student's idea and let them know you were engaged with their response.

- "Build student-student rapport," (Guide, 10).

  ○ Consider in-class activities that have them conversing and working with their peers, whether it is a think-pair-share or a group activity.

  ○ Create activities that allow students to bring their past research experiences and knowledge to the table and share with their classmates.

- "Treat each student as an individual," (Guide, 10).

  ○ Ensure you are "pronouncing their names correctly." Allow students to self-identify if they feel comfortable, but do not assume their identity group (Guide, 10).

- "Avoid making assumptions about students' abilities based on stereotypes," (Guide, 10).

  ○ "Be mindful of existing stereotypes," (Guide, 11). What assumptions do we have about students' research abilities, and how do we perpetuate them? For example, we assume students will wait until the last minute to do their research. This assumption can create a deficit mindset approach, however, that leads us to stress to them that research takes time and to start early.*

---

* *Deficit mindset* refers to the practice of labeling certain groups of students as "at risk" because of their struggles to conform to the cultural norms of academia. It places emphasis on the students needing to assimilate and change, as opposed to the institutional culture and barriers. For more on the pervasiveness of deficit mindset in LIS literature, see resources such as the book *Academic Library Services for First-Generation Students* and the article "Dismantling Deficit Thinking: A Strengths-Based Inquiry into the Experiences of Transfer Students in and out of Academic Libraries" listed in the suggested further readings at the end of this essay.

- o Focus instead on "behavioral and controllable actions"—for example, suggesting students schedule a research consultation for more help (Guide, 11).

- "Convey the same level of confidence in the abilities of all your students," (Guide, 11).

  - o Set high standards for all students. When teaching an upper-level class, we might reemphasize some searching basics because we assume some students have not had library instruction before. Instead of lowering standards to meet your assumptions about these groups, give assurance of your support and belief in students' abilities, and emphasize your ability to help them succeed (Guide, 11).
  - o Scaffold instruction in your sessions and throughout the curriculum to help in avoiding assumptions and encourage student success.

- "Address challenging classroom moments head-on," (Guide, 11).

  - o Name microaggressions. The library instruction classroom is not immune to microaggressions and offensive behaviors. If it happens on your watch, make sure to stop, name what happened, and give students space to reflect and recoup (Guide, 11).
  - o Make sure any discussions focus on "issues or comments, not individuals," (Guide, 11).
  - o Follow up with the faculty after the class if needed.

Considerations and Challenges in the One-Shot

Library instruction faces challenges when considering course climate, like time and being a guest in someone else's classroom space. The biggest challenge facing librarians with one-shot library instruction is often the clock. An inclusive course climate requires careful consideration of who is in your space and what experiences students bring with them. We often have little time to cover even what we feel is necessary for students to learn and are only seeing these students once. So how can we reasonably learn enough about the students to create an inclusive course climate in our short time with them?

We have to work to find a balance between covering the content for that particular session and giving students the space and ability to utilize their voice and knowledge. This balance can be challenging to achieve in the face of faculty who have a list of topics they want covered and are offering only one class session for us to present this information. One option might be to work with the faculty to prioritize what is important to learn in person and offer asynchronous materials to cover the other requested topics. This approach could then free up space and time for more reflective activities.

We additionally have to take into consideration the course climate that is already being established by the teaching faculty member and how our teaching practices either fit or digress from these established norms. We may be able to grasp some of the elements of the course climate in our planning conversations with faculty, but things such as tone or attitude do not always come out explicitly. Likewise, we might ask faculty about their students beforehand, but it is hard to grasp the various dimensions of students' identity through the eyes of another.

Principle 2: Set Explicit Student Expectations

Communication in terms of learning objectives and assessment can help students be motivated and successful. Course goals should be clearly articulated, and the assignments should reflect those set for the course (Guide, 14). Instructors should pair each assignment with clear criteria for assessment so students understand how they will be graded (Guide, 14). Scaffolding assignments and giving timely feedback can help ensure students are on the right track and have the skills they need to be successful (Guide, 15). Other ways to be transparent in communicating expectations include giving "examples of exemplary work," "discussing common mistakes," and creating "community agreements" so that students have a participatory role in creating the expectations and norms for the classroom (Guide, 16, 14, 15, 14).

Adapting Relevant Teaching Strategies from the Guide

- "Articulate assessment criteria," (Guide, 15).

  - Ask the teaching faculty for the rubric in addition to any assignment instructions so you know how the research component will be graded to reinforce and reiterate any requirements during your library instruction session.
  - Consider in-class activities that help reinforce their assignment's rubrics. For example, have students practice evaluating a source to see if it fits the assignment, or give them an example bibliography and form groups of students to see how it might be graded based on the assignment's rubric.

○ Discuss with faculty if their rubric is realistic when it comes to source requirements and other research components. Sometimes teaching faculty assume there are plenty of sources for a given assignment when in fact the topic might not be as widely covered as they expect or are not available in your library's subscriptions.

- "Provide timely feedback," (Guide, 15).

○ Build in time to assess any activities you plan, such as reporting out, so you can make sure students are on the right track before they leave the classroom. Make sure you are clearly communicating any kind of reporting out you expect from the onset of any planned activities.

○ Be reflective in how you might need to modify your teaching moving forward when receiving student feedback (Guide, 15).

○ Incorporate formative feedback strategies during your session.*

- "Provide examples of exemplary work," (Guide, 16).

○ Provide models of disciplinary research papers or annotated bibliographies so students have an idea of expectations around certain types of assignments. A supplementary research guide is helpful for showcasing these examples and allows students to see what successful research might look like and the types of sources their professor expects.

- "Model expected behaviors," (Guide, 16).

○ Model the skills students are expected to demonstrate during an in-class activity.

○ "Be aware that you are modeling expected behavior," (Guide, 16). Reflect on how your behavior, intentional or not, can impact how they view research, and make sure your behavior imitates the established course climate. However, keep in mind that white cultural norms are centered in academia.

Considerations and Challenges in the One-Shot

A big part of this principle involves establishing community agreements and discussion guidelines as a joint effort between instructor and students. These guidelines give students a sense of agency over the course environment and provide direction in moments of discomfort. During one-shot instruction, we are entering into the course climate set by the teaching faculty. Even when we bring students into our

---

* See *Classroom Assessment Techniques for Librarians* in suggested further readings.

own spaces, the norms and expectations set by their instructor prior to coming to us are still in play. Communicating with faculty ahead of time to see what their established guidelines or agreements for communication are is a great place to start to make sure we are modeling the expected behavior. The syllabus often has codes of conducts or behavioral expectations if you are not able to get this information from the faculty directly.

We need to make sure our instruction session aligns with the skills and knowledge students are expected to take away from the course to ensure clearly articulated course goals and learning objectives. Sharing our instruction learning objectives at the start of class helps students know what to take away from the session and how any skills they gain relate back to their assignment and course. Any planned activity for the session should also include articulating your expectations on what students will accomplish.

Feedback is just as important as objectives and goals in setting expectations. Try to provide feedback within the instruction session; however, if you run out of time to do so, follow up with the faculty member after. Formative feedback strategies can allow for clarity on any muddy points during the class, but think strategically about what strategies will provide the best level of feedback for your instruction plan and how you plan to communicate the results.

Principle 3: Select Course Content That Recognizes Diversity and Acknowledges Barriers to Inclusion

The heartbeat of a course is found in the supporting learning materials. Course content comes in the form of readings, documentaries, spoken examples, movies, songs, poems, learning activities, LibGuides, and other relevant learning media. The content shared in classrooms influences learning outcomes, student perceptions of content, and the classroom environment. An inclusive classroom cannot be achieved if the learning content itself is not inclusive and sensitive to multiple experiences (Guide, 18).

Instructors with established courses will need to critically examine the content they provide to their students. It is important to note that this applies to all subject matters. There are no neutral subjects, and everything should be taught through a critical lens. Addressing shortcomings and being transparent about how disciplines fall short in acknowledging diversity is a good place to start. Instructors should not include marginalized voices to tokenize them when developing new courses or introducing new material but should, instead, make sure to actively engage and validate marginalized authors into the course content.

Adapting Relevant Teaching Strategies from the Guide

- "Select content that engages a diversity of ideas and perspectives," (Guide, 19).

  ○ Remind students that educational degrees are not the only way folks have the authority to speak on a subject matter. This teaching strategy for library one-shot instruction sessions ties directly into the Association of College and Research Libraries' (ACRL) *Framework* concept Authority Is Constructed and Contextual.[7] Published peer-reviewed articles are not the only reliable sources of information students can depend on for supporting their arguments or thesis statements. We must be mindful of whose ideas and perspectives we are advocating for student use.

  ○ Ask students to critically consider whose voices are being represented in the sources they locate in their search results, and whose voices might be absent.

  ○ When necessary, use sample searches that highlight research from non-majority perspectives.

- "Select content by authors of diverse backgrounds," (Guide, 19).

  ○ Use examples from diverse authors or researchers. For example, if you are leading a class session on evaluating web resources, you might use information from *Algorithms of Oppression: How Search Engines Reinforce Racism* by Safiya Umoja Noble to explain the biases found in search engine algorithms and how it distorts individual search results.

  ○ Encourage students to select studies conducted by authors with diverse backgrounds for their research projects. Explain the significance of incorporating a wide breadth of voices to support their argument.

- "Use multiple and diverse examples that do not marginalize students," (Guide, 20).

  ○ Use examples relevant to the course and class assignment that can be understood across different identity groups. Be mindful that cultural references might not be understood universally.

Considerations and Challenges in the One-Shot

This principle asks the instructors to take on the critical thinking and evaluation role. Reflecting on the content we provide to students, such as providing sample research topics, is imperative in creating an inclusive class environment. We need to be aware of how we speak about topics that make us uncomfortable. If we are confined by the project topic, that does not mean we cannot acknowledge diverse voices and the work they contribute to their disciplines. As information professionals, we are in the unique position to help teaching faculty through collection management see what voices are highlighted in their fields and whose are not. We can use this position to offer advice on how to diversify their course content and students' research assignments. For example, consult with the teaching faculty and have a discussion around allowing students to include at least one web-based source that brings in an authoritative voice who may not have an educational degree but has the experience and research to make them an expert on the topic.

Our greatest opportunity to incorporate this principle into our one-shot sessions is to hear from the diverse and varying perspectives of the students. Incorporate the students' opinions, ideas, and perspectives on the topic you are guiding their research on. Learn more from the student: Why are they interested in this topic? Do they have a personal connection to the topic? What pieces of information are important for them to include? This can be done out loud in front of the class as an example, or it can be done on an individual basis when you are allowing students free time to research during the session. The one-shot session is about the students and their needs, so be sure to include their perspectives as they often vary from your own.

Principle 4: Design All Course Elements for Accessibility

Accessibility touches every element of teaching. Student learning modalities are equally as diverse as their cultural backgrounds. As instructors, we must continue learning how to provide accessible and functional course material, such as presentations, video tutorials, and handouts. Appert and colleagues highlight the universal design for learning (UDL) pedagogy in this principle and explain that UDL "means making no assumptions about learners' abilities or experiences …and eliminating biases in methods of expression, such as only accepting written work," (Guide, 22). UDL asks instructors to think objectively about student learning abilities and allow their course materials to be more adaptable. UDL also addresses clearly outlining bigger topics into smaller, digestible pieces for content comprehension. Incorporating accessibility practices allows for easy adjustability from a face-to-face modality to an online modality. Infusing accessibility and UDL practices into lesson plans, or full courses, adds to an inclusive classroom environment and allows both instructor and students to digest course information through multiple perspectives.

Adapting Relevant Teaching Strategies from the Guide

- "Provide multiple means of representation," (Guide, 23).

  o Reflect on how your lesson plan may favor only one learning modality. For example: Do you send a text transcript along with your video tutorials to the teaching faculty? Or do you make sure the YouTube closed captioning is correct and provides proper grammar? Are you filling out the alt text on your LibGuide or presentation images? If you use a handout for a learning activity, are you able to provide it digitally and physically? Are you being mindful of color contrast in your content?

  o Ensure your materials are accessible by persons with disabilities. For example, make sure a screen reader can capture text in any document or handout you create.*

  o Do not assume the knowledge of your students. Repeating concepts throughout the session and clearly outlining the information you are teaching is helpful and needed.

  o Be sure to provide information in multiple formats (Guide, 23). If you use a presentation during class, send it along to the teaching faculty afterward so they can post it to their learning management system (LMS).

  o Set aside some time to learn about accessibility practices.

  o Collaborate and meet with your institution's instructional designer and the accessibility office staff.

  o Integrate accessible materials slowly into your lessons, if this is new to you.

- "Provide multiple means of action and expression," (Guide, 23).

---

* A great resource to test for screen reader accessibility is NaturalReader. A free software download is available for your own use to test readability of the following files: .pdf, .docx, .txt, and ePub. Additionally, a web add-on is available for download. For more information, please visit https://www.naturalreaders.com.

○ Be clear in your expectations for participation and completion of assignments and class activities, as discussed in Principle 2 (Guide, 23).

○ Scaffold between "mechanics and big picture outcomes in a learning experience," (Guide, 24). For example, if you have a learning outcome for your session to help students create a solid search strategy, then you might scaffold the skills needed to reach this outcome by having them brainstorm keywords, create search strings, and consider where to search.

- "Provide multiple means of engagement," (Guide, 24).

  ○ Check for understanding throughout sessions. Read body language and see if you need to reframe a concept or activity for understanding.

  ○ Ask students about their current search strategies when in a one-on-one session with them. We can learn a lot from what they are already doing and build off those skills.

  ○ Consider how students might prefer to engage with your course content. For example, if you are asking students to answer a question, some students might want to write down their answer rather than saying it out loud. Digital tools like Padlet and Kahoot! are popular means of engagement, but they need to be looked at and considered from an accessibility lens. Gathering feedback from students on their preferred method of engagement and modalities can be valuable in how you approach sessions.

Considerations and Challenges in the One-Shot

A main challenge surrounding accessibility for one-shot sessions lies within not knowing the abilities of each student coming into the classroom that day. Most course instructors do not relay accessibility accommodations to the librarian who is teaching. In order to minimize last-minute adjustments to course materials, librarians should begin incorporating accessible practices into all of their lesson planning. Automatically including UDL in library instruction materials will foster a more inclusive space for learners. Some accessibility practices including closed captions on instructional videos, providing a suggested step-by-step timeline for research projects, providing class materials in multiple formats (digitally and physically), checking documents for screen readability, and outlining learning outcomes for the class session. These practices do not have to be implemented all at once and can be approached one by one.

Principle 5: Reflect on One's Beliefs about Teaching to Maximize Self-awareness and Commitment to Inclusion

The fifth principle focuses on critical reflection to improve teaching. As mentioned at the beginning of this reflective essay, everyone possesses biases and assumptions, and those are often embedded, intentionally or not, into our lesson plans. Reflecting on the beliefs and habits we bring into the classroom will help us not only grow as instructors but also be more inclusive. Without taking the time to reflect, we have the tendency to "mirror our own learning preferences" and teach in a way that is similar to how we were taught (Guide, 26). If left unchecked, this can create a perpetual cycle of upholding the learning preferences and modes of a monocultural, white majority.

Adapting Relevant Teaching Strategies from the Guide

- "What are my identities, and how do others/my students perceive me?" (Guide, 27).

  o Understand how the facets of your identity and positionality can impact your perceptions of others and their perceptions of you (Guide, 27). Is there a power dynamic between you and the students? What assumptions might someone make about you?

  o Be mindful of how you present yourself and what information you share with the students. As mentioned before, sharing information about yourself can help create rapport. Consider what information you are choosing to share and why. For example, if you only share your educational degree accomplishments, students might have a hard time relating to you, and it reinforces an academic hierarchy. If you feel comfortable, you can share a hobby or interest of yours to connect with students in the classroom.

  o Recognize the importance of cultural competence to acknowledge various student dynamics.

- "What are my implicit (or explicit) biases? Do I propagate, neutralize, or challenge stereotypes in my class?" (Guide, 27).

- O Take an implicit bias test to understand where your bias lies.[*]
- O Recognize stereotype threats and how to address them if they arise (Guide, 27).
- O Seek out training on how to identify and deal with microaggressions— and we mean deal with them. Do not let snide remarks or harmful microaggressions slide under the radar without addressing the language. Microaggressions are important to understand if you encounter them in the classroom as well as in the library space.

- "How might the ways I set up classroom spaces and activities foster inclusion or disinclusion?" (Guide, 28).

  - O Consider the classroom space and how it is set up. If you are visiting someone else's classroom, consider taking a look at the space prior to your instruction session. Pay attention to how the space may or may not facilitate collaboration: are the seats stationary or movable? Are there tables or individual desks? How does the space help or hinder an activity you have planned? How does the space accommodate students with disabilities?
  - O Examine how you would position yourself in this space. Do you stay behind a podium the whole time? Do you walk through the classroom? Would students perceive you as open or closed based on your body language? For example, if standing at the front of class is most comfortable while teaching, then try sitting next to the student when they ask you a question during the in-class activity so you are at their level. These questions, however, do have an ableist assumption element to them and should be adjusted accordingly.
  - O Scrutinize any activities you plan for the lesson. Are you providing multiple types of engagement opportunities (group, pairs, individual, etc.) (Guide, 29)? Are your activities getting the level of engagement you are hoping for, and if not, how might you adapt the activities to better meet student preferences for engagement?

Considerations and Challenges in the One-Shot

How we present ourselves and our identity should be consistent across all classes even though the nature of our one-shots have us constantly meeting with different

---

[*] Project Implicit allows you to take free implicit bias tests through its website to see where you have biases related to topics such as skin tone, gender, religion, weight, race, disability, etc. You can take the test and learn more at https://implicit.harvard.edu/implicit/.

groups of students. It is important to constantly reflect on our assumptions and positionalities regardless of the different student identities we interact with. Our own positionality in the classroom can be challenging because students may not view us with the same level of authority as they do their instructor. This guest lecturer persona can cause students to make assumptions about our positionality that might be inaccurate. For example, students might view our authority on par with that of a substitute teacher and therefore might not be as attentive or engaged, especially if the professor is absent.

Another challenge is how we think about student research and engagement with our library databases and how this can lend to us treating students monolithically. Students are the greatest asset to our learning environments, so it is crucial to include their voices in our instruction sessions. The best way to not assume students' information literacy skill level is by asking and learning from them. Be open to changing lesson plans on the fly to meet their needs and reflect on what to adjust for future sessions. In critically reflecting, we must not put the blame on the students if a lesson does not go as planned and be willing to reexamine our own teaching in how we can better meet the needs of the students.

Conclusion

The *Guide for Inclusive Teaching at Columbia* offers a great starting point for how to approach inclusive teaching even if some of the suggestions are irrelevant or hard to implement in one-shots. Inclusive environments need to span beyond the classroom setting, but making impactful changes to curriculum is a good place to start.[8]

The authors of the inclusive teaching guide acknowledge that the guide is meant to be "ever-evolving" and there are a few areas for future consideration we want to mention (Guide, 7). First, there is opportunity for more conversations around the intersectionality of student identities and how that impacts creating an inclusive course climate and addressing student needs. Second, inclusive teaching would benefit from being examined through a Critical Race Theory (CRT) lens.[†] Third, some of the suggested approaches in the guide come from a more able-bodied mindset, which presents another opportunity for the guide's principles to expand and be considerate and knowledgeable in relation to students with disabilities. Finally, there are some suggestions in the guide that create challenges around setting high expectations and academic rigor while also meeting students where they are at. The guide does not address how to navigate between these two conflicting goals; however, this is another opportunity for future consideration and research.

---

† After submitting the first draft of this reflective essay, we presented at the 2022 Connecticut Information Literacy Conference, "Inclusive Pedagogies Through a Critical Race Theory Lens," in which we applied the CRT tenets to the contents of this essay.

As a reminder, inclusive teaching requires careful consideration and reflection on the part of the instructor. Therefore you do not need to completely revamp your lesson plans and teaching overnight. You can become more inclusive in your teaching through small steps and an open mind. If you would like to learn more about inclusive teaching and some of the concepts introduced in the guide, please check out the list of further readings offered at the end of this chapter. This list is not exhaustive, but might offer other resources to explore.

Suggested Further Reading

Arch, Xan, and Isaac Gilman. *Academic Library Services for First-Generation Students*. Santa Barbara, CA: Libraries Unlimited, 2020.

Bowles-Terry, Melissa, and Cassandra Kvenild. *Classroom Assessment Techniques for Librarians*. Chicago: Association of College and Research Libraries, 2015.

CAST. "The UDL Guidelines." 2018. http://udlguidelines.cast.org.

Drabinski, Emily. "What Is Critical about Critical Librarianship?." *Art Libraries Journal* 44, special issue no. 2 (2019): 49–57. https://doi.org/10.1017/alj.2019.3.

Heinbach, Chelsea, Brittany Paloma Fiedler, Rosan Mitola, and Emily Pattni. "Dismantling Deficit Thinking: A Strengths-Based Inquiry into the Experiences of Transfer Students in and out of Academic Libraries." *In the Library with the Lead Pipe*, February 6, 2019. http://www.inthelibrary-withtheleadpipe.org/2019/dismantling-deficit-thinking/.

Noble, Safiya Umoja. *Algorithms of Oppression: How Search Engines Reinforce Racism*. New York: New York University Press, 2018.

Pagowsky, Nicole, and Kelly McElroy, eds. *Critical Library Pedagogy Handbook*, 2 vols. Chicago: American Library Association, 2016.

Spina, Carli. *Creating Inclusive Libraries by Applying Universal Design: A Guide*. Lanham, MD: Rowman & Littlefield, 2021.

State Universities of New York. "Your Resources for Remote Learning During COVID-19." SUNY Accessibility Week: Designing Inclusive Digital Course Content #accessibilitymatters. Accessed June 4, 2021. https://sunycpd.eventsair.com/QuickEventWebsitePortal/suny-accessibility-week/site/ExtraContent/ContentPage?page=6.

Wright, Andrea, Laura Baker, Libby Young, Sara Swanson, James Sponsel, DebbieLee Landi, Lucretia McCulley, et al. "Complete Annotated Bibliography." Inclusive Pedagogy for Library Instruction. Last modified June 5, 2020. https://library.sewanee.edu/ip4li/annotated_bib.

Notes

1. Diane Ceo-DiFrancesco, Mary K. Kochlefl, and Janice Walker, "Fostering Inclusive Teaching: A Systemic Approach to Develop Faculty Competencies," *Journal of Higher Education Theory and Practice* 19, no. 1 (2019): 32–33; Gwen Lawrie et al., "Moving towards Inclusive Learning and Teaching: A Synthesis of Review," *Teaching and Learning Inquiry* 5, no.1 (2017): 10–11, https://doi.org/10.20343/teachlearninqu.5.1.3.

2. Lawrie et al., "Moving towards Inclusive Learning," 10–11.

3. Brandy S. Bryson, Lindsay Masland, and Susan Colby, "Strategic Faculty Development: Fostering Buy-In for Inclusive Excellence in Teaching," *Journal of Faculty Development* 3, no. 3 (2020):

107–8, Ingenta Connect; Amber Manning-Ouellette and Cameron C. Beatty, "Teaching Socially Just Perspectives in First Year Seminars: A Faculty Guide to Strengthen Inclusive Teaching Methods," *Journal of Faculty Development* 33, no. 2 (2019): 21, ProQuest.

4. Bryson, Lindsay, and Colby, "Strategic Faculty Development," 112; Ceo-DiFrancesco, Kochlefl, and Walker, "Fostering Inclusive Teaching," 33; Manning-Ouellette and Beatty, "Teaching Socially Just Perspectives," 21.

5. Lucy Appert et al., *Guide for Inclusive Teaching at Columbia* (New York: Center for Teaching and Learning, 2017), 7, https://cpb-us-w2.wpmucdn.com/edblogs.columbia.edu/dist/8/1109/files/2020/02/Guide-for-Inclusive-Teaching-at-Columbia_Accessibility-Revisions_15-January-2020_FINAL.pdf. (Because there are so many citations of the *Guide for Inclusive Teaching at Columbia* in this chapter, following this note it will be cited parenthetically in the text.)

6. While this essay focused on the print guide, there is also an online course taught through edX entitled "Inclusive Teaching: Supporting All Students in the College Classroom," which goes into more depth and features testimonies from experts in the field.

7. Association of College and Research Libraries, *Framework for Information Literacy for Higher Education* (Chicago: Association of College and Research Libraries, 2016), https://www.ala.org/acrl/standards/ilframework.

8. Kevin Gannon, "The Case for Inclusive Teaching," *Chronicle of Higher Education*, February 27, 2018, https://www.chronicle.com/article/the-case-for-inclusive-teaching/.

Bibliography

Appert, Lucy, Christine Simonian Bean, Amanda Irvin, Amanda M. Jungels, Suzanna Klaf, and Mark Phillipson. *Guide for Inclusive Teaching at Columbia*. New York: Columbia Center for Teaching and Learning, 2017. https://cpb-us-w2.wpmucdn.com/edblogs.columbia.edu/dist/8/1109/files/2020/02/Guide-for-Inclusive-Teaching-at-Columbia_Accessibility-Revisions_15-January-2020_FINAL.pdf.

Association of College and Research Libraries. *Framework for Information Literacy for Higher Education*. Chicago: Association of College and Research Libraries, 2016. https://www.ala.org/acrl/standards/ilframework.

Bryson, Brandy S., Lindsay Masland, and Susan Colby. "Strategic Faculty Development: Fostering Buy-In for Inclusive Excellence in Teaching." *Journal of Faculty Development* 3, no. 3 (2020): 107–16. Ingenta Connect.

Ceo-DiFrancesco, Diane, Mary K. Kochlefl, and Janice Walker. "Fostering Inclusive Teaching: A Systemic Approach to Develop Faculty Competencies." *Journal of Higher Education Theory and Practice* 19, no. 1 (2019): 31–43. Education Database.

Gannon, Kevin. "The Case for Inclusive Teaching." *Chronicle of Higher Education*, February 27, 2018. https://www.chronicle.com/article/the-case-for-inclusive-teaching/.

Lawrie, Gwen, Elizabeth Marquis, Eddie Fuller, Tara Newman, Mei Qiu, Milton Nomikoudis, Frits Roelofs, and Lianne van Dam. "Moving towards Inclusive Learning and Teaching: A Synthesis of Recent Literature." *Teaching and Learning Inquiry* 5, no. 1 (2017): 9–21. https://doi.org/10.20343/teachlearninqu.5.1.3.

Manning-Ouellette, Amber, and Cameron C. Beatty. "Teaching Socially Just Perspectives in First Year Seminars: A Faculty Guide to Strengthen Inclusive Teaching Methods." *Journal of Faculty Development* 33, no. 2 (2019): 19–23. ProQuest.

CHAPTER 39

Teaching from the Outside

Inclusive Pedagogy and the Adjunct Instructor

Nicole Pagowsky, Shanti Freundlich, Rachel Gammons, and Emily Drabinski

Introduction: The Syllabus as a Lens through Which We Analyze Our Practice

A master's degree in library and information science (MLIS) represents more than the credentials needed to become a librarian. It is often the point of entry into the profession, when graduate students are introduced to the cultural values, expectations, norms, and standards of behavior for librarians. What and how we teach students in our programs has much to do with the frames of mind new librarians bring to their work in the information literacy classroom and beyond. MLIS programs, like much of higher education, are increasingly reliant on adjunct instructors to teach courses on topics such as academic librarianship, teaching and pedagogy, discipline-focused searching, and many others. An aspect of equitable and inclusive pedagogy that can often be overlooked is the role of librarian adjunct instructors in MLIS programs and the influence they will also have on the pedagogy of future librarians. We four coauthors are academic librarians who serve as adjunct instructors in MLIS programs, and each of us has varying levels of agency within

our associated programs and with course design. We explore how our positionality within the MLIS program impacts our abilities to integrate inclusive pedagogies into our adjunct teaching. We consider inclusive pedagogy paramount to our teaching philosophies. Although each of us endeavors to use inclusive teaching practices as we do in our work as full-time librarians, our ability to actualize these pedagogies is often curtailed by our tenuous position as adjunct instructors. We authors chose to collaborate together through community and a collective sense of joy in engaging with this work, when typically our experiences would be siloed teaching different courses at different campuses.

Using the concept of a syllabus as a lens to analyze our practice, we first ground our own purpose in the teaching philosophy, which Nicole also assigns to her students as a semester-long process in LIS 581: Information Literacy Pedagogy at the University of Arizona School of Information. A discussion on assignments follows, considering how to incorporate agency from the perspective of being both an insider and outsider as an adjunct for Rachel in LBSC734: Seminar in the Academic Library at the University of Maryland College of Information Studies. Then, we contemplate expectations for standardized language and how it influences our focus in teaching practices, and Emily reflects on grappling with required templates and resistance relating to her class at Rutgers University School of Communication Studies. Last, following standardized language, we consider required policies and power imbalances from the students' perspective and Shanti discusses ways she intentionally uses those discussions as part of the pedagogical experience in her class LIS 407: Information Sources and Services at Simmons University. There are many facets of navigating the work of precarious adjunct teaching within the experience and agency of a practitioner. When we put forward inclusive pedagogies as our purpose and expectation, we believe we are the most successful and effective as educators for the benefit of our students.

Teaching Philosophies (Nicole Pagowsky)

My experience seems to be unusual in adjuncting for the University of Arizona School of Information, where I have had a great deal of creative freedom and agency. I was invited in to help develop a new graduate certificate in teaching and instruction[1] and was able to design my class (LIS 581: Information Literacy Pedagogy) from scratch. It is an instruction elective on its own but also makes up three of the twelve credits for the certificate. There was a previous information literacy instruction course that served as the elective for many years. Rather than needing to continue the structure for that class, I was able to create something new based on my teaching philosophy and what I believe to be important for future librarians to know, do, and value, from the perspective of a practitioner in my full-time job. Bringing forward the importance of having a teaching philosophy as an interactive, scaffolded larger assignment, students craft their own teaching philosophy based on what is important to them combined with what they learn through participating in the class. To ground practice in theory and have a guide, the teaching philosophy serves as a living document to always be amended. It demonstrates its importance for both student learning and a path forward in adjuncting. It gives some stability in carrying out the labor of precarity, which is often overlooked or dismissed.

Emphasizing a teaching philosophy can help rouse the labor of adjunct teaching from invisibility and devaluation. A teaching philosophy helps make the connection between intent and action, stating what we value and how to put these inclusive pedagogies into practice. Gannon highlights the importance of praxis: "Theory has to be embodied in tangible practice to be meaningful. A pedagogical philosophy must be more than sloganeering; it has to pervade our decisions and actions as well."[2] Considering how philosophy as a discipline actually fits into developing a teaching philosophy provides a multidimensional and authentic view of how to approach praxis. If we can grasp what drives our beliefs, we can better understand how we construct our classrooms and subsequent interactions, as well as being able to see what might need improvement or more reflection. Teaching philosophies highlight the behind-the-scenes thinking and planning that is not always assumed to exist from an outsider perspective of teaching. This can be seen in adjuncting since being paid a fixed rate makes it appear that all labor exists solely within the confines of class meetings and grading, when in reality there is so much planning, designing, and care-work throughout and beyond the semester. Additionally, with the ephemeral nature of adjunct work, having a teaching philosophy can ground an instructor despite changing foci or limitations on what they are able to design and carry out in the classroom. Particularly for adjuncts grappling with precarity and considering agency, as Maxine Greene describes, "a teacher in search of his/her own freedom may be the only kind of teacher who can arouse young persons to go in search of their own."[3] This would also apply in andragogy as adult learners benefit from agency in their learning and freedom in their own lives, too. Approaching our teaching from the perspective of imagining inclusivity of our own status makes for more inclusive pedagogy for all.

A teaching philosophy can have a community impact. As Beatty, Leigh, and Dean explain, it is often viewed as personal and reflecting on a teacher's identity, but sharing our philosophies in community establishes a foundation from common understandings of teaching theories and practice.[4] When a teaching philosophy is developed over time throughout a semester, such as in the assignment in my class, students build their learning in common understandings of teaching theories as stated above through discussion, reflection, and class community. In my assignment, students begin with a rough, free-form discussion post sharing what they think their teaching philosophy could be. They are asked not to do any prior research or reading and to just think creatively based on their experience. Midway through the semester, they revise their original, including incorporation of what they've been learning, and discuss their thought process (and receive feedback from me). Then, the final assignment is to revise again, updated with what they have learned over the entire semester. They reflect on what they are or are not changing from the original draft, and why; and what might have surprised them, and why. This gives students a great deal of agency to be creative, to focus more on the readings and theories that interest them and apply what they are learning to the area of librarianship or information work they hope to pursue. Students have been enthusiastic about this assignment and consistently leave positive feedback about the experience of reflection and revision to think about their philosophy.

We, the authors, hold similar teaching philosophies based within inclusive pedagogy. There are different limitations for each of us, depending on our positions and program structures, but our philosophies, centering on a few main principles, are consistent. For example, we hold that as adjuncts simultaneously working in the field while teaching, we view our students as future colleagues. This can change perspective on how a syllabus is structured or how class discussions are held, for example, depending on the amount of flexibility and agency an adjunct has. With that, we do not want to micromanage students and hope to use the syllabus as a living document to also uphold inclusive and socially just teaching practices, rather than using the syllabus as a fixed contract that does not take individual students' identities and needs into consideration as the semester goes on. When we are able, we try to give students choice in how they engage with the coursework and offer agency and flexibility to our students, as we hope to have as adjuncts in the liminal space between practitioner and educator.

Assignments (Rachel Gammons)

In qualitative research, insider/outsider epistemology situates the researcher in relation to the population being studied. An insider shares common identities, roles, or experiences with the participants, while an outsider is separated from the group through space, time, or experience. Being an insider lends legitimacy to the research and encourages vulnerability from participants, but an outsider brings objectivity and emotional distance, which allows them to observe what an insider might not. Most researchers find both sameness and difference with their population. This "space between"[5] is complex and holds the enormity of the researcher's shifting social identities, lived experience, and self-understanding. As adjuncts in an MLIS program, we stand in this liminal space; as practitioners, we are insiders with the community to whom we teach, but as adjuncts, we are outsiders to the program itself, with limited ability to impact the curriculum, content, or direction of the program as a whole.

My first experience adjuncting was at the University of Maryland, where I was invited to teach LBSC602: Serving Information Needs, an MLIS course focused on information behavior theory and reference. Because LBSC602 was a "core-course," it used a standard syllabus of readings and assignments, which ensured that students would meet the same learning objectives across multiple sections of the course. The primary assignment was a "pathfinder": a team-based and scaffolded assignment that asked students to identify, research, and meet the information needs of a specific user population. The course also included smaller individual assignments, such as performing a reference skit based on an imagined reference encounter. In addition to my work as an academic librarian, I am also a part-time doctoral student. As an instructor for LBSC602, I struggled to find myself anywhere in the standardized syllabus. As a student, I found the assignments frustrating; as a teacher, I found it difficult to find meaning and purpose in the curriculum; and as a practitioner, I felt disconnected from the material of the course. Although, as an adjunct, I viewed myself as an outsider to the MLIS program, to my students, my presence as their instructor positioned me as an insider. I found these conflicting identities and positionalities difficult to reconcile. Although I made changes to the syllabus where I could, I always felt (as Emily later describes) "adjunct to it, and it to me."

A few years later, I had the opportunity to redesign and teach LBSC734: Seminar in the Academic Library. Given the opportunity to build my own syllabus, I wanted the course to feel authentic to the different aspects of my identities. When I started the design process, one of the first curricular decisions I made was to extend agency to students by allowing them to select their own deadlines for assignments (see appendix A). As a practitioner, my day-to-day deadlines are largely self-imposed and self-enforced. Allowing students to select their own due dates demonstrates respect for the complexity of their lived experiences and is an affirmation of my teaching philosophy, to treat my students as future colleagues. For me, this small act is an expression of inclusive pedagogy; it destabilizes the power imbalance between student and instructor and extends agency to students in an environment in which they are typically subject to sanctions and scrutiny. As an instructor, I expected that student-led deadlines would be difficult to manage. However, because students select not only the dates, but also the order in which they would like to complete and submit assignments, I have found that student-led deadlines reduce my grading fatigue by introducing variety into what can otherwise be a redundant process.

One of the challenges of graduate education is in the range of experiences that students bring to their learning processes. As instructors in MLIS programs, our courses include students who are new to the field, others who are beginning second or third careers, and yet others who bring extensive experience gained through paid or volunteer work in libraries. It can be difficult to design an assignment, or even series of assignments, that offers sufficient learning, depth, and rigor for all members of the learning community. For LBSC734, I adopted assignment themes, which offer multiple pathways for students to meet the expectations of the assignment while also serving their individual goals and needs. Each set of assignments focuses on building practical materials that could prepare students for a career in academic librarianship. The first is the Career Portfolio (see appendix B), which offers three pathways:

1. Job Application: Identify an academic library position advertised in the last year and compile a (mock or real) job application portfolio for the position, including background research on the institution, curriculum vitae, cover letter, prepared list of questions for the hiring committee, and list of three references.

2. First Year on the Job: Identify an academic library position advertised in the last year and develop plan for how you would approach your first year on the job in that position, including background research on the institution, short analysis of institutional and individual priorities, a proposal for a new project that you would undertake in the first year, and a brief work plan for how you would meet the expectations for the position.

3. Design Your Own Project: This might take the form of a literature review, a research proposal, an applied project, or other equivalent product.

The second set is Scholarship and Creativity (see appendix C), which can be used to make progress on a current project or goal or explore a new intellectual or creative space. Students are asked to complete two of the following:

1. Conference Proposal: You can choose to complete a draft of a real conference proposal that you plan to submit, or a mock proposal based on an imaginary (but feasible) project you might complete as a librarian.

2. Teaching Philosophy: A reflective (one-to-two-page) document that summarizes your approach to and beliefs about teaching.

3. Research Hero: Select a librarian (or other scholar) whose research/publications you admire and write a (one-to-two-page) overview of their work, highlighting two or more articles or publications.

4. Job Talk Observation: Attend an academic library job presentation and write a (one-page) summary of the presentation and your observations.

5. Design Your Own Project: This might take the form of a blog post, informational interview, personal website, zine, or other creative product.

While I struggled with my earlier experience with assignments in standardized syllabus for LBSC602, the assignments for LBSC734 feel authentic to my lived experience as an academic librarian, and because of that, they resonate with my students. Extending agency to my students by providing flexibility with deadlines and assignment choice allows me to demonstrate respect for my students, which helps me to feel grounded as an instructor.

Standardized Expectations (Emily Drabinski)

From the student perspective, because I teach in the LIS program they are fully enrolled in, I am also fully *of* the program. From my own perspective and that of full-time faculty, I am ancillary to it. My primary job is a library job. My days are concerned with these fundamentals, selecting and acquiring research materials, describing and inscribing them into our knowledge organization structures, making decisions about how long they can circulate and to whom, when they must be replaced or discarded or preserved for some other future. I am a librarian. When I enter the classroom on behalf of the profession, my task is to teach the next librarians to do what I do, to reproduce my approach to library work by way of their own practice. I labor at the intersection of the academy and its infrastructure. I gnaw at a very small corner of that apple.

This is not to say that I have total control over what happens in that classroom. I do not. My syllabus does not start with the proverbial blank page but with a template that I did not design and that I cannot change. Here's an example template, from a course I teach at Rutgers School of Communication and Information.

Course Delivery: Note if course is fully face-to-face, fully online, or hybrid

Course Website: Give URL of Course Management System site (e.g. http://canvas.rutgers.edu or http://sakai.rutgers.edu)

Instructor: FirstName LastName

Email: user@email.com

X-hour turnaround on email correspondence (for online courses, it is recommended that it be 24-hour turnaround)

Office Phone: xxx-xxx-xxxx

Office Hours: Day, time, location; or live chat in online course by appointment; etc.

Instructional Asst: If relevant - FirstName LastName

The template opens with restraints on where I can teach and makes demands on
my labor without my negotiation. In order to teach, I must complete this template
and submit it in advance, deciding in advance how committed I will be to responding
to e-mail from students that forms only a tiny adjunct element of my working life.

Standardized language also codifies practices that I must comply with even if I
would rather not. In my pedagogy, grading raises stakes such that students become
more interested in hitting rubric marks than they are in the messy and iterative
process of making meaning together through social engagement with shared texts.
In order to submit an approved syllabus, I am required to fill out a table aligning
assessments with course objectives and determining in advance how much each
will count (see table 39.1). What if I want to design these course elements with my
students? Or push back against making grades required? Because I am an adjunct
faculty member, the status of standardized language is not subject to my control. I
am adjunct to it, and it is adjunct to me.

Table 39.1
Required syllabus component

Assignment	Corresponding Course Learning Objective	Weight
Title of Assignment	Indication of which # course learning objective(s) the assignment corresponds with	% or pts
Title of Assignment 2 Part A: Title (% or pts) Part B: Title (% or pts)	Indication of which # course learning objective(s) the assignment corresponds with	% or pts
	TOTAL	100% or point total

In order to teach my course, I must reproduce language generated by the department around issues like access to disability services, grading policies, plagiarism penalties, and others. If language itself is always subject to contestation, this demand can evacuate those statements of meaning. They are reprinted again and again in my syllabus and every other one in the program. But we also know that language isn't binding, that as an instructor I regularly break with the contract set forth by the university with the student, not necessarily because I see it as worth resisting, but because it is not mine to begin with so I do not really know it or embrace it.

Policies (Shanti Freundlich)

Receiving a full-formed and policy-rich copy of the syllabus from the most recent time a course was taught has been a reassuring constant in my experiences as an adjunct instructor. Sometimes an old syllabus is the only documentation I've received, but it's always my introduction to the teaching and learning that has come before and the policies that set the boundaries in a given course. Most syllabus policies are outside the control of adjunct instructors, but to me the importance of being transparent about their different purpose, authorship, and enforcement has only become more apparent. Trusting students with the knowledge of which course policies are shaped by the program and which ones are customizable shows respect for the students we get to teach, fosters a more empowering learning environment, and demonstrates good workplace communication. These reflections, suggestions, and challenges are helping me add transparency to brand-new, quietly rewritten, and regularly updated syllabus policies.

The power imbalances are uncomfortably clear through the one-sided nature of the written expectations in syllabi: much is explicitly expected of students and very little is spelled out for instructors. It is *understood* and *implied* that instructors will try to return graded materials and respond to e-mail promptly, and that sometimes we make grammatical or citation errors, but I've never experienced immediate consequences that parallel losing one point every day for a late assignment. Instructors usually receive the grace to be imperfect; we could offer that same professional courtesy to our future colleagues.

Consider making implicit offers of exceptions or extensions the stated policy for all students.[6] It might seem clear to me that when I add "if you need to miss a class, just let me know!" to a strict attendance policy the implicit offer is that I will make an exception to the stated policy, but students need to know about and how to read the hidden curriculum in order to see what I think is clearly offered.[7] For example, some variation of "this is not a contract and the professor will post to the LMS if or when readings or assignments change" is a common syllabus language. While I've definitely needed the flexibility offered by such ambiguous phrasing in order to make midsemester changes to reading assignments, deadlines, or other improvements to the course, we can also make it explicit that unanticipated changes will not increase workloads or shorten deadlines.[8] Another phrase that gives instructors flexibility in the face of rigid imposed policies is "instructor discretion," which could easily be "instructor discrimination" in practice. Instead of forcing students to share personal and medical information and then judging if their lived experiences are worthy enough for compassion, consistently offer everyone the understanding a good supervisor would offer you and believe them.[9] The implication of incomplete or incorrect policy information is that instructor time is more valuable than students' time; that I don't have time to waste on finding accurate information, but students, especially students in crisis, do have the time. What additional stress are we creating for our students in order to lessen our own?

Collectively annotating and then discussing syllabus policies could be an opportunity to teach about higher education, the institution, program, and course design process. Removing or rewriting policies is not an option for me, but I try to use a combination of facilitated discussion and social annotation tools to layer explanations, context, and my interpretation onto immovable policies. Students add initial questions and can return to these annotations later in the semester to reflect, critique, and make suggestions based on their experience with the course. This learner-centered, multilayered discussion is an opportunity for students to normalize sharing tips on how to best use institutional services, helps instructors clarify policy vagueness, and leads to a frank discussion of the realities of adjunct instructor in higher education—a highly relevant topic for future academic librarians.[10]

While we may write and rewrite our syllabi with the most inclusive of pedagogical intentions, students read each new syllabus through decades of educational experiences and concurrently with the syllabi of all their courses.[11] They know arbitrary rules and rigid enforcement is always available to instructors, and without instructor transparency it is quite literally impossible to differentiate between the policies that are not *really* enforced, which are inconsistently followed, and which are actually important. Transparency might seem like a small change, but it has great potential for nurturing kindness and improvements through an exploration of "why" when it comes to course policies. A course and its learning environment are where students do the work of learning—Could you do your best work under the policy conditions it imposes?

Conclusion

MLIS programs are primarily professional, with the end goal of students becoming librarians and information professionals. Although much of a program might be practice-focused, the degree incorporates theory to provide guidance and grounding in navigating the conventions of libraries—hopefully with mindfulness toward enacting needed change. For the four of us, our experiences are shaped by balancing our insider/outsider roles as working librarians and adjuncts, while also attempting to balance practice and theory in our teaching. We must take into consideration the conflict between how we hope to teach and how we might be required to teach in programs where we may or may not have full creative agency in course design, and attempt to do this through a few entry points in our pedagogy. Teaching philosophies need to be returned to regularly in order to refine and ground practice—both our own, and students crafting theirs. This grounding can be both an aspirational space for creative agency and an anchor in the chaos of academic precarity. Through syllabus and assignment design, we might need to engineer structure between navigating required busywork and creating more authentic assessments based on current library practices. The language we use and policies we employ affect students' empowerment to control their own learning and assessment and to push back on potentially rigid policy expectations that set the tone for students' first impressions of a course. Although some of the strategies may seem small, these acts of grounded and shared respect for students are a way that enacts an inclusive pedagogy and cocreates an equitable learning space.

Appendix A: Personal Deadlines Assignment Description

You will be selecting your own deadlines for this course. This works in service of two goals. First, it allows you to select due dates that complement your existing work, academic, and personal schedules. Second, it models professional practice, in which many of your deadlines will be self-identified. The last possible date for submission is the last day of the semester. Although these deadlines are self-imposed, please take them seriously and, to the best of your ability, consider your schedule and available bandwidth before committing to a date. However, we get that life is wild right now. If you need to shift a deadline, just let us know.

As you prepare your deadlines, please take into account your personal learning goals. Please note that selecting earlier deadlines will support our ability to provide detailed feedback on your work. This may be more important to you for some projects than others. Your deadlines are entirely a matter of personal preference. You may choose to spread them out, or stack them together at the end of the semester. Please select the dates that work best for you.

By the second week of class please complete the "Project Selection and Personal Deadlines" quiz in Canvas. This will let us know (1) which projects you will be completing for the Career Portfolio and Scholarship and Creativity Assignments and (2) the dates that you plan to submit each component of the learning assessments. If you plan to design your own for any of the learning assessments, please communicate these intentions before submitting your quiz. Although we ask that you select which options you will be completing for each of the assignments, this can be adjusted over the course of the semester. Just e-mail us if you need to make a switch.

You are welcome (and encouraged!) to come to us with questions about these assignments or to submit drafts for feedback. We ask that drafts be submitted at least one week before your chosen deadline to give us time to thoughtfully review your work (and so that you have time to incorporate that feedback).

Appendix B: Career Portfolio Assignment Description

Career Portfolio: 40 pts total (20 pts per part)

Use what you have learned in class to get a head start on preparing yourself for the job market. Each project begins by selecting an academic librarian job ad published within the last two years. Make sure that you will be able to meet the minimum qualifications for the job by the time you graduate. From there, you will either assemble a portfolio to apply for the job or prepare materials to succeed in your first year in that job.

If you have a compelling reason for why the above options will not be helpful in achieving your professional goals, you have the option to design your own learning assessment.

Part 1: Background Research on the Institution (20 pts)

One of the most important parts of interviewing/starting a new job is to do your research ahead of time. It seems tedious, but this makes an enormous difference in the quality of your interview.

Make a copy of this slide deck (https://go.umd.edu/LBSC734BGResearch) to use as a template—feel free to rearrange the slides, customize the theme, and/or include different bullet points than the ones suggested. Although you can add slides as needed, please do so sparingly. The background research is important, but it should not be super time-consuming. Keep it simple and try to focus on what is really important.

Rubric: Background Research	20 pts
Organization: Does the slide deck effectively organize and present information?	2 pts
Focus: Does the slide deck highlight meaningful information about the institution, library/library system, and position?	3 pts
Significance: Is the information presented relevant to the specific position?	3 pts
Comprehension: Does the slide deck include relevant and significant information about the institution and library system to the extent that it is available? If not, does the student provide a rationale for why the information was not available or accessible?	3 pts

Rubric: Background Research	20 pts
Quality: Is the information well-researched? Are the questions in each section addressed?	7 pts
Presentation: Does the slide deck demonstrate an appropriate amount of time and effort? Does it include relevant hyperlinks or supplementary materials, as appropriate?	3 pts

Part 2: Career Portfolio (20 pts)

Select **one** of the following:

OPTION 1: JOB APPLICATION PORTFOLIO

For students preparing for the job market, this is an opportunity to prepare your materials. In addition to the background research, completed portfolios should include

- ❏ **Job Ad:** Include a PDF copy of the job ad you have selected.
- ❏ **Curriculum Vitae (CV):** A CV is a standard part of any academic job application. CVs are longer and more detailed than résumés and, in addition to your work experience, include sections such as education, scholarship, and service.
- ❏ **Cover Letter:** A well-written cover letter can make or break a job application. Cover letters are typically 1–2 pages and are tailored to the specific position. Use details from your background research to make your letter stand out from the crowd!
- ❏ **List of Questions:** Academic job interviews are long and include lots of time for questions. Prepare a list of 5 to 10 questions to ask the hiring committee during your interview.
- ❏ **References:** List of three references and brief descriptions as to why you selected each person.

Rubric: Job Application Portfolio	20 pts
Job Ad: Does the portfolio include a copy of the job ad?	2 pts
Curriculum Vitae (CV): Does the portfolio include a well-organized curriculum vitae that includes (1) education, (2) work experience, and (as appropriate) (3) scholarship, (4) service, and (5) awards? Is the CV free of grammatical errors? Is it up-to-date?	6 pts
Cover Letter: Does the portfolio include a well-organized 1-to-2-page cover letter that is tailored to the specific position? Is it free of grammatical errors? Does it demonstrate thought and attention?	6 pts

Rubric: Job Application Portfolio	20 pts
List of Questions: Does the portfolio include 5 to 10 thoughtful questions for the hiring committee?	3 pts
References: Does the portfolio include a list of (at least) three references and brief rationales for why these individuals were selected?	3 pts

OPTION 2: YEAR ONE ON THE JOB

For students who may already be on the job search, Year One on the Job offers an opportunity to start thinking strategically about what happens *after* you get the job. Using the position you selected in part 1, then chart a plan for how you would succeed in your first year on the job. Your portfolio should include

- ❑ **Job Ad/Position Description:** Include a PDF copy of the job ad or position description.
- ❑ **Year One on the Job Packet:** One of the strangest parts of starting your first librarian position is your first day of work: you show up to an empty inbox and calendar, you sit down at your desk, and you have to decide how you are going to fill your time. Imagine this is day one of your new job and you are preparing to meet with your new supervisor. What would you like to work on? What do you need from them for you to be successful? Think of this more as a thought experiment, rather than creating official documentation. To help guide you through the process, we have developed a template (https://go.umd.edu/LBSC734Year1) for you to follow.
- ❑ **Strategic Priorities:** Using the university, library, or departmental strategic plan, 3–5 strategic priorities that are applicable to your new position.
- ❑ **Work Plan:** List of goals, projects, and day-to-day responsibilities.
- ❑ **One Specific Initiative:** Pick one of the strategic initiatives listed above and develop a brief proposal for a project that addresses that goal. This could be an event (such as an outreach opportunity, workshop, or class), a new tool or resource, partnership on campus, or a smaller-scale project that would be easy to implement in your own work.
- ❑ **Librarianship:** Pick 5–10 things that you are going to work on this year. These could be direct from the job ad or responsibilities you infer based on your background research from part 1.
- ❑ **Service:** Based on your job ad, background research from part 1, and knowledge of the organization, identify 1 to 3 opportunities for service to the library, the campus, and the profession.
- ❑ **Scholarship:** Select 2–3 learning opportunities (conferences, workshops, courses, etc.) and 1 research idea you would like to pursue over the next year.

Rubric: Year One on the Job	20 pts
Job Ad: Does the portfolio include a copy of the job ad or position description?	2 pts
Strategic Priorities: Does the portfolio include an analysis of the institution, library, and/or departmental strategic priorities? Does the student indicate these priorities are applicable to their position?	4 pts
Proposal for Specific Initiative: Does the portfolio include a proposal for a specific initiative or project? Can this project be accomplished in the first year on the job? Is it connected to at least one of the strategic priorities? Does it include relevant details, such as a justification, potential partners, needs, and assessment?	6 pts
Work Plan: Does the portfolio include a one-year work plan with goals and objectives? Does this work plan reflect the positional responsibilities as outlined in the job ad? If there are gaps in the work plan due to a lack of information, does the student provide a plan for how they would locate the information?	6 pts
Presentation: Are the portfolio materials well-written and free of grammatical errors?	2 pts

Alternate Assignment: Design Your Own (40 pts)

If you feel the above options will not be helpful in achieving your professional goals, you have the option to create your own prompt to complete this learning assessment. This might take the form of a literature review or annotated bibliography, draft of an article or book chapter for submission, applied project, or other equivalent product. If you select this option, you must meet with us to discuss your project before submitting your project selection and personal deadlines.

Your submission should include

- ❏ A project of equivalent length, depth, and scope to the career portfolio.
- ❏ Rubric by which I will assess your project modeled after the rubrics for the background research, job application portfolio, and year one on the job portfolio, due one week before the submission of your final project.

Appendix C: Scholarship and Creativity Assignment Description

Scholarship and Creativity: 30 pts total (15 per project)

As an academic librarian, you will be expected to produce works of scholarship and/or creativity. This project will help get you a head start on that process! Please select **two** of the following:

Option 1: Conference Proposal (15 pts)

Academic librarians have the opportunity to attend and present at conferences locally, nationally, and internationally. For this assessment, you'll be creating a conference proposal. You can choose to complete a draft of a real conference proposal that you plan to submit or a mock proposal based on an imaginary—but feasible—project you might complete as a librarian.

Please follow the proposal guidelines outlined for an upcoming (or recently completed) conference. I recommend that you look through the proceedings from previous years' conferences to get a feel for the kinds of proposals that get accepted. As a new librarian, you might find poster proposals to be more accessible than presentations. Posters can be an opportunity to get feedback on a work in progress or preparation for a more rigorous conference presentation or article. You could also submit a presentation, workshop, lightning session, roundtable discussion, or other conference sessions.

Your submission should include

- ❑ A PDF or screenshot of the conference proposal form or requirements. If you can't get to the proposal requirements or submission form, just include a link to the conference and stick to the basic proposal requirements: title, 100-word abstract, 500-word description, 1–3 learning outcomes for participants.
- ❑ Conference proposal following submission guidelines for the conference.
- ❑ A list of 1 to 3 questions that you have about the proposal, things you struggled with, or areas you would like me to focus on in our feedback.

Rubric: Conference Proposal	15 pts
Background: Does the proposal include a copy of the proposal guidelines, submission form, or (at minimum) a link to the conference?	1 pt
Feedback: Does the proposal include a list of 1–3 questions or areas of focus for reviewers?	2 pts

Rubric: Conference Proposal	15 pts
Significance: Does the conference proposal relate to the conference theme? If there is a track identified, does the proposal align with the criteria?	2 pts
Comprehension: Does the proposal describe a specific research or professional project? Is the information included relevant to potential reviewers?	5 pts
Quality: Does the proposal meet the requirements as outlined in the submission guidelines?	3 pts
Presentation: Is the proposal well-written and free of grammatical errors?	2 pts

Option 2: Teaching Philosophy (15 pts)

A teaching statement (https://cft.vanderbilt.edu/guides-sub-pages/teaching-statements/) is a reflective document that summarizes your approach to and beliefs about teaching. While these documents are a staple for academic faculty, it is not uncommon to see a teaching philosophy or statement listed as a requirement for a job application for an academic librarian position. Because academic libraries are situated within the context of higher education, teaching is at the heart of all of our services. Even if you do not plan to pursue a teaching-focused position, a teaching philosophy provides an opportunity to reflect on how teaching and education fit into your practice.

Your submission should include
- ❑ 1-to-2-page teaching philosophy
- ❑ A list of 1 to 3 questions that you have about the teaching philosophy, things you struggled with, or areas you would like me to focus on in my feedback.

Rubric: Teaching Philosophy	15 pts
Feedback: Does the submission include a list of 1 to 3 questions or areas of focus for the reviewer?	2 pts
Focus: Does the philosophy focus on the student's beliefs, practices, and/or values about teaching?	5 pts
Comprehension: Does the philosophy demonstrate an understanding of teaching within an academic library setting?	3 pts
Quality: Does the philosophy meet the length requirements?	2 pts
Presentation: Is the philosophy well-written, free of grammatical errors, and formatted with appropriate citations (if required)?	3 pts

Option 3: Research Hero (15 pts)

The great thing about being an academic librarian is that we get to work with smart and talented people. This assignment is an opportunity for you to geek out! Select a librarian whom you admire and tell us about what makes them awesome. Although there are many amazing people who have not published, for this assignment, focus on someone who has produced scholarship (articles, books, conference presentations, etc.) that has inspired or pushed you to think about something in a new way.

Your submission should include

- ❑ 3–5 sentence bio of your Research Hero. Try to hit the big things: name, title, type of work they do, what they are known for, where you can find them on the internet (Twitter handles, website). If you aren't sure who to pick, our list of guest speakers is a great place to start!
- ❑ 1–2 examples of scholarship. Read something they have published and tell us what you admire in each of the pieces. This is not about summarizing the article/presentation/book—but instead, connecting with something specific. Do you like their research method? The way they write? The things they say? What is it that speaks to you?
- ❑ 5–7 sentence summary/analysis. Wrap it up and take us home. What makes this person your hero? How might their approach to scholarship influence your own? How do they push, challenge, or provoke the discourse in LIS?

Rubric: Research Hero	15 pts
Focus: Does the analysis highlight a scholar in LIS?	5 pts
Comprehension: Does the analysis demonstrate an understanding of research within an academic library setting?	5 pts
Quality: Does the statement meet the length requirements? Does it highlight 1–2 examples of scholarship?	3 pts
Presentation: Is the statement well-written, free of grammatical errors, and formatted with appropriate citations?	2 pts

Option 4: Job Talk Observation (15pts)

As we have discussed, academic job interviews are very long full-day affairs. One component of the interview process is a presentation or job talk. These presentations are typically open to library staff, and occasionally the broader campus community. If you have the opportunity, observing a job talk can give you a lot of insight into the interview process. If you are invited to observe one of these during the spring semester, we encourage you to attend!

Your submission should include

❑ PDF of the job ad for the position.

❑ 1 page summary of the job talk and your observations. Consider the following: How did the candidate address/not address the prompt? What questions were they asked, and how did they respond? What questions did they ask attendees? How did they engage/not engage the audience? What would you have done differently? What did you learn about academic job interviews?

❑ A list of 1 to 3 questions that you have about the presentation, interview, or related items.

Rubric: Job Talk Observation	15 pts
Feedback: Does the submission include a list of 1 to 3 questions for the reviewers?	1 pt
Focus: Does the summary highlight relevant aspects of the presentation?	5 pts
Comprehension: Does the analysis demonstrate an understanding of the academic job interview process and aspects of a strong presentation?	5 pts
Quality: Does the summary meet the length requirements? Does it include a copy of the job ad?	2 pts
Presentation: Is the statement well-written and free of grammatical errors?	2 pts

Option 5: Design Your Own (15 pts)

As always, you have the option to create your own prompt to complete this assignment. This might take the form of a blog post, informational interview, book review, ALA Emerging Leader application, or other equivalent product. If you select this option, you must e-mail us to discuss your project before submitting your project selection and personal deadlines (Feb. 10).

Your submission should include

❑ A project of equivalent length, depth, and scope to the other options.

❑ A list of 1 to 3 questions that you have about your final project, things you struggled with, or areas you would like us to focus on in our feedback.

❑ Rubric by which we will assess your project modeled after the rubrics for the conference proposal, teaching philosophy, and research statement. This will be due two weeks before the submission of your final project.

Notes

1. University of Arizona School of Information, "Instruction and Teaching for Librarians and Information Professionals Certificate," May 10, 2019, https://ischool.arizona.edu/graduate-certificates//instruction-and-teaching.
2. Kevin M. Gannon, *Radical Hope* (Morgantown: West Virginia University Press, 2020), 25.
3. Maxine Greene, *The Dialectic of Freedom* (New York: Teachers College Press, 1988), 14.
4. Joy E. Beatty, Jennifer S. A. Leigh, and Kathy Lund Dean, "Philosophy Rediscovered: Exploring the Connections between Teaching Philosophies, Educational Philosophies, and Philosophy," *Journal of Management Education* 33, no. 1 (February 2009): 105, https://doi.org/10.1177/1052562907310557.
5. Sonya Corbin Dwyer and Jennifer L. Buckle, "The Space Between: On Being an Insider-Outsider in Qualitative Research," *International Journal of Qualitative Methods* 8, no. 1 (March 1, 2009): 54–63, https://doi.org/10.1177/160940690900800105.
6. Milton A. Fuentes, David G. Zelaya, and Joshua W. Madsen, "Rethinking the Course Syllabus: Considerations for Promoting Equity, Diversity, and Inclusion," *Teaching of Psychology* 48, no. 1 (January 2021): 69–79.
7. Gannon, *Radical Hope*, 137.
8. Kathy Lund Dean and Charles J. Fornaciari, "The 21st-Century Syllabus: Tips for Putting Andragogy into Practice," *Journal of Management Education* 38, no. 5 (October 2014): 724–32, https://doi.org/10.1177/1052562913504764.
9. Catherine Denial, "A Pedagogy of Kindness," *Hybrid Pedagogy,* August 15, 2019, https://hybridpedagogy.org/pedagogy-of-kindness/.
10. Aaron S. Richmond et al., "Project Syllabus: An Exploratory Study of Learner-Centered Syllabi," *Teaching of Psychology* 46, no. 1 (January 2019): 6–15, https://doi.org/10.1177/0098628318816129.
11. Logan E. Gin et al., "It's in the Syllabus …or Is It? How Biology Syllabi Can Serve as Communication Tools for Creating Inclusive Classrooms at a Large-Enrollment Research Institution," *Advances in Physiology Education* 45, no. 2 (June 2021): 224–40, https://doi.org/10.1152/advan.00119.2020.

Bibliography

Beatty, Joy E., Jennifer S. A. Leigh, and Kathy Lund Dean. "Philosophy Rediscovered: Exploring the Connections between Teaching Philosophies, Educational Philosophies, and Philosophy." *Journal of Management Education* 33, no. 1 (February 2009): 99–114. https://doi.org/10.1177/1052562907310557.

Denial, Catherine. "A Pedagogy of Kindness." *Hybrid Pedagogy*, August 15, 2019. https://hybridpedagogy.org/pedagogy-of-kindness/.

Dwyer, Sonya Corbin, and Jennifer L. Buckle. "The Space Between: On Being an Insider-Outsider in Qualitative Research." *International Journal of Qualitative Methods* 8, no. 1 (March 1, 2009): 54–63. https://doi.org/10.1177/160940690900800105.

Fuentes, Milton A., David G. Zelaya, and Joshua W. Madsen. "Rethinking the Course Syllabus: Considerations for Promoting Equity, Diversity, and Inclusion." *Teaching of Psychology* 48, no. 1 (January 2021): 69–79. https://doi.org/10.1177/0098628320959979.

Gannon, Kevin M. *Radical Hope: A Teaching Manifesto*. Morgantown: West Virginia University Press, 2020.

Gin, Logan E., Rachel A. Scott, Leilani D. Pfeiffer, Yi Zheng, Katelyn M. Cooper, and Sara E. Brownell. "It's in the Syllabus …or Is It? How Biology Syllabi Can Serve as Communication Tools for Creating Inclusive Classrooms at a Large-Enrollment Research Institution." *Advances in Physiology Education* 45, no. 2 (June 2021): 224–40. https://doi.org/10.1152/advan.00119.2020.

Greene, Maxine. *The Dialectic of Freedom.* New York: Teachers College Press, 1988.

Lund Dean, Kathy, and Charles J. Fornaciari. "The 21st-Century Syllabus: Tips for Putting Andragogy into Practice." *Journal of Management Education* 38, no. 5 (October 2014): 724–32. https://doi.org/10.1177/1052562913504764.

Richmond, Aaron S., Robin K. Morgan, Jeanne M. Slattery, Nathanael G. Mitchell, and Anna Grace Cooper. "Project Syllabus: An Exploratory Study of Learner-Centered Syllabi." *Teaching of Psychology* 46, no. 1 (January 2019): 6–15. https://doi.org/10.1177/0098628318816129.

University of Arizona School of Information. "Instruction and Teaching for Librarians and Information Professionals Certificate." May 10, 2019. https://ischool.arizona.edu/graduate-certificates//instruction-and-teaching.

SECTION 7
Professional Development

Introduction

Ariana Santiago

As librarians we constantly engage in professional development—both as participants engaging in continual learning and as designers and facilitators of professional development opportunities for our communities. Each chapter in this section focuses on a form of professional development and shares theories, practices, or reflections on ensuring these are inclusive and equitable learning spaces. I hope you find something here that inspires community building and inclusivity in the professional development you design, facilitate, or engage with.

The first two chapters discuss professional development created and led by librarians for the communities we serve and collaborate with. In Chapter 40, "Enabling Inclusive and Equitable Teaching Practices through Instructor Development," Jane Hammons, Amanda L. Folk, Katie Blocksidge, and Hanna Primeau outline two instructor development programs at The Ohio State University Libraries—Meaningful Inquiry and Teaching Information Literacy. By highlighting the equity-minded pedagogies these programs are grounded in, the authors underscore the importance of identifying hidden curricula and focusing on increasing transparency to make learning more equitable for all students. With program templates and activities, this chapter provides an excellent example of library-led instructor professional development programs designed to bring inclusivity to information literacy and research-based assignments.

In Chapter 41, "Designing and Managing Inclusive Group Projects," Laura Saunders discusses research-based benefits and challenges of group projects—including the disproportionately negative impacts on students of color, as well as challenges for adult learners and online students—and shares practical strategies using an example group project from a graduate-level course on academic libraries. Saunders takes us through the many decisions involved in designing group projects and how they affect inclusivity, including transparency with students about the goals of the group project, facilitating inclusive teamwork, guiding students in providing effective peer feedback, and more. The strategies and resources shared in this chapter will be valuable for librarians who teach credit-bearing courses, as well as those who wish to design inclusive group projects in other settings.

The second two chapters in this section shift to professional development by and for practicing librarians, starting with Chapter 42, "Engaging through Conversation: Community Building for Inclusive Library Instruction" by Christopher Lowder, David X. Lemmons, and Ashley Blinstrub. The authors, all librarians at George Mason University, created a community of practice called Conversations of an Inclusive Nature (COIN) to provide a space for library instructors to discuss topics related to inclusivity in library instruction and inspire action for change in practice. COIN is a thoughtfully planned discussion series that enables participants to learn about relevant topics (e.g., feminist pedagogy, vocational awe) from a variety of resources, reflect on and share their own experience, and learn from each other in community. This chapter will be particularly helpful for considering how to develop this type of program at your own institution.

We close this volume with Chapter 43, "It Starts with Us: Exploring Inclusive Pedagogies through Relational Learning Approaches among Library Workers" by Lalitha Nataraj, Torie Quiñonez, April Ibarra Siqueiros, Talitha R. Matlin, Judy Opdahl, Amanda Kalish, Yvonne Nalani Meulemans, Allison Carr, and Tricia Lantzy. The authors take an autoethnographic approach to exploring validation theory and relational-cultural theory in their work at the University Library at California State University, San Marcos, particularly how these theories inform the Teaching and Learning Department's Teaching Academy. The authors reflect on their experiences with the Teaching Academy, surfacing themes of personal identity and values, trust and safety with colleagues, and collaboration and autonomy. This chapter underscores the significance of relational approaches, sharing how they help us create inclusive and equitable learning environments, contribute to valuable relationships with faculty and students, and enable continued professional growth along with colleagues.

CHAPTER 40

Enabling Inclusive and Equitable Teaching Practices through Instructor Development

Jane Hammons, Amanda L. Folk, Katie Blocksidge, and Hanna Primeau

In The Ohio State University Libraries, we support inclusive and equitable teaching practices through instructor development.[1] The Libraries' Teaching and Learning department offers two formal university-wide, cross-campus instructor development programs, Meaningful Inquiry and Teaching Information Literacy. In this chapter, we outline our programs, highlight the equity-focused pedagogical strategies that we incorporate, and provide activities and templates readers can use to support equity and inclusion in their own work with instructors.

Meaningful Inquiry is a five-part workshop developed in collaboration with Writing Across the Curriculum and The Ohio State Newark Library intended to support instructors in developing equitable and meaningful research or inquiry-based assignments. Originally an in-person workshop, in 2020 Meaningful Inquiry was redesigned into a virtual series due to COVID-19. Our second program, Teaching Information Literacy, is a self-paced online course intended to help participants strategically incorporate information literacy into their courses and, in doing so, create a more equitable learning environment for all students. Our university's Drake Institute for Teaching and Learning offers credentials, known as teaching endorsements, for faculty and staff who complete professional development programs. Both

Meaningful Inquiry and Teaching Information Literacy are available as teaching endorsements and are open to all instructors and faculty, graduate teaching associates, librarians, instructional designers, and staff from across the university.[2]

In each program, we incorporate pedagogical strategies aimed at increasing equity and inclusion, among them Estela Mara Bensimon's cognitive frames, the Decoding the Disciplines model developed by Joan Middendorf and David Pace, and the Transparency in Learning and Teaching (TILT) framework developed by Mary-Ann Winkelmes and colleagues.[3] We combine these strategies with the *Framework for Information Literacy for Higher Education* to support instructors' capacity to teach information literacy and create more equitable and transparent assignments.[4]

Equitable Strategies/ Pedagogies

We believe that the ways of thinking and knowing articulated in the *Framework for Information Literacy* remain part of a hidden curriculum for many students, including those whose identities have been marginalized in higher education.[5] Instructors develop assignments and expectations for performance based on these ways of thinking and knowing, but they are not always explicitly or transparently taught or discussed with students. Instructors may assume that students have already learned these ways of thinking or knowing or that they are learning them in another course. Furthermore, most instructors have likely internalized these ways of thinking and knowing—they have crossed those conceptual thresholds—and might not be able to remember a time when they did not incorporate them into their work. One of the shared goals in both Meaningful Inquiry and Teaching Information Literacy is to increase equity by encouraging instructors to explicitly identify, model, and discuss the practices and expectations that are included in this hidden curriculum.

Bensimon's Cognitive Frames

To achieve this goal, we draw upon Dr. Estela Mara Bensimon's cognitive frames to provide us with an equitable foundation for our instructor development programming.[6] Dr. Bensimon outlines three frames that instructors, administrators, and staff might use to develop programming or services to close racial equity gaps in higher education. The first is a deficit frame, in which the programming or service attempts to fix the student. In this frame, the student is viewed as deficient, and they might be subjected to programs like remedial or developmental education. The second is the diversity frame, in which the solution is to fix the workers or employees. In this frame, employees celebrate diversity but are also required or encouraged to attend workshops and training. While there is nothing inherently wrong with many of the activities in this frame, they ultimately do not move the needle to equity because they do not address systemic or cultural issues that create inequities among different student populations. In other words, activities in the diversity frame do not address the root causes of the inequities. In the equity frame, the goal is to fix the culture, including systems and processes that continue to reproduce inequities.

There is a lot of overlap among these frames, and our instructor development programming has elements of both the diversity and equity frames. This programming is quite literally a series of workshops or modules for course instructors that address elements of their practice.[7] However, we do truly believe that we are working toward culture change within classrooms across the university by highlighting the potentially tacit nature of information literacy for many students and discussing its possible role in reproducing persistent equity gaps. We intend to normalize reflection on students' information literacy, their performance on research assignments, and changes to teaching practices to create a more equitable and transparent learning environment. In other words, as Bensimon describes, we are trying to make the "invisible visible and undiscussable discussable."[8]

Decoding the Disciplines

A key aspect of both Meaningful Inquiry and Teaching Information Literacy is encouraging instructors to identify the bottlenecks within their disciplines and course content that students consistently find challenging. Decoding the Disciplines provides a structure for these discussions, asking instructors to consider the mental tasks they expect students to perform in order to successfully complete research assignments.[9] We believe that these tacit assumptions create challenges for students as they do not yet have the mental models that an expert would have in these situations. Instructors need to think back to their own experiences as novices to determine how they learned to complete these research tasks; after identifying bottlenecks, instructors can consider how they would model these hidden tasks for students and provide them with opportunities to practice and receive formative feedback.

We make a point to link the *Framework for Information Literacy* to Decoding the Disciplines by asking participants to identify the threshold concepts and dispositions from the *Framework* that are most important for helping students move past research bottlenecks. Prioritizing the research practices necessary for student success is crucial, as students may not receive formal research instruction before arriving at a university; additionally, students may be asked to engage with discipline-specific research practices. This work helps instructors identify how they can make their research assignments more equitable and connect topics in their disciplines to the classes that they teach.

Transparency in Learning and Teaching (TILT)

A main focus in each program is helping instructors uncover the hidden ways of thinking and knowing in their specialization. This can be as large as the task that it is to learn how to be a part of a discipline, or as small as the process it takes for a novice to understand and engage with the content in a course, a process that may be contributing to student learning bottlenecks if hidden. Once instructors have identified the bottlenecks and considered their disciplinary knowledge, we introduce TILT (Transparency in Learning and Teaching).[10] TILT encourages instructors to explicitly outline three components of research assignments for students. First, the PURPOSE of the assignment, including how it connects to course or program learning outcomes. Second, the TASKS that students will need to complete as part of the assignment. And third, the CRITERIA by which students' grades will be determined.

A student has little to no chance of success in an assignment if the goals for it, along with descriptions of an expected outcome, are not explicit. TILT provides instructors with guidance for how they can be transparent about all details of research assignments. This means ensuring learning outcomes are written for a student audience, providing detailed and organized explanations of how the final product will be graded, and sharing examples of the work expected, knowing that these changes can help shift a student's motivation for assignment completion.

While TILT is included in both programs as a means to encourage instructors to clarify their expectations, thus increasing the ability of all students to successfully complete research assignments, in Meaningful Inquiry, TILT is also used to support an additional workshop goal, the creation of research assignments that are meaningful. We encourage instructors to reflect upon what their purpose is for a research-based assignment, if they consider their assignments to be meaningful to students, and if not, how they could become so. With emphasis on providing students with authentic tasks, we ask instructors to begin to think about how to connect the materials to students' lives and current interests as well as their future lives, post-graduation.[11]

This gentle approach to shifting what lies behind the curtain of teaching, to sharing openly with students, encourages instructors to be more thoughtful about assignment purpose and final design, and thus creates a more equitable opportunity for all students. It is important to note that, although we have described Decoding and TILT separately, in practice, we use them together, building off of each to ensure instructors have a robust tool kit to address changes in their courses' content. Repeatedly in feedback, participants mentioned Decoding hand in hand with TILT, showing how deeply intertwined the concepts were in application to their own courses and assignments. Many participants also indicated their plans to redesign or reconsider course assignments with a focus on transparency in order to create a more positive experience for all students.

Meaningful Inquiry Redesign Template

An overview of the basic assignment redesign process that participants use in Meaningful Inquiry is provided in table 40.1, indicating where specific pedagogical strategies or frames are incorporated.

Table 40.1

Meaningful Inquiry assignment redesign process

Step	Goal	Action	Pedagogical Frame or Strategy
1	Identify student achievement gaps	Consider achievement gaps in higher education and approaches to overcome gaps	Bensimon's Cognitive Frames
2	Uncover learning bottlenecks	Identify places where students get stuck or fail to meet expectations	Decoding the Disciplines
3	Identify ways of thinking or knowing that contribute to bottlenecks	Use the Framework for Information Literacy to highlight key concepts, knowledge practices, or dispositions related to learning bottlenecks	Decoding the Disciplines, the Framework for Information Literacy
4	Identify characteristics of meaningful assignments	Consider factors that contribute to making assignments meaningful (aligned with students' interests or future goals)	
5	Consider the purpose	Reflect on the purpose of their research assignments	Decoding the Disciplines, TILT
6	Outline assignment revisions	Identify changes they can make in order to integrate information literacy, overcome bottlenecks, add meaning	Framework for Information Literacy, Decoding the Disciplines

Table 40.1

Meaningful Inquiry assignment redesign process

Step	Goal	Action	Pedagogical Frame or Strategy
7	Apply TILT	Clarify the purpose, tasks, and criteria for assignment	TILT & Decoding the Disciplines

Meaningful Inquiry Activities

In this section, we share examples of activities from the Meaningful Inquiry workshop intended to help instructors identify learning bottlenecks and make explicit connections to the *Framework for Information Literacy for Higher Education*.

Reflective Prompt (Table 40.1, Step 2)

First, participants complete a reflection designed to help them connect their own experiences as an instructor with workshop content, by responding to the following prompt: What are some of the common ways in which students fall short of meeting your expectations on research assignments?

Activity: Connecting Bottlenecks with the Framework (Table 40.1, Step 3)

After identifying initial bottlenecks, participants are encouraged to connect the bottlenecks with the *Framework* by answering the following questions:

1. Which of the information literacy frames are most relevant to the common ways in which students fall short of meeting your expectations on research assignments? Why do you feel this frame (or frames) is relevant?
2. Explore the dispositions and knowledge practices for the selected threshold concept. Which of these do you think are most important for helping students to move past the bottleneck that you've identified? Which of these do you believe may be tacit for students who struggle with the bottleneck?

We have found this activity is more successful if we first provide very brief overviews of each frame. The librarians at Bucknell University have created posters we have found to be helpful for providing a quick introduction to the *Framework*.[12] After an instructor has identified the relevant frames, they can then turn to the *Framework* to read a more complete description, including the dispositions and knowledge practices.

Reflective Prompt (Table 40.1, Steps 5–7)

In this reflective activity, participants consider their own assignments in relation to what they have learned about Decoding, TILT, and meaningful assignments throughout the workshop by answering the following questions:

1. When you assess student performance, what are you rewarding?
2. How do you give students practice with and feedback on those things that you are rewarding in their performance on the final assignment?
3. Do you give students the opportunity to reflect on what they're learning or how they're growing?

At the end of the workshop, participants are encouraged to submit an action plan where they indicate how they intend to incorporate content from the workshop in order to create more meaningful and equitable assignments. Although the action plan can take a variety of formats, we have structured prompts for each of the main topics within the workshop for the participants to apply their learning to their courses. These prompts are

1. How could you more purposefully integrate information literacy into your course?
2. What are some things that you could do to help students overcome the bottlenecks you have identified?
3. How could you better clarify the purpose, tasks, and criteria for your research assignment?
4. How could you make your research assignments more meaningful for students?
5. What kinds of support would you need to make these changes to your assignment(s)? What do you need to learn more about?

Teaching Information Literacy Redesign Template

As with Meaningful Inquiry, one of the foundational aspects of the Teaching Information Literacy course is that instructors' expectations for student performance are often based on understandings and assumptions about research and scholarship that are broadly shared across experienced researchers, but which may not be familiar to novice learners. However, rather than just attempting to fix the students (as with the deficit frame described by Bensimon), the goal is to change the approach that instructors take to teaching information literacy in order to create a more equitable learning environment for all students.

Participants follow a course or assignment redesign process (outlined in table 40.2), in which they learn about the core information literacy concepts from the *Framework for Information Literacy,* identify information literacy–related learning bottlenecks related to the core concepts, and recognize the hidden assumptions or expectations they have that may be contributing to these bottlenecks. Finally, participants develop strategies or activities that they can use to support all students' capacity to move past these bottlenecks.

Table 40.2

Teaching Information Literacy assignment or course redesign process

Step	Goal	Action	Pedagogical Frame or Strategy
1	Identify learning bottlenecks	Assess previous assignments and student performance to identify places where students get stuck	Decoding the Disciplines
2	Identify expectations and disciplinary knowledge	Use the Framework to identify expectations, assumptions, and disciplinary knowledge that may contribute to learning bottlenecks	Framework for Information Literacy, Decoding the Disciplines
3	Identify information literacy goals or learning outcomes	Determine what students need to understand or be able to do related to information literacy	Framework for Information Literacy
4	Identify assessment options	Consider a range of assessment methods to determine whether students are meeting goals	
5	Develop learning activities or assignments	Develop or revise one or more activities to help students meet learning outcomes	Framework for Information Literacy, Decoding the Disciplines
6	Apply TILT	Use TILT to clarify the purpose, tasks, and criteria for their draft activities or assignments	TILT

Teaching Information Literacy Activities

This section outlines two activities that participants complete as part of the course that are intended to help make hidden expectations visible and transparent for all students.

Activity: Identifying Hidden Disciplinary Knowledge (Table 40.2, Step 2)

After learning about the core concepts from the *Framework*, participants attempt to surface the knowledge they have about research practices in their discipline. The activity is based on the work of Sara D. Miller, who combined the Decoding the Disciplines model with the *Framework* to develop a series of reflective questions that instructors can use to identify their tacit disciplinary knowledge.[13] Without realizing it, instructors may be holding students accountable for not meeting the standards of research in their field, even though students have not yet been exposed to those standards.

In their workbook, participants consider questions, based on those developed by Miller, that are related to each of the core concepts and are designed to draw out the disciplinary knowledge that participants have. For the purposes of the activity, the wording of some questions has been revised slightly from Miller's original wording. Questions include the following:

AUTHORITY IS CONSTRUCTED AND CONTEXTUAL

- Who are the authorities in your field? What makes them authorities?
- What processes contribute to the construction of authority in your field?

INFORMATION CREATION AS A PROCESS

- What information are most common in your field?
- Are some formats considered more authoritative?

INFORMATION HAS VALUE

- What are the for attribution in your field?
- Is access to in your field limited in some way? If so, who has access and who does not?

RESEARCH AS INQUIRY

- What does it to research in your field?
- What counts as in your field?

SCHOLARSHIP AS CONVERSATION

- How do the in your field take place? Who are the participants?
- In what types of do the conversations appear (books, journals, websites)?

SEARCHING AS STRATEGIC EXPLORATION

- What information tools resources are most relevant to your field?
- What search behaviors or search strategies are commonly used in your field?

Participants then respond to the following question: How do you think your hidden knowledge may be contributing to the bottlenecks you see?

Asking participants to reflect on these questions is intended to help them to identify what information literacy looks like in their field. It also brings awareness to how much knowledge participants have gained about researching in their field since they were a novice. More importantly, it is intended to help them acknowledge the ways in which their disciplinary knowledge could be creating unrealistic expectations for novice learners and identify ways to address these issues in their teaching.

Activity: Incorporating TILT (Table 40.2, Step 6)

One of the ways that instructors are then encouraged to make their hidden expectations visible is by using TILT. After developing a draft assignment or activity, participants answer the following questions:

- What terminology may cause difficulties for students?
- What is the specific PURPOSE of the assignment or activity?
- What TASKS will students need to do in order to complete the activity?
- What CRITERIA will their performance be evaluated on?

Combining the *Framework for Information Literacy*, Decoding the Disciplines, and TILT in this way gives participants direction for how they can integrate information literacy into their courses in a way that will be more equitable because the expectations will be clear to all students. Participants are encouraged to explicitly share information on the purpose, tasks, and criteria as part of the instructions or guidance they provide to students when they assign research or inquiry-based projects.

Conclusion

Since 2019, sixty-three participants have completed the Meaningful Inquiry workshops and twenty-seven participants have completed the Teaching Information Literacy course. Participant feedback has been positive, and we are aware, anecdotally, of several courses in which participants have used strategies learned in the workshops to revise learning outcomes and assignments.[14]

Our instructor development programs are only one example of our efforts to support equity and inclusion in our work. While we value the opportunity to provide instruction directly to students and continue to do so both through curricular and cocurricular programming, we also recognize the challenges of reaching all students directly, especially at an institution the size of Ohio State. For this reason, we have made instructor development one of the key activities of the Teaching and Learning department. By teaching instructors, our reach to undergraduates is amplified and our ability to promote equitable and inclusive teaching practices is increased. Through this work, we inspire instructors to approach their teaching through an equity lens.

Although not all academic libraries will have the opportunity to offer full professional development programs such as Meaningful Inquiry and Teaching Information Literacy, there are opportunities at multiple types of institutions to incorporate an equity focus into instructor development work. Pedagogical models such as Decoding the Disciplines and TILT offer easily approachable and adaptable guidelines that instructors can use to help make their research or inquiry-based assignments more equitable and inclusive for all students. Librarians who work with instructors on course or assignment design projects can follow the model above to support instructors and can also incorporate these strategies into their own work as instructors.

Notes

1. We use the term *instructor development*, rather than *faculty development*, to indicate that many of those who teach or provide instructional support (including many who participate in our programming) do not have faculty status.
2. For a more detailed overview of the goals and structure of each program, see Amanda L. Folk and Jane Hammons, "Expanding Our Reach: Implementing Instructor Development Programming," *International Information and Library Review* 53, no. 1 (2021): 69–78.
3. Estela Mara Bensimon, "Closing the Achievement Gap in Higher Education: An Organizational Learning Perspective," *New Directions for Higher Education* 131 (2005): 99–111; Joan Middendorf and David Pace, "Decoding the Disciplines: A Model for Helping Students to Learn Disciplinary Ways of Thinking," *New Directions for Higher Education* 2004, no. 98 (Summer 2004): 1–12; Decoding the Disciplines home page, accessed October 15, 2021, http://decodingthedisciplines.org/; Mary-Ann Winkelmes et al., "A Teaching Intervention That Increases Underserved College Students' Success," *Peer Review* 18, no. 1/2 (Winter/Spring 2016), ; "TILT Higher Ed home page, accessed May 4, 2021, https://tilthighered.com/.
4. Association of College and Research Libraries, *Framework for Information Literacy for Higher Education* (Chicago: Association of College and Research Libraries, 2016), https://www.ala.org/acrl/standards/ilframework.
5. Amanda L. Folk, "Reframing Information Literacy as Academic Cultural Capital: A Critical and Equity-Based Foundation for Practice, Assessment, and Scholarship," *College and Research Libraries* 80, no. 5 (2019): 658–73.
6. Bensimon, "Closing the Achievement Gap."

7. Participants in our workshops include instructors from across the university with a variety of appointments, including tenure-stream and tenured faculty, associated and contingent faculty, and graduate teaching associates. In addition, we welcome participants who serve in teaching and learning support roles, including library employees, instructional designers, educational technologists, and instructional consultants.
8. Bensimon, "Closing the Achievement Gap," 99.
9. Middendorf and Pace, "Decoding the Disciplines"; Decoding the Disciplines home page.
10. Winkelmes et al., "A Teaching Intervention"; TILT Higher Ed home page.
11. Susan A. Ambrose et al., *How Learning Works* (San Francisco: Jossey-Bass, 2010).
12. Bucknell University Library, "About the Framework," https://researchbysubject.bucknell.edu/framework.
13. Sara D. Miller, "Diving Deep: Reflective Questions for Identifying Tacit Disciplinary Information Literacy Knowledge Practices, Dispositions, and Values through the ACRL Framework for Information Literacy," *Journal of Academic Librarianship* 44, no. 3 (2018): 412–18.
14. For Meaningful Inquiry, we are currently in the process of analyzing participant responses to pre- and post-workshop surveys but are not yet able to share conclusions about the impact of this work on instructors. For both programs, long-term, formal assessment of the impact of this work on student learning is challenging, as we must rely on instructor reports of impact.

Bibliography

Ambrose, Susan A., Michael W. Bridges, Michele DiPietro, Marsha C. Lovett, and Marie K. Norman. *How Learning Works: Seven Research-Based Principles for Smart Teaching*. San Francisco: Jossey-Bass, 2010.

Association of College and Research Libraries. *Framework for Information Literacy for Higher Education*. Chicago: Association of College and Research Libraries, 2016. https://www.ala.org/acrl/standards/ilframework.

Bensimon, Estela Mara. "Closing the Achievement Gap in Higher Education: An Organizational Learning Perspective." *New Directions for Higher Education* 131 (2005): 99–111.

Bucknell University Library. "About the Framework." https://researchbysubject.bucknell.edu/framework.

Decoding the Disciplines home page. Accessed October 15, 2021, http://decodingthedisciplines.org/.

Folk, Amanda L. "Reframing Information Literacy as Academic Cultural Capital: A Critical and Equity-Based Foundation for Practice, Assessment, and Scholarship." *College and Research Libraries* 80, no. 5 (2019): 658–73.

Folk, Amanda L., and Jane Hammons. "Expanding Our Reach: Implementing Instructor Development Programming." *International Information and Library Review* 53, no. 1 (2021): 69–78.

Middendorf, Joan, and David Pace. "Decoding the Disciplines: A Model for Helping Students to Learn Disciplinary Ways of Thinking." *New Directions for Teaching and Learning* 2004, no. 98 (Summer 2004): 1–12. https://doi.org/10.1002/tl.142.

Miller, Sara D. "Diving Deep: Reflective Questions for Identifying Tacit Disciplinary Information Literacy Knowledge Practices, Dispositions, and Values through the ACRL Framework for Information Literacy." *Journal of Academic Librarianship* 44, no. 3 (2018): 412–18.

TILT Higher Ed home page. Accessed May 4, 2021. https://tilthighered.com/.

Winkelmes, Mary-Ann, Matthew Bernacki, Jeffrey Butler, Michelle Zochowski, Jennifer Golanics, and Kathryn Harriss Weavil. "A Teaching Intervention That Increases Underserved College Students' Success." *Peer Review* 18, no. 1/2 (Winter/Spring 2016): 31–37.

CHAPTER 41

Designing and Managing Inclusive Group Projects

Laura Saunders

Group projects are a popular assignment format purported to have many benefits for students. However, unless they are carefully designed and managed, they are unlikely to achieve those benefits and can be a source of unnecessary stress for students, stresses that may disproportionately impact students from historically marginalized groups. This chapter provides research-based and practical advice for addressing common pitfalls to create meaningful and inclusive group projects. The focus is on group projects as a graded assignment, as opposed to ungraded group activities.

Group Projects: Benefits and Challenges

Group projects offer many benefits to students. A type of collaborative learning, which is considered a high-impact educational practice, group work is associated with positive student outcomes.[1] They facilitate social interaction, which has been posited as the basis of knowledge construction,[2] and a number of studies with students ranging from elementary school to college age suggest that collaborative projects can lead to deeper learning as well as a greater ability to transfer skills into new contexts.[3] When structured properly, group work can positively impact critical thinking abilities and the competencies needed for successful collaboration and socialization, including interpersonal skills, empathy, and perspective taking.[4] These skills are highly sought by employers and could lead to more success in the job market.[5] Further, lower-performing and other disadvantaged students often

show disproportionate gains with cooperative versus competitive or individualistic learning.[6]

However, group work, and especially graded group projects, can present challenges to both students and instructors. Many instructors expect the social and collaborative outcomes to be a natural side product of group work and do not teach students how to work in teams.[7] Unless those skills are explicitly taught, along with the content, students will not necessarily achieve the intended outcomes. Many students report disliking group work. They are often concerned that their grades will be negatively affected by "social loafing," or group members not contributing equitably to the workload.[8] Others do not see the benefit of contributing to the group or feel their input is not valued by their team members and withdraw.[9] While the research is mixed with regard to whether there are gender disparities in outcomes for group work,[10] some research suggests that students of color are more likely to receive lower ratings from their team members in peer evaluations and may feel tokenized if they are the only student of color on a team.[11] Further, some students report facing microaggressions in group work.[12] Concerns about the time involved in meeting and planning may be exacerbated for adult learners, who are often juggling many commitments, as well as for online students, who may be located across various time zones.

Designing Successful Group Projects

Instructors can structure group projects to glean the benefits while minimizing challenges. Such design takes time and effort, but the research-supported benefits of group work make the effort worthwhile. The rest of this chapter illustrates how to put the criteria for effective group projects into practice, using an example of a group project from a graduate-level course on academic libraries that I teach and drawing on existing research to support design choices. The project is structured as committee work (a search committee, space planning committee, marketing committee, etc.), with a charge outlining their responsibilities and the deliverables. Committees are expected to meet throughout the semester and must submit meeting minutes roughly every two weeks. Each committee proposes a budget to support their activities. At the end of the semester, committees submit written reports and supporting materials showing how they fulfilled their charge and share their activities verbally at a whole-class "staff meeting."

Goals and Transparency

The first step, before any designing begins, is to decide whether and why to design a group project. Despite the benefits of collaborative learning, not all courses need to have graded group assignments, and not all assignments are equally well suited to a group approach. One consideration is the intended learning outcomes of the project and the course. If communication skills, teamwork, leadership, and other inter- and intrapersonal skills are expected outcomes, then a group project might make sense, whereas if the focus is more on domain or content knowledge and skills, an individual assignment might be more appropriate. Transparency and relevance are important for helping students understand the purpose of assignments and can help ease anxieties and increase motivation.[13] When assigning group projects, instructors should find opportunities to explain clearly and explicitly why a group project has been assigned and what students will gain from the experience.[14]

In my class, I chose to incorporate a semester-long group project in part because much of the work in academic libraries, and higher education in general, is done in committees. A group project mimics that professional environment and requires students to engage in and develop the interpersonal and collaborative skills necessary for successful committee work. I explain this reasoning in multiple places through-out the course, including in the syllabus and in an opening lecture in which I talk about my own committee experiences, including the time I was assigned to the committee on committees to review the purpose and charges of my department's existing committees. I remind students of this reasoning throughout the semester. In this way, I work to help the students understand the purpose of the assignment and to see its relevance to their career goals.

Choice

Giving students some choice in assignments allows them some self-direction and can increase their motivation and sense of control.[15] Students might be allowed to form their own groups, although in such cases there is a risk that students will gravitate to peers with whom they are familiar and might form relatively homog-enous groups without regard to the needs of the project. Conversely, students can engage in a skills inventory to identify their areas of strength and then form groups of people whose skills complement each other and align with the skills necessary to complete the project. For instance, the instructor could use guiding questions or reflective writing to help students identify their strengths as well as the areas in which they might benefit from support and then facilitate an interactive session to help connect students with complementary skills. This skills identification might also help students from marginalized groups or introverted students surface and be recognized for their abilities and contributions. Another option is to form groups based on students' general availability for meetings. This option can work especially well for adult students and online learners, whose availability might be restricted by jobs, family commitments, and differing time zones. For the Academic Libraries class, students select the committee on which they want to serve. This option allows them to choose a committee that aligns with their areas of strength, background knowledge, and ultimate career goals. In addition to student interest, complementary schedules, and the mix of skills, instructors might also want to restrict the number of students in a group. The ideal size of the group depends in part on the scale of the project, but in general groups of three to four tend to work well. Larger groups often have a harder time coordinating schedules.

Project Scope and Interdependence

Teams need to feel a sense of interdependence, as if each person must contribute for the project to be successful.[16] As a result, the project must be large enough to support multiple people.[17] At the same time, the individual elements of the project should be integrated so that students cannot simply divide up the tasks and do them individually. The committee assignment fulfills the criteria for scope and interdependence by providing committees with detailed charges that cover a range of responsibilities and deliverables relevant to the committee's area of focus. For example, the search committee is tasked with hiring a new assistant director. They must write a job posting and find outlets to post it; determine a salary range; source three potential candidates; justify their choices; and plan campus visits, including a schedule of activities, interview questions, and any necessary travel arrangements. The charges and deliverables are interrelated so that, for instance, students cannot develop interview questions without some understanding of the job description or develop a travel budget without knowing who the potential candidates are. Each charge naturally embeds a number of decision points that require group discussion and consensus. Further, committees are required to submit meeting minutes several times throughout the semester, which helps ensure that discussions and decision-making are occurring.

Team Building and Roles

Too often, instructors expect students to develop interpersonal and collaborative skills as a by-product of group work, without any explicit instruction. However, when they are placed in teams without direction, students will often jump into the tasks of the project without attending to issues of team building and process. Further, one or two students tend to assume dominant roles, directing the project, assigning tasks, and potentially marginalizing or silencing others, often those from already marginalized groups such as students of color and women.[18]

Instructors can facilitate inclusive teamwork by providing tools and direct instruction on how to work successfully as a team. For instance, group contracts, in which teams establish guidelines for interactions and processes for getting work done, can facilitate success.[19] Although written for business professionals, Mary Shapiro's *HBR Guide to Leading Teams* offers comprehensive advice, including templates for a contract and cultural audit.[20] In my class, the committee's first task is to create a contract in which they come to consensus about process, decision-making, and accountability. For example, the team agrees to when, where, and how meetings will be held; the protocol for alerting the team if you have to miss a meeting; and the steps for being accountable for any discussions that are missed. In the semesters since I implemented this contract, I have had far fewer complaints and concerns from groups about issues of social loafing, and peer evaluation forms suggest that students are generally holding themselves accountable to the contracts.

Assigning roles can also alleviate some of the common pitfalls of teams,[21] as it facilitates task divisions, helps to clarify each person's contribution, and thus increases accountability. These roles can also help students who might be hesitant to participate or more likely to be silenced or marginalized define their position on the team and highlight their contributions. In my course, the committees rotate the chair position about every two weeks until every student has had a turn as chair, thus ensuring every student an opportunity in a leadership role. During their rotation, the student serving as chair takes a leadership role and is responsible for convening meetings, setting an agenda, and submitting minutes.

Scaffolding and Opportunities to Intervene

Group projects need to be large and complex enough to support the participation of the group. To avoid students becoming overwhelmed or getting off track, these large projects should be scaffolded with shorter-term goals.[22] To ensure the committees are making regular progress, I integrate regular check-ins, both graded and ungraded. As noted, committee chairs submit meeting minutes roughly every two weeks. Not only does this provide some scaffolding, it also gives each student an opportunity to earn an individual grade related to their project work. Each committee is also required to submit a preliminary budget as part of one of the chair reports for approval about one month before the final project is due. In addition, each student fills out an ungraded midterm and end-of-semester assessment report in which they can identify issues or concerns with the team or the project. These mechanisms offer an opportunity to monitor progress and provide feedback on both the content of the work and the group process.

Time and Tools

Students are often concerned about the logistics of group projects, including finding time to meet. Instructors can help groups find, adopt, and learn to use collaborative tools to manage their time and the project. Shared online folders, platforms for synchronous meetings and asynchronous discussions, shared calendars, and messaging systems can facilitate the communication and coordination necessary for a successful project. However, the instructor should keep in mind that students might not have equitable access to online tools or the hardware to connect with them, and some tools might have a steep learning curve.[23] We can build in instruction time or provide access to tutorials for these tools, and we can survey students about their technology needs and work with individuals to ensure they have the appropriate access or to help them find alternatives. In face-to-face or synchronous online courses, instructors can consider setting aside class time for group meetings. Not only does this alleviate some of the pressure for students, especially those with work and family obligations, but it also allows the instructor a chance to check in with groups in real time, answer questions, and help resolve issues.

Assessment and Feedback

Assessment and feedback both from the instructor and from peers help build accountability, show students the value of their contributions, and motivate participation. Feedback should focus on both the content of the work produced and the student's engagement with the group process.[24] However, instructors should be aware that students from historically marginalized groups, including students of color and women, might be judged more harshly by their peers, and we should integrate instruction into what constitutes meaningful feedback. We can help students learn to give good peer feedback by modeling effective feedback in class and on assignments and sharing effective feedback models like SPARK, which suggests students provide feedback that is specific, prescriptive, actionable, referenced, and kind, or Plus Delta or Do again/Do better, in which the reviewer begins with positive notes and then provides feedback structured on change for improvement.[25] We can also discuss the importance of including both positive and fairly worded constructive feedback and might alert students to issues of implicit bias in feedback and encourage them to be reflective as they assess their peers. For the committee project, students provide a brief, general assessment halfway through the semester on how well the group is functioning. At the end of the semester, they provide more detailed feedback, assessing their own and each team member's overall participation, contributions, and leadership.

Lessons Learned and Continuous Improvement

While my committee project meets many of the criteria for successful and inclusive group projects, it did not start out that way. In the first run-through, I randomly assigned students to groups, I did not provide direct instruction or activities focused on how to work in teams, and I did not provide much framing for why I was assigning this work as a group project. Not surprisingly, student anxieties ran high, and course evaluations were not strong. My first instinct was to revert to an individual assignment. However, I knew that I had a strong reason for this project to be done in groups, and I was fortunate to have observed a colleague who is an expert on teamwork facilitate these processes in another course. Based on what I learned, I have added the elements and framing I described above, and not only have course evaluations improved, but some students have also actually commented on how much they have learned from the project and how relevant it is to their career goals. More importantly, the group process seems to be working well in general, and the work coming out of the committees is outstanding.

Going forward, I hope to improve the project in several ways: I would like to add more specific roles to the group, such as a secretary and treasurer. I want to integrate a fuller debrief session at the end of the semester, including asking students what they learned from both the process and the content of the project, what went well in the teams, and what they might do differently the next time they work on a team. To date, I have always assigned a group grade, without taking individual contributions into account. Going forward, I would like to explore using the feedback and reflection forms to provide individual grades to acknowledge each student's work, along with a group grade for the overall project. Managing this project is an intense experience for both me and my students, but ultimately, I believe the benefits are worth the work.

It is important to note that this chapter focuses on group work with graduate students in a semester-long course. However, most of the criteria and techniques are relevant to students at different levels, and to different settings, including single-lesson group work. Considerations such as scheduling and outside obligations might not impact group work in a one-shot session, but developing a rich activity, creating a group with complementary skills, ensuring that all group members have a role to play and an opportunity to contribute, and providing time and guidance for feedback are still integral to an effective group experience.

Notes

1.   Kathryn E. Linder, Chrysanthemum Mattison Hayes, and Kelvin Thompson, *High-Impact Practices in Online Education* (Sterling, VA: Stylus, 2018).

2.   Lev Vygotsky, *Mind in Society* (Cambridge, MA: Harvard University Press, 1978).

3.   Nancy Frey, Douglas Fisher, and Sandi Everlove, *Productive Group Work* (Alexandria, VA: ASCD, 2009); Katherine McWhaw et al., "From Co-operation to Collaboration: Helping Students Become Collaborative Learners," in *Cooperative Learning: The Social and Intellectual Outcomes of Learning in Groups*, ed. Robyn M. Gillies and Adrian F. Ashman (New York: Routledge, 2003), 69–86.

4.   David W. Johnson, Roger T. Johnson, and Edythe Johnson Holubec, *Circles of Learning* (Alexan-

dria, VA: Association for Supervision and Curriculum Development, 1984).

5. McWhaw et al. "From Co-operation to Collaboration."

6. Hannah Shachar, "Who Gains What from Cooperative Learning: An Overview of Eight Studies," in *Cooperative Learning: The Social and Intellectual Outcomes of Learning in Groups*, ed. Robyn M. Gillies and Adrian F. Ashman (New York: Routledge, 2003), 103–118; Linder, Hayes, and Thompson, *High-Impact Practices*.

7. Johnson, Johnson, and Holubec, *Circles of Learning*, 29-45.

8. McWhaw, et al., "From Co-operation to Collaboration."

9. Shachar, "Who Gains What."

10. See, e.g., David W. Johnson and Roger T. Johnson, "Cooperative Small-Group Learning," *Curriculum Report* 14, no. 1 (October 1, 1984): 1–6; Renee P. Petersen, David W. Johnson, and Roger T. Johnson, "Effects of Cooperative Learning on Perceived Status of Male and Female Pupils," *Journal of Social Psychology* 131, no. 5 (1991): 717–35, https://doi.org/10.1080/00224545.1991.9924655.

11. Sue V. Rosser, "Group Work in Science, Engineering, and Mathematics: Consequences of Ignoring Gender and Race," *College Teaching* 46, no. 3 (1998): 82–88, https://doi.org/10.1080/87567559809596243.

12. Stacie Anne Harwood et al., *Racial Microaggressions at the University of Illinois at Urbana-Champaign* (University of Illinois at Urbana-Champaign, 2015), https://hdl.handle.net/2142/79010.

13. Marilla D. Svinicki, *Learning and Motivation in the Postsecondary Classroom* (San Francisco: Anker, 2004).

14. Johnson, Johnson, and Holubec, *Circles of Learning*, 30; Flower Darby and James M. Lang, *Small Teaching Online* (San Francisco: Jossey-Bass, 2019).

15. Johnson, Johnson, and Holubec, *Circles of Learning*; Flower Darby and James M. Lang, *Small Teaching Online* (San Francisco: Jossey-Bass, 2019).

16. Johnson, Johnson, and Holubec, *Circles of Learning*; McWhaw et. al. "From Co-operation to Collaboration."

17. Johnson, Johnson, and Holubec, *Circles of Learning*, 79.

18. Veena S. Singaram et al., "'For Most of Us Africans, We Don't Just Speak': A Qualitative Investigation into Collaborative Heterogeneous PBL Group Learning." *Advances in Health Sciences Education: Theory and Practice* 16, no. 3 (August 2011): 297–310, https://doi.org/10.1007/s10459-010-9262-3.

19. Darby and Lang, *Small Teaching Online*.

20. Mary Shapiro, *HBR Guide to Leading Teams*, Harvard Business Review Guides (Cambridge, MA: Harvard Business Review Press, 2015).

21. Darby and Lang, *Small Teaching Online*.

22. Darby and Lang, *Small Teaching Online*; Linder, Hayes, and Thompson, *High-Impact Practices*.

23. Linder, Hayes, and Thompson, *High-Impact Practices*.

24. Frey, Fisher, and Everlove, *Productive Group Work*, 13–22.

25. Mark Gardner, "Teaching Students to Give Peer Feedback," Edutopia, October 8, 2019, https://www.edutopia.org/article/teaching-students-give-peer-feedback; Alan Mossman, "Using Plus/Delta for Feedback and Improving Social Processes," *Lean Construction Blog*, September 12, 2019, https://leanconstructionblog.com/Using-Plus-Delta-for-Feedback-and-Improving-Social-Processes.html

Bibliography

Darby, Flower, and James M. Lang. *Small Teaching Online: Applying Learning Science in Online Classes*. San Francisco: Jossey-Bass, 2019.

Frey, Nancy, Douglas Fisher, and Sandi Everlove. *Productive Group Work: How to Engage Students, Build Teamwork, and Promote Understanding*. Alexandria, VA: ASCD, 2009.

Gardner, Mark. "Teaching Students to Give Peer Feedback," Edutopia, October 8, 2019. https://www.edutopia.org/article/teaching-students-give-peer-feedback.

Harwood, Stacy Anne, Shinwoo Choi, Moises Orzoco, Margaret Browne Huntt, and Ruby Mendenhall. *Racial Microaggressions at the University of Illinois at Urbana-Champaign: Voices of Students of Color in the Classroom*. University of Illinois at Urbana-Champaign, 2015, https://hdl.handle.net/2142/79010.

Johnson, David W., and Roger T. Johnson. "Cooperative Small-Group Learning." *Curriculum Report* 14, no. 1 (October 1, 1984): 1–6.

Johnson, David W., Roger T. Johnson, and Edythe Johnson Holubec. *Circles of Learning*. Alexandria, VA: Association for Supervision and Curriculum Development, 1984.

Linder, Kathryn E., Chrysanthemum Mattison Hayes, and Kelvin Thompson. *High-Impact Practices in Online Education: Research and Best Practices*. Sterling, VA: Stylus, 2018.

McWhaw, Katherine, Heidi Schnackenberg, Jennifer Sclater, and Philip C. Abrami, "From Co-operation to Collaboration: Helping Students Become Collaborative Learners." In *Cooperative Learning: The Social and Intellectual Outcomes of Learning in Groups*, edited by Robyn M. Gillies and Adrian F. Ashman, 69–86. New York: Routledge, 2003.

Mossman, Alan. "Using Plus/Delta for Feedback and Improving Social Processes." *Lean Construction Blog*, September 12, 2019. https://leanconstructionblog.com/Using-Plus-Delta-for-Feedback-and-Improving-Social-Processes.html.

Petersen, Renee P., David W. Johnson, and Roger T. Johnson. "Effects of Cooperative Learning on Perceived Status of Male and Female Pupils." *Journal of Social Psychology* 131, no. 5 (1991): 717–35. https://doi.org/10.1080/00224545.1991.9924655.

Rosser, Sue V. "Group Work in Science, Engineering, and Mathematics: Consequences of Ignoring Gender and Race." *College Teaching* 46, no. 3 (1998): 82–88. https://doi.org/10.1080/87567559809596243.

Shachar, Hannah, "Who Gains What from Cooperative Learning: An Overview of Eight Studies." In *Cooperative Learning: The Social and Intellectual Outcomes of Learning in Groups*, edited by Robyn M. Gillies and Adrian F. Ashman, 103–18. New York: Routledge, 2003.

Shapiro, Mary. *HBR Guide to Leading Teams*. Harvard Business Review Guides. Cambridge, MA: Harvard Business Review Press, 2015.

Singaram, Veena S., Cees P. M. van der Vleuten, Fred Stevens, and Diana H. J. M. Dolmans. "'For Most of Us Africans, We Don't Just Speak': A Qualitative Investigation into Collaborative Heterogeneous PBL Group Learning." *Advances in Health Sciences Education: Theory and Practice* 16, no. 3 (August 2011): 297–310. https://doi.org/10.1007/s10459-010-9262-3.

Svinicki, Marilla D. *Learning and Motivation in the Postsecondary Classroom*. San Francisco: Anker, 2004.

Vygotsky, Lev. *Mind in Society: The Development of Higher Psychological Practices*. Cambridge, MA: Harvard University Press, 1978.

CHAPTER 42

Engaging through Conversation

Community Building for Inclusive Library Instruction

Christopher Lowder, David X. Lemmons, and Ashley Blinstrub*

Introduction

Beginning

Library instructors often do not have a formal education in instructional pedagogy when they begin delivering lessons through library instruction.[1] Learning how to be a good library instructor can also be insular, with individual librarians testing new techniques and completing classes in silos without much input from other library instructors. Widespread change requires broad participation from librarians who are focused on diversity, inclusion, and equity in their instructional practice.

As library instructors new to George Mason University, we saw a gap in library instruction communities of practice, since none focused on both library instruction and diversity, equity, and inclusion. At the institution, there were general trainings about these issues, but none that focused on actionable plans for library instructors

---

* All the collaborators responsible for this chapter are white. We benefit from the white supremacy and suppression maintained in librarianship and higher education. There are limits and hidden biases at work that stem from our privileges and perspectives. We also have other identities that play a role in our writing. Christopher is a cis, able-bodied, queer man. Ashley is a cis, able-bodied, heterosexual woman. David is an able-bodied and queer nonbinary person.

that would give us the skills to directly apply our learnings to the classroom. In response, we created Conversations of an Inclusive Nature (COIN) to provide a space for library instructors to build a community focusing on the intersection of their jobs and social justice.

Definitions

Throughout this chapter, we use *library instructors* to mean faculty librarians as well as library staff who teach classes or workshops. Our definition of inclusion draws heavily on the definitions from Mason's Office of Compliance, Diversity, and Ethics and C4DISC.[2] For our context, we highlight that inclusion "decenters majority perspectives and structures";[3] is "active, intentional, and ongoing";[4] creates "opportunities for historically excluded groups";[5] and is a "commitment to diversity at all levels."[6] Daniel Solórzano and Tara Yosso's definition of majoritarian narratives as stories that have been privileged by race, class, gender, and other privileges guides our work.[7] This encompasses white supremacy, ableism, and colonialism, as well as other forms of systemic oppression. By decentering majoritarian narratives, library instructors may begin to understand how their own stories and intersecting identities affect their experiences.[8]

Chapter Structure

In this chapter, we discuss the shortcomings of inclusion trainings in libraries and outline COIN, a conversation series centered on discussions of improving inclusion in library instruction. We also cover the creation and logistics of COIN, outcomes of the program, and how to adapt it to your context.

Current Situation

Problems related to prejudice and discriminatory practices are usually denied by members of the dominant white group. Such denials tend to be reinforced by the belief among whites that equal employment opportunity and affirmative action legislative policies have opened doors for minorities and erased discriminatory practices in these organizations.

—E. J. Josey[9]

Librarians and scholars from marginalized communities have long said that not enough is being done to bring about justice and equity institutionally to libraries and library and information science (LIS) programs, which has affected library instruction.[10] Todd Honma explains how librarianship pretends to be a haven for justice while it upholds and mimics racist structures found in the rest of the country.[11] For example, libraries often collect Indigenous artifacts and systems of knowledge and fail to recognize the colonial history of their institution.[12] Future librarians are not receiving the education to remedy this. Social justice pedagogies have yet to become fully integrated into LIS curricula, but many scholars have presented methods to change this.[13] One way that libraries have attempted to answer this criticism of the institution is through internal cultural awareness workshops for staff.

Stephane Shepherd's study on the effects of cultural awareness workshops in the medical field concluded that the workshops are ineffective at making significant changes to workplace inclusion.[14] April Hathcock explains that diversity programs in libraries are too intertwined with whiteness to effectively recruit and retain librarians from underrepresented groups.[15] Cultural awareness workshops fail at destabilizing the majoritarian systems intrinsic to traditional library instruction. In order to demonstrate a commitment to inclusivity, the library field (well intentioned or not) came to the false conclusion that one-time inclusivity trainings or webinars are effective at creating inclusive instructors and instruction practices.

At our institution, library instruction often consists of single sessions with students, or the one-shot model. As a result, we hope to make as much of an impact as possible during our single classroom visits. We created COIN to be a place where library instructors can discuss inclusivity issues and connect them to their jobs and instructional practices, while keeping the limitations of the single-session instruction model in mind across our discussions.

COIN Creation

As a response to the issues we recognized with inclusion trainings at our institution, we created COIN to engage with a community of people about inclusivity issues in library instruction settings. We created a series focused on libraries and library instruction, which concentrates on one issue at a time and is grounded in community participation and action. We chose to limit COIN's scope to instruction because this is an area where we can make both individual and programmatic changes without administrative buy-in. The COIN facilitators are all members of our library's Teaching & Learning Team, so we have a voice in higher-level decisions surrounding library instruction. There were several factors that assisted us in the creation of this program: the team had an existing interest in DEI-related issues, there was already a framework in place for this type of work, and we were given the necessary time and space to plan these meetings.

First, there was already an interest in learning about inclusive teaching practices on our team. The Teaching & Learning Team previously designed a well-attended workshop series about universal design for learning, and library instructors regularly attended other diversity trainings as well. Further, some library instructors would regularly and informally discuss these trainings in relation to issues surrounding inclusivity in library instruction and how they might change their practices as a result of what they learned. Originally COIN was intended to be held in person to mimic this lunchtime discussion, but soon after our inaugural meeting in early 2020, most employees at our institution began teleworking due to COVID-19, which led to COIN being held online. A major goal of COIN was to expand these conversations so that all library instructors would have the opportunity to participate, and this online environment (while unplanned) helped expand the conversation beyond the silos created by workplace location.

Our library also had an existing framework for communities of practice that assisted in the creation of COIN. A community of practice is defined as a

> social learning communit[y] …driven by collaboration [that] may include sharing work or ideas or observing each other's work. Central to communities of practice are learning skills and concepts, but the building and transfer of cultural knowledge within the community enable them to thrive.[16]

This definition guided our creation of COIN.

It is important to remember that "training culturally competent and socially responsible library and information science (LIS) professionals requires a blended approach that extends across curricula, professional practice, and research."[17] While COIN is one example of the inclusion efforts at our library, it cannot solve these issues alone; it must happen in conjunction with other initiatives.

COIN Logistics

COIN is a monthly discussion series, with each meeting focusing on a different inclusivity theme. In this section, we outline how the series runs, including how participants and facilitators interact, how we engage participants in the discussion, and the changes that we made as a result of the COVID-19 pandemic.

The theme of COIN changes each month, but in each discussion, we focus on inclusivity issues in library instruction. Examples of past themes include academic ableism, feminist pedagogy, and race in the Association of College and Research Libraries' (ACRL) *Framework for Information Literacy*. These themes come from a variety of sources: scholarly literature, conversations in the library world via Twitter, broader world issues, and a list of topic ideas generated by our COIN community.

Once the facilitators settle on a theme, we select resources to share with our community. We include resources in a variety of formats, including scholarly articles, podcasts, videos, and news articles. We prioritize choosing materials created by the communities most affected by the issue we discuss. We also provide our community with a document containing discussion questions beforehand so that learners who may need more time to process information have adequate time to think about these questions in advance. This document initially includes three to five questions based on the facilitators' reading and viewing of the resources.

An example of a COIN theme we used recently was vocational awe, centered by Fobazi Ettarh's work both in her original article and in a podcast where she discussed her ideas.[18] During the meeting, we prepared questions asking participants where they saw vocational awe in our institution, how we could follow Ettarh's advice and start collaborating more across departments on instruction, and other questions that related to her work and ours.

While we started with our questions, our discussion quickly expanded into our participants sharing their own personal experiences with this topic, both at our institution and outside it. We, in fact, asked only one of our prepared four questions and instead allowed participants to share. This is an example of our facilitation style at work: giving participants the space and flexibility to share their own thoughts is a crucial part of our work. We also used anonymous whiteboard tools, allowing participants who were not comfortable sharing aloud to still be heard during the meeting.

Community of COIN

Since COIN was founded as a community of practice, we made it a priority to build our community and constantly adapt to its needs. This group was founded to discuss inclusivity issues in library instruction, but also to be inclusive of all library instructors and our wide array of experiences and personal knowledge. In creating that inclusivity, we advocate for welcomeness and do not limit conversations to being centered on only scholarly articles. Instead, we also encourage our community to share their stories around these topics.

In order to build the community and allow it to flourish, we created a space in which people can share their thoughts, experiences, and ideas in a variety of ways. This community encourages everyone to continue discussions and work outside of COIN meetings. We frame the meetings as a starting discussion of the topic, but the application of the work happens in library instruction settings. We also created an online messaging channel to encourage continued discussion of topics and sharing of resources. These opportunities hopefully allow colleagues to get to know one another as people, not just coworkers and scholars, which is one of COIN's major goals.

In a community of practice, keeping participation voluntary allows participants to spread what they learn throughout the library.[19] Even with the voluntary nature of COIN, the learning and benefits are widespread due to the collaborative nature of library instruction at Mason.[20] We advertised COIN through e-mails to library instructors and presented about it department-wide. In these avenues, we discussed what happens in this community and went over the guidelines for discussions. The social learning approach of COIN also allows library instructors to learn and practice the skills we are discussing within their own contexts.

Six months into COIN, we distributed an anonymous survey to all library instructors to evaluate the program and find ways to improve. In this survey, we gathered a list of suggested topics the community wanted to learn about. After we received the survey results, the facilitators held a special meeting to organize the data. Then, as a community, we discussed the results and came up with recommendations to improve the program. The community asked for a space to continue these conversations with each other and brainstormed the best ways to do this.

We also had a request for more guest facilitators from across the library and the university. We encouraged our community to volunteer to guest-facilitate in order to provide this diversity of experiences of facilitators. The guest facilitator roles are always completely voluntary—in doing this, we hope to avoid tokenizing our colleagues and asking them to speak for their entire community, a burden that falls especially disproportionately on our colleagues of color.[21] We also introduced collaborative discussion questions so that those who do not feel comfortable facilitating can still help focus the discussion based on their interpretations of materials. Currently, we do not have a budget to pay for guest speakers, so we are careful not to ask others to freely exert their time and emotional labor. Overall, the group discussions about the survey and the reaction of the list of recommendations helped strengthen the COIN community. Members reach out more often to discuss COIN topics outside the sessions, share over our online messaging system, and provide feedback on how to keep improving the program.

Instruction Projects Originated from COIN

Not every COIN is expected to result in a significant change in instruction pedagogy, but some have led to larger projects and assessments of instruction practices. Here we will focus on three different projects that have originated from COIN to demonstrate how it has impacted our institution.

Lesson Plan Review

One of the first outcomes of COIN resulted from our discussion on feminist pedagogy in library instruction. During this conversation, the community shared how individual lesson plans should be reviewed and altered to have a stronger focus on student authority and expertise. Since that discussion, library instructors have worked to both alter existing lesson plans and create new lessons grounded in this work.

Finding Diverse Voices Guide

During a COIN discussion on majoritarian narratives, library instructors decided that students should be taught about the oppressive systems of academic publishing, the importance of locating diverse authorship for their research, and ways to find these authors. This inspired a group of instructors to create the "Finding Diverse Voices in Academic Research" LibGuide and an accompanying lesson plan. Subject-specialist librarians have adapted this guide to their own fields, and one department has already requested workshops specifically on using this guide in their classrooms.

Anti-racist Pedagogy Module

COIN attempts to support other inclusion projects in the University Libraries, too. As a result of national and local discussions of anti-racism, some library instructors began working on an asynchronous learning module in Blackboard on how to be an anti-racist library instructor at Mason. In order to introduce this module, a COIN was held and facilitated by the creators of the module. This COIN has helped shape the creation of the module to be focused on the needs and gaps at Mason.

Bringing COIN to You

Because COIN is an adaptable program and format, we encourage you to adapt it at your own institution. As you think through this possibility, we want to take a moment to highlight some of our considerations as we started our series.

Before beginning this process, consider your internal work environment and purpose.[22] Each institution is at different stages, especially regarding inclusivity work. For example, if your institution is in the initial stages of becoming anti-racist, begin by defining concepts like inclusivity or white supremacy. Be prepared to set expectations for the discussions and consider how you will decenter majoritarian voices, counter harmful statements, and allow anonymous responses (see appendix for COIN discussion guidelines). Think about what your motivations are for creating this at your institution and what allyship looks like for your community.[23] If your institution can maintain consistent work toward decentering majoritarian narratives, then your COIN could focus on structural changes such as adjusting job application requirements, name of use policies, and promotion processes.[24]

Our community members have been crucial in improving COIN along the way. Through a large survey as well as informal check-ins during meetings, we have learned how our community feels about COIN, what topics they are interested in discussing, and what we can do to make their experience better. We recommend this community approach, coupled with assessing your community's needs and participation during COIN discussions and activities.

Finally, consider if and how you want administrators to participate. When management gets involved in these personal and sometimes controversial discussions, the power dynamics at play can stifle conversation.[25] We prevented this from happening by allowing many opportunities for anonymous feedback, while still allowing administrators to participate. Perhaps there could be a secondary COIN for administrators and managers, or supervisor-free COIN meetings. Whatever you choose, make sure to always emphasize your commitment to the community and the marginalized voices in the library.

Conclusion

For this chapter, we attempted to bring together relevant diverse perspectives in our sources. As we learn and advance our community's pedagogical practices, we hope to listen to the voices leading the movement of systemic change and to acknowledge the work of those who have been fighting against oppression in libraries long before us. Changing our instruction strategies and working together to introduce new teaching expectations will help to begin change at our level.

Racism and oppression did not start with, nor will they end with, one outwardly racist person. Racism and oppression are systemic. We see COIN as a step beyond education into action; action that we can take in our community and in our teaching. In addition to programs like COIN, which encourage more inclusive teaching practices, we need systematic change to the deep-rooted oppression evident in hiring practices, promotion criteria, and retainment.[26] Committees and initiatives must have the power and sustainability to confront the issues and imagine a better future for all learners.

Appendix: COIN Discussion Guidelines as of Fall 2021

1. Learn from each other. This happens through listening, acknowledging differences, and realizing differences increase awareness.
2. Understand that there are different approaches to solving problems. If you are uncertain about someone else's approach, ask a question to explore areas of uncertainty. Listen respectfully to how and why the approach could work.
3. Be careful about putting others on the spot. Do not demand that others speak for a group that you perceive them to represent. Conversely, if you are a member of a group relevant to the discussion, you can choose to speak up or not depending on your comfort level.
4. Recognize that we are all still learning. Be willing to change your perspective, and make space for others to do the same.
5. If challenging something that has been said, do not challenge the individual sharing this idea or practice. Instead, challenge the idea or practice itself.
6. Accountability is important to growth. People will be given grace but will also be held accountable. If someone challenges something you said, this is an opportunity to grow not to become defensive.
7. Step Up, Step Back. Be mindful of taking up much more space than others.
8. Do not generalize about people. Be aware that even within groups, people have different lives and experiences.
9. Speak from your own experiences. Trust that your and others' experiences are important and valued; they are enough.
10. This is a confidential space. Don't share what others talked about without permission. Ask individually for permission to share others' stories.

Notes

1. Dani Brecher and Kevin Michael Klipfel, "Education Training for Instruction Librarians: A Shared Perspective," *Communications in Information Literacy* 8, no. 1 (2014): 43–49, https://doi.org/10.15760/comminfolit.2014.8.1.164.
2. George Mason University Office of Compliance, Diversity, and Ethics, "Diversity and Inclusion FAQs," accessed May 7, 2021, https://diversity.gmu.edu/diversity/diversity-and-inclusion-faqs; Coalition for Diversity and Inclusion in Scholarly Communications, "Joint Statement of Principles," accessed May 7, 2021, https://c4disc.org/principles/.
3. Coalition for Diversity and Inclusion in Scholarly Communications, "Joint Statement of Principles."
4. George Mason University Office of Compliance, Diversity, and Ethics, "Diversity and Inclusion FAQs."
5. Coalition for Diversity and Inclusion in Scholarly Communications, "Joint Statement of Principles."
6. Coalition for Diversity and Inclusion in Scholarly Communications, "Joint Statement of Principles."

7.   Daniel G. Solórzano and Tara J. Yosso, "Critical Race Methodology: Counter-storytelling as an Analytical Framework for Education Research," *Qualitative Inquiry* 8, no. 1 (February 2002): 28, https://doi.org/10.1177/107780040200800103.

8.   Vani Natarajan, "Counterstoried Spaces and Unknowns," in *Knowledge Justice: Disrupting Library and Information Studies through Critical Race Theory*, ed. Sofia Y. Leung and Jorge R. López-McKnight (Cambridge, MA: MIT Press, 2021), https://doi.org/10.7551/mitpress/11969.001.0001.

9.   E. J. Josey, "Diversity in Libraries," *Virginia Libraries* 48, no. 1 (2002), https://doi.org/10.21061/valib.v48i1.847.

10. Todd Honma, "Trippin' over the Color Line: The Invisibility of Race in Library and Information Studies," *InterActions: UCLA Journal of Education and Information Studies* 1, no. 2 (June 21, 2005), https://escholarship.org/uc/item/4nj0w1mp; Nicole A. Cooke, Miriam E. Sweeney, and Safiya Umoja Noble, "Social Justice as Topic and Tool: An Attempt to Transform an LIS Curriculum and Culture," *Library Quarterly* 86, no. 1 (January 2016): 107–24, https://doi.org/10.1086/684147.

11. Honma, "Trippin' over the Color Line."

12. Sandra Littletree, Miranda Belarde-Lewis, and Marisa Duarte, "Centering Relationality: A Conceptual Model to Advance Indigenous Knowledge Organization Practices," November 2020. https://digital.lib.washington.edu:443/researchworks/handle/1773/46601.

13. Cooke, Sweeney, and Noble, "Social Justice as Topic and Tool"; Paul T. Jaeger et al., "Diversity and LIS Education: Inclusion and the Age of Information," *Journal of Education for Library and Information Science* 52, no. 3 (Summer 2011): 166–83. ProQuest.

14. Stephane M. Shepherd, "Cultural Awareness Workshops: Limitations and Practical Consequences," *BMC Medical Education* 19, no. 1 (January 8, 2019): article 14, https://doi.org/10.1186/s12909-018-1450-5.

15. April Hathcock, "White Librarianship in Blackface: Diversity Initiatives in LIS," *In the Library with the Lead Pipe* 1, no. 1 (October 7, 2015), http://www.inthelibrarywiththeleadpipe.org/2015/lis-diversity/.

16. Maoria J. Kirker, "Cultivating Teacher-Librarians through a Community of Practice," in *The Grounded Instruction Librarian: Participating in the Scholarship of Teaching and Learning*, ed. Melissa Mallon, Lauren Hays, Cara Bradley, Rhonda Husman, and Jackie Belanger (Chicago: Association of College and Research Libraries, 2019), 312.

17. Cooke, Sweeney, and Noble, "Social Justice as Topic and Tool," 107.

18. Fobazi Ettarh, "Vocational Awe and Librarianship: The Lies We Tell Ourselves," *In the Library with the Lead Pipe*, January 10, 2018, https://www.inthelibrarywiththeleadpipe.org/2018/vocational-awe/; Michelle Velasquez-Potts, "Imagine Otherwise: Fobazi Ettarh on the Limits of Vocational Awe," *Ideas on Fire* (blog), October 23, 2019, https://ideasonfire.net/98-fobazi-ettarh/.

19. Christina H. Gola and Lisa Martin, "Creating an Emotional Intelligence Community of Practice: A Case Study for Academic Libraries," *Journal of Library Administration* 60, no. 7 (October 2020): 752–61, https://doi.org/10.1080/01930826.2020.1786982.

20. Gola and Martin, "Creating an Emotional Intelligence Community of Practice."

21. Jaena Alabi, "From Hostile to Inclusive: Strategies for Improving the Racial Climate of Academic Libraries," *Library Trends* 67, no. 1 (2018): 131–46, https://doi.org/10.1353/lib.2018.0029.

22. Nicole A. Cooke, "Developing Cultural Competence," in *Information Services to Diverse Populations: Developing Culturally Competent Library Professionals*, Library and Information Science Text Series (Santa Barbara, CA: Libraries Unlimited, 2017), 11–26.

23. Mia McKenzie, "No More 'Allies,'" *Black Girl Dangerous* (blog), September 30, 2013, http://www.blackgirldangerous.com/2013/09/no-more-allies/; Keith Edwards, "Aspiring Ally Identity Development," May 5, 2015. https://www.keithedwards.com/2015/05/05/aspiring-ally-identity-development/.

24. Hathcock, "White Librarianship in Blackface"; Stephen G. Krueger, *Supporting Trans People in Libraries* (Santa Barbara, CA: Libraries Unlimited, 2019), https://www.abc-clio.com/ABC-CLIOCorporate/product.aspx?pc=A5898P.
25. Frances J. Milliken, Elizabeth W. Morrison, and Patricia F. Hewlin, "An Exploratory Study of Employee Silence: Issues That Employees Don't Communicate Upward and Why," *Journal of Management Studies* 40, no. 6 (September 2003): 1453–76, https://doi.org/10.1111/1467-6486.00387.
26. Hathcock, "White Librarianship in Blackface."

Bibliography

Alabi, Jaena. "From Hostile to Inclusive: Strategies for Improving the Racial Climate of Academic Libraries." *Library Trends* 67, no. 1 (2018): 131–46. https://muse.jhu.edu/article/706992.

Brecher, Dani, and Kevin Michael Klipfel. "Education Training for Instruction Librarians: A Shared Perspective." *Communications in Information Literacy* 8, no. 1 (2014): 43–49. https://doi.org/10.15760/comminfolit.2014.8.1.164.

Coalition for Diversity and Inclusion in Scholarly Communications. "Joint Statement of Principles." Accessed May 7, 2021. https://c4disc.org/principles/.

Cooke, Nicole A. "Developing Cultural Competence." In *Information Services to Diverse Populations: Developing Culturally Competent Library Professionals*, 11-26. Library and Information Science Text Series. Santa Barbara, CA: Libraries Unlimited, 2017.

Cooke, Nicole A., Miriam E. Sweeney, and Safiya Umoja Noble. "Social Justice as Topic and Tool: An Attempt to Transform an LIS Curriculum and Culture." *The Library Quarterly* 86, no. 1 (January 2016): 107–24. https://doi.org/10.1086/684147.

Edwards, Keith. "Aspiring Ally Identity Development." May 5, 2015. https://www.keithedwards.com/2015/05/05/aspiring-ally-identity-development/.

Ettarh, Fobazi. "Vocational Awe and Librarianship: The Lies We Tell Ourselves." *In the Library with the Lead Pipe*, January 10, 2018. https://www.inthelibrarywiththeleadpipe.org/2018/vocational-awe/.

George Mason University Office of Compliance, Diversity, and Ethics. "Diversity and Inclusion FAQs." Accessed May 7, 2021. https://diversity.gmu.edu/diversity/diversity-and-inclusion-faqs.

Gola, Christina H., and Lisa Martin. "Creating an Emotional Intelligence Community of Practice: A Case Study for Academic Libraries." *Journal of Library Administration* 60, no. 7 (October 2020): 752–61. https://doi.org/10.1080/01930826.2020.1786982.

Hathcock, April. "White Librarianship in Blackface: Diversity Initiatives in LIS." *In the Library with the Lead Pipe* 1, no. 1 (October 7, 2017). http://www.inthelibrarywiththeleadpipe.org/2015/lis-diversity/.

Honma, Todd. "Trippin' over the Color Line: The Invisibility of Race in Library and Information Studies." *InterActions: UCLA Journal of Education and Information Studies* 1, no. 2 (June 21, 2005). https://escholarship.org/uc/item/4nj0w1mp.

Jaeger, Paul T., Mega M. Subramaniam, Cassandra B. Jones, and John Carlo Bertot. "Diversity and LIS Education: Inclusion and the Age of Information." *Journal of Education for Library and Information Science* 52, no. 3 (Summer 2011): 166–83. https://www.jstor.org/stable/41308894.

Josey, E. J. "Diversity in Libraries." *Virginia Libraries* 48, no. 1 (2002). https://doi.org/10.21061/valib.v48i1.847.

Kirker, Maoria J. "Cultivating Teacher-Librarians through a Community of Practice." In *The Grounded Instruction Librarian: Participating in the Scholarship of Teaching and Learning*, edited by Melissa Mallon, Lauren Hays, Cara Bradley, Rhonda Husman, and Jackie Belanger, 311–19. Chicago: Association of College and Research Libraries, 2019.

Krueger, Stephen G. *Supporting Trans People in Libraries*. Santa Barbara, CA: Libraries Unlimited, 2019. https://www.abc-clio.com/ABC-CLIOCorporate/product.aspx?pc=A5898P.

Littletree, Sandra, Miranda Belarde-Lewis, and Marisa Duarte. "Centering Relationality: A Conceptual Model to Advance Indigenous Knowledge Organization Practices." November 2020. https://digital.lib.washington.edu:443/researchworks/handle/1773/46601.

McKenzie, Mia. "No More 'Allies.'" *Black Girl Dangerous* (blog), September 30, 2013. http://www.blackgirldangerous.com/2013/09/no-more-allies/.

Milliken, Frances J., Elizabeth W. Morrison, and Patricia F. Hewlin. "An Exploratory Study of Employee Silence: Issues That Employees Don't Communicate Upward and Why." *Journal of Management Studies* 40, no. 6 (September 2003): 1453–76. https://doi.org/10.1111/1467-6486.00387.

Natarajan, Vani. "Counterstoried Spaces and Unknowns." In *Knowledge Justice: Disrupting Library and Information Studies through Critical Race Theory*, edited by Sofia Y. Leung and Jorge R. López-McKnight. Cambridge, MA: MIT Press, 2021. https://doi.org/10.7551/mitpress/11969.001.0001.

Shepherd, Stephane M. "Cultural Awareness Workshops: Limitations and Practical Consequences." *BMC Medical Education* 19, no. 1 (January 8, 2019): article 14. https://doi.org/10.1186/s12909-018-1450-5.

Solórzano, Daniel G., and Tara J. Yosso. "Critical Race Methodology: Counter-storytelling as an Analytical Framework for Education Research." *Qualitative Inquiry* 8, no. 1 (February 2002): 23–44. https://doi.org/10.1177/107780040200800103.

Velasquez-Potts, Michelle. "Imagine Otherwise: Fobazi Ettarh on the Limits of Vocational Awe." *Ideas on Fire* (blog), October 23, 2019. https://ideasonfire.net/98-fobazi-ettarh/.

CHAPTER 43

It Starts with Us

Exploring Inclusive Pedagogies through Relational Learning Approaches among Library Workers

Lalitha Nataraj, Torie Quiñonez, April Ibarra Siqueiros, Talitha R. Matlin, Judy Opdahl, Amanda Kalish, Yvonne Nalani Meulemans, Allison Carr, and Tricia Lantzy

Introduction

Since 2020, the Teaching and Learning (TAL) Department at the University Library at California State University, San Marcos, has committed a few days each January to reflect on and grow our collective expertise in teaching. We fondly refer to this professional development activity as the Teaching Academy. Research and service are required to earn tenure and promotion, but when we tie those activities to national-level service, we buckle under the weight of the expensive conference fees and often must pass on several opportunities.[1] However, the Teaching Academy provides free, targeted professional development based on what *we* think we need (as opposed to opportunities created and provided by others) and is also a chance for us to share our expertise with others in the unit. Topics range from the nuts and bolts of teaching, such as active learning strategies and creating performance support tools, to more philosophical discussions, such as contemplating teaching identities and uncovering our assumptions about learners. In the second Teaching Academy, we focused on engaging in anti-racist work and envisioning a philosophy of co-liberation in our work within the department and the library as a whole.

Throughout the course of our discussions, we observed that in a collaborative profession such as librarianship, our growth as educators hinges on the strength of our professional relationships with our colleagues; essentially, we need to validate one another in order to develop as educators. Validation theory (VT) describes a process that enables, confirms, and supports students' academic and personal development.[2] Initially applied to college students from underrepresented backgrounds, it was intended to address any anxiety about feelings of belonging in the academy. Relational-cultural theory (RCT) is a therapeutic, feminist ethic of care framework developed in the late 1970s at the Stone Center at Wellesley College that posits growth through mutually empowering relationships.[3] If we wish to create learning environments for students that are inclusive and equitable, it is imperative that library workers apply relational approaches to our own professional development and learning. Engaging in frank and open conversations with each other around racial and social justice in information processes is vital to transforming our teaching. We enact such transformation by shedding the idea that lived experiences don't factor into our pedagogies, something that Laura Rendón refers to in her work as creating familia learning environments in validating first-generation Latinx students.[4] We posit that familia is a relational construct that also extends to collegial and institutional support so that Black, Indigenous, and People of Color (BIPOC) library faculty can push back against Eurocentric epistemologies.[5] If we ever hope to help our students feel like they belong in the classroom, BIPOC faculty must be collegially supported and also be able to feel as though we belong, too.

As of the time of the publication of this chapter, TAL is made up of ten librarians: seven of us are tenure-track or tenured and three of us are full-time lecturers. Our racial/ethnic makeup is slightly more diverse when compared to librarianship as a whole (which is 86% white according to the 2012 ALA *Diversity Counts* report)[6]— two librarians are Latinx, three librarians are Asian Pacific Islander Desi American, and five librarians are white. We are all cisgender women. It was important for us all to recognize, consider, and reflect upon all of these identities as we set about to reimagine what professional development looked like when we approached it collaboratively for our own personal learning and growth as a group. As teaching librarians, we value both autonomous and cooperative learning; though we are all autonomous professionals, we recognize that library work is inherently collaborative. To feel supported in our autonomous learning, we must foster agency and trust within our group and also be given the space to do this work without top-down directives. For us to engage in cooperative learning that moves us all forward while honoring our individual areas of expertise and experience, we need to have psychological safety to be vulnerable and open with our colleagues. The ability to be authentic in our collegial relationships is fundamental to a co-liberatory praxis, something that we are striving for within TAL and that we hope will inform our work throughout the library.[7] Catherine D'Ignazio and Lauren Klein note that a co-liberation model pushes back against hierarchical leadership grounded in white privilege in order to share and disseminate knowledge in more equitable ways that amplify and validate marginalized voices.[8]

In this chapter, we use autoethnography to explore how RCT and VT inform our approach to the Teaching Academy and how this approach values all of our contributions to our development as librarians and educators. Validation is a relational practice because enhancing someone's self-worth is vital to creating meaningful connections among ourselves and with our students. "We feel validated and aware of our own worth when someone welcomes us, joins with us, and responds to our unique being, thoughts, and feelings."[9] These experiences then, in turn, inform and guide the use of inclusive pedagogies with our students. According to Deitering, autoethnography allows us to use "deep reflection and rigorous analysis to create knowledge."[10] Autoethnography also contrasts with the universalized positivist research methodology that requires researchers to distance themselves from the subjects they're examining.[11] It is also a relational methodology given that "the autoethnographer is constantly negotiating relationships with others."[12] We would also argue that, from an RCT lens, autoethnography is a manifestation of relational competence, which Judith Jordan defines as "capacity to move another person, to effect a change in a relationship, or effect the well-being of all participants in the relationship."[13] By sharing our teaching successes and failures through autoethnography, we demonstrate that we are open to being influenced by each other and that vulnerability is a site of strength and potential growth.[14] While other grassroots professional development methods encourage instructional improvement such as teaching squares, they focus purely on the instructional improvement or process and not explicitly on relational cultural practice, which is relevant to inclusivity in the unit.

In many ways, the Teaching Academy itself is also an autoethnographic exercise because we individually and collectively reflect upon our own practices and identities, noting how those intersect with our work with students. Engaging in this type of communal, deep reflection helps us to uncover and make clear what we have learned through the Teaching Academy as well as new directions we may want to explore going forward.

How It All Started

- **YNM:** I never set out to be a manager/leader. Yet I have been since 2010. Prior to this, I was the science librarian for eight years in the same department that I now lead. As with many other instruction coordinators (and similar library positions), I have no formal supervisory capacity. While this initially felt like a limitation, over time I concluded that it requires me to center the people within the department, not my perceptions of what needs to be managed or led. I do not determine the work of the department; my colleagues do, and my role is to provide resources, support, and coordination of the work that the department wants to do.

To this end, it was clear that my colleagues wanted an opportunity to thoughtfully reflect on their instructional efforts, but it did not feel possible during the academic semester. Additionally, my colleagues found each other to be valuable sources for this reflection as well as for new ideas. Lastly, as a white woman who had followed a relatively traditional path into academic librarianship, I was cognizant that my ability to mentor and support our racially/ethnically diverse colleagues, and those who had taken more nontraditional career paths, was limited. These reasons resulted in the creation of a three-day "teaching academy" that occurred during our winter break. I and two other tenured librarians coordinated creating the agenda and selecting some initial readings, but it must be noted that each person in the department was vital in determining the structure and activities.

- **TRM:** There were a few things that helped bring about the Teaching Academy. First, as a group, we'd been talking a lot about how to mentor or onboard new librarians, not just to logistical parts of working at CSUSM, but also to our philosophical grounding and values. We didn't want to bring people into a sink-or-swim type of environment because that just didn't feel right. Also, there were lots of changes happening in first-year programs, and we wanted to come together as a group to figure out our way forward in working with those programs. Lastly, our department already had a history of self-led professional development, such as sharing our conference presentations with each other, leading mini-workshops for the group based on workshops we had attended as individuals, etc.

  Much of what we choose to center and focus on during the Teaching Academy stems from our conversations during meetings and organically sharing our experiences with our work. This encourages collaboration, instead of competition, and sharing our expertise, instead of having lead experts. In recent years, topics have included teacher identity, teaching philosophy, assumptions about learners and teachers, data feminism, co-liberation, validation theory, and relational-cultural theory.

Teaching Academy as a Validating Practice

- **YNM:** As previously noted, the curriculum for the Teaching Academy was only initially crafted by veteran librarians, after which each person in the department made contributions to content and approach. The task of creating the Teaching Academy itself revealed each person's particular expertise. Topics included developing our individual and collective teaching identities, assumptions about teaching and learning, writing concise teaching philosophies, and providing engaging instruction for content that is very procedural (e.g., where to click in a database). Instead of feeling like the planning and implementation was on my shoulders as the department head, I felt that this required everyone to define for themselves their contribution and roles in the group and further their individual professional interests as an instructional librarian. Instead of me, as department head, being essential to the department, I knew my primary value was to be available if needed, but otherwise, I was a fellow librarian. My manager/leader identity shifted in a way that informed my teaching identity; leader/teachers are most important when they recognize it's time to step aside and truly center the colleague/learner.

RCT favors "power with" relationships in which cooperative connections are valued over competitive individualism.[15] By fostering cooperation rather than competition with one another, we actively disavow the raced, meritocratic, and gendered systems that have historically disenfranchised Black, Indigenous, and People of Color (BIPOC), queer, and disabled communities.[16]

Applying validation to the academic library setting, Quiñonez, Nataraj, and Olivas describe validating practice through relational peer mentoring to "create authentic, validating, and supportive mentoring relationships among colleagues of color."[17] Combining validating practices with an RCT framework, Quiñonez, Nataraj, and Olivas reinforced the value of each other's experiences and expertise and provided safe opportunities for continued collaboration and learning.

Inspired by their colleagues, Quiñonez, Nataraj, and Olivas, TAL focused a Teaching Academy on ways to infuse our work with validating and relational practices. This became an opportunity for others in the department to listen to and learn from their BIPOC colleagues and see the connection with previous work we have engaged in together. As a result, we are in different stages with incorporating being relational and validating with each other and in our work with students.

The Teaching Academy was an opportunity for us to learn together and work through areas where we felt stuck and become unstuck and empowered through growth-enhancing relationships, engaging in mutual empowerment, and becoming interdependent, which include mutual reliance, leadership and vision.[18]

- **TQ**: I came to academic librarianship reluctantly. My MLIS was completed with an emphasis on archives and special collections, and my intention was to go into the profession via community archives or the nonprofit arts world. I cut my teeth at places like the Center for the Study of Political Graphics, the Woody Guthrie Archives, and the City Heights Community Development Corporation, with no desire to teach or otherwise work within higher education. This was a political decision as much as a professional one. I wanted to contribute to radical history and to sustain the institutions that serve grassroots communities. My background in community organizing influences my enduring orientation as a communitarian, participatory, and locally focused contributor to any group I belong to, including my workplace. I can't help but bring with me the traditions of DIY punk, feminist consciousness-raising, and anarchist organizing.

  Ending up in academe threw me, as I had to spend a few years first bumbling dazedly like I'd come dressed for the wrong costume party, to queasily getting my footing and playing along, to finally realizing that I could not remain in a bureaucratic and hierarchical setting unless I could express my values through the way I work. Luckily, I had landed in what seems continually to be an extremely rare place for the academic librarian: a nonhierarchical, noncompetitive, empowered, "life first, work second," collaborative, autonomous workplace. There was zero hand-holding when I first started here, which at first had me panicking like I'd been left out in the woods with nothing but a match and a knife. But I got good at using those tools, and when I doubted myself I was constantly told, "You are here because we believe you will do good work." Seven years along, I have forged my own path, with utmost support from my colleagues in the department as well as from my dean. I've been encouraged to try and fail and use my mistakes to make something new and different. I, like the rest of my department, am respected as the faculty member I am by my liaison faculty in the colleges and by my students.

  Our library's commitment to students is, above all, the singular factor that brings us all together to do the good work we're known for. This is the place where I could see first-generation students grappling with understanding academic culture and values (me, too, friend!), and have the support and openness of my colleagues to allow me to adapt the curriculum of our first-year information literacy courses to better explain the gatekeeping nature of the culture we're all swimming in. This is where I was trusted to collaborate with my liaison faculty in the School of Arts to design unconventional but extremely customized instruction and research help for our students.

It's where we are empowered to respectfully push back on expectations that do disservice to students and workers alike. Those seemingly outsider skills I brought with me to my professional practice have been welcomed in forums like the Teaching Academy, which is in itself an expression of the trust, curiosity, and desire for growth that shapes our work in TAL.

TAL developed a Teaching Academy that allows our diverse ways of knowing, pedagogical approaches, and subject knowledge to be shared. We use an inclusive approach of curriculum development to address shared common values and objectives for professional growth as individuals and as a unit. Collaborative academy planning allows the topics most important to us to surface and encourages those ready to engage in leadership to rise because we have the space to do this work without mandates or top-down directives. We foster agency and trust within our group through these practices. Reenvisioned understandings of TAL's teaching values and philosophies, learning theories related to our instruction, and different teaching approaches are some of the results of our efforts. In essence, our work is co-liberatory; as a collective we are greater than individuals.

- **LN:** When I transitioned to full-time university library work, I brought with me eleven years of experience as a public librarian and adjunct community college librarian. While I learned a lot in those roles, I lacked agency in terms of developing reflective, meaningful ways of connecting with users to determine their information needs. And much of that has to do with a heavy emphasis on customer service, which is really about satisfying the user with an answer, rather than focusing on teachable moments. In TAL, I had to unlearn a lot of those values, because our work isn't about finding answers, but empowering and validating students to enter liminal spaces that may initially feel unfamiliar and help them navigate that discomfort. Relational collegiality is something I'm deeply invested in because my previous work experiences in the public library taught me that unless you have the full support of your colleagues, it is difficult to feel motivated or even invested in your work or the people you're trying to help. Having psychological safety within TAL means that I have the support of my colleagues to try out new things without fear of rejection. While I previously lived in fear of being seen as incompetent, here, my nascent ideas were valued. In fact, I would argue that in TAL, *not* trying, or continuing to engage in staid practices, might be met with raised eyebrows, ha ha!

The Teaching Academy has allowed us to feel validated and safe among TAL colleagues and in doing so has made us more productive, creative, and confident in our abilities. It has allowed us to have agency and group autonomy in that we can now take control of our work and define norms. We feel empowered to challenge the ways of doing things that do not align with our principles and values. For instance, we have created a new co-liberatory data statement that qualifies our perspective on assessment and metrics and ensures that we are taking into account the full story of our work as librarians, not just the expected quantifiable numbers and data collected expected of us to justify our existence; numbers simply don't reflect the full picture of us. Our statement pushes further into ethics and ensures that we do not cause students harm by data. BIPOC students, staff, and faculty in particular can be harmed by quantitative data as it can be reductive when there is no accompanying qualitative data that is more humanizing and tells a story; plain numbers remove context.

- **JO:** The Teaching Academy provides time to engage, listen, ideate, and later try new ideas in my professional practice. The diversity of our experiences is greater than any one of us individually. I value the ability to learn from one another. I have found myself in growth mode personally and professionally as an outcome. An activity from an initial Teaching Academy was the development of an abbreviated teaching philosophy shared with our colleagues. "Get messy, make mistakes, have fun, and learn!" goes with me everywhere; in my e-mail signature, I say it to set the stage for instruction: mistakes = learning. This seemingly simple work created great conversations and genuine insight into each other's ways of being in our teaching. Recent work has pushed boundaries further into areas of anti-racism and social justice. I have been trying new technologies such as Mentimeter (shared by a colleague) and by inviting students to use chat in Zoom (sending direct messages for privacy reasons) to get more involvement and allow for more diverse (particularly BIPOC) participation. Some students are uncomfortable talking in class but feel comfortable typing their thoughts. I am contemplating finding ways to use these virtual methods to continue keeping voices involved when we return to the physical library (post-COVID). There are also collaborative efforts, within TAL, to discuss ways of knowing throughout our first-year programs and into subject instruction. Ideas for incorporation are discussing epistemologies being left out of academic discourse or discussing the conflicts when a student studying, for example, health or science finds their held Indigenous epistemologies (such as relationality and holism) in internal conflict with traditional scientific epistemologies.[19] The Teaching Academy provided a place for conversations on examining the value placed on scholarship that may be centered in whiteness, for examining the privilege of peer-reviewed journal articles over oral traditions and other ways of knowing that are so important and valued in other cultures. The Teaching Academy has spurred my interest in taking an anti-racist lens to my LibGuides. There is a multicampus approach to reviewing LibGuides with which our campus is now beginning to engage by developing a rubric for reviewing and improving our guides.

Collaboratively working toward translating our values of anti-racism into these spaces is a direct result of participation in the Teaching Academy.

- **AK:** I try to make students feel comfortable from the very beginning of the class by showing a silly picture of myself at home with my dog and explaining to them from the outset that I have an extremely precocious son who might be interrupting at any time. I think it humanizes me and shows that I understand what it is like working from a virtual environment where any of us can be distracted or interrupted and that's OK and understandable. I do this to make the students feel like we are in this together and in the hopes that they will then feel like they can approach me with any questions or concerns.

- **AIS:** It was first my BIPOC library colleagues, both inside and outside of my department, who recognized my lived experience and interests in a way that was affirming. Because I have a background different from traditional students and, by extension, academic librarians, such as being the first in my family to attend college, low income/working class, and having Mexican immigrant parents with family across the US-Mexico border, it is meaningful and validating to feel like I matter and am seen by my colleagues in ways that are authentic. My fellow BIPOC colleagues encouraged me to be open about how this affected my librarianship and to include it in my research agenda. They also invited me to present at conferences and publish research along with them, which is not something that was extended to me in previous positions. When we made space to engage with the research that they had already done within validation theory and relational-cultural theory in libraries for the Teaching Academy, there was a collective interest in intentionally incorporating it into our own work. This also revived my interest in developing a more detailed onboarding process and documentation for new librarians in our department, partially informed by my experiences, that goes beyond logistical aspects but also introduces resources, tools, and concepts that we've shared as a department while also making space for incoming librarians to include their own.

  When we are relational and validating with each other as colleagues, it becomes a firsthand example that demonstrates how to extend those same transformative practices with students. Proactively cultivating a sense of belonging by learning their needs and experiences can be especially important for BIPOC students who are underrepresented and marginalized in higher education. Some ways we do this is by being open about the challenges and unspoken expectations in learning to be a student-scholar, such as how to read and analyze a scholarly article and understand terminology specific to a profession. We also let them know that their lived experience is an asset and engage with them to help us identify their needs in ways where they feel seen.

I've learned what students care about, as well as small parts of their life and experiences, by talking to them about their research topics for their assignments with genuine interest because it often turns out they've chosen something that's personal to them or close to their communities.

We can validate and be relational with students by sharing our overlapping experiences with them, but that is not the singular approach since much of this work takes engaging with students in ways where we learn about who they are. It's just as important to learn how to do so when we don't share the same culture or experiences. When we have instruction sessions with students, part of our role is to share our expertise and knowledge of research strategy as it relates to their assignment, but it's been my experience that during this process I learn so much from them because we are all in a community of learners. I let them know that I'm there to guide them and share my expertise but ask them what existing skills, knowledge, and experiences they bring to the table. In this way, I try to position myself as another learner with them. Some of the impacts of this approach that I've observed are an increase in student confidence in their research abilities and openness to share their ideas and ask questions.

- **TRM:** As one of the more senior librarians in the group, what I really appreciate about not just the Teaching Academy, but overall our approach to working with one another, is the chance to learn from librarians who are newer to the organization who bring in their unique skills, interests, and areas of expertise. And not necessarily just their skills that they've gleaned from past library work or library school, but their unique perspectives just based on their personal experiences, lives, and interests. I feel like I learn so much from everyone in the group.

Inclusive Outcomes Born Out of Relational and Validating Practices

- **TRM:** I feel like over the last couple of years, we've tried harder to work in a less hierarchical way within our department and also done a lot of work to develop a workplace environment where people feel psychologically safe. This enables us to try out new things without a fear of being punished for failing, be vulnerable about what we don't know, and provide the space for people to share their interests and expertise. The Teaching Academy is just one example of how this relationship building takes place, but I think we intentionally try to engage in relational and culturally validating practices in most of our work. Obviously, this is a work in progress and we are never done with validating one another, and I still have a lot of areas of weakness. But I so appreciate people in our department who have provided us with these theoretical frameworks that help us to make sense of what we're trying to do and give us a way to approach our interdepartmental dynamics with intentionality. In general, I would say that it has helped me to have a greater understanding of how I can connect with students in order to provide them with validating experiences, and it always makes me consider the curriculum and lesson plans with the idea of ensuring different perspectives are represented, that people aren't left out, etc.

- **AK:** I was raised with the expectation that I would go to a four-year college and most likely get a higher degree too, just as my parents, aunts and uncles, sister, and cousins all had done before me. I, of course, had gone to school with people who were first-generation college students and those who had taken a more circuitous path than I had, but I had never really heard their stories and therefore didn't fully understand how those untraditional paths could be assets in the college setting. The Teaching Academy gave me the opportunity to hear the stories of my colleagues who had taken a windier road to college than I had, and it became clear to me how their experiences along the way benefited them, the college, and their students. It opened my eyes to the fact that academic scholars are not the only experts we can look to and use in our studies. Because of this I think I look at my students in a different, more appreciative light. I understand, in a way I never have before, that by listening to my students and making them feel that their experiences and expertise are heard and validated that I can help make their college experience positive and successful.

- **JO:** Prior to the Teaching Academies, I had participated in professional development opportunities on campus such as decolonizing your syllabus, advancement via individual determination (AVID) techniques, and critical pedagogy, just as many of my colleagues have, but most impactful has been the practice of sharing our identities (personal and teaching), how this informs how we work to validate our students and one another professionally; creating a workplace that provides acceptance and measurable comfort. Learning from colleagues in how they validate students and one another has produced many insights. Trying a technique or technology that a colleague uses in my instruction or pedagogy has improved my work. The iterative nature of the Teaching Academy has placed at the forefront the values of TAL moving our practice forward each year. Introspectively I am finding new connections and thoughts on how to work together, how I can improve myself to better facilitate collaborations with colleagues, and a more willing spirit to share out, try new things, make mistakes (share those out), and learn.

Conclusion

We are creating an environment where people want to do good work, where there is no shaming or isolation of people, where there is no external accountability within the group, and where individuals get to define for themselves what "successful" means. We have cultivated a sense of self-accountability where we hold ourselves (rather than others) accountable and know that we can seek advice and guidance in a safe environment because we created these relationships. A hallmark of our group is peer-led professional development. RCT and VT have not only informed our teaching and service philosophies, but are also infused into the way our department defines itself, the way we interact with and treat each other, and, inevitably, the way we interact with and treat students. It is visible in our focus on relationship building with our liaison faculty, something that is notoriously difficult for many academic librarians. Diaz and Mandernach observe that building enduring relationships with liaison faculty involves a "constellation of traits, values, and skills"[20] including the librarian's ability to "go the extra mile."[21] But as Meulemans and Carr observe, above-and-beyond service rarely impacts the liaison faculty-librarian relationship in a positive way; if anything, a service model that continually "fulfills an uninformed request …perpetuate[s] faculty ignorance."[22] Rather, a relational approach to collaboration that centers the shared goal of developing students' critical information literacy skills while simultaneously respecting the librarian's unique expertise in this effort will likely lead to valuable (and validating) connections between faculty and librarians.[23] Further, this approach is evident in the quality-over-quantity approach that we take toward determining the need for library instruction, as well as research appointments with students, where the overall number of consultations in a given semester is not the sole data point in assessing our work with students. It is paramount in our development as practitioners and colleagues, as we do the work to understand, support, and learn from each other.

Teaching Academy, as we have purposefully cocreated it, provides exactly the kind of professional development that we believe we need as a group. Arising from informal conversations or as outgrowths of other educational experiences, the process of identifying what we need or want to learn is in itself relational. Each aspect of the Teaching Academy is cocreated in this collaborative manner, which gives librarians the opportunity to share their expertise with others. It is important to note that how individual librarians apply (or choose not to apply) what they learn during the Teaching Academy is up to them. We do not hold one another accountable for meeting particular metrics or goals, but rather strive to create an environment where individuals can interpret for themselves how best to address any relevant retention, tenure, and promotion policies. There is no one right way to meet these goals, and the Teaching Academy helps us to work with one another to see the multiplicity of valid and valuable ways in which we might go about our work. These relational approaches enact a learning environment and process that is inclusive and equitable, which is exactly what we want to provide for our students. If we wish to create learning environments for students that are inclusive and equitable, it is imperative that library workers apply relational approaches to our own professional development and learning.

In particular, it has been transformative for us as a department to address the problem of racism and white supremacy in information processes and institutional policies. Engaging in frank and open conversations was the first step and continues to serve as a constant process of reassessment and accountability. Additionally, by attending to the experiences of BIPOC faculty, we acknowledge that higher education, like all Western institutions, has been constructed with the assumption of whiteness as a standard. Looking at our work through the lens of people who do not conform to the standard challenges all of us to rethink the equity and justice of our approaches, not just with respect to our students, but to our colleagues, as well.

We had to consider the interplay of all of our identities while reimagining our professional development as peer education. We discovered that power could be constantly redistributed according to who possessed the knowledge and experience we wished to learn from. It seems almost certainly naïve to propose that everybody everywhere should aim to be vulnerable and open with their colleagues. At best, many workplaces foster civil and friendly relations between their workers, while all too often academic librarians, especially BIPOC or otherwise marginalized people, face extremely toxic work environments. It cannot be overstated that we are invested in a common goal of psychological safety, to the extent that we are able to agree that it is essential for cooperative learning that allows us to move forward as a group. It helps that we have an understanding that the preservation of our autonomy partly rests on the success of our endeavors as a collaborative unit.

The work of co-liberation pushes back against hierarchical leadership grounded in white privilege in order to share and disseminate knowledge in more equitable ways that amplify and validate marginalized voices.[24] This is not possible without collaborating in nonhierarchical, relational ways. The Teaching Academy is one example of how we try to take a nonhierarchical and relational approach to our work with one another and helps us to bring inclusion and equity into both our work and with our students.

Appendix A: Reflection Prompts

We encourage others to consider the following reflective questions so that they may determine how they might incorporate validating and relational practices in their own instructional pedagogies:

- What do you think you need to develop as a practitioner/educator? What can your colleagues teach you? What can you teach them?
- How might building relationships with your colleagues inform your work with students?
- Has your (department/unit/library) examined how white supremacy enacts itself in your policies and practices? Has your (department/unit/library) engaged in the authentic and non-performative work of examining how white supremacy enacts itself in the lives of each individual within it?
- Do your BIPOC colleagues feel a sense of belonging in your department? If you are not BIPOC, how might you change your consciousness to under-stand how the experiences of BIPOC in higher education are likely unequal to yours, no matter if they are students or faculty?
- How do the varying identities within your colleague group impact the experience of those individuals in the workplace?
- How might your colleagues work together to build a sense of psychological safety conducive to relational work environments? How autonomous do you think you can be, as a group and as an individual, in avoiding what we call "top-down directives"?
- Is nonhierarchical and relational collaboration possible in your current place of work? Are there other networks that include folks outside of your institution, where co-liberatory work can transpire? How do you ensure that your work is values-driven?

Appendix B:
2021 Data Statement Zine

One of the outcomes from the 2021 Teaching Academy was the creation of a *Data Statement* zine. This was not necessarily something we had envisioned creating at the beginning of the three days of Teaching Academy, but something that came about organically as we set about learning about traditional data collection practices in higher education and feminist approaches to data collection and analysis and also reflected upon what was important to us as a group that would guide our involvement in projects requiring us to collect data from our students. The zine is shared through CSUSM's institutional repository ScholarWorks: http://hdl.handle.net/20.500.12680/xs55mj21w.

Notes

1. Brigette Comanda et al.,"Service Ceiling: The High Cost of Professional Development for Academic Librarians," *In the Library with the Lead Pipe*, June 9, 2021, https://www.inthelibrarywiththeleadpipe.org/2021/service-ceiling/.
2. Laura I. Rendón, "Validating Culturally Diverse Students: Toward a New Model of Learning and Student Development," *Innovative Higher Education* 19, no. 1 (September 1994): 33–51, https://doi.org/10.1007/BF01191156.
3. Jean Baker Miller Training Institute, "The Development of Relational-Cultural Theory: Beginnings: Self-in-Relation," accessed August 31, 2021, https://www.wcwonline.org/JBMTI-Site/the-development-of-relational-cultural-theory.
4. Laura I. Rendón, *Sentipensante (Sensing/Thinking) Pedagogy* (Sterling, VA: Stylus, 2012).
5. Torie Quiñonez, Lalitha Nataraj, and Antonia Olivas, "The Praxis of Relation, Validation, and Motivation: Articulating LIS Collegiality through a CRT Lens," in *Knowledge Justice: Disrupting Library and Information Studies through Critical Race Theory*, ed. Sofia Y. Leung and Jorge R. López-McKnight (Cambridge, MA: MIT Press, 2021), https://direct.mit.edu/books/edited-volume/chapter-pdf/1956588/c001300_9780262363204.pdf.
6. American Library Association, Office for Research and Statistics and Office for Diversity, *Diversity Counts* (Chicago: American Library Association, 2007, upd. 2012), https://www.ala.org/aboutala/offices/diversity/diversitycounts/divcounts.
7. Catherine D'Ignazio and Lauren F. Klein, *Data Feminism* (Cambridge, MA: MIT Press, 2020), https://data-feminism.mitpress.mit.edu/.
8. D'Ignazio and Klein, *Data Famism*.
9. Harriet L. Schwartz, *Connected Teaching* (Sterling, VA: Stylus, 2019), 19.
10. Anne-Marie Deitering, "Introduction," in *The Self as Subject: Autoethnographic Research into Identity, Culture, and Academic Librarianship*, ed. Anne-Marie Deitering, Robert Schroeder, and Richard Stoddart (Chicago: Association of College and Research Libraries, 2017), 3.
11. Deitering, "Introduction," 3.
12. Deitering, "Introduction," 13.
13. Judith V. Jordan, "Toward Competence and Connection," in *The Complexity of Connection:*

Writings from the Stone Center's Jean Baker Miller Training Institute, ed. Judith V. Jordan, Maureen Walker, and Linda M. Hartling (New York: Guildford Press, 2004), 15.

14. Jordan, "Toward Competence and Connection," 15.

15. Quiñonez, Nataraj, and Olivas, "Praxis of Relation."

16. Quiñonez, Nataraj, and Olivas, "Praxis of Relation."

17. Quiñonez, Nataraj, and Olivas, "Praxis of Relation," 249.

18. Nikki M. Fedele, "Relationships in Groups: Connection, Resonance, and Paradox," in *The Complexity of Connection: Writings from the Stone Center's Jean Baker Training Institute*, ed. Judith V. Jordan, Maureen Walker, and Linda M. Hartling (New York: Guildford Press, 2004), 196; Joyce K. Fletcher, "Relational Theory in the Workplace," in *The Complexity of Connection: Writings from the Stone Center's Jean Baker Training Institute*, ed. Judith V. Jordan, Maureen Walker, and Linda M. Hartling (New York: Guildford Press, 2004), 275; adrienne maree brown, *Emergent Strategy* (Chico, CA: AK Press, 2017), 87.

19. Erin A. Cech et al., "Epistemological Dominance and Social Inequality: Experiences of Native American Science, Engineering, and Health Students," *Science, Technology, and Human Values* 42, no. 5 (September 2017): 743–74, https://doi.org/10.1177/0162243916687037.

20. José O. Díaz and Meris A. Mandernach, "Relationship Building One Step at a Time: Case Studies of Successful Faculty-Librarian Partnerships," *portal: Libraries and the Academy* 18, no. 2 (2017): 280, https://doi.org/10.1353/pla.2017.0016.

21. Díaz and Mandernach, "Relationship Building," 281.

22. Yvonne Nalani Meulemans and Allison Carr, "Not at Your Service: Building Genuine Faculty-Librarian Partnerships," ed. Jennifer Rosenfeld and Raida Gatten, *Reference Services Review* 41, no. 1 (2013): 83, https://doi.org/10.1108/00907321311300893.

23. Meulemans and Carr, "Not at Your Service," 83.

24. D'Ignazio and Klein, *Data Feminism*.

Bibliography

American Library Association, Office for Research and Statistics and Office for Diversity. *Diversity Counts*. Chicago: American Library Association, 2007, upd. 2012. https://www.ala.org/aboutala/offices/diversity/diversitycounts/divcounts.

brown, adrienne maree. *Emergent Strategy: Shaping Change, Changing Worlds*. Chico, CA: AK Press, 2017.

Cech, Erin A., Anneke Metz, Jessi L. Smith, and Karen deVries. "Epistemological Dominance and Social Inequality: Experiences of Native American Science, Engineering, and Health Students." *Science, Technology, and Human Values* 42, no. 5 (September 2017): 743–74. https://doi.org/10.1177/0162243916687037.

Comanda, Bridgette, Jaci Wilkinson, Fraith Bradham, Amanda Koziura, and Maura Seale. "Service Ceiling: The High Cost of Professional Development for Academic Librarians." *In the Library with the Lead Pipe*, June 9, 2021. https://www.inthelibrarywiththeleadpipe.org/2021/service-ceiling/.

Deitering, Anne-Marie. "Introduction." In *The Self as Subject: Autoethnographic Research into Identity, Culture, and Academic Librarianship*, edited by Anne-Marie Deitering, Robert Schroeder, and Richard Stoddart, 1–22. Chicago: Association of College and Research Libraries, 2017.

Díaz, José O., and Meris A. Mandernach. "Relationship Building One Step at a Time: Case Studies of Successful Faculty-Librarian Partnerships." *portal: Libraries and the Academy* 18, no. 2 (2017): 273–82. https://doi.org/10.1353/pla.2017.0016.

D'Ignazio, Catherine, and Lauren F. Klein. *Data Feminism*. Cambridge, MA: MIT Press, 2020. https://data-feminism.mitpress.mit.edu/.

Fedele, Nikki M. "Relationships in Groups: Connection, Resonance, and Paradox." In *The Complexity of Connection: Writings from the Stone Center's Jean Baker Training Institute*, edited by Judith V. Jordan, Maureen Walker, and Linda M. Hartling, 194–219. New York: Guildford Press, 2004.

Fletcher, Joyce K. "Relational Theory in the Workplace." In *The Complexity of Connection: Writings from the Stone Center's Jean Baker Training Institute*, edited by Judith V. Jordan, Maureen Walker, and Linda M. Hartling, 270–98. New York: Guildford Press, 2004.

Jean Baker Miller Training Institute. "The Development of Relational-Cultural Theory: Beginnings: Self-in-Relation." Accessed August 31, 2021. https://www.wcwonline.org/JBMTI-Site/the-development-of-relational-cultural-theory.

Jordan, Judith V. "Toward Competence and Connection." In *The Complexity of Connection: Writings from the Stone Center's Jean Baker Miller Training Institute*, edited by Judith V. Jordan, Maureen Walker, and Linda M. Hartling, 11–27. New York: Guildford Press, 2004.

Meulemans, Yvonne Nalani, and Allison Carr. "Not at Your Service: Building Genuine Faculty-Librarian Partnerships," edited by Jennifer Rosenfeld and Raida Gatten. *Reference Services Review* 41, no. 1 (2013): 80–90. https://doi.org/10.1108/00907321311300893.

Quiñonez, Torie, Lalitha Nataraj, and Antonia Olivas. "The Praxis of Relation, Validation, and Motivation: Articulating LIS Collegiality through a CRT Lens." In *Knowledge Justice: Disrupting Library and Information Studies through Critical Race Theory*, edited by Sofia Y. Leung and Jorge R. López-McKnight, 241–61. Cambridge, MA: MIT Press, 2021. https://direct.mit.edu/books/edited-volume/chapter-pdf/1956588/c001300_9780262363204.pdf.

Rendón, Laura I. *Sentipensante (Sensing/Thinking) Pedagogy: Educating for Wholeness, Social Justice and Liberation*. Sterling, VA: Stylus, 2012.

———. "Validating Culturally Diverse Students: Toward a New Model of Learning and Student Development." *Innovative Higher Education* 19, no. 1 (September 1994): 33–51. https://doi.org/10.1007/BF01191156.

Schwartz, Harriet L. *Connected Teaching: Relationship, Power, and Mattering in Higher Education*. Sterling, VA: Stylus, 2019.

Yosso, Tara J. "Whose Culture Has Capital? A Critical Race Theory Discussion of Community Cultural Wealth." *Race Ethnicity and Education* 8, no. 1 (March 2005): 69–91. https://doi.org/10.1080/1361332052000341006.

A Call to Action

This book started with a call to action by Nicole A. Cooke and Miriam E. Sweeney:

> "We challenge you to be the instructors our students need."[1]

The editors would like to issue a similar call to action to readers of these volumes. We encourage you to consider how you might apply some of the pedagogical strategies, such as reflecting on methods of fostering an anti-racist classroom, using primary source materials to engender empathy for different voices, and/or considering potential partners on your campus to increase the accessibility of your instructional materials. We posit several questions for contemplation and action:

- How does your own positionality affect the way you approach equitable and inclusive pedagogies?
- How have the theories and practices related to equitable and inclusive pedagogies inspired your teaching in the past, and might continue to inspire it in the future?
- How can you thoughtfully articulate your teaching practices to promote an inclusive and equitable classroom for all learners?
- How can we, as academic librarians, lift up and amplify the voices of our students, our colleagues, and learners all over the world?

We hope the chapters in this manuscript have inspired you as much as they have inspired the editors. No matter what has resonated, we encourage you to make positive changes, to include a philosophy of inclusive and equitable teaching and learning in your praxis, and, above all, to center the learner.

Notes

1. Nicole A. Cooke and Miriam E. Sweeney, *Teaching for Justice: Implementing Social Justice in the LIS Classroom*, Library Juice Press 2017. p. 288.

Bibliography

Cooke, Nicole A., and Miriam E. Sweeney. *Teaching for Justice: Implementing Social Justice in the LIS Classroom*. Library Juice Press, 2017.

About the Editors

Robin Brown, BSFS, MLS, MA is professor and head of public services for the library at Borough of Manhattan Community College (CUNY). She identifies as a person with disabilities and has published significant work on universal design for learning and disabilities studies. She identifies as a white, cis gender person and acknowledges that she has benefited from privileges on many different levels.

- Brown, R. and S. Sheidlower. *Seeking to Understand: A Journey into Disabilities Studies and Libraries.* Sacramento: Library Juice Press, 2021.
- Brown, R, Z. Welhouse, and A. Wolfe. "Keeping up with Universal Design for Learning." ACRL, 2020. http://www.ala.org/acrl/publications/keeping_up_with/udl
- Brown, R. "Wheelchair Warrior: Gangs, Disability, and Basketball." In *Disability Experiences: Memoirs, Autobiographies, and Other Personal Narratives*, edited by G. Thomas Couser and Susannah B. Mintz, 825-828. Vol. 2. Farmington Hills, MI: Macmillan Reference USA, 2019.
- Brown, R. and S. Sheidlower. "Claiming our Space: A quantitative and qualitative picture of disabled librarians." *Library Trends* (67:3, Winter 2019).

Elizabeth Foster, MSLS, is the social sciences data librarian at the University of Chicago. She serves as the subject expert for sociology and provides research and instructional support for data-driven research. Her research interests include anti-racist pedagogy, reflective practice, and data privacy.

Melissa N. Mallon (she/her), MLIS, is associate university librarian for teaching & learning at Vanderbilt University. She has published, presented, and taught professional development courses in the areas of online learning, instructional design, and the impact of information and digital literacies on student learning. Her previous books include *Partners in Teaching & Learning: Coordinating a Successful Academic Library Instruction Program* (2020); *The Pivotal Role of Academic Librarians in Digital Learning* (2018); and the co-edited volume, *The Grounded Instruction Librarian: Participating in the Scholarship of Teaching & Learning* (2019). Positionality Statement: I identify as a white, cis-gendered woman, which affords me an acknowledged place of privilege. Through my teaching and research, I strive to use this privilege to give voice to those that may be underrepresented or unheard in both libraries and higher education. I strive to lead with empathy and humility, and endeavor to not stop listening and learning.

Jane Nichols provides research and instructional support as a humanities librarian and a liaison to the Undergrad Research & Writing Center at Oregon State University. Reflecting the variety of roles she has taken over her career, she has published and presented on myriad topics aimed at improving library services and spaces for all. Her scholarship extends to editing "The Americas" volume of *Women's Lives around the World: A Global Encyclopedia*. A white, cis-gendered queer lesbian, she lives and works in the traditional homelands of the Marys River or Ampinefu Band of Kalapuya.

Ariana Santiago (she/her) is the head of open education services at the University of Houston Libraries. She has published, presented, and contributed professional service in the areas of open educational resources, information literacy, and library outreach. Ariana earned an M.A. in applied learning and instruction from the University of Central Florida and an M.A. in library and information science from the University of South Florida.

Maura Seale is the history librarian at the University of Michigan, providing research and instructional support for students and faculty in the history department. Maura holds an M.S.I. from the University of Michigan School of Information, an M.A. in American studies from the University of Minnesota, and a graduate certificate in digital public humanities from George Mason University. Her research focuses on critical librarianship, library pedagogy, political economy and labor in libraries, and race and gender in libraries. She is the co-editor, with Karen P. Nicholson, of *The Politics of Theory in the Practice of Critical Librarianship* (2018). Her work can be found at www.mauraseale.org and she welcomes comments via @mauraseale.

About the Authors

Andrea Baer is a public services librarian at Rowan University in the Campbell Library and has been an academic instruction librarian for over ten years. She has worked at both teaching-centered and research-intensive universities. Andrea holds a master's in information sciences from the University of Tennessee and a PhD in comparative literature from the University of Washington. Prior to entering librarianship, she taught and studied comparative literature and writing, which has informed her approach to information literacy education. Her research interests include the intersections between information literacy and writing studies, digital literacies, affect and learning, critical reflective practice, and librarians' development as teachers. For more about her research please see https://orcid.org/0000-0002-6361-948X.

Kelsa Bartley is the education and outreach librarian in the Learning, Research and Clinical Information Services Department at the Louis Calder Memorial Library, University of Miami Miller School of Medicine. Her role includes providing library education and research services, in addition to outreach and promotion of library services and resources. Her research interests include diversity, equity and inclusion in libraries, library marketing, outreach and social media, library instruction and instructional design and also wellness and wellbeing in libraries.

Randi Beem is the instruction archivist at University of North Carolina at Charlotte, where she uses primary document instruction in her Reading Room classroom across various subjects from the African American experience post-1865 to feminist resistance theory in cartography. A born and bred Hoosier, Randi attended Saint Mary's College, Notre Dame, Indiana, receiving a bachelor's in history, and Indiana University Bloomington, receiving a master's in library science with a specialization in archives and records management.

Selinda Adelle Berg is currently the university librarian at the University of Windsor, Canada. She holds a PhD in library and information studies from Western University, a master's in library and information studies from the University of Alberta, and a bachelor of science in nutrition from the University of Saskatchewan. Selinda maintains an active research program that intersects with her professional interests, including research culture in academic libraries, information inequities for 2SLGBTQ+ communities, and tacit knowledge in the health and information professions.

Ashley Blinstrub (she/her) is the student success and inclusion librarian at George Mason University Libraries. She has a master of science in information from University of Michigan. Her research interests include accessibility of information, inclusive teaching practices, and assessment of student learning.

Katie Blocksidge is the library director at The Ohio State University at Newark and Central Ohio Technical College. As part of this role, she works with colleagues and faculty to integrate information literacy into the student learning experience. Katie has an MLIS from Kent State University and an MA in learning technologies from The Ohio State University.

Faith Bradham is a community college librarian in California. Originally a Texan, she obtained her MLS from Indiana University Bloomington before moving to the West Coast. As a community college librarian, she has a role that extends into reference, instruction, liaisonship, and outreach. Her research interests focus on critical librarianship and inclusive teaching practices. When she's not in the library, Faith can be found on one of California's many beautiful hiking trails.

Frances Brady, MS, is the reference and instruction librarian at Adler University, where she coordinates, teaches, and assesses scaffolded information literacy sessions for graduate students and mentors student workers as peer teachers. Her research interests include information literacy instruction, social justice, and mentoring student workers as co-teachers.

Ava Brillat is the program lead for information literacy and instructional design. She also serves as a liaison librarian to the departments of English, English composition, theatre arts, and classics. Ava Brillat received her MLIS from the University of South Florida in 2010 and her MA in liberal studies from the University of Miami in 2019. Prior to coming to the University of Miami, she worked as an instructional design librarian. Born and raised overseas in Saudi Arabia, she enjoys the cross-cultural experiences Miami has to offer. Her personal research is focused on mentoring, collaboration, and diversity in librarianship.

Angie Brunk is an experienced public services librarian who also holds a MAS in human factors. Her primary research interest is accessible and inclusive design in libraries.

Sam Buechler, MLIS (they/them), is the student success faculty resident librarian at Washington State University, Vancouver. Prior to their current position, Sam worked in circulation and access services departments at a variety of four-year and community college libraries. Sam is also a member of the Library Freedom Project. These experiences provide the foundation for their research interests, which center privacy and surveillance on college campuses, outreach services, and critical information literacy.

Heather Campbell is a mother, teacher, librarian, and educational developer. She is an uninvited settler on lands connected with the London Township and Sombra Treaties of 1796 and Dish with One Spoon Covenant Wampum, the traditional lands of Anishinaabek, Haudenosaunee, Lūnapéewak and Chonnonton peoples. Now Curriculum Librarian at Western University, Heather worked as a library assistant, librarian, and educational developer at Brescia University College from 2006 to 2020. Heather's work in supporting the creation of Brescia's first-year seminar, along with her leadership in Brescia's articulation of values-based degree outcomes, helped solidify her teaching identity as a feminist pedagogue. Heather spends her professional time navigating academia's third-space, with the hopes of contributing to the decolonization and Indigenization of the academy. She is happiest, though, when playing LEGO with her five-year old son.

Allison Carr serves as the Academic Transitions Librarian at California State University, San Marcos. Her current area of research is centered around the sense of belonging of transfer students and creating a robust Common Read program. She has a Master of Library and Information Science from San Jose State University.

Liz Chenevey is a health and behavioral studies librarian at James Madison University in Virginia. She is interested in affective learning, ethics of care, zines, and critical pedagogies. Outside of the library, she enjoys gardening, quilting, and making up silly songs for her daughter.

Melissa Chomintra is an assistant professor in the Purdue Libraries and School of Information Studies. She received an MA in criminal justice from the University of Nevada, Las Vegas, and her MLIS from Kent State University.

Maggie Clarke is the reference services coordinator, an instruction librarian, and liaison to the humanities at CSU Dominguez Hills. She has worked in both academic and public libraries since 2016 and is currently pursuing research focused on the politics of student workers in academic libraries.

Scott R. Cowan is an information services librarian at the University of Windsor, Canada. His research has centred around teaching and learning within a library context; information and access needs of the LGBTQ2S+ community; and social justice issues within the classroom. In his previous career, Scott taught middle school and high school instrumental and vocal music in Saskatchewan. He received his master of library and information science (MLIS) from Western University and his bachelor of music education and bachelor of education from the University of Saskatchewan. Currently, Scott is also working on a PhD in educational studies.

Breanne Crumpton is the Information Literacy Librarian for the Humanities and Assistant Professor at Appalachian State University. She is a cis, settler, able-bodied, white, middle class, heterosexual female. Her research interests include DEIA work in libraries, social and racial justice to overcome systemic barriers, inclusive pedagogy practices and critical information literacy.

Kyle Denlinger is the digital pedagogy and open education librarian at Wake Forest University's Z. Smith Reynolds Library, where he collaborates with faculty and students to develop scholarly digital projects, advocates for and supports open educational practices, and contributes to the library's information literacy efforts through teaching and student support.

Emily Drabinski is interim chief librarian at the Graduate Center, City University of New York.

Kate Drabinski is principal lecturer in Gender, Women's, and Sexuality Studies at UMBC, where she also directs the Women Involved In Learning and Leadership (WILL+) program. She teaches courses in sexuality studies, queer theory, transgender studies, and activism. She is coeditor with Nicole King and Joshua Davis of *Baltimore Revisited: Stories of Inequality and Resistance in a U.S. City*.

Alissa Droog, MLIS, MA, BEd, BA, is an assistant professor and the education and social sciences librarian at Northern Illinois University, where she works primarily with faculty and graduate students in the College of Education. Alissa's research interests include information literacy, library assessment practices, LGBTQ+ children's literature, biblical reception history, and children's Bible stories.

Sara Durazo-DeMoss is the director of mentoring and academic advising at California State University, San Bernardino. Her work focuses on student mentoring and college transition, experiential learning and career readiness, and academic advising for undergraduate students. Her research interests include representations of higher education in popular culture, leadership identity development of college women, critical mentoring, and the dualism of mentoring as both an oppressive and liberating practice.

Erin Durham is a reference and instruction librarian at the University of Maryland, Baltimore County (UMBC), and provides research instruction and support to the history, english, music, theatre, dance, and language, literacy, and culture departments. She received an MLIS and MA in History from the University of Maryland, College Park. Her research interests include critical pedagogy, open educational resources, the intersection of libraries and writing centers, and she seeks to engage in conversations about information privilege and inequities. In addition to her library pursuits, Erin is a violin performer and teacher and an enthusiast for the outdoors.

Christine R. Elliott is a reference and instruction librarian at UMass Boston. Christine's interests include universal accessibility, library marketing, innovative technologies, information literacy instruction, and open educational resources. She loves cross-stitching, and her favorite flavor of toaster pastry is blueberry.

Rachel Fager is Head of Resources Management at Saint Joseph's University. She first became interested in accessibility while working with students at a community college ten years ago and has continued to seek opportunities to learn and to support students. She has co-presented accessibility webinars for national and regional organizations..

Carol Fisher, MLIS (she/her), is a collections and technical services librarian at Washington State University, Vancouver. She holds an MLIS from University of Washington and a BS in psychology from Penn State University. Prior to working in academic libraries, Carol served on active duty in the United States Navy, where she worked in tropical cyclone forecasting. Her research interests currently involve veteran identity and the intersection with academic libraries, focusing on outreach and programming.

Rebecca Fitzsimmons is special collections librarian and liaison to the Women's, Gender, and Sexuality Studies program at Illinois State University. She is the curator of the Children's and Historical Textbooks Collection and works extensively with the Rare Books and Manuscripts Collection. She provides instruction, reference, and collection development services and engages in a variety of digital projects and initiatives in the library.

Amanda L. Folk is an assistant professor and head of teaching and learning at The Ohio State University Libraries. Amanda works with her teaching and learning colleagues to develop a vision and strategy for developing students' information literacy through instructor development, reference interactions, cocurricular programming, credit-bearing courses, and learning objects. Amanda has both an MLIS and a PhD from the University of Pittsburgh.

Shanti Freundlich is an assistant professor and the assistant director for online learning and assessment at MCPHS University in Boston, Massachusetts.

Joanna Gadsby works as the instruction coordinator/reference and instruction librarian at University of Maryland, Baltimore County. Her research interests include relational practice, critical and constructivist pedagogies, and gendered labor in librarianship. She is coeditor, along with Veronica Arellano Douglas, of the recently published volume *Deconstructing Service in Libraries: Intersections of Identities and Expectations.*

Rachel W. Gammons is head of teaching and learning services at the University of Maryland (UMD) Libraries, an affiliate faculty member in the UMD College of Information Studies (iSchool), and a PhD candidate in higher education, student affairs, and international education in the UMD College of Education.

Sheila García Mazari, is the online learning librarian at the University of California, Santa Cruz. Formerly, she was a professional programs liaison librarian at Grand Valley State University. Sheila has an MLIS from Wayne State University and is a 2016 American Library Association Spectrum Scholar as well as a 2019 Emerging Leader. She is an active member of the Asian Pacific American Librarians Association (APALA) and the Michigan Academic Library Association (MiALA) and has served as the 2020–2021 Residency Interest Group convener of the Association of College and Research Libraries (ACRL).

Jane Hammons is an assistant professor in the University Libraries at The Ohio State University. As the teaching and learning engagement librarian, she focuses on supporting the integration of information literacy into the curriculum through instructor development. Jane has an MSLIS from the University of Illinois Urbana-Champaign and an MS in instructional design from Western Kentucky University.

Beth Heldebrandt has been the public relations director at Booth Library since 2012. She is the sole person responsible for the library's PR, publicity, and communications, with her work including social media, photography, graphic design, media relations, grant writing, and internal communications. Prior to working at Booth Library, Beth was a newspaper editor for more than twenty-two years. She also works as a media research specialist for Ad Fontes Media, home of the Media Bias Chart, and is an adjunct instructor of journalism at Eastern Illinois University.

Barbara Herrera is the coordinator of the Student Mentoring Program at California State University, San Bernardino. Her work focuses on the hiring, training, and supporting professional development of student mentors. She has partnered with the library to co-facilitate the Library Ambassador Initiative.

April Ibarra Siqueiros is the User Experience Librarian at CSU San Marcos and was formerly in reference and instruction. She has a Master of Library and Information Science with a User Experience concentration from Pratt Institute. Her research interests range from zines to critical user experience design in libraries.

Darren Ilett is a Teaching and Outreach Librarian and Assistant Professor at the University of Northern Colorado. He serves as a liaison for two TRIO programs supporting first-generation students (Student Support Services and McNair Scholars Program), the DREAMer Engagement Program (supporting DACAmented and undocumented students), and Go On and Learn (supporting students with intellectual and developmental disabilities), as well as the College of Education and Behavioral Sciences. Darren teaches information literacy credit courses and one-shot instruction sessions. His research centers on how librarians can work with students typically underserved and underrepresented in higher education, particularly first-generation students.

Allison Jennings-Roche is the library instruction coordinator for Towson University and a PhD student in information studies at the University of Maryland. Her research interests include information policy, advocacy, and human rights, critical information literacy, and inclusive leadership. She has an MLIS with a focus on diversity and inclusion from the University of Maryland, as well as an MA in legal and ethical studies and a graduate certificate in organizational leadership from the University of Baltimore. Allison has professional experience in higher education, libraries, and undergraduate teaching, and has previously worked at UMBC and the University of Baltimore.

David Kelly, Jr. is the writing services coordinator at the University of Baltimore. He received his MS in negotiations and conflict management from the University of Baltimore. Focusing on writing as a conflict in institutions of higher education, David works to transform students' relationships with writing through advocating writer autonomy; collaboration; and development of rhetorical awareness, genre expectation, and audience identification; through demystifying the curriculum of higher education. Some of his interests include rock climbing, hiking, daydreaming, and finding meaningful ways to interrogate and disrupt the everyday practice of racism and white supremacy in higher education spaces. I do what I do for my people. You know who you are!

Amanda Kalish has a BA in History and a Master's of Library and Information Science from UCLA. She has worked in both public and academic libraries and is currently an Instruction & Reference Librarian at California State University, San Marcos. Her research interest revolves around figuring out the best methods of effectively teaching information literacy that can cut through the deliberate disinformation spread through social media, foreign influences, and other bad actors.

Sara C. Kern is the student success and outreach librarian at Juniata College in Huntingdon, Pennsylvania. She earned her MA in history from the Pennsylvania State University and her MSLIS from Syracuse University. She loves library instruction and hiking, and her favorite flavor of toaster pastry is cinnamon.

Maria Kingsbury, PhD, works at Southwest Minnesota State University in Marshall, Minnesota, where she serves as the director of the Center for Online Teaching and Learning in the McFarland Library.

Stacey Knight-Davis is the head of circulation services at Booth Library, Eastern Illinois University. She also serves as the systems librarian and as the librarian for nursing and public health. She earned an MS in library and information science from the University of Illinois at Urbana-Champaign and an MS in technology from Eastern Illinois University. Stacey joined the EIU library faculty in 2002 as a reference librarian.

Glenn Koelling is an instruction librarian and English department liaison at the University of New Mexico in Albuquerque. Her research focuses on information literacy and instruction.

Debbie Krahmer is the diversity and inclusion research librarian at Cornell University in New York State. As a white, queer, fat, trans, and disabled librarian, D has been incorporating social justice into D's librarianship for many years and using IGD actively since 2016. Debbie has presented on accessibility, instructional technology, queer and trans issues, and assessment at library and higher education conferences for many years.

Pamela Nett Kruger is the institutional repository librarian at California State University, Chico, Meriam Library. She has an MA in anthropology from California State University, Northridge, and an MLIS from San José State University. Her research interests include communities of practice, tech equity, and inclusive and constructivist pedagogies.

Sharon Ladenson is gender and communication studies librarian and coordinator of diversity, equity, and inclusion education at the Michigan State University Libraries. Her commitment to equity, diversity, and inclusion and anti-racist practices informs her work, particularly in the areas of teaching and learning. She has presented independently on intersectionality and critical information literacy at the California Conference on Library Instruction and collaboratively at the European Conference on Information Literacy and at the Charleston Conference. Her writing on feminist pedagogy and information literacy is included in works such as *Critical Library Instruction: Theories and Methods* (from Library Juice Press) and the *Critical Library Pedagogy Handbook* (from the Association of College and Research Libraries).

Tricia Lantzy is the Health Sciences & Human Services Librarian at California State University San Marcos. She has a MS in Information Studies from the University of Texas at Austin and a BA in Anthropology from the University of California, San Diego. Her current research focuses on investigating how students learn and experience their education in a variety of different learning environments.

David X. Lemmons (he/they) is the instruction coordinator for George Mason University Libraries. They have a master of science in library science from the University of North Carolina at Chapel Hill and a master of arts in political science from Appalachian State University. Their research interests include student-centered pedagogy and critical information literacy.

Lindsey Loeper has served as the reference and instruction archivist at the University of Maryland, Baltimore County (UMBC), since 2019, following her role as the special collections archivist since 2007. In this position she coordinates the Special Collections reading room, reference and researcher services, and instruction and archival literacy and serves as the primary student supervisor. She has previously written and presented on EAD-XML finding aids, participatory learning in archival literacy instruction, and team-based instruction portfolios.

Christopher Lowder (he/him) is the online learning specialist at George Mason University. He has a master of library and information science with a specialization in diversity and inclusion from the University of Maryland. His research interests include information accessibility, online learning, and inclusive teaching in library instruction.

Elaine MacDougall is a lecturer in the English department and director of the Writing Center at the University of Maryland, Baltimore County (UMBC). She is currently a doctoral student in the Language, Literacy, and Culture program at UMBC with research interests in mindfulness and writing studies, embodiment pedagogy, tutor and student self-efficacy and advocacy, and anti-racist pedagogy in the writing center and writing classroom using frameworks from critical race theory and feminist theory, especially Black feminism. Additionally, her background as a yoga instructor influences her practices in the writing classroom and made her more aware of the importance of being present with and listening to her students. Elaine is excited to continue growing from and learning about positionality in her roles as a writing center director, instructor, colleague, and student.

Kelleen Maluski is a student success and engagement librarian at University of New Mexico Health Sciences Library.

Francesca Marineo Munk is the education liaison and humanities and social sciences librarian / coordinator of library student research assistants at the University of California, Los Angeles. She wrote this chapter while in her previous position of teaching and learning librarian for online education at the University of Nevada, Las Vegas, one of the nation's most diverse universities for undergraduates. In addition to her MLIS, she holds an MS in educational psychology, which is where she was first introduced to motivation theory. She is a first-generation college student and an emerging mid-career librarian. Her current research focuses on fostering a culture of educational equity through communities of practice and designing inclusive learning experiences especially within an online environment. Francesca is a white, Canadian-born dual citizen of the United States and Canada. She is a queer, cis, and able-bodied woman, and her pronouns are she, her, hers.

Talitha R. Matlin is the STEM Librarian at CSU San Marcos. She has a Master's of Learning, Design, and Technology from San Diego State University and a Master's of Library and Information Science from San Jose State University. Her research interests focus on applying instructional design methodologies to nontraditional instructional settings.

Allison McFadden-Keesling received her BA from Albion College (1982) and MLIS from the University of Michigan (1984) and has been a reference librarian for thirty-eight years at academic and public libraries. An active member of Diversity, Equity, Inclusion and Justice initiatives, she was honored and humbled to receive the Oakland Community College (OCC) Diversity Champion award in 2017 for her work on the Human Library. She read about the Human Library in an article in a London paper in 2008. Impressed and intrigued by the concept, she researched and contacted the Humanlibrary.org and facilitated her first Human Library in 2009 at OCC in Michigan. She has facilitated over thirty Human Library events over the last thirteen years. Recognizing the immediate and positive effects for all involved, she continues to be passionate about meeting and vetting potential human books and facilitating human libraries. These events foster empathy and understanding in both the reader and the human book.

Samantha Minnis is the information literacy and outreach librarian at Grand Rapids Community College. After working in a variety of areas of librarianship in both public and academic libraries, she earned her MLIS from Kent State University in 2016. Samantha is an active member of Michigan Academic Library Association (MiALA). Her research interests include critical librarianship and critical pedagogy.

Michelle K. Mitchell is the Reference and Instruction Librarian at Syracuse University. She holds a MSLIS from Simmons College and a BA in English from Le Moyne College. She is a cis, settler, able-bodied, white, middle-class female. Michelle is passionate about critical librarianship, inclusive instruction techniques and practices, assessment strategies, and technological literacy.

Madeline Mundt is head of the Research Commons at the University of Washington Libraries, where she is responsible for planning, managing, and coordinating services for student researchers in this interdisciplinary physical and virtual space. She is also particularly interested in bringing graduate student researchers into public and open scholarship. She is a cis white woman who has been working in libraries for fifteen years.

Megan Mulder is the Special Collections Librarian at Z. Smith Reynolds Library, Wake Forest University. She teaches classes on the history of material texts and provides instruction for undergraduate and graduate students, and she collaborates with teaching faculty to embed primary source materials from Special Collections and Archives into the classroom and the curriculum. She holds an MA in English literature from the University of Virginia and an MLIS from the University of North Carolina at Chapel Hill.

Yvonne Nalani Meulemans has been the Head of Teaching and Learning at the University Library at California State University at San Marcos since 2010. Her research interests include the use of threshold concept framework to support students' transformational learning and reflective practice in library leadership and management.

Lalitha Nataraj is the Social Sciences Librarian at California State University, San Marcos. She holds an MLIS from UCLA and a BA in English and Women's Studies from UC Berkeley. Her research interests include relational-cultural theory, critical information literacy, and South Asian Americans in librarianship.

Clanitra Stewart Nejdl is head of professional development and research services librarian at the Alyne Queener Massey Law Library at Vanderbilt University, as well as a lecturer in law at Vanderbilt Law School. She teaches both first-year and advanced legal research classes. Clanitra presents and publishes on topics related to academic law libraries and legal research instruction, including cultural competence and DEIA awareness for law students, legal information preservation, and professional development for law librarians. Clanitra is the 2021 recipient of both the American Association of Law Libraries (AALL) Emerging Leader Award and the AALL Spectrum Article of the Year Award. She is also the 2017 recipient of the AALL Minority Leadership Development Award. Clanitra is an active member of the American Association of Law Libraries, the Southeastern Chapter of the American Association of Law Libraries, the Mid-America Association of Law Libraries, and the Chicago Association of Law Libraries. She is a licensed attorney in Georgia and in South Carolina.

Zach Newell served as dean of library services at Eastern Illinois University from 2018 to 2022 and is currently dean of libraries and learning at the University of Southern Maine. Zach earned a BA in philosophy from Susquehanna University, Selinsgrove, Pennsylvania; an MA in history of art from University of Massachusetts Amherst; and an MS in library science from Clarion University, Clarion, Pennsylvania. He is a PhD candidate in library and information science at Simmons University, Boston, Massachusetts.

Judy Opdahl is the Business and Economics Librarian for the College of Business and Department of Economics Department at California State University San Marcos. Her research interests include practices of embedded librarianship and how the academic library can support ADHD and other neurodiverse students.

Nicole Pagowsky is an associate librarian at the University of Arizona Libraries and adjunct faculty with the University of Arizona School of Information.

Roxane Pickens is the community engagement librarian and head of External Engagement at New York University Libraries, having formerly served as the director of the Learning Commons at University of Miami Libraries. She received her MA and PhD in American studies at the College of William and Mary, and her scholarly work explores identity and festivity in Harlem Renaissance/Jazz Age literature and expressive culture. Her current research and teaching interests include library outreach and engagement, interdisciplinarity and cultural literacies in library settings, teaching with primary resources, diversity/equity/inclusion in academic spaces, American studies, African American literature/culture, US identity construction, and the rhetorical dimensions of ethnic festive/expressive culture.

Hanna Primeau is the instructional designer at The Ohio State University Libraries. In this role, she is involved in a range of projects from redesigning for-credit online courses to consultations with fellow librarians on how to best use teaching technology in their sessions or how to transition from in-person to virtual instruction. Hanna has an MSI from the School of Information at the University of Michigan.

Torie Quiñonez is the Arts and Humanities Librarian at CSU San Marcos. Her research interests include exploring the role validation plays in the intellectual development of learners of all kinds.

Madeline Ruggiero is a collection development librarian at Queensborough Community College in Queens, New York. In addition to an MLS from Pratt Institute she also has a masters degree in Art History from SUNY Stony Brook. Her research and publications focus on ways to support community college students academically and holistically.. In addition to an MLS from Pratt Institute She also has a masters degree in Art History from SUNY Stony Brook. Her research and publications focus on ways to support community college students academically and holistically.

Zohra Saulat is a graduate of the School of Information Sciences at the University of Illinois, Urbana-Champaign. She is the student success librarian at Lake Forest College. Her passions include student success, the first-year experience, and critical library pedagogy.

Laura Saunders is a Professor at Simmons University School of Library and Information Science, where she teaches and conducts research in the areas of reference, instruction, information literacy, and intellectual freedom. She has a strong interest in the connections between information literacy and social justice issues, as well as in the impact of mis- and disinformation.

Her most recent books include *Reference and Information Services: An Introduction*, 6th edition, co-edited with Melissa Wong, and the open access textbook *Instruction in Libraries and Information Settings: An Introduction*, co-authored with Melissa Wong. Her articles have appeared in a variety of journals, including *College & and Research Libraries*, The *Journal of Academic Librarianship*, and *Communications in Information Literacy*. Laura has a PhD and a Master of Library and Information Science, both from Simmons College, and a Bachelor of Arts in English Literature from Boston University. She has served a Trustee for the Somerville Public Library in Somerville, Massachusetts. She is the 2019 recipient of Simmons University's Provost Award for Excellence in Graduate Teaching.

Gina Schlesselman-Tarango is a librarian at Des Moines University and was previously the coordinator of library instruction at California State University, San Bernardino. In addition to co-facilitating the Library Ambassador Initiative in partnership with the Student Mentoring Program, she facilitated library instruction and led professional development for faculty on topics related to critical information literacy. Her research interests include gender and race in librarianship, critical library pedagogy, and information labor as it relates to reproductive failure.

Melanie Sellar is head of instruction and assessment at University Library, Santa Clara University. In this role she develops, enhances, and implements the Library's instruction and assessment programs and priorities. She has twelve years of accrued experience specializing in the public services of academic libraries, with scholarships interests spanning inclusive and critical pedagogy, algorithmic literacy, and instructional design.

Anne Shelley is scholarly communication librarian and music librarian at Illinois State University, where she manages the institutional repository ISU ReD, gives workshops, and provides instruction, reference, and collection development services. She has written or cowritten book chapters published by ALA Editions, ACRL Publications, IGI Global, Neal-Schuman, and A-R Editions.

Kathy Shields is the Research and Instruction Librarian for History and Social Science and Research Services Lead at Wake Forest University's Z. Smith Reynolds Library. In those roles, she provides research and instruction support to students and faculty, primarily in the areas of History and Psychology, teaches credit-bearing information literacy courses on primary sources and social science research, and coordinates the library's liaison program. Her scholarship has primarily focused on the value of collaboration between librarians and disciplinary faculty. She holds an MLIS from the University of North Carolina at Greensboro.

Tierney Steelberg is a Digital Liberal Arts Specialist at Grinnell College's Digital Liberal Arts Collaborative. Prior to joining Grinnell, she was the Digital Pedagogy & Scholarship Technologist at Guilford College's Hege Library. She is passionate about supporting the critical and thoughtful implementation of technology in teaching and learning, as well as empowering students to create digital projects across disciplines and modalities. She earned her MSI from the University of Michigan in 2016.

Elliott Stevens is the English studies and research commons librarian at the University of Washington, Seattle. With Madeline Mundt, he has done research and written about the value of undergraduate student library workers doing written reflections while on the job. He is also interested in the digital humanities and digital scholarship and to what degree they are accessible. He is a forty-year-old, white, cis, able-bodied man who is six years into full-time library work.

Alicia G. Vaandering is an assistant professor and the student success librarian for the University Libraries at the University of Rhode Island. In her role, she supports the learning and research of students, with an emphasis on undergraduate first-year, international, first-generation, and transfer students. She received a bachelor of arts in history from Willamette University and master of library and information studies and master of arts in history at the University of Rhode Island. Her research interests include the history of public libraries, the representation of the LGBTQIA+ community in children's picture books, library collaborations with academic services, and the use of dialogic pedagogy in information literacy instruction.

Kari D. Weaver, MLIS, EdD, is the learning, teaching, and instructional design librarian at the University of Waterloo, where she oversees the development of online instruction, advances teaching culture, and explores strategic partnerships related to teaching and learning. Her research interests include accessibility, censorship, co-teaching, information literacy, and academic integrity, particularly in the STEM disciplines.

Megan Wilson is an assistant professor and research and instruction librarian at Murray State University. She serves as the library liaison for the Jones College of Science and the Hutson School of Agriculture as well as serving as an instructor for courses about information literacy and intellectual property. Her research interests include virtual reference, inclusive teaching and learning, library outreach, and online learning.

Lauren Wittek is a librarian and instructor at Central Washington University's James E. Brooks Library. She earned her MLIS from the University of Washington in 2018 and has worked in higher education for over 15 years. Her research interests include addressing accessibility and privacy issues in the library.

Mir Yarfitz is an Associate Professor in the Department of History at Wake Forest University and the Director of the Jewish Studies Program. His teaching and scholarship bridge Latin American History, Gender and Sexuality Studies, and Jewish History. He incorporates library visits into undergraduate classes at all levels, collaborating with librarians to make primary source research accessible to every student. His current research explores multiple interpretations and assertions of what might fruitfully be framed as trans lives in Argentina circa 1900-1930. His monograph Impure Migration: Jews and Sex Work in Golden Age Argentina was published in 2019 by Rutgers University Press. He holds a PhD in History from UCLA.

Perry Yee is the senior online learning support manager at the University of Washington, Seattle. As part of the libraries' Instructional Design unit, he designs, develops, and delivers online learning opportunities for UW students, staff, and faculty while providing digital pedagogy and instructional technology training and support to libraries staff members. He offers his viewpoint as a mixed-race, cisgender, able-bodied man who has been working in libraries for seven years.